GW00724671

# THE KU KLUX KLAN

# THE KU KLUX KLAN

## AN AMERICAN HISTORY

### KRISTOFER ALLERFELDT

For Maja, Hamish, Lily and Phoebe Holman.
The bravest people I know.

First published 2024

The History Press
97 St George's Place, Cheltenham,
Gloucestershire, GL50 3QB
www.thehistorypress.co.uk

British Library Cataloguing in Publication Data.
A catalogue record for this book is available from the British Library.

ISBN 978 1 80399 016 3

Typesetting and origination by The History Press
Printed and bound in Great Britain by TJ Books Limited, Padstow, Cornwall.

Trees for LYfe

## Publisher's Note

*The Ku Klux Klan: An American History* is an exploration of one of the darkest recesses of American culture. To present and analyse such a history honestly, we believe that the full context of language and events must be available and so have not censored or downplayed them within these pages.

# CONTENTS

# PREFACE

The Ku Klux Klan (KKK) doesn't fit neatly into any group. It is not a political party, a social movement or a charity. In many respects, the Klan should be seen as an 'order': a sinister, bigoted and ultra-violent version of the Rotary Club. It claims it was founded as a fraternity and argues it is still one today. And, given its attempts to overthrow post-Civil War reconstruction and desegregation in the Deep South, it is even fair to call the Ku Klux Klan an insurgency.

If finding the right pigeonhole for the Klan is difficult, it's made doubly tricky because the Klan is not consistent. Another of the Klan's unique qualities is its ability to reinvent itself and re-emerge. Its history is not linear. Membership has risen and declined, peaking three times. In each one of these peaks, the Klan attracted members by vilifying a distinct and different section of US society, proposing simplistic and more often than not violent solutions.

The first of these surges in membership was from 1866 to the mid-1870s, beginning merely months after the Klan's foundation. This 'Reconstruction Klan' emerged as a secretive paramilitary group dedicated to a violent response to what they perceived as the imminent collapse of the social, political and racial order of the 'Old South'. They saw themselves as fighting the predatory, avaricious, Northerners, along with their Southern 'toadies' and bestial African American stooges. With the removal of the protections for the former slaves in the 1870s and reinstatement of the old hierarchies from 1877, Klan membership dropped, remaining relatively dormant until its second incarnation.

The '1920s Klan' offered itself up as a conservative response to the rapidly changing modern world which threatened the old certainties and securities of middle America. The organisation seemed to have solutions for problems as diverse as mass immigration, the disintegration of family values, political sleaze and rural poverty. The message was popular. For a brief period in the early 1920s the Klan became a national movement attracting millions. It assumed for itself the role of traditionalism – a natural defender of conservative, God-fearing native-born Protestant Americans. Not much later the Klan spectacularly imploded – fuelled by exposés of sexual and financial improprieties and persistent reports of shocking violence.

Its final real flourish in terms of numbers happened in the 1950s and 1960s as the Klan repositioned itself as the focal point for hardline opposition to the pressures for racial equality, most notably in the South. This 'Civil Rights Klan' is probably the one with which most people are most familiar. This is the Klan of countless movies and TV programmes: an overtly racist, ultra-violent, domestic terrorism outfit. This Klan was dedicated to bombing and murdering its way across the South in the second half of the 1950s and early 1960s before collapsing in the surging wave of popular pressure behind the civil rights and peace movements.

Even today many people think of the Klan as a powerful organisation with cells (Klaverns) throughout the country and with members in the highest levels of society telegraphing their membership through secret handshakes and coded language.

The reality is that the Klan has been in decline since the 1960s. Other white nationalist groups see the Klan's costumed secrecy and ritual as something of an embarrassment. To them the Klan is more interested in creating an aura of secrecy than in actually being covert. And yet, while other equally savage, equally repellent groups have faded away, the Klan has been able to regenerate itself by using its own mythology.

Even when near extinction, the Klan is preserved in folklore. It is perhaps the most instantly recognisable racist organisation in the world. Law and public opinion severely limit its operation. It retains the reputation of being one of the most notorious and ultra-violent terrorist groups, even though today that is demonstrably little more than a myth. However, this is a myth capable of crossing continents and oceans.

I first heard of the Klan as a 6-year-old boy in England. Older boys described some sort of gruesome act the Klan had committed and told me the name 'Ku Klux Klan' came from the noise made by the cocking of a Winchester repeating rifle. Years later I was astonished to come across an obscure nineteenth-century pamphlet with this very story.[1] It is almost certainly apocryphal, but my childhood self would have found proof enough in the wisdom of my elders – boys who may have been all of … 12.

I encountered Klan folklore once more as a teenager furtively smoking in the grounds of an English boarding school. Like many of my generation, my brand of choice was Marlboro Reds. Standing in a lonely wood

– probably in the rain – a friend showed me how when the pack was tipped at certain angles the iconic red triangles made up the three 'K's of the Ku Klux Klan. As we stood under the dripping trees my friend explained the sinister symbolism: red was the blood of African Americans, white was the unity of the white race.[2]

In my twenty years of research, I have become more and more convinced that the Klan's peculiar name and iconography was, and remains, a crucial element of its success. Like the Mafia, the Klan drew on its age-old traditions. For the Mafia it was the code of silence or *Omertà*, the sacrilegious burning of images of the saints and the hierarchical Godfather system that enabled it to prevail as the ultimate organised crime group. For the Klan it was the instantly recognisable three 'K's, the robes, the burning crosses and white hoods which simultaneously concealed the members' identity and terrorised their victims. Throughout the Klan's ghastly, blood-soaked, history its symbols are, to use a military term, the 'force multipliers' enabling the Klan to remain the headline white supremacist group.[3]

Our view of the Klan today is rooted in the past. It is the image of the sweaty Southern 'good ole boys' driving battered old pickup trucks down dusty tracks to a clandestine meeting place. It is Imperial Wizards, white robes and hoods, racist mumbo-jumbo and cross burning in films like Alan Parker's *Mississippi Burning* (1988) and Spike Lee's *Blackkklansman* (2018). We feel unified in our hatred for these groups and perhaps also enjoy a tremor of fear. If sex sells, in many cases terror is a pretty close second.

The reality is that the vast majority of Klansmen now operate as part of small, sad groups of internet trolls whose main threat comes from leaflet dropping. Ignoring that, we opt instead for the Klan as a single, identifiable, scapegoat for 'evil'. And it appears there's a squadron of writers, filmmakers and journalists ready to fulfil that urge for unity. When depicting the enemies of society, it's best to make them *powerful*.

And finally, when looking at the USA's long and violent legacy of racism it is perhaps easier to look at the very worst of groups than to look within. This means that even we, who despise the Klan, inadvertently promote it. Consider this fact – the combined US Klan groups from across the nation could only muster twelve members for the rather ironically titled showcase 'Unite the Right Rally' in Charlottesville in August 2017.

And this is not an anomaly. As far as it is possible to tell – and it is never easy to estimate Klan membership – the numbers of Klansmen are now in sharp, maybe terminal, decline. According to the Southern Poverty Law Center (SPLC), a non-governmental organisation dedicated to tracking and prosecuting hate groups, 'The number of Ku Klux Klan (KKK) chapters continued to fall for the third year in a row, down to 51 chapters in 2018 from 130 in 2016.'[4] Yet there is still a feeling that the Klan's numbers grew under the presidency of Donald Trump.

In any discussion of US race-hate, sooner or later the Klan's ugly, trademark hooded head will pop up. So pointing out the truth is important, and it is not just a moral imperative: it can hopefully have an effect on the Klan itself. As well as detailing its atrocities, this book will show the Klan's spectacular defeats and the brevity of its self-proclaimed glory days.

If we see the Klan for what it truly is, and what it really was, we have a far better chance of neutralising its toxic but resilient message. When a more subtle Klan history begins appearing in the media, imagine how a foolish, diminished, ineffective Klan image will affect those attempting to co-opt its legacy for racially based violence. To see the Klan for what it is gives us the chance to finally break the whack-a-mole re-emergence of the Klan after periods of near-extinction.

That is why *The Ku Klux Klan: An American History* seeks to understand and demystify one of the most hated, feared and, to my mind, poorly understood organisations in US history. And there is need for this. As I write this, in 2022, there is no single history of the KKK that spans its origins in post-Civil War Tennessee to the present day. This book seeks to be that history.

## PART I

# STANDING OVER A SLEEPING VOLCANO 1865–1867

Our visitor appeared to be about nine feet high, with a most hideous face, and wrapped in an elegant robe of black silk, which he kept closely folded about his person. He wore gloves the color of blood, and carried a magic wand in his hand with which he awed us into submission to any demand he might make … We tried to say no, but a wave of his wand made us tell the truth.

Description of KKK Grand Cyclops Frank McCord,
*Pulaski Citizen*, 19 April 1867

# CHAPTER 1

There is a rather grand double-fronted townhouse on Spofford Street, in the small rural town of Pulaski, Tennessee. Legend has it, that it was here, on the wet and chilly night of Christmas Eve, 1865, that six old friends met up. These were the 'Pulaski Six', the original members of the KKK. Although only one of them had reached his 30s, they were all former Confederate soldiers who had each seen and suffered through nearly four years of active service in the bloodiest conflict the USA had ever known.

Three of them, Lieutenant John C. Lester and Privates Richard Reed and John B. Kennedy, had enthusiastically joined a locally raised regiment, Colonel Clack's 3rd Confederate Infantry, at the very start of the Civil War. All would serve on the frontlines until the end of the war. Together they hunkered down under six weeks of continuous heavy federal bombardment at the siege of Port Hudson, reduced to eating first the mules, then the dogs and finally rats. Later, they survived two days of slaughter at Chickamauga where nearly a third of their regiment was wounded, captured or killed. Finally, in April 1865, starving and in rags, they surrendered in Greensboro, North Carolina.

Calvin Jones, their host, was the son of the building's owner, an affluent local judge. Compared to his friends, Calvin had served in relative comfort as an adjutant in the 32nd Tennessee Infantry, though he, too, had survived the bloodbath at Chickamauga and faced the full ferocity of the Union assaults at Lookout Mountain and Missionary Ridge.

There was also a genuine war hero in the group. James R. Crowe had joined the 4th Alabama Infantry as a private in the first weeks of the war and risen through the ranks to become a captain in the 53rd Tennessee Infantry. Crowe was involved in the Confederate victory at Manassas. And at Shiloh in April 1862, he led his men headlong into the whirlwind of musket and cannon fire of the Union positions. He was wounded, and badly enough to be discharged. However, he was back with his regiment within months.

By the end of the year Crowe was thrown into the worst three days of slaughter the war was to see – at Stones River. Again, he was wounded and discharged. Again, he recovered and quickly rejoined his regiment. In October 1863, in Central Tennessee, he was captured carrying detailed plans of the enemy's positions. Taken to his hometown, Pulaski, he was tried as a spy alongside another Confederate officer, Sam Davis. Although specifics are vague, it appears Crowe was acquitted, escaped and made his way back to his regiment. Davis was less fortunate. He was hanged – in the town square, where a monument still stands to this Confederate martyr.[1]

At some unknown battle later in 1863, Crowe was once more wounded and once again discharged from active duty. This time he could not return to his regiment. Promoted to the rank of major, he spent the rest of the war in the safety of a desk job in Richmond, Virginia. From here, on the surrender of the Confederacy, he was demobilised and sent back to Pulaski – a hero.

The final man present was the oldest and had been the least fortunate. As a private soldier in the 9th Kentucky Infantry, 33-year-old Frank Owen McCord had been badly wounded, most likely at the Battle of Chickamauga.[2] The war left McCord with a pronounced limp and permanent blindness in one eye.[3]

Now, on Christmas Eve, eight months after the Confederacy surrendered, the young friends were together. Pulaski was a small town where many had backed the losing side. It had been socially and economically devastated by the war. Many houses in Pulaski would have had empty chairs at Christmas dinner, places where husbands, brothers or fathers might have sat. Even those where the menfolk had returned found themselves with less to celebrate than usual. Times were hard. Businesses had closed, bread-winners had been killed or disabled: money was tight. But for all this, the six friends were fortunate. They'd survived.

For young men now used to the terror and exhilaration of battle, the sleepy town of Pulaski would have been something of a culture shock. Bored, with plenty of time on their hands, the six had met to find some sort of distraction from the tedium of rural life. According to at least one, they had the idea to form a fraternity. By the end of the night, they had done just that.

Forming a fraternity was not unusual at the time. Four of the six had gone away to college and were familiar with the enduring fashion for 'Greek Letter' fraternities. In fact, 'frat houses' had originated in Europe, but they'd quickly become a real US tradition, as old as the nation itself. The first

US college fraternity, Phi Beta Kappa, had been founded at William & Mary College in Virginia the same year as Thomas Jefferson made his historic declaration in 1776. By 1780, there were some twenty chapters in the South and within another year the fraternity had reached Harvard and Yale. From there, frat houses had spread west, picking up imitators until, by the outbreak of the Civil War, the USA was experiencing a genuine boom in fraternities – and not just on college campuses.[4]

The appeal of fraternities was obvious to US manhood in peacetime. They could be used to provide society, entertainment and valuable connections. In the devastation of the post-war world these benefits were even more apparent. With their emphasis on camaraderie, loyalty, recklessness and manliness, it is hard to imagine ideals that would have had more appeal to war veterans all over the nation.

Filling a space somewhere between a gentlemen's club, pressure group, trade union and amateur dramatic society, fraternities gradually became a dynamic part of US society. Millions of men would join, and to fill the need more and more of them emerged. Well-known fraternities like the Knights of Pythias (founded 1864) fed this desire for comradeship. Others, like the rural reform fraternity the Grange (1867), emerged out of post-war desire to build a better world. Others, like the Knights of Labor (1869), would serve the function of trade unions. In the craze for fraternities many came and went. Who remembers the Veterans of Future Wars, the Jolly Corks or the Knights of Reciprocity?[5]

Forming a fraternity would have been seen as a positive thing for the six young men to do in 1865. There were no ominous associations with such an act. By the end of the night, they had not only formed their fraternity, they had given it a name: the Ku Klux Klan.

The name was not, as my school friends had claimed, based on the sinister cocking noises made by the Winchester repeater, but rather, drew on benevolent fraternal traditions of brotherhood and mutual obligation. It was not connected to the violence and terror we universally associate with the Klan today.

# CHAPTER 2

Historians continue to debate the origins of the actual name 'Ku Klux Klan'. There are many persuasive arguments for the name's origins which, upon closer examination, can't be true – for the explanations are based upon what the Klan would come to be in later years, not what it was on 24 December 1865.

One of the more gruesome of these post-facto theories argues that the name originated in pre-Columbian Mexico, apparently from a Meso-American feather-covered snake-god, Kukulcan. There are a great many carvings and images of the serpent Kukulcan dotted around the Yucatan and other areas of the Mayan Empire and this explanation seems to draw on the terror inspired by the name centring as it does on the gory reputation this bird-snake has as the recipient of human sacrifices. But this explanation's roots are spurious, typical linguistic 'reverse-engineering'.

It is probable that the theory stems from somebody noticing how similar 'Kukulcan' and 'Ku Klux Klan' sounded, a connection made at the height of the Klan revival in the early 1920s, when numbers of Klansmen were counted in the millions and 'Klannishness' was a true craze. The Meso-American snake-god connection should be seen as one of many origin myths. It sits alongside allusions to Klansmen on the *Mayflower*, at the Sermon on the Mount and at the signing of the Declaration of Independence.[1]

The evidence for the association is particularly scanty. Besides, it's unlikely that a group of ex-soldiers, no matter how well educated, would be familiar with this obscure Mayan god.[2] And certainly the retro-spectively invented bloodthirstiness of Kukulcan would not have sat well with the Klan of the 1920s, which was attempting to position itself as a benign mass movement with mainstream political views. So this theory for the origin of the name has largely been abandoned.

Another name theory came from an 1868 *Memphis Appeal* article suggesting that the name dated back as far as Old Testament times, when the Israelites were enslaved by the Egyptians. The newspaper claimed to have uncovered an ancient Jewish text, the snappily titled *A True and Authentic History of the Great Rebellion of the Hebrew Against the Ancient Egyptian King Pharoah [sic], BC 2000*. In this work, apparently, there is mention of a 'Cu Clux Clan', which could be translated into the 'Straw Club'. This explanation would have appealed to Klansmen, since it equated the misery of the South under Union occupation with the suffering of the Israelites in their Egyptian exile.

This is a particularly interesting root, since it fits well with the fraternal practice of giving orders pedigrees reaching back to ancient times. Freemasons trace a pedigree back to the building of the Temple of Solomon, so why shouldn't the Klan trace its heritage back to Moses? As another Tennessee paper explained, this foundation myth gave the Klan 'a saintly livery' – a divine heritage and a readily identifiable moral high ground to exploit.[3] While unlikely, this divine blessing for the Klan's mission has echoed down through the ages, perhaps most vividly in the final, rather trippy, section of David Wark Griffith's 1915 film *The Birth of a Nation*.

Then there's the Clopton myth, which though equally obscure, ties the Klan's roots more solidly to its future behaviour. In this interpretation the name derives from a Native American clan, the unlikely sounding Co-Cletz. The tribe was renowned for its hell-raising lifestyle, and their one-eyed chief, Clopton, was the wildest of them all. But when he got so drunk that he killed the servants around him, Clopton literally raised hell. The Prince of Evil was so thrilled by Clopton's wickedness he kidnapped the entire tribe, along with their horses and their hounds. From then onwards they became ghostly hunters, doomed forever to become the eternal slaves of the god, serving to perpetually hunt down his enemies.

At first glance it seems unlikely that this story is relevant to the birth of a white supremacist terror group, but there is a strand of logic in this connection. The story of wicked Clopton and his spectral posse had already been adopted by pre-Bellum slave hunters. Among these were some Native American trackers – some could have come from the Co-Cletz tribe itself. It is equally plausible that Native Americans, enslaved and working alongside African American slaves, could have told the legend to those with whom they laboured.

Any mention of connections with the spirit world would probably have had an impact on runaway African slaves. Slave hunters would have used their knowledge of African animist beliefs and their pantheon of spirits – benign and evil – to terrorise their quarry. These manhunters very possibly pretended to be the ghostly chieftain with his minions, hounds and horses in order to frighten and discourage runaway slaves.[4] And this connection leads us down into an important historical rabbit hole. There is increasing historical evidence of an association between slave bounty-hunters and the Klan, indicating that the 'Ku Kluxers' had existed before the end of the war, and certainly before the Pulaski Six met to form the initial Klan 'den'.[5]

To better understand this, it helps to take a leap forward to the 1930s, when as a part of his efforts to jump-start the stagnating Depression economy, Franklin Delano Roosevelt (FDR) sanctioned the Works Progress Administration (WPA). Recordings were made of the last remaining survivors of plantation slavery, freed by abolition more than three generations earlier. Those who could remember the horrors of slavery were reaching old age and many had already died. The WPA audio recordings and transcripts provide invaluable descriptions about everyday life under slavery.

Several of these testimonies describe how slave-catchers operated. One stands out – that of an ex-slave, Joseph Samuel Badgett. Interviewing him in the 1930s, a recorder in Little Rock, Arkansas, Samuel S. Taylor, was struck by the 72-year-old Badgett's remarkably vivid and lucid account. He'd had a relatively fortunate youth for a part-'Indian' former slave. A local judge had noticed the child's intelligence and sent Badgett to a private boarding school in Pine Bluff. That level of education was very rare among slaves, and Taylor was struck by the clarity of the old man's testimony, which he wrote about some years later.[6]

Among other things, Badgett told Taylor about the policing of slaves in the Plantation South. He explained that the 'Pass System' established at that time required slaves moving around outside their plantation to produce on demand a paper signed by their master. The so-called 'slave patrollers' employed to enforce this were usually funded and controlled by the region's slave-holders.

However, as Badgett told Taylor, there were also two categories of mercenary 'freelance' slave-catchers. Badgett summarised this in an invaluable testimony:

> The jayhawkers were highway men or robbers who stole slaves among other things. ... The jayhawkers stole and pillaged, while the Ku Klux stole those Negroes they caught out. The word 'Klan' was never used in their name. ... [By contrast] The Ku Klux Klan was an organization which arose after the Civil War. It was composed of men who believed in white supremacy and regulated the morals of the neighbourhood. ... They took the law into their own hands.[7]

Taylor added his own notes to the transcription:

> Badgett's definite and clear-cut memories, however, led me to believe
> that many of the Negroes who were slaves used the word Ku Klux to
> denote a type of person who stole slaves. It was evidently used before it
> was applied to the Ku Klux Klan.[8]

Another ex-slave, J.T. Tims, agreed:

> Before the war that I knew 'bout the Ku Klux. There wasn't no difference
> between the patroles [sic] and the Ku Klux that I knows of. If th'd ketch
> you, they all would whip you. I don't know nothin' about the Ku Klux
> Klan after the War.[9]

Both testimonies argue that the Klan was in existence *before* the war, *before*
Pulaski and *before* that fateful meeting that Christmas Eve.

Although many of the Ku Klux Klan name origin stories sound convincing, the most widely accepted name origin story has no retrospectively
applied menace. According to later accounts by the Pulaski Six, the reason
for choosing the name was, in fact, exceedingly ordinary: they were copy-
ing the name of a fraternity they admired.

It is astonishing to consider the shortlist of names from which the name
'Ku Klux Klan' was chosen. We have come to associate the group with such
horrific levels of violence and racism that it is hard to believe the other
names under consideration included 'The Secret Circle', 'The Pulaski Social
Club' and, believe it or not, 'The Thespians'.

It was James Crowe who came up with the name we know and hate. It
was a name combining the high-minded concepts of fraternalism with the
fashion for all things ecclesiastical and scholarly, a gaudy approximation of
academic jargon and allusions to Ancient Greek.[10]

It stemmed from the ancient Greek word for circle – *kuklos*. This classical
allusion would have appealed to Crowe's fellow college graduates, John
Kennedy, Richard Reed and Calvin Jones, not least because it echoed one
of the most famous college fraternities in the South, *Kuklos Adelphon*. That
name translates as 'Circle of Friends', a clear reference to the vaunted fraternal values of loyalty, dependability and brotherhood.

It's worth mentioning one final, less benign origin myth steeped in
pseudo-academic imagery, a vivid scene depicted by the classical Roman
historian Pausanias. The story goes that in the fifth century BCE on the night
before an impending battle, 600 Phocian night raiders slipped into their
enemy's camp. In order to distinguish friend from foe, they had painted

themselves with chalk. Seeing the Phocians glowing white in the moonlight, their enemies thought they were gods and offered no resistance to the attack. Their piety made no odds. They were slaughtered anyway.[11]

This story draws on the Greek word for 'circle', coming from the Greek phrase *ton kuklon tes selenes*, which translates as 'the circle of the moon'.[12] This phrase linguistically echoes the accounts of the original six, who each later affirmed their group's name had come from the Greek word *kuklos*.

It is certainly plausible. At least one of the 'Jolly Six', John B. Kennedy, had sufficient classical knowledge to have inspired these allusions. This is backed up by Calvin Jones who, speaking to an academic writing a history of the order, later said that one of the six 'up at Pulaski got up a piece of Greek and originated it, and then General [Nathan Bedford] Forrest [alleged first Grand Wizard, commander-in-chief of the KKK] took hold of it'.[13]

# CHAPTER 3

Though there is a great deal of debate about the origins of 'Ku Klux', there is far less about the origin of the word 'Klan'. The word drew upon a rage for the idealised imagery of Scottish clans. It had Highland peaks and glens and wild tartan-clad tribes in perpetual blood feuds, loyal to their chiefs and brethren to the death – and beyond. While this image was drawn from romanticised stories, it was an especially appealing brand of fiction. Fed by the massive Scottish diaspora, which was in turn caused by the enclosure of farmland in the Highlands and islands, this genre was especially appealing to emigrant Scots, or those with Scottish ancestry – and there were many of them in Tennessee.

There is little doubt the 'Pulaski Six' would have been familiar with the popular poems of the mythical 'Homer of the North', Ossian, and the highly romanticised medievalism of Walter Scott. Scott's long page turners, in achingly romantic settings, appealed to those spending their monotonous, sweltering days in dull towns and isolated plantations. Scott created an escapist world populated by aristocratic heroes and villains who lived, struggled and died demonstrating fierce loyalty and unswerving morality. It was the perfect literature for a proud but defeated readership – and perfect for the make-believe world of an upstart fraternity.[1]

Now the six had a name for their group, their task was to recruit. They used initiation rituals borrowed from happier, pre-war days in college fraternities. During these rituals, blindfolded initiates, in a darkened room, crashed into furniture, bounced off walls and tripped through doors. Their victims' faces were painted with soot and they were given donkey's ears then made to repeat absurd, meaningless oaths and call each other by weird names. In short, the Klan 'hazed' their recruits, made them figures of fun and, according to their own recollections, humiliated them – in a good-natured fashion.[2]

Such silliness drew on strong traditions of minstrelry, circus and carnival that had long histories in the South.[3] Within months the Klan began to parade, exciting more interest than disapproval. While fraternities all over the country had similar outlandish rites, one can't help wonder if the local parades like Mardi Gras made Southerners more at home with the absurdities of the Klan's costumes and absurd rituals. And even though Pulaski may have been typically buttoned up and parochial in its day-to-day small-town existence, it is likely the town's porch-sitters would have barely blinked at the sight of young men in costume parading down the street in the topsy-turvy, joyous spirit of carnival.

Yet as we recently learned, only too clearly, even a missionless group unified by a hodgepodge of pseudo-myths can quickly become something far more menacing. Consider the storming of the US Capitol Building on 6 January 2021. An air of carnival pervaded – people wore costumes, face paint, horned hats and flags as capes, filmed themselves and tweeted messages, showing their friends at home what fun they were missing. And yet, even as they broke into offices, sat with their feet on desks and tweeted photos of themselves, four people died.

Similarly, we begin to see the nascent violence underlying the Klan's supposed fraternalism in the fantasy titles given to one another. By his own account, cotton-broker James Crowe became the 'Grand Turk', drawing on the bloodthirstiness and brutality stemming back to the Ottoman threat to Europe.[4] Attorney Richard Reed was made a 'Lictor', after the bearer of the insignia of authority in republican Rome. Associate editor of *The Pulaski Citizen* Frank McCord, being blind in one eye, was made the 'Grand Cyclops', for the man-eating one-eyed giants who gulped down many of Ulysses' crew in Homer's epic *The Odyssey*. In this capacity he was supported by the clerk John Kennedy, his 'Grand Magi', a title rather incongruously taken from the wise men who visited the baby Jesus in Bethlehem.

But it is with the remaining two that we find the first signs of the racist thuggery of the Klan we recognise today. The lawyers Calvin Jones and John Lester were appointed 'Night Hawks' of the Ku Klux Klan, a designation hearkening back to the night-riding slave patrollers of the pre-war South. Lester and Jones said it was not long after this that Klan members began going out into the town and, for their own amusement, preying upon the gullibility and superstition of newly freed slaves with cruel pranks, demanding food and drink from the terrified freedmen while dressed in ghoulish costumes and pretending to be the spirits of dead Confederates.

Small wonder, then, that so many of the name origin theories of the Klan have been retrospectively imbued with violent intentions. Even the grossly sanitised accounts of the Pulaski Six themselves cannot disguise the quick cohesion of their underlying white supremacist values.

# CHAPTER 4

It was almost inevitable that some form of insurgency would emerge in the post-war South: the legacy of war seemed so monstrous to the defeated Confederacy. It had killed one in ten US adult males, maimed countless more and left the nation exhausted and broken. Nowhere was that wreckage more apparent than in the former rebel states.

The source of their wealth – the plantations – had ceased to function: casualties of slave migration. There were countless land disputes as widows and families came to terms with the devastation of war. The demand for cotton had entirely collapsed. Those plantations that had managed to survive limped on. They produced little, sold less. The fate of Mississippi, the most important of the cotton states, demonstrates this clearly.

In 1860, Mississippi had sold nearly three-quarters of the USA's cotton crop, the nation's most important export. Yet by 1866 it has been calculated that the state earned more money from the manufacture, sale and export of artificial limbs than it did from cotton. After five years of war, the South's cotton-producing states went from being the hub of the US economy to becoming the down-at-heel backwaters of the USA. They would remain that way for decades.

Large areas of what had been thriving cities like Atlanta, Georgia; Richmond, Virginia; and Charleston, South Carolina, were reduced to ruins. All that remained of entire blocks of wooden houses were the stone chimneys and piles of rubble. As troops on both sides passed through farmlands, they consumed what they needed. Northern troops destroyed what they didn't want, or couldn't remove, as was all too memorably illustrated by William Tecumseh Sherman's promise to 'make Georgia howl'.[1]

Sherman's devastating 'March to the Sea' was the epitome of the Union's strategy of 'total war'. Starting by burning down nearly 50 per cent of Atlanta, Sherman's troops then cut a 50-mile-wide swathe of utter destruction through central Georgia on their southward march to Savannah. In November and December 1864, 60,000 of Sherman's men lived off the land, consuming all the resources they needed. They burnt homesteads, killed the surplus livestock and ruined the standing crops. It was an effective strategy.

When taken to task for his devastation of the region, Sherman snapped, 'War is cruelty. There is no use trying to reform it: the crueller it is, the sooner it will be over.'[2] But the fear, suffering and lasting hatred inspired by Sherman's actions would do much to feed the concepts of Northern barbarity that would fester in the next decades.[3]

Further west, in Louisiana, things were no better. The thriving docks of New Orleans, thrumming with activity before the war, were now quiet. Crops rotted in the fields or sat in warehouses and barns, waiting for an imaginary market. Still more lay exposed to the elements on wharves on the Mississippi River or on the jetties of the formerly thriving ports of Mobile, Houston, Savannah and Charleston.

Even if there had been demand for these decaying stacks of burlap-covered bales, the South couldn't get them to market in New Orleans or ship them to Liverpool or elsewhere. Most of the region's ships were in disrepair, having been forcibly blockaded in their ports during the war. Stuck in harbours and as liabilities for their owners, the ships had rapidly become unseaworthy and, in many cases, needed to be scrapped.

Much of the region's rail system had been deliberately vandalised by Union forces or retreating Confederates. Any usable equipment had been taken north for the federal war effort. The rest, destroyed. Locomotives were left useless, their boilers blown up. Rails were irreparably twisted and bent. Those lines which had not been deliberately destroyed couldn't be used for lack of rolling stock which had, in many cases, simply been burnt.

A useful horse or a mule was just as difficult to find. Nearly a million of them died in battle, requisitioned as cavalry mounts. Others, draft animals, succumbed to disease or, as fodder became scarcer, starvation. Desperate Confederate troops resorted to slaughtering horses and mules and eating them along with huge numbers of purloined pigs, cows, sheep and other domestic animals. Many had been wantonly killed by federal troops and left exposed, rotting and bloated.

The Confederate military was no more, its loss jeopardising any sense of security for Southern whites. It has been estimated that between 75 and 85 per cent of white males between the ages of 15 and 55 served in the formal or informal Confederate forces. About half of all white men between the ages of 15 and 30 in former Confederate states had been killed or maimed.[4] All this made the racial dominion of the South's conservative whites increasingly difficult to hang on to.

There were no more bosses, no more driving masters to maintain 'order' with their whips. There were no more slave patrols to prevent the freedmen exacting revenge on the white community for their years under the lash. Yet many Southern whites were now more deeply committed to the continuation of the caste system than they had ever been. They felt betrayed by their leaders and threatened by the rise of what they saw as the ignorant mass of brutal freedmen.

To the defeated South, no sooner had the war ended than the North had steamrolled through legislation that threatened their very way of life. As the Pulaski Six met in Spofford House, the Thirteenth Amendment was ratified, freeing the slaves. With the First and Second Freedmen's Acts (1865 and 1866), the Radicals had set up expensive and expansive funding for their benefit. They had even tried to grant them full citizenship with the Civil Rights Bill of 1866.

Things only got worse for them. In July 1868 the North passed the Fourteenth Amendment entering a new era of Reconstruction. This amendment granted citizenship and legal rights to the former slaves. It also banned former members of the rebel armed forces from any military activities: even the forming of militias. Worse still, ex-soldiers were prohibited from serving in any law enforcement capacity.

These 'vindictive' prohibitions unleashed violent emotions in the ardent Southern veterans. They saw the North's triumphalism – its seeming ignorance of Southern traditions, Southern values – as simply too much. And unsurprisingly, it was ex-soldiers who were the most prominent supporters of the values of Confederacy. Men like the Pulaski Six now took it upon themselves to reassert white, Southern pride. To them, this was the only way the South could recover.

Plantations, once the engine of Southern prosperity, now lacked the slave labour on which they had so utterly depended. The harvest of 1866 rotted in the fields. There was no one to plant and tend the next year's crop, let alone harvest and process that which had already been planted. Stunned plantation owners complained they had treated their slaves like family. They'd fed, clothed and protected their slaves. They knew them and their children by name, providing for them all in sickness and old age. This *Gone with the Wind* fairy-tale reality was presided over by the slave-holder. He was the 'massa' in a benign world of simple, happy slaves: a make-believe figure of elegant sophistication and gentlemanly codes of honour.

Most former slaves had, naturally, fled the site of their torment. Some wandered around the region searching for loved ones and family members.

Only a few remained on the plantations – too accustomed to the way of life, or too old, scared or damaged to leave.

Yet the overwhelming support among whites for the old ways was in some manners, odd. For all its influence, the Southern slave-holding population was remarkably small. One estimate puts the number at the outbreak of the Civil War at no more than 43,000 planters, with only a wealthy elite owning more than twenty slaves. The vast majority of the nearly 5.5 million whites in the Confederate South were hardscrabble farmers, manual labourers and urban poor. These people owned no slaves at all.[5]

Stories spread from the plantations to the Southern white population of obdurate former slaves demanding crazy sums in wages or refusing to work at all. Oddly, it was those who had never come close to owning slaves who seemed the most outraged – frequently even more so than those whose 'property' had been taken from them. With a logic not unlike the trickle-down capitalism of today, these poor Southern whites supported slavery with the most visceral and vocal of faiths.

An English visitor during the cotton boom of the 1850s noted this, writing that 'for all practical purposes we may still regard Southern society as consisting of aristocratic planters and "white trash"'. He pointed out that the 'white trash of the South, though not themselves holding slaves, have all the passions and prejudices of the slave-holders in the most exaggerated form'.[6]

It is a startling thought: a small minority of privileged whites were able to use over 3.5 million slaves to keep around 5 million poor whites largely compliant. From this logic, it naturally followed that emancipation would mean a threat to the lives of *all* Southern society, not just the lives of the now-beleaguered planters. And this was crucial to the development of the Klan in the years to follow.

# CHAPTER 5

In the twenty-first century, a wrinkled and stained photograph came to light in Giles County, Tennessee. It pictured a group of seven men, obviously friends, posing with musical instruments, bottles and glasses. Local historian Bob Wamble felt that six of these men could well have been those who'd met in Spofford House in Pulaski the previous Christmas.[1]

But, the Klan: a *band*?

This is not as far-fetched as it might sound. In 1908 an interview with one of the Six, James Crowe, revealed the group – all bachelors – would 'frequently meet' for 'music and songs'. Sometimes, he said, they'd just roam the town serenading 'the pretty girls of Pulaski'.[2] But, the name inscribed at the bottom of the photograph allows for a very different and far more sinister interpretation. Dated 3 September 1866, the caption reads, 'The Midnight Rangers'.

Historian Elaine Frantz Parsons points out that the combination of the words 'midnight' and 'rangers' would have meant something a great deal less benign to people in Pulaski – especially those freedmen whom the Ku Kluxers tormented.

The Six – veterans all – would almost certainly have been aware that rangers had – to put it politely, a mixed reputation.

During the Civil War, 'ranger' was a term used for local, irregular, troops. These units were extensively used by both sides, but especially by the Confederacy. At one end of the spectrum rangers were 'light infantry' and 'irregular cavalry', units under the command and control of the Army of the Confederate States, bound by military discipline and subject to military law. At the other extreme, rangers were best seen as paramilitary bandits, linked to the Confederacy only to cover their pillaging.

As Anthony Minghella vividly showed in his 2003 film of Charles Frazier's novel *Cold Mountain*, irregular bands of 'Home Guards' brutally controlled the policing of desertion. They enforced the requisitioning of supplies and the day-to-day inspiration of loyalty to the Confederate cause on the home front. With slave-holders and their foremen away at the Front, it also fell to the rangers to perform another increasingly important function: the 'disciplining' of the 4 million or so slaves, and the maintenance of the caste system that underpinned the South's entire cause.

The duties of slave patrolling had always been clear. An 1825 Arkansas directive stated they were 'to patrol and visit all Negro quarters and other places suspected of unlawful assembly of slaves' and prevent their 'straying from one plantation to another without a pass'.[3] Slave regions had strict curfews since the cover of darkness enabled more secrecy for slave movement, and this patrolling usually took place at night. The patrollers were also aware that the night was the most effective time for inducing terror in the superstitious slaves. Therefore, for the 'band' of seven to call themselves the *midnight* rangers was to highlight a long tradition of nocturnal terror in slave-holding regions – 'night-riding'. And the war played a big part in its resurgence.

Abraham Lincoln's January 1863 Emancipation Proclamation had freed the enslaved in Confederate-held regions. Immediately, around half a million slaves ran away from their bondage. Nearly 100,000 joined the Union forces. Most other runaways sought some form of federal protection.[4] On the plantations there was a surge in sabotage and increasing insubordination. Across the region a noticeable fragility emerged between slave and slave-holder.[5]

Against this backdrop, the retention and control of slaves became ever more vital to the survival of the Southern cause. The slightest disturbance met with savage reprisals.[6] With the majority of the white male population away at the Front, controlling and punishing the slaves fell to the Home Guard – the rangers – and they tended to be even more brutal than their pre-war slave patrol counterparts. Perhaps this was foreseeable, for as the South's situation worsened, the rangers lashed out.

Slaves became not just tokens of all the South stood to lose but, more worryingly, they seemed in league with their enemies. What was more, unlike the slave patrols of the past, the wartime rangers were not chosen and funded by the slave-holders. Also, during the war they'd been under the control of the military. Now, with defeat, the post-war rangers felt less constrained – and they could be even more ruthless than their notoriously cruel predecessors.[7]

Given this background, for the Klansmen to call themselves 'midnight rangers' makes perfect sense. The Pulaski Six, like the tens of thousands of veterans who'd served, suffered and been wounded for the Southern cause, were inevitably the most resentful over the failure of that cause. The Klan's bloody history begins with this deep-seated resentment. With this feeling, their mission comes into focus: the persecution of the group they saw as the beneficiaries of the war and the root cause of their suffering – the now freed slaves.

So, to return to that photo. At the time it was taken, in September 1866, it is possible to detect an upsurge in Black political activity and a corresponding rise in violent white attempts at its suppression. Federal government agents stationed in the region reported this was especially pronounced in Tennessee's Giles and Maury Counties, focused in the area surrounding Pulaski in particular.

Which begs the question: why this region? What made it such a breeding ground for racial violence?

# CHAPTER 6

Civil wars cannot just end. The South had rebelled and attempted to break up the Union, the US nation. There could be no treaty, only total surrender and forced reintegration. There could only be victory for the North and defeat for the South. There could only be the imposition of one set of ideals on the other – if necessary, by force.

To the Pulaski Six, such a prospect was horrific. They had fought the federal government and lost. They were now forced to obey those laws the victors created – no matter how odious. The only alternative was essentially another treason, a new rebellion – or at least an insurrection – and they found their way towards this through 'ranging'.

Even moderates who ultimately accepted, or acquiesced to, the South's defeat found themselves sympathising with those advocating insurrection. Rumours flew in conservative circles about plantation property being confiscated. It seemed that the Northern Radicals not only supported ex-slaves in their demands for actual wages for the work they did, but the Radicals seemed to be edging ever closer to granting them full political equality. Most terrifyingly, there were signs that the Black population was being armed in order to take and defend those rights by force.

Tennessee was a particularly ripe breeding ground for violence. It was a point where the two perspectives on how the peace should be enacted met, most clearly. The state had been recaptured *before* Lincoln issued his Emancipation Proclamation in January 1863. That edict set free all slaves in *rebel-held* territory. As a result, Tennessee's 20,000 slaves were already part of the Union when Lincoln made the Proclamation, and so could not be declared free.[1] Ironically, until Tennessee's February 1865 Constitutional ratification, slavery wouldn't be abolished in the state.

These years of indecision created a sense of complacency in the white population and frustration in the Black population. The Black community experienced an upsurge in political activity, leading to a violent white backlash. The situation became even more explosive in March 1866, when Congress passed one of the most momentous Acts in US history. With the Civil Rights Act anyone born in the USA gained citizenship. In one fell swoop, another 10 per cent of the people who lived within its borders became US citizens: the ex-slaves.[2] The white response was immediate.

In Memphis, a skirmish between the police and uniformed Black Union soldiers prompted a violent white backlash. Three days' rioting left nearly fifty Black men and women dead and a further seventy-five seriously injured. Black women had been raped. All the city's Black churches and schools had been burnt to the ground and over 100 Black homes had been looted.[3]

Further south, in Mississippi, reports from the first six months of 1866 claimed at least one freedman had been killed each day with over 100 people massacred in one incident. Alabama and Louisiana also reported huge upsurges in white-on-Black violence. Even in Gallatin County, Kentucky – a Union state in the Civil War – a mob of 500 forced the 200 Black residents to leave the town of Warsaw at gunpoint.[4]

Accounts of the unrest were frequently reported in shocking terms by the Southern press. For example, in late July 1866 a convention was called in New Orleans to rewrite the 1864 Constitution to enfranchise the male Black population of Louisiana. The overwhelming majority of whites opposed such a move, with the local papers predicting 'negro domination' and other horrors.

On 30 July, with shouts of 'Kill the Yankee nigger' and 'Shoot the nigger sons of bitches', New Orleans firemen and policemen pulled Black people off streetcars and beat them to death. They chased women and children down alleyways and attacked them, leaving many for dead. According to several accounts, some 200 Black men, women and children were killed that day. Crucially, the following day's *New Orleans Tribune* clearly asserted, 'All of the dead belong to the unarmed crowd. Not one single person died on the other side.'[5]

In Memphis and New Orleans there were federal inquests into the events, both of which found overwhelming evidence clearly pointing to white-on-Black violence. Unsurprisingly, no white men were prosecuted. Instead, the violence merely sped up the process of virtual re-enslavement already under way in Mississippi by 1865. Across the former slave-holding Southern states, the notorious 'Black Codes' started to emerge.

If these Codes didn't actually reintroduce slavery, they came very close to it. For example, under these Codes an ex-slave could be required to produce written evidence of employment at any time. Failure to show this meant imprisonment for 'vagrancy'. Echoing the pass systems of slavery, it clearly reasserted the Black workers' ties to a plantation, and the white boss. It made sure the terms of the freedman's employment were never the same as those of white men. Under the Black Codes the freedman had to fulfil the entirety of a contract – regardless of treatment or conditions – or forfeit all wages due.

Yet state Black Codes reintroduced the caste system at the very moment Congress sought to dismantle it. In most of the former slave states, freedmen now faced imprisonment for breaching 'race etiquette' (essentially the recognition of white superiority) in their speech, actions, even their facial expressions and body language. And imprisonment increasingly meant that the convict could be sold to the highest bidder.

But there were differences between this 'leasing' and the slave auction. Firstly, and most obviously, it was the name. These men were 'convicts', and they were being 'leased'. They were not referred to as 'slaves'. To its advocates, this system passed on to private individuals the burden of looking after law-breakers, saving the state from an ever-increasing tax bill. It kept criminals off the street and made them earn their keep. Further, the fact that they were 'convicts' reinforced the idea that the freedman was inherently untrustworthy and in need of being controlled.

Secondly, there was the money. Under slavery, the prices paid were so high, as a slave's labour was immensely valuable and their well-being worth preserving. A healthy, fit slave was an investment. Under slavery, oddly, greed mitigated some of the worst abuses. After all, who would pay good money for a 'product', only to destroy it, either wilfully or through neglect? The convict, on the other hand, was cheap. There was little incentive to look after them. If they were injured, got sick or died, then it was possible to simply lease a replacement.

While they had much in common with each other, each state's Black Codes had their own unique emphasis. Florida's codes were based on the idea of slavery as a 'benign' system. Texas' codes ordered that the entire family of a field hand must be available for work on the plantation when required. A Louisiana code demanded that all labour disputes with Black 'employees' were to be decided by the employer.[6] But, in essence, they had the same goal: the resubjugation of the freedman.

# CHAPTER 7

By the end of 1866, it seemed like the South was being permitted to reshape its post-war world in a way that suited it, ignoring the fact that they had lost that war. Soon the federal government would take away the carrot and apply the stick. This would further fuel a growing white rage and in turn a greater desire to bring the South to heel and remind them of why the war had been fought. Yet it looked like the war was about to restart.

Even in Washington, the battle lines were clearly visible. The man in the White House, Andrew Johnson, continued his policy of leniency towards the South. In Congress, the dominant clique, the Radical Republicans, saw this as a betrayal of the legacy of Union heroes killed in the war for emancipation. As one Radical New England editor bluntly put it, Johnson was defending the South's 'glorious privileges of flogging women and buying and selling children'.[1]

A mere month after the assassination of Lincoln, Johnson's presidential decree stated that he would grant amnesty and pardon to those 'who directly or indirectly participated in the rebellion'. Johnson told Congress explicitly that he intended to restore not only pardons but all legal rights and property – other than slaves. All the former Confederates needed to do was swear a binding oath to:

> Henceforth faithfully support, protect and defend the Constitution of the United States, and the Union of the States thereunder; and … abide by, and faithfully support all laws and proclamations which have been made during the existing rebellion with reference to the emancipation of slaves …[2]

Johnson was as good as his word. Over the next year or so, across the region, the former elites gradually resumed power and began to exert renewed control over the freedman, becoming increasingly violent as they did so. For these fundamentally conservative Southerners in search of continuity amid the turmoil of reconstruction, Johnson's decrees seemed to make things better.

These actions roused the emerging clique of powerful, outspoken Radical Republicans, coalescing around the effective leadership of Thaddeus Stevens in the House and Charles Sumner in the Senate. To these men and other Radicals, President Lincoln's plea in his second inaugural speech to 'bind the wounds' of the nation had not just been a call for healing but a demand that the South make reparations for the horrors of slavery and the destruction of the war.

These Radicals were Republicans, but not Lincoln's folksy, conciliatory type of Republicans. The time for that had passed. These Republicans were not interested in making deals and compromising, certainly not with the president, nor with the South. These men were very ready, willing and more than able to force Lincoln's visionary goals through Congress. Without real change, Stevens, Sumner and others wondered what the North's 'victory' had meant. Why had so many died? What was it for?

The mid-term elections of 1866 clearly demonstrated the South's lack of repentance and keen yearning to return to the pre-war system. Not only was the former vice-president of the Confederate States of America elected, but also six members of his Cabinet as well as some fifty-eight former Confederate congressmen along with four former Confederate Army generals. All of them were conservative Democrats.

The extent of Northern fury became tangible with the results of their own mid-term elections in 1866. Republicans won a staggering 75 per cent of all the seats in Congress. This, it should be noted, is more seats than any party has ever won, before or since, in any election in all of US history.

In the summer of 1867, a visitor to the galleries of the US House of Representatives or Senate could not help but notice the large number of empty seats in the chamber. Listening to the accents of the speakers, the visitor may well have found a reason for the poor attendance: the South was not represented. Almost all of the Southerners elected were either prevented from leaving their home states for Washington or found themselves arrested on their way to the Capitol and not allowed to take their seats.[3] This had not been unusual when the Southern states were in rebellion, but the war had ended more than two years beforehand.

With no congressional opposition, the Radicals ruthlessly set to work. Between March and July 1867 Congress enacted two 'Reconstruction Acts' authorising the US Army to turn the former Confederate South into an occupied territory. The legislation divided the South into five military districts under the full control of a federal military governor. Some 20,000 federal troops were deployed to ensure Southern compliance.

The Acts stipulated that these military governments would remain in place until Congress deemed the Southern states eligible to rejoin the USA. This would be done on an individual basis. Once two-thirds of Congress voted for change, the states within that region would once more become a part of the USA.

In order to qualify for readmission to the Union, a state was required to ratify the Fourteenth Amendment granting full citizenship to all African Americans as well as institute full voting rights to Black males over 21. And, in order to show they intended to enforce these rights, the state had to enshrine these changes in a new State Constitution.

There was one other important change: until Congress decided otherwise, men who had 'engaged in insurrection or rebellion' against the USA were barred from voting. They could not become a 'Senator or Representative in Congress, or elector of President and Vice-President, or hold any office, civil or military, under the United States, or under any State'.[4]

Former Confederates were now excluded from government at all levels, in their own states and nationally, as well as barred from service in the military, the militia or the judiciary. Not least, until these changes were made every former supporter of the Confederacy was denied the right to vote.

Not long after the passage of the Radicals' Acts, a local newspaper vividly conveyed the chaos these new laws had wrought upon Southern society. The scene was a grand house in Raleigh, South Carolina. The setting was a dinner party. It was a glittering affair attended by three former state governors, a former justice of the South Carolina Supreme Court, several former congressmen and a few other dignitaries and their wives. This star-studded cast was not the reason the party made the papers. It was newsworthy because, as the journalist pointed out, 'The only person in this august gathering who could vote was the black man waiting on the tables'.[5]

For the Klan and many Southern conservatives these intolerable new laws were a call to action. The Klan plotted the creation of an underground army with units all over the former slave-holding areas of the region. The aim of these units would be the subjugation of the local freedmen – a task it had arguably already been carrying out. The difference was the level of urgency. This was the second period of Reconstruction – and both the Klan and Southern conservatives in general believed the time had come for the containment, intimidation and, if necessary, punishment of those puppets of Washington, the local Republican activists and their sympathisers.

From its supporters' perspective, the years from 1867 to 1869 are the period when the Klan was most effective. This period 'ended' in January 1869 when the order's first Imperial Wizard issued General Order No. 1: a call to disband. According to this sympathetic and deeply unreliable narrative, the Klan ceased to exist as a force in the 1870s and would remain dormant until the next century. In this narrative of Klan history, the enforcement of the Republican Congress' 1867–69 occupation of the South spurred the white population of the region into fury, channelled into an effective paramilitary response by a heroic Klan.

To most observers, the USA was just as polarised in 1867 as it had been when it hurtled towards war in 1860. Many predicted catastrophe. One ex-Confederate general, a veteran of Shiloh and Sherman's March to the Sea, told his neighbours in Alabama that he thought it was going to get rough: 'I advise you to get ready for what may come. We are standing over a sleeping volcano.'[6]

## PART II

# KU KLUXERS
# 1867–1869

The fact is inevitable that bloodshed will follow. Reconstructed governments are bad enough with negro legislators, negro magistrates, negro police, and negro Commissioners of Education and other matters; but when armed negroes appear as military forces to keep white men in order ... the spirit ... must revolt.

*New York Herald*, 1 October 1868

# CHAPTER 8

To my mind, no one summed up the dangers of the brutal treatment of the defeated South better than the ardent New England abolitionist Herman Melville. He warns the North not to behave in 'any way akin to that of the live dog to the dead lion'.[1]

But, by 1867, that was exactly how many Southerners felt the situation was evolving. They detected increasing signs that Northern dogs were sniffing around the carcass of the Southern lion. President Andrew Johnson's concentration on reunification, his pardons and reintegration, were rapidly giving way to something which seemed to Southerners far harsher and far more provocative.

The concentration on protecting and nurturing the South's Black minority over the white majority seemed unjustified and spiteful. The division of the South into military districts and their occupation by federal troops – some of them Black – was an unbearable provocation. The exclusion of the Southern elites from representing their homelands, either in state or federal government, was unconstitutional. Their reaction was a mixture of distress, resignation and fury.

The Klan's response was an absolute rejection of the North's goal for Southern reintegration into the Union and the terms the North imposed on the South to achieve this goal. With the beginning of the second Reconstruction period in 1867, the various Klans shrugged off their innocent-looking chrysalises. Then, like some particularly venomous insects, they emerged reconfigured as the ultra-violent, night-riding white supremacists we think of today.

The escalation of violence was so extreme that by 1870 the term 'Ku Klux' and the practice of 'Ku Kluxing' had become the universal expressions for paramilitary white supremacist terrorism across the South. Ku Kluxers with their hoods and robes threatened any attempts by freedmen to assert their rights, or any efforts of Republicans of either colour, to enable that assertion.

The Ku Kluxers used such a potent mixture of broadcast threats and clandestine actions that they quickly gained a reputation for being ubiquitous, omnipresent, omnipotent and *ultra*-violent. The strategy was made even more effective by giving what was a widely dispersed, shadowy and diffuse organisation a single and very memorable name. The term 'Ku Klux' acted as a force multiplier. Just as the pre-war slave patrollers – the so-called 'Patarollers' – had drawn on the superstitions and ignorance of the slaves to instil irrational but visceral fears, so the Ku Kluxers used theatrical costumes, supernatural names and the power of rumour to cultivate the same instincts in the freedmen. Their main tactic was terror – plain and simple.

In an interview years later, a former Tennessee slave named Frankie Goole confirmed he remembered 'the Ku Klux Klan and the Patarollers. They would come around and whip the niggers with a bullwhip.'[2] The war had brutalised the South and nowhere was this more apparent than on the plantations. To some extent it was the inevitable result of the relentless constriction of all necessities by the North. Naval blockade, military conquest and deliberate vandalism took their toll, and the symbol of that Northern cause was the slave. Therefore, the slaves suffered.

But it was also driven by the sincere belief on the part of Confederates that they could and would win the war, and therefore needed to keep their human 'property'. They needed to keep that property subservient, compliant and obedient. They did not need to kill them. They needed to keep that property on the plantation, working.

But after the war ended and the slaves were freed, Ku Kluxers could take the violence to a different level. Self-proclaimed Ku Kluxer Charlie Jeff Harvey told a revolting tale to a Federal Writers Project interviewer in 1938. Without a trace of remorse, Harvey described the Ku Kluxers' treatment of captured, armed, Black militia-men:

> The Ku Klux made a boat twenty-five feet long to carry the negroes down the [Broad] river. They would take the negroes' own guns, most of them had two guns, and tie the guns around the negro's neck ... with wire, ... When the captain would say 'A-M-E-N', over the side of the boat the negro went with his guns and bullets, taking him to a watery grave in the bottom of the Broad River. The wooden parts of the guns would rot, and sometimes the bodies would wash down on the rocks [downstream]. Old gun stocks have been taken from there as mementoes.[3]

This was no attempt to terrorise men into submission – no one survived to pass on the warning. The violence wasn't about preventing runaways, keeping a workforce or protecting 'property'. It wasn't about productivity or production. Now it was about terrorism, voter suppression and eliminating a political enemy. It was the brutality of the defeated. It was the brutality of those who are helpless and enraged and who hurt for the pleasure it brings. It was sadism. But sadism with a purpose.

# CHAPTER 9

It was a pleasant spring evening in April 1867 when civilian-clad Klansmen strolled into Nashville's swanky, new Maxwell House Hotel. Secret circulars calling the meeting had been sent by the Pulaski mother den to all other dens. They had been summoned to talk about a problem: how to best resist the Radicals' agenda for the South. The time and venue had been chosen to coincide with the nomination of Democratic candidates taking place in the city, a deliberate strategy. It was thought that a mass presence of known conservatives in Nashville would serve as the perfect smokescreen for the gathering of Klansmen.[1]

According to a variety of accounts, including those of members of the original Pulaski Six, a 30-year-old lawyer and Confederate war hero from Pulaski was the meeting's driving force. Although he was a relatively new Klansman, George Washington Gordon was one of the most ardent and active opponents of the Radicals' agenda in the South.

In 1864, Gordon had become the youngest one-star general in the Confederate Army and had served with courage in all of the major battles fought by the ill-fated Army of Tennessee. In November of that year, after an ill-advised and very bloody frontal assault at the Battle of Franklin, the Army of Tennessee was 'shattered'. Gordon was – perhaps mercifully – captured.[2] He would spend the final months of the war as a prisoner of war, only to be released in the summer of 1865. Straightaway, Gordon returned to his hometown of Pulaski.

Perhaps because he did not experience the deprivation, suffering and collapse of the Confederacy, he remained rabidly committed to the cause of the South after his return to civilian life. He went straight from fighting for a glorious cause to eulogising that cause. So firmly entrenched was his view that he would later refer to the Civil War as an 'unavoidable and defensive war'.

Gordon became a passionate advocate for the memorialisation of the Confederate cause. It was not unusual for him to kneel, hat over heart, at the unveiling of memorials, publicly mourning the passing of the old order and the glorious dead of the Confederate Army. Long after the passage of the Thirteenth Amendment abolishing the ownership of one human being by another, Gordon would often publicly lament the demise of slavery.[3]

Gordon had been recruited by the Pulaski Six themselves and played a pivotal role in moving the Klan away from a seemingly harmless fraternity and towards becoming a brutal insurgency. Like many others, Gordon was infuriated by the treatment of his fellow Southerners and vowed that the Klan would become the means to fight back against the federal government's tyrannous 'occupation'. Indeed, his role was so central that after his death his wife would claim that he, not Forrest, was the first Grand Wizard.[4]

The timing of the meeting was precipitated by Congress, which weeks before had passed the Military Reconstruction Act. That measure marked the end of federal patience with the South and spelled the end of congressional leniency. Gone were the legislatures in Confederate states made up of pardoned ex-Confederate grandees: now these men were not even allowed to vote, let alone hold office. Gone were the Black Codes that re-enslaved the freedmen: now freedmen were being trained to get the vote. To enforce these changes the region was divided into five military districts, each presided over by a military governor, with sweeping powers.

To the Radicals in Washington, it was the dawning of a new colour-blind and democratic nation. To the former Confederates and racial conservatives in the South, it was vindictive tyranny, designed to subjugate and humiliate the region. Southerners like Gordon saw the Reconstruction Act as an outrage, a virtual redeclaration of war.[5] And even today it is difficult to imagine a law, even a law in support of civil rights, that would be accepted with the threat of military force written into it.

In the North, the rhetoric was just as heated. Republican congressman – later US president – James A. Garfield told Congress that the situation in the former rebel states was out of hand. He argued it was now essential to arm the freedmen so they might defend their rights. Normally a measured man, he spoke of 'a cordon of bayonets ... [and advocated] putting a bayonet at the breast of every rebel murderer in the South to bring him to justice'.[6]

By contrast, the Klansmen gathering in Nashville seemed calm and rational – eerily calm and rational. Cannily employing the rhetoric of compromise, a pamphlet put together by George Gordon seemed like a kind of constitution for the Klan. In reality, the pamphlet was a subtle, coded call to arms.

The Klan's *Prescript* contained lines like, 'We recognize our relations with the United States Government, and acknowledge the supremacy of its laws' and 'To the lovers of Law and Order, Peace and Justice, we send greeting'. Alternately patriotic, inoffensive, bland and laughable, Gordon had invented even more ridiculous-sounding levels of rank above that of the Grand Cyclops: Grand Turk, Grand Magi and Lictors presided over by 'a Grand Council of Yahoos and a Grand Council of Centaurs'.[7]

At the pinnacle of the new ranks was the Grand Wizard – a kind of field marshal or supreme commander of the Klan. Below him came the Grand Dragons, Titans, Giants, Monks, Exchequers, Scribes, Sentinels and Ensigns. Enlisted Klansmen were acknowledged as the GIs of the Klan, the 'Ghouls' of the new, self-styled 'Invisible Empire'.[8] Infantile as these names sound, in reality they show a clear understanding of the military and the necessity of effective chains of command.

Even the absurdity of these ranks was a ploy, designed to make the group come across as too silly to be a threat. The *Prescript* was deliberately vague. The word 'Klan' never appeared, only an asterisk inserted a few times where the order's name would have been. Nor was there any allusion to freedmen, Republicans or Radicals. Instead, the *Prescript* spoke in generalised terms of an obligation to 'protect the weak ... to defend the Constitution of the United States ... and the people thereof from all invasion'.[9]

Georgia's Grand Dragon John Brown Gordon (no relation to George W. Gordon) demonstrated this obfuscating rhetoric when he testified at an 1872 Joint Congressional Committee that the Klan was merely:

a brotherhood of property holders, the peaceable, law abiding citizens of the state for the purpose of self-protection ... a combination of the best men of the county. [It was] purely a peace police organization ... [Its objectives were to resolve] conflict growing out of a personal difficulty between a black man and a white man ... and restore the peace without any violence to anybody.

The *Prescript*'s promise to defend the US Constitution is doublespeak for a defence of the *pre*-Civil War Constitution, a document which, in many respects, was as coy as the *Prescript* itself, first and foremost on the issue of slavery. The Constitution before the war devoted considerable ink to defending the institution of slavery. But it is interesting to note that the first actual mention of the word 'slavery' was in the Thirteenth Amendment – the very measure that outlawed it. Both the pre-Civil War Constitution and the *Prescript* use the word 'property' instead of the word 'slave'. It was as profound an example of the power of language as seems imaginable. Another instance of *Prescript* doublespeak is in its offering of 'protection' from the threat of 'invasion'. The latter word was code for the North's imposition of military districts and the stationing of federal troops in the South.[10]

Grand Dragon John Brown Gordon's 1872 testimony is enlightening. His 'property holders' were actually the disenfranchised 'plantocracy' of the pre-war South – the region's former aristocrats. This class was well represented in the Klan. Most of the leading Klan officials appointed on that day at Maxwell House in 1867 would later become prominent politicians in the white supremacist, post-Reconstruction South. An overwhelming majority of Grand Dragons – state-level commanders – would go on to serve as either senators or representatives in the post-Reconstruction US Congresses.[11]

When John Gordon talks of 'personal difficulties' he's really complaining about the freedman's refusal to work without pay and their protest of the reimposition of 'discipline' with the 'Black Codes'. It is not hard to imagine how these 'troubles' would be 'quelled'. For many white 'property holders' the solution to the freedman's resistance would always involve violence or the threat of violence.[12]

# CHAPTER 10

The interpretation of George Washington Gordon's pamphlet as a covert call to arms becomes even more apparent when considering the man who was likely chosen as the supreme leader on that day. According to later accounts by Klan apologists, the meeting at the Maxwell House Hotel involved the selection of the Klan's first Grand Wizard, none other than the former slave trader and perpetrator of the infamous massacre at Fort Pillow – Nathan Bedford Forrest.

Like the vast majority of those who had lived well on slave labour, this charismatic 'wizard of the saddle' had hit hard times. The life he was leading in 1867 was a far cry from his glory days in the Civil War. The war had left Forrest, in his own words, 'all used up', physically and financially. He'd tried to recover his cotton plantation fortune after the war – with predictable results. He'd invested in a lumberyard, which fared little better. By the time he was approached to become the figurehead of the Klan, he was promoting the Memphis, Okolona and Selma Railroad and selling insurance.

This was some climb down. The pre-war Forrest was a very wealthy man. It was estimated he had around $1.5 million in assets. By its end he was $30,000 in debt. His plantation's crops would not pay off even a fraction of that amount. His estate was run down, with large holes in the levees and weed-ridden, overgrown fields. Like most of the planters who'd once enjoyed the pre-war economic boom made possible by slave labour, Forrest found it challenging to deal with the newly freed workforce.

Forrest's personality was particularly ill-suited to the style of management in plantation slavery's replacement: sharecropping. And though the system of sharecropping was inherently weighted against the field hands and their families, managers needed to use a subtle mixture of deception and patronising bonhomie to make this new arrangement profitable. This did not suit the irascible, cruel and deeply chauvinistic ex-slave trader. Forrest could deceive outsiders, but he would not indulge in any form of familiarity with those he felt were barely human – the Black freedmen. He reluctantly paid his ex-slave workforce, but he avoided any changes that might improve the lot of his tenants or give them further rights – essentially, anything which might lead him to concede an inch more of his land than was necessary.

In his rigidity, Forrest was swimming against the tide. Under the share-crop system, which was starting to spread rapidly across the South, the former slaves seemed, at least initially, to have achieved the means to build lives for themselves. A system was evolving which would allow them to rent small parcels of the large plantations, allegedly benefiting both land-owner and worker.

In theory the worker paid rent and expenses after harvest with part of the value of their crops – which the landlord marketed for them. In practice, plantation owners invariably short-changed the tenants, fleecing them by claiming ever higher costs to take crops to market. Year by year, the croppers were squeezed, first losing their savings and eventually ending up in a spiral of debt and obligation from which there was no exit. Legally, the sharecroppers were tenants; in reality they were little more than slaves. The main difference between their period in bondage and their post-emancipation status was that now they were enslaved by debt rather than fear of the whip. Often, they were subject to both.

Sharecropping might have saved Forrest financially. It seems he cared more about keeping his workers within the caste system he'd fought to preserve than in making a profit. Forrest never even paid lip service to the standing of the freedmen, driving his field hands just as hard and just as brutally as he had done when they had been slaves. Forrest was even accused of killing one of his Black field hands, Thomas Edwards, with an axe.

Forrest never denied killing the man, but he did put forward different reasons for his action – depending on his audience. To his fellow white Southerners, he claimed Edwards had 'insulted him', adding that the field hand was well known as a leader of a group of around 100 or so local 'resentful Blacks'. To the local Republican authorities, he was more circumspect, telling the story that he'd intervened when he discovered Edwards drunk and beating his wife. When Edwards threatened him with a knife, Forrest claimed, he hit the freedman with an axe in self-defence. Edwards' wife denied this. Incredibly, the local Freedmen's Bureau investigation found Forrest to be 'indulgent' with his workers, even allowing them to carry arms.[1]

Historians dispute many details about the Maxwell House meeting and Nathan Bedford Forrest himself. But they are unanimous in one thing: in the spring of 1867 the nature of the Klan was fundamentally altered. The Klan was no longer – if it ever had been – a social organisation. It had become an insurgency. From this time onwards the Klan would beat, whip, rape, torture or murder thousands of Black and white men, women and children, intimidating whomever they saw as standing in its way.

To the Klan, Forrest had many assets. He was a dashing figure dedicated to the cause of the 'Fallen South'. He was a great tactician. And he was already a Klansman. James Crowe, one of the Six, claimed Forrest had been inducted into the Klan in the early autumn of 1866. Forrest had another asset, sinister in its utility. Unlike many other former Confederate war veterans, he was able – under the guise of his railroad work – to travel freely around the South.

Most accounts of the Maxwell House meeting claim Forrest took little persuading. By a vote he was appointed the supreme commander of the insurrection. If there is any doubt as to Gordon's intentions and the deliberately underplayed mission of the group evinced by the bizarre *Prescript*, there is no ambiguity in the election of a man like Nathan Bedford Forrest. The idea of insurgency delighted him, not for its own sake, but as a means to an end. After telling Gordon that this newly repurposed Klan was a 'damn good thing', Forrest added delightedly, 'We can use it to keep the niggers in their place.'[2] There is no evidence that anyone present at that meeting disagreed.

# CHAPTER 11

The shocking viciousness of Forrest and other Ku Kluxers was not limited to Black victims. On 24 May 1870, Republican North Carolina judge Albion Tourgée wrote a letter to his friend in the US Senate, General Joseph Abbott. It contained a graphic description of the murder of their mutual friend, Republican state senator John W. Stephens. The setting was so unlikely it added an element of surreal horror to the story: Caswell County's beautiful Italianesque courthouse in Yanceyville, North Carolina. As people debated and proposed the nominees for sheriff in the main chamber, Stephens was beckoned by a former sheriff he was hoping to persuade to run for the office – as a Republican. Pretending to consider the matter, the man lured Stephens to the courthouse basement.

There, he was ambushed by a group of masked men and shoved into a dank storeroom. Stephens was told the gang were local Ku Kluxers whose den had tried him as a race traitor and found him guilty *in absentia*. The sentence was death unless Stephens confessed his guilt and repudiated his ideals. Stephens refused.

The masked men attacked him with knives and clubs and wrestled him to the ground. Stephens squirmed and fought off their blows, but eventually they managed to get a noose around his neck. They stabbed the rapidly weakening Stephens, garrotting him and then stabbing him in the jugular vein. Next, they dragged the dying Stephens across the room, leaving trails of blood on the earthen floor. Finally, they hoisted Stephens onto a hook on the wall and left him dangling there to bleed to death. In the morning, Stephens' brother discovered his bloody and mutilated corpse.[1]

Stephens was an ideal political target for the Klan's terror. A loyal Southerner during the war, he'd been a recruiter for the Confederate Army. But with his hardscrabble background, after the South's defeat he increasingly sympathised with the local freedman's predicament, eventually becoming one of their most prominent supporters. This shift in perspective was reflected in his politics.

A Democrat before the war, he stood as the Republican candidate in Caswell County, in 1868. Winning the seat, he replaced the veteran Democrat candidate, Bedford Brown – a conservative of the 'good ole boy' type. Brown had dominated the region for so long that he essentially regarded the county as his fiefdom. By replacing Brown, and openly supporting the Yankees, Stephens was viewed as a traitor to his race and his country, and as a collaborator with the invaders.

Stephens found himself increasingly ostracised by the local whites. Seemingly oblivious to the danger, he openly advocated and enforced the policies of North Carolina's Radical Republican governor, William Woods Holden. Both men came from a poor white background. Both were former Confederates and Democrats. Both were on a collision course with the white supremacist vigilantes of North Carolina.

As Holden's agent, Stephens had helped investigate and prosecute over fifty Ku Kluxers.[2] Holden was, therefore, a prime target of those committed to 'Home Rule' for the South. Yet if the Ku Kluxers were not particularly worried about the colour of their victims, those charged with controlling them certainly were. Murdering a white government official in such a brutal and public way could not be allowed to go unpunished.

The situation that lay behind the murder of Stephens can be seen as a microcosm of the political situation of the South as a whole. For most of its history the South was essentially a one-party state. Before the war, the Democratic party had held a stranglehold over Southern politics. After the war, the emerging opposition in the South had to build its political infrastructure from scratch. Enfranchised under the Civil Rights Act of 1866, the freedmen wanted to help. In the heady early days of Reconstruction, the freedmen were supported by white Southern Republicans, politicians eager to flaunt their contempt for the region's all-pervasive caste system.

Southern Republicans saw it was their task to empower and educate the freedmen on the wonders of democracy. As a vehicle for this revolution, Southern Republicans chose the Union League. It had been founded in the early years of the war to promote the Union cause. After the war, Union Leagues spread across the South, mobilising and registering freedmen to vote – and vote Republican. To many conservatives, the Leagues became the symbol of all that was reprehensible about Reconstruction.

The Leagues 'banded ignorant dupes into midnight conspiracy against intelligence, virtue and property'. They were 'a shelter for thieves and plunderers' which 'licensed arson, assassination and rape'. But perhaps most importantly, they had 'turned loose upon the impoverished and humiliated community of the South a horde of depraved carpetbag adventurers to eat out their scanty subsistence and fill public stations with imbecility, corruption and malignity'.[3] They were 'the slimy reptiles of the pestilential den which creep and crawl around ... for the accomplishment of evils which alone can keep them in power are endeavouring to sustain their infamous project' – namely the corrupting and misleading of the freedmen.[4]

Across the South conservatives saw the obliteration of the Leagues as paramount. This strategy is clearly outlined in an editorial in a conservative Alabama paper in 1868. The *Athens Post* urged its readers to:

Organize! Organize! ... Political clubs should be formed in every neighbourhood where ten people can be got together. ... They may be 'Seymour [named after the 1868 Democrat presidential candidate] Clubs' or 'Blair [Seymour's running mate] Clubs' or 'Liberty Clubs' or even 'Ku Klux Clubs', if you choose. ... [But whatever name they took] the First object of these clubs should be to break up the Loyal Leagues.[5]

Organise they did, ultimately managing to convince state legislatures to demolish the fragile structures the Leagues had put in place. They used a variety of methods, sowing confusion among the freedmen about the role of the Leagues and discouraging potential members from joining the Union and Loyal Leagues. One method was to tell potential members that, if they joined, they would be made to serve in the US Army. They used this threat on potential voters as well, telling them that the mere act of registering would get them conscripted.

Another tactic was to infiltrate the Leagues themselves, joining in order to undermine and subvert the League's own programmes. The Klan and its allies were often more direct, putting pressure on the freedmen's employers and families, stipulating that they would not employ Union League members. They also forced freedmen to prove they intended to vote Democrat – or not vote at all.

But the main tactic used against the Leagues was simply violence. Targeting activists and political leaders was largely carried out at night, by disguised men – the now ubiquitous Ku Kluxers. In 1871, James E. Boyd gave evidence to the US Senate about this. In his testimony Boyd said he'd been a member of a 'Ku Klux' group in Alamance County, North Carolina. He explained how Klansmen intimidated Republicans and freedmen, describing the raids carried out to neutralise the 'radical' vote in the region:

by riding around in the night-time disguised to the houses of poor white men and negroes, and informing them that if they went to the election, such and such would be their fate – proceedings of that kind; and by whipping and at the same time informing them that a part, at least, of their offense was having voted the Republican ticket.[6]

The political ramifications of that strategy were swift and dramatic. As early as 1869, one freedman from Graham, North Carolina, admitted that the local League was 'all broke up'.

And that violence was widespread across the South. In April 1871 a Mississippi woman wrote to her sister from Oakland in the north of that state. She cheerfully told her that a 'scalawag' had been shot dead by Klansmen in the middle of delivering a speech at a night-time lecture to Black Union Leaguers. She then asked, 'How are the radicals getting along in your part of the country?' And told her sister, 'We have slain them here in Oakland. Every vote that was given in here was *Democratic*.'[7] In Tuscaloosa County, Alabama, at least eight – almost certainly more – Republicans were killed.

Within a matter of months across much of the South, the Union and Loyal Leagues were a thing of the past.[8]

# CHAPTER 12

The murder of John W. Stephens was not an aberration. In the late 1860s the Klan developed a pattern of particularly vindictive violence against that most hated of traitors to the Southern cause, the 'scalawag'.

A good example of this is their campaign against North Carolina's governor William Woods Holden, friend of the murdered Stephens. Governor Holden was the epitome of a scalawag.

From the Southern conservative's point of view, Holden's record as a 'true Southerner' seemed patchy at best. Holden had vowed to fight to the bitter end for Southern independence in 1861. In the wake of the bombardment of Fort Sumter he had been one of the unanimous voters for succession at the North Carolina State Convention.

Like so many others, Holden was swept up in the surge of Southern patriotism. He was outraged by Lincoln's inflammatory call for 75,000 volunteers to 'redress wrongs already long enough endured'.[1] Holden had been happy to go to war. He was a real 'fire-eater' – one of those Southerners, implacably opposed to giving up any cherished beliefs, come what may.

As the war dragged on, his enthusiasm for the cause dimmed. By 1865, as inevitable defeat loomed, Holden advocated Confederate surrender. He seemed to be moving ever closer to the enemy's federal standpoint. To the horror of his former allies, in 1866 Holden stood and won the gubernatorial election as a *Republican*. By shifting his allegiances, Holden made enemies of diehard Confederates, especially the man who would become the alleged Grand Dragon of North Carolina, Zebulon Baird Vance.

The two were closely linked. Holden, like many politicians of his day, had started his work life as a newspaperman and then progressed to become an editor. His Raleigh-based *North Carolina Standard* was one of the most influential papers of North Carolina. Holden's backing had enabled Vance, standing on a *very* conservative ticket, to win the governorship in 1862. The pair's position was so conservative that Vance stood not for the traditional 'Whig' Party, with its focus on the protection of the planters, but on a highly idealistic new 'Conservative' Party, dedicated to the sanctity of the pre-war US Constitution and set in opposition to Lincoln's defiling of those sacred texts.

When the war ended in 1865, Holden committed the ultimate act of betrayal. He took the appointment as governor from US President Andrew Johnson. To his enemies this confirmed his position as a pawn of the 'occupational government'. From that day forward he was seen as an irredeemable scalawag. In 1868 Holden compounded this reputation when he was elected Republican governor. In taking office he swore to uphold North Carolina's new constitution, pledging support for mixed-race public schools; mixed-race marriages; voting rights for freedmen; and higher taxation to pay for these measures.

This proved too much for many of his opponents. Not surprisingly, almost as soon as Holden entered the Governor's Mansion in late 1868, North Carolina Klans became active. By the end of the year, they were terrorising almost all regions of the state. We know this because Holden employed more than twenty private detectives to keep him informed of Klan activity, hoping to stay one step ahead of the night-riders. The reports submitted by his fleet of detectives give us clear accounts of Klan tactics, revealing an effective and brutal playbook which would be used across the South throughout Reconstruction.[2]

State investigators reported 'murder after murder in such frequency' that the local and poorly equipped militias were frequently overwhelmed.[3] In contrast the Klans, comprised in part by ex-Confederate soldiers, were often well led. Many of the night-riders had their own modern weapons and military training. These groups were led by experienced soldiers with at least some knowledge of tactics.

Ranged against them were inexperienced, if enthusiastic, militia. In North Carolina, these were often entirely composed of freedmen. Although Southerners in general were not committed to the violent methods of the Ku Kluxers, they were even less likely to serve alongside Black militia-men. The idea of armed Black ex-slaves was just too reminiscent of Civil War tales of rebellious slaves engaged in wanton acts of murder, rape and mayhem. The militias tended to lack military experience. Ex-Confederates would certainly not serve in these bodies, and Union veterans were thin on the ground in rural North Carolina.

When North Carolina's night-riders were not killing, they were terrorising, usually in disguise and always at night. In March 1869 state investigators in Alamance County reported:

a great many outrages [were] committed on the loyal people of the County by unknown men who go masked at night for the purpose of whipping the poor colored men, and taking from them what little they have made since they have been free ... Calvin [Caswell] Holt, colored, taken from his family and unmercifully whipped ... Sandy Sellers, colored, whipped and hung by the neck ... Joe McAdams, JP [Justice of the Peace] had a coffin placed at his door upon which the following words were written – 'Hold your peace, or this shall be your resting place.'[4]

Sometimes it was not partisan politics but the claim of protecting their communities that the Klan offered as justification for their acts of violence. In Lenoir County, thirty Klansmen broke into a Kingston jail and abducted five Black prisoners at gunpoint. The men were awaiting trial for murder and grave robbery. The Ku Kluxers dragged them to a nearby bridge and, after torturing them to death, dumped their bodies in the river.[5]

The more the detectives investigated, the more apparent it became that the Klansmen were well connected. It is probable that the Klansmen at Kingston had help from the jailers and it was reported that at least one of the masked men was a local professional – a lawyer named Adolphus Munroe. In many cases it would prove impossible for opponents of the Klans to secure convictions, no matter how compelling the evidence.

Local friends would provide alibis and give false evidence. White juries might simply refuse to convict. Local investigators would often just ignore the crimes altogether. In November 1869, in Lenoir County, Munroe managed to successfully delay the trial of twenty-six of his fellow Klansmen until January 1872, when Holden had left office. The case was quietly dropped by his conservative successor.[6]

Where the Klan didn't control political appointments, or if it encountered stubborn resistance, it would often just kill its opponents. In Jones County, local law enforcement was in the hands of two prominent Republican brothers who'd moved south from New York at the end of the war. The pair, David and Orson Colgrove, were targets for the local Klansmen – after all, they were carpetbaggers.

In May 1869, things came to a head when Sheriff Orson Colgrove imprisoned two well-known Ku Kluxers for stealing a mule. Two days later the prisoners were busted out in broad daylight by an armed group of whooping Klansmen. Within a week, Colgrove was killed in broad daylight on a public road in a military-style ambush. After the murder, his brother and other prominent local Republicans received death threats warning them to leave the county. They did.[7]

Taking heart from this victory, the Klan stepped up its violence, particularly to the north in the Piedmont's Alamance County. Here, on 26 February 1870, about 100 masked Klansmen rode into the city of Graham. They stopped outside the house of a Black Republican, town commissioner Wyatt Outlaw. They dragged him to the courthouse and hanged him in the town square with a note reading, 'Beware, you guilty, both black and white.'

In the following weeks Klansmen rampaged across the county, killing, threatening and whipping. The authorities seemed powerless as the Klan resorted to familiar techniques. Suspects provided plausible alibis. Courts were bullied into dropping charges. Militias proved powerless. When the federal troops arrived, Klansmen disappeared. Then John Stephens was murdered. Holden was in danger of losing control, and he knew it. He had to act.

In June, Holden took drastic measures and enlisted the help of George Washington Kirk. Kirk had been a Union ranger in the war and had used his experience to suppress Klan activity in Tennessee. He enlisted nine companies of experienced soldiers to form the 2nd Carolina State Troops. They were given uniforms and new Springfield rifles, and they would be more than a match for the Klan. Adding to their effectiveness, they were supported by the ruthless powers of the Shoffner Act. Under this controversial piece of Carolina law, *habeas corpus* was suspended, giving the governor the power to declare a state of emergency and utilise whatever measures deemed necessary to 'secure the better protection of life and property'.[8]

Kirk delivered. His troopers restored peace in Alamance and Caswell Counties. They detained eighty-two suspects and were joined by six companies of federal troops. There were no casualties, but the action backfired spectacularly on Holden.

While in the Piedmont, Kirk oversaw elections which resulted in an overwhelming Democrat victory. It was an ominous sign for Holden. He now found himself under fire in the press and, by September, there were demands for the arrest of Kirk on charges of false imprisonment. Holden faced calls for his impeachment.

By the beginning of December, Kirk had surrendered himself and the charges were dropped. Holden was not so fortunate. He was facing eight articles of impeachment – introduced by a well-known Klansman, Frederick Strudwick. On 19 December he was impeached on charges including the false declaration of a state of emergency in order to 'stir up civil war and subvert personal and public liberty and the Constitution'.[9] He became the first governor in US history to be impeached and removed from office.

In 1872 Holden's friend Albion W. Tourgée managed to indict eighteen Klansmen for the murder of Wyatt Outlaw. It was a short-lived victory. The following year the now Democrat and truly conservative, white supremacist General Assembly passed the Amnesty Act. It pardoned all convicted Klansmen in North Carolina. It seemed like the reign of the carpetbaggers, scalawags and freedmen was coming to an end, but events elsewhere showed they would not go without a fight.

# CHAPTER 13

The experience of Holden is instructive, but it was not unique. Tennessee was the last state to secede from the Union in 1861 and the first hostile state to fall back under the control of the Union Armies in 1863. Its position in Reconstruction is no less important. Much of that is due to its election of the scalawag Republican governor and Methodist preacher William Gannaway Brownlow.

An unforgiving and deeply religious man, 'Parson' Brownlow had been one of the most violently outspoken critics of secession. Brownlow made Tennessee the first state to ratify the Fourteenth Amendment, famously telling opponents that 'a loyal Negro was more deserving than a disloyal white man'.[1] Opponents claimed he supported the measure to be able to exploit the naïve freedmen into providing a voting pool deep enough to make sure his position was unassailable.

As if that were not enough to ensure the enmity of the racial conservatives, he then used an all-Black, sometimes mixed-race, militia to form his so-called state guard. This militia was tasked with rounding up many of Tennessee's former Confederate leaders and imprisoning them, making a point in the process that the former leaders had been brought to 'justice' by armed ex-slaves.

Reaction to Brownlow's 'provocations' took some time to become apparent. In 1867 Tennessee held gubernatorial elections. It was a test of Brownlow and the Republicans' ability to promote their radical plans. If the Republicans could not protect the Black voters, they would suffer a collapse since their success or failure hinged on the enfranchised freedmen. A classic example of this struggle took place in Maury County south of Memphis in the central region of Tennessee.

The county had long been a racially conservative stronghold. After the war it would go on to become the most virulent hotbed for Klan activity in Tennessee. But in this election, it was the scene of a triumph for the Radical policies of Brownlow. In great measure this was due to Brownlow's superb organisation and targeting of largely Black militias. Neutralising conservative threats with a combination of a show of strength and a cunning that belied their actual weaknesses, Brownlow's allies managed to draw in and protect the freedmen from intimidation and trickery. They also managed to make sure that the ballot was legitimate both at the polls and in the way in which the result was counted.

First, in Maury County, two Black militia detachments, and a further fifty federal troops, oversaw the election. They were effective. While Black voters were 'jeered and insulted', they suffered little actual physical violence. Maury voted overwhelmingly Republican and Brownlow polled over 2,800 votes. His opponent got a little under 240 votes. The figures for Brownlow's majority in each county directly correspond with the numbers of militia he deployed. Given the levels of protection provided in August 1867, it should come as no surprise that this election saw twice as many voters go to the polls as had voted in any other election in Tennessee history.[2]

This prompted Maury's Samuel Arnell, the victorious Radical candidate for Congress for the district, to call the election a 'civil revolution'. Convinced this was the beginning of a new era of race equality, Arnell proclaimed the election had been a demonstration that 'the chattel [slave] had become a human creature'.[3] But he was premature in calling the revolution over – and sadly mistaken in his optimism.

Galvanised by their humiliating electoral defeat, the following year conservatives organised and their response was well planned. They refrained from any direct action until they saw their compliance had lulled the authorities into disbanding and withdrawing Brownlow's militias. They knew this would give them a clear field for night-riding and other terrorism. Then they ostentatiously signalled their power.

On 5 March 1868 at around 11 p.m., 100 hooded and robed Ku Kluxers rode through the streets of Nashville. Simultaneously, small bands of disguised night-riders began to move around Middle Tennessee under the cover of darkness unleashing a campaign of terror.[4] Most raids followed a particular pattern. The group would arrive at an ex-slave cabin or the house of a Republican activist as stealthily as possible. They would then kick in the door and, at gunpoint, they'd drag the intended target outside and then whip and beat their victims.

Some of the Ku Kluxers had military training and would station pickets to keep guard some distance from the target they were raiding. They could warn of approaching militia. Other Klansmen, their thirst for violence buoyed by 'Dutch courage', shot their victims, not aiming to kill, but to terrorise and control. Murder, they also knew, would bring unwanted attention.

Nevertheless, the violence was shockingly brutal. In one case they gave a freedman 900 lashes. In another, nearly sixty Ku Kluxers garrotted a young Black man, tied a stone around his neck and threw him in a nearby river, drowning him. While usually stopping short of murder, those who survived were often permanently disabled or scarred and many eventually died of their wounds.

Even if freedmen survived the first raid, it was not necessarily the end of the violence. The Klansmen usually demanded a show of 'contrition' on the part of their victims. Where their targets were suspected of ignoring the message given by a whipping or beating, they were more likely to be murdered. This was the case with one freedman, Henry Fitzpatrick. Henry's house was raided and he was dragged outside and given 200 lashes. Within weeks the night-riders returned, accusing Henry of having burnt two local white-owned barns since their last visit. This time they hanged him from a nearby tree, leaving his body exposed as a grim lesson to others.[5]

Few victims continued to resist. The odds were so enormously and overwhelmingly against them – rarely less than ten to one. Fighting back led to greater levels of violence and increased the likelihood of not only their own death but their families' as well. As early as March 1868, it was obvious to most Republicans that, in Middle Tennessee, the power of Brownlow's militias had been largely broken. Republicans increasingly found themselves openly challenged, and almost invariably vanquished.

A new contempt for the militias became apparent. When the local Union League attempted to hold a pre-election parade in the Franklin County seat of Winchester, the militia guarding them was taunted by heavily armed and hostile white onlookers. As the parade reached the town square, Brownlow's militia were halted by a line of armed opponents. Behind the marchers, the windows of the courthouse opened to reveal more rifles ranged on the unarmed Union Leaguers. As the Leaguers and the militia tried to leave the square they were attacked. It was a bloodbath.

This open display of power had concrete results. When elections took place for the Franklin County tax collector and county trustee later in March, the result was far closer than may have been predicted at the start of the month. The turnout was greatly reduced and, although Brownlow's Radicals retained their posts, the election nearly resulted in a riot. It was a portent of what was to come.[6]

Sometimes Klans were foiled by their own overconfidence. The Maury County Klan felt they had sufficiently intimidated the Black population and their allies into silence. Together with other bands of Ku Kluxers across

Tennessee, they organised a 4 July parade in the county seat, Columbia. In a rare pre-emptive strike, twenty or so armed freedmen ambushed them on their way back from a rural rendezvous with another Klan group.

A fire-fight ensued. The 200 or so Klansmen were so caught off guard that three or four of them were wounded and one killed before they were able to launch a counter-attack. They gradually drove the freedmen back, first to a fortified camp and then to the protection of a detachment of federal infantry on the outskirts of Columbia. The situation deteriorated into a standoff, with armed Klansmen facing armed blue-coated troops.

At dusk, the Klansmen were forced to back off. They didn't have the stomach for a fight with the better-armed, better-trained federal troops, nor did they know what the penalties of such an engagement might be. Sadly, this minor victory in 1868 was to prove the swansong of Black resistance in Tennessee that year.

By the end of the summer the Klan had essentially eradicated Union League activity in Maury and neighbouring counties. They had forced the closure of most Black schoolhouses. They had terrified a large proportion of the freed population so badly that the freedmen took to overnighting in rough shelters in the woods rather than face a raid on their homes. It was estimated that over 200 freedmen and their families had fled their homes in Maury County and sought sanctuary in Nashville, where, without work, the best they could hope for was to live as beggars.[7]

# CHAPTER 14

Before we leave Tennessee for the numerous instances of Ku Kluxing all over the South, it is important to make a point about the name, which had come to serve as both noun and verb. Across the state Ku Kluxers became a generic term for all white supremacist terrorists. It was used by newspapers hostile to the Klan's activities both within and outside of the state. It was applied to the Pale Faces in the central districts around Maury County and the Red Caps in nearby Humphreys County. In DeKalb County, to the east of central Tennessee, it included the Knights of the Golden Circle, while in Giles County, to the south of the central area, there was the original Ku Klux Klan.

The use of the term Ku Klux or Klan for groups like this is not unique to this period. While some more attentive historians since have highlighted the distinctions between the Pale Faces, Red Caps, Knights of the Golden Circle and the Klan, the press at the time used the term 'Ku Kluxing' as a universal term: a verb for acts of white supremacist terror. All white supremacist terrorists tended to be called Ku Kluxers. Certainly, there were subtle differences in each group's organisation and appearance, but the objectives, ends and means were pretty much the same among all of them.[1]

It could be argued historians lay too much emphasis on such distinctions like this, but there are dangers in conflating all white supremacists and racists or turning them into one body, as it were. By normalising this blend, by universalising it, we unwittingly give more power to these groups, and imply a centralised movement that doesn't really exist. To attribute all white supremacist crimes, today or in the past, to the Ku Klux Klan risks teaching the public that the Klan is larger, more widespread and more organised than it really ever was – or indeed is. And that cannot be a good thing, either in terms of disrupting its actions or preventing its spread.

There is no doubt that in Tennessee in 1868 the activity of disparate white supremacist groups yielded the same horrible results. Ku Kluxing, in all regions of Tennessee, began to significantly ramp up and reporters from outside the region tended to amalgamate the different organisations. White supremacists took advantage of this sloppiness.

By March 1868, there were reports that the Klan had issued General Order No. 1, a rather grandiose title that would become famous in another context less than a year later. In this order, the Great Grand Cyclops declared war on all Republicans and their Black 'stooges', and did so with a typically ghoulish, and rather unintelligible, message: 'The bullet red and right are ours.'[2] This theatricality was meant to suggest a universal code and call to arms understood only by the initiated.

There were even indications that this gobbledegook was more than wishful thinking. In areas where there had never been any reported Klan activity in the past, threatening signs appeared. In the heartland of Brownlow's regime, in Knoxville, in the eastern section of the state, Ku Klux notices began to be seen in the streets. In western Tennessee at least sixty Klansmen roved under ex-Confederate Major John Robson, suffering no consequences and with no opposition.

This was clearly demonstrated when Ku Kluxer and ex-guerrilla leader William Duncan was thrown into the Dyer County jail after a violent clash in which the son of local sheriff James Tarkington had been killed. A few weeks later Duncan was sprung from the jail by Ku Kluxers. Tarkington was unable – for lack of resources – to raise a posse or get assistance from Brownlow to go to neighbouring Madison County, where he knew Duncan was sheltering. Tarkington stepped down as sheriff in March 1868, publicly stating that without sufficient military forces it would never be possible to suppress the insurgents.[3]

It seemed that the Klan was already aware of this. In the previously peaceful mid-northern region of Sumner County, freedmen had felt relatively safe under the Republican sheriff backed by powerful militia. In reality, they proved unable to prevent conservative authorities from arresting the militia leader on trumped-up charges of murder. Nor could militias stop Klansmen abducting and whipping the sheriff in Rutherford County to the south.

It was becoming clear that even Brownlow was powerless. By March 1868, he had been reduced to making a plea for residents of mid- and western Tennessee to 'defend themselves ... within the limits of the law'. He urged them to keep notes on all Klan depredations and promised prosecution sometime in the future.[4]

With little to fear from the militia or federal troops, the Ku Kluxers could now dedicate themselves to the reinstatement of white supremacy. The tactics night-riders had honed in the period after the 1867 election were ideal. Only now, they were far less squeamish about murder.

Between January and August 1868, the Ku Kluxers carried out hundreds of atrocities all over the state. They set about whipping, beating, shooting, raping and lynching both freedmen and their scalawag enablers. They robbed houses, burnt down schools and disrupted church services, dragging out enemies and whipping them. They threatened, maimed and killed anyone they suspected of supporting the Radical agenda. The Union Leagues were all but wiped out in central Tennessee and, when identified and found, their leaders were tortured and murdered.

Not content with annihilating support for Republican machines at a local level, the night-riders put on traditional shows of strength. In middle Tennessee on 4 July, the Klan staged several parades, including one notorious incident at Bedford County where around fifty costumed Ku Kluxers galloped into Shelbyville. Halting outside the homes of two Radical officials, they dragged out James Franklin, a Black activist and former slave, and J.C. Dunlap, a white teacher who'd moved south to work for the Freedmen's Bureau. They publicly whipped them, giving them each over 100 lashes. Then, they chased the two stumbling and weak men, raw-backed, semi-naked and covered in dust and blood, down the main street in front of their parade.[5]

The militias occasionally still fought back. In Columbia, in Maury County, several hundred robed riders paraded through the city and held a large parade in the main street of neighbouring Murfreesboro. But in Murfreesboro they came under fire from freedmen who wounded several Klansmen. Not surprisingly, reports told of the gunmen being later hounded down in Nashville, and killed.[6]

In June 1868, the Klan felt powerful enough to attempt to lynch Tennessee's Radical Republican congressman, Samuel Arnell. Openly armed with pistols and carrying rope, Ku Kluxers stopped and searched the train on which he was meant to be returning from Washington DC. As shocked passengers looked on, they made no secret of their intentions. Luckily for Arnell, he was not on board the train. Badly shaken, he reported the event to Brownlow, demanding protection.[7]

The Klan carefully targeted their actions at those whose intimidation would make a real difference. In Marshall County in the central region, the county registrar – responsible for registering and certifying those who could vote – wrote a letter to Brownlow, telling him that 'the Ku Klux are all through the county'.

Out of fear for his personal safety, the registrar handed in his resignation and left the region. He had good reason. Shortly afterwards, the registrar in neighbouring Overton County was killed by the Ku Kluxers. By contrast, the registrar in Fayette County gave in to threats and added several well-known rebels to the electoral roll, in spite of legislation expressly forbidding their enfranchisement.[8]

There was another strand to the Klan's campaign of terror. Nathan Bedford Forrest, the putative leader of the Ku Kluxers, published a warning that 'if the militia are called out, we cannot but look upon it as a declaration of war'. He went on to warn that 'There will be war, and a bloodier one than we have ever witnessed. … Not a Radical will be left alive.'[9] The threats had an impact. Conservative Republicans persuaded their Radical colleagues that the consequences outweighed the costs and stalled the legislation necessary for mobilising Brownlow's state guard. As long as Ku Kluxers didn't night-ride, the politicians would restrain Brownlow's militiamen. The result was a virtual, if uneasy, standoff: a truce.

# CHAPTER 15

On 20 January 1869, Grand Wizard Nathan Bedford Forrest disbanded the Klan by issuing General Order No. 1. It:

> ORDERED AND DECREED that the masks and costumes of this order be entirely abolished and destroyed. And every (den leader) shall assemble the men of his den and require them to destroy in his presence every article of mask and costume and at the same time shall destroy his own.

There are probably as many reasons why Nathan Bedford Forrest published this order as there are biographies of Forrest himself. In the surge of controversies surrounding the monuments, buildings and commemorations of Forrest it was estimated in 2011 that there were over thirty full-length biographies of the man.[1]

I read Nathan Bedford Forrest's General Order No. 1 as strategic. The way in which he disbanded the Klan neutralised Tennessee, which could have become a hostile state, perhaps even drawing in federal forces. When Forrest wrote the order, Klan violence was on the brink of turning even the local Democrats against them. Indeed, politicians had long argued that Klan atrocities were playing into the hands of the Radicals, enabling them to call up the state guard and protect, even perhaps expand, the rights of the freedmen, particularly at the ballot box. Effective insurgency needs to know when to stop.

To give one example, at the height of the Klan violence in 1868 in Maury County, a vehemently anti-Radical ex-Confederate white farmer, Nimrod Porter, spoke out against the vigilantes. He confided to his diary that he had abandoned his condemnation of the militia for inciting the freedmen to riot. In fact by summer 1868 he demanded that the Klan 'be stopt [sic] some way. ... I greatly dread the consequences. I fear the result.'

Nor was he alone. In that summer of violence, in Carroll County in the Klan heartlands of West Tennessee, it was reported that several ex-Confederate veterans had been among the Radicals parading in condemnation of Ku Klux vigilante activity. Uniformed, hard-bitten, battle-scarred, white supremacist, ex-Confederate soldiers, they publicly marched against the Klan: they were marching against the very organisation founded by ex-Confederates to represent their interests.[2] Such stories must have reached Forrest, and could feasibly have motivated his decision to close down the Klan.

But there are other reasons given for Forrest's action. Pro-Forrest biographer and Klan apologist James T. McNutt claims he had a change of heart in 1868, arguing that the callous, short-tempered ultra-racist was mellowed and softened by the death of his beloved mother. McNutt claimed that for the last ten years of his life, until his death in 1877, Forrest was a different man. According to McNutt, the slave trader and perpetrator of the massacre at Fort Pillow was now apparently committed to abolition and race equality.

McNutt and other apologists don't tend to deny Forrest was a Grand Wizard; they simply argue that he was more committed to defeating the Radicals than terrorising the freedmen. Some Klan apologists interpret General Order No. 1 literally, when it mentions 'bad men' and their 'depredations' while disguised as Ku Kluxers. To them Forrest's disbanding of the Klan was aimed at preventing acts of terror aimed at sullying the 'honourable and patriotic' name of the Klan.[3] Lastly, there is an apologist theory based on a totally opposite premise. It holds that the Klan was beyond the power of one man.

For all that is contested about the Klan, two things are clear: it is one of the most bigoted and brutal racist organisations in US history, and it is secretive. Because of the latter, most other aspects of its history can be contested, not least the role of Forrest. Forrest himself always denied any direct connection with the Klan. He did so when interviewed for the *Cincinnati Commercial* on 3 and 6 September 1868. And he would go on to repeat his lack of ties to the 'Invisible Empire', as it was increasingly styling itself, when interviewed by the US Congress on 27 June 1871 as a part of the Joint Committee Hearings on the Ku Klux Klan Conspiracy.

But arguably, the only verifiable part of Forrest's denial is that the Klan was beyond the power of any individual. As has been shown, the Ku Kluxers were regional and they had different agendas and different strategies. One man couldn't hope to unify and control such disparate groups, especially because these groups comprised their region's most disaffected, violent and unrestrained characters. It would be more strategic for Forrest to disassociate himself. By disbanding the Klan as a whole, Forrest would no longer be held accountable for the actions carried out in his name as the nominal head of the order.

And so, having essentially restored a pre-war, Democrat regime in Tennessee, Nathan Bedford Forrest could leave in glory. By claiming he had disbanded the Klan, he would remain forever unsullied by its future exploits – his reputation improved by knowing when to quit. And in reality, as he must have well known, his dissolving of the order would have little effect on Ku Klux violence in Tennessee, let alone elsewhere. It must have been clear to him that it was totally immaterial whether those carrying out the will of the white supremacists were the 'official Klan' or not. What mattered was what they did, not the name in which they did it.

## PART III

# THE ROAD TO REDEMPTION 1869–1877

A lawlessness which, in 1865–1868, was still spasmodic and episodic, now became organized. … Using a technique of mass and midnight murder, the South began widely organized aggression upon the Negroes.

W.E.B. DuBois, *Black Reconstruction*[1]

# CHAPTER 16

One of the greatest ironies surrounding Forrest's disbanding of the Klan in January 1869 is that his timing coincided with an explosion in the levels, frequency and violence of Ku Kluxing activities in most Southern states. This was a period of time when the Southern white elites had been re-enfranchised. The freed slaves and their Republican protectors were trying to cling on to their limited and rapidly disappearing hints of equality. The result is a brutality which escalates and brings about the death of hope for integration and a horrible resignation that the African American will have to return to subservience, if not slavery.

The violence is captured vividly by the Radical Republican judge, activist and novelist Albion Tourgée, who noted enough had been killed 'to furnish forth a battlefield'. They'd all been 'killed with deliberation, overwhelmed by numbers, roused from slumber at the murk midnight, in the hall of public assembly, upon the river-brink, on the lonely woods road … shot, stabbed, hanged, drowned, mutilated beyond description, tortured beyond conception'.[1]

The Yale historian David Blight has calculated that between 1868 and 1871 over 400 Black men and women were lynched across the South, with some regions showing much higher numbers of violence than others. In central Kentucky alone some 100 Black people were beaten, branded, whipped, raped or lynched in that same time period. In Jackson County, Florida, as many as 150 Black men suffered similar violence. In Alabama, beatings – or worse – took place nearly every day. In Mississippi thirty Black men were killed in a single day, the day of an election.

But perhaps the epicentre of this violence was South Carolina, where Blight claims that thirty-eight Black men were killed between November 1870 and the spring of 1871.[2] South Carolina held a unique position in the South: the Black population out-numbered whites. Enfranchising the former slaves had

had a dramatic effect: it toppled white supremacy, state-wide. In the 1867 election, voters had returned seventy-six Black legislators and only forty-eight whites. More than anywhere else in the South, the former elites of South Carolina were now excluded from power.

The bitterness this created is reflected in (probably apocryphal) comments reported in the *Raleigh Sentinel* that told of a dinner party:

> attended by three former governors, a former justice of the state Supreme Court, one or two former members of Congress, and several other former distinguished men. The only person in this august gathering who could vote was the black man waiting on the tables.[3]

Hardly surprisingly, South Carolina became a hotbed of white supremacist activity and the figures tell their own story.

One of the first historians to take advantage of statistics compiled at the time was DuBois. He drew heavily on the *Testimony Taken by the Joint Select Committee to Inquire into the Condition of Affairs in the Late Insurrectionary States*.[4] This report was commissioned by President Grant and created in March 1871. It was one of the largest investigations in congressional history, comprising seven senators and fourteen congressmen. Subcommittees visited Alabama, Georgia, Mississippi, Florida and South Carolina, taking evidence from atrocity scenes and holding interviews.

Since the hearings were held in public, they generated heavy press commentary. Testimony from victims was problematic since they received frequent and very real threats. Also, since witnesses were given a $2 per diem and mileage allowance, conservative newspapers argued that it was simply an income source for the 'vagabond negroes' to exhibit themselves 'marked with stripes which in many cases no doubt was done years ago at the pillory for crime'.[5]

Submitted in February 1872, the report remains one of the most vivid and shocking pieces of primary evidence. Its thirteen volumes display the true horror and tragedy of the Klan's reign of terror which had taken place in most Southern states leading up to 1869, and in many cases was still continuing, especially in South Carolina. Here, the situation was obviously beyond the control of the authorities since:

> in the nine counties covered by the investigation for a period of approximately six months, the Ku Klux Klan lynched and murdered 35 men, whipped 262 men and women, otherwise outraged, shot, mutilated, burned out, etc., 101 persons.[6]

With its large Black population, South Carolina is a microcosm enabling us to view the evolution of white supremacist violence in Reconstruction. It starts with violent retaliation to former slaves trying to demonstrate their new equality with their former masters. A Black man might walk into a white-owned business, only to find himself assaulted, or worse. A white man may feel his former slave shows too little respect for him or his family and violence breaks out.

Each of these actions builds. Whites lash out at challenges to their authority or 'uppishness' in Black communities. It might be demands for wages or political organising. Most frighteningly it could be Black military training and drilling with firearms. As DuBois points out, violence does not disappear as the Black population asserts its rights from 1868 to 1870: it grows. It becomes more organised, more targeted, more effective.

Yet the figures from the report cited by DuBois only hint at the scale of mayhem. The freedmen trying to assert their rights were met with so much violence in South Carolina that Grant was eventually compelled to call in federal forces. By the spring of 1871, Republican governor Robert Kingston Scott lost control of about half of the state. In York, Union, Newberry, Spartanburg, Chester, Lancaster, Chesterfield, Fairfield and Laurens counties in the Piedmont district, it looked like civil government was genuinely on the brink of real collapse.

Armed ex-Confederate soldiers and other racial conservatives excluded from office during Reconstruction now seized the levers of power. Many of these men had been Klansmen and they continued the Ku Klux traditions. They all wanted the forceful, violent, overthrow of the Republican administrations and the reimposition of white supremacy. And in several states, it worked. In 1868 the population was so cowed that the Republican administration was replaced in Georgia by Democrats. In 1869 the Tennessee Radical Brownlow had been replaced and his reforms undone. But South Carolina, with its huge Black population, was different.

Between 1868 and 1870, South Carolina reported less white supremacist violence than its neighbours. But after the October 1870 election the state was shaken by a huge wave of violence. Ku Kluxers began hounding Republicans of both colours out of office. Some were threatened, others beaten up or whipped. Some were simply killed, their bodies left unburied in public spaces as warnings to their supporters. Many disappeared, their bodies thrown into ravines, rivers or other convenient places. Others, terrified, just ran away.

Klans operated in precise and well-co-ordinated groups patrolling the Piedmont region. They set up roadblocks, interrogating anyone moving around and crushing any attempts by militia-men. Republican officials found themselves outnumbered and out-gunned. Frightened sheriffs and constables dared not intervene, even when men were being shot in the street. Ku Kluxers broke into the local jails, killing Black prisoners. Law enforcers watched helplessly as Ku Kluxers beat, whipped and often murdered local freedmen and known Republicans in broad daylight, in full view of the local citizenry.

The judiciary was equally powerless. Even if the perpetrators of this violence could have been apprehended, the courts could not sit. When juries were summoned, the results were a foregone conclusion. No one dared give evidence. No jury would dare convict. And if they did convict, the results would be dire. Judges who tried to intervene were whipped or beaten. Attempts to suppress the Klan would be 'a signal for a general uprising and slaughter of those not in sympathy with the marauders'.[7]

In Washington it seemed that South Carolina's Republican governor was simply letting the white supremacists run roughshod over the freedmen. After all, with the passing of the South Carolina Militia Law of 1869, he was granted the power to raise necessary forces to tackle just such an emergency.

Yet Governor Scott had no options: he seemed paralysed. He couldn't police large areas of the state since he had no reliable forces. White men would be intimidated by their peers and very few would join, especially if the militia was of mixed races. Mustering Black militia-men risked escalating the situation: ex-slaves bearing arms was the stuff of nightmare to most white residents of South Carolina. As the then senator and future US Attorney General, George H. Williams, had warned Scott, 'the formation of Negro regiments ... would unquestionably lead to a war of the races'.[8]

His only option was to appeal to President Grant for federal forces. Stalling for time, Scott appeased the paramilitaries, promising not to declare martial law, while writing to Grant, begging for federal troops. Grant proved as reluctant to commit federal forces as Scott was to use all-Black militias. The president was in a difficult position. His 1868 election campaign had been run on the slogan, 'Let us have peace'.

Grant was known as one of the architects of 'total war' on the South. He had been the leader of a triumvirate of Northerner warlords along with 'Fighting Phil' Sheridan and William Tecumseh Sherman. Together they'd waged war on the Southern economy, its infrastructure, its culture and its civilian population. But it was Grant as the 'Generalissimo' who'd unleashed that ruthless, unrelenting, mayhem on the South. To his supporters, Grant's initials, 'U.S.', meant 'Unconditional Surrender'. His detractors called him the 'butcher'.

But now, as a politician, Grant was loath to entangle federal forces in another war, especially as he headed towards re-election in 1872. But Grant needed the freedmen's votes, and failure to act against the Ku Kluxers would not get him those votes. So, on 26 March 1871, some two weeks after Scott promised to avoid martial law, the federal 7th Cavalry arrived in York County under the command of Major Lewis Merrill.

Grant had finally changed his mind because of a series of outrages that had taken place at around 2 a.m. on 6 March 1871 in South Carolina's upcountry. Led by former Confederate surgeon J. Rufus Bratton, fifty Klansmen wearing 'black gowns with heads, false faces and horns' charged into Yorkville, the county seat of York County. Whooping, they drew to a halt outside the shack of a freedman, Andy Timmons. A Ku Kluxer yelled, 'Here we come, straight from Hell', and they kicked in the door. Hauling Timmons from his bed, they started to beat him, all the while shouting, 'We want to see your captain, tonight!'

With his wife and children screaming at the raiders, the bloodied and battered Timmons told them where James Williams, the commander of the local Black militia, lived. The Ku Kluxers were particularly mad with Williams because his men 'constantly drilled and frequently moved about the country districts'. Williams had also ordered white women to 'make way for the [Black] soldiers'. He was considered by the local white supremacists to be 'a bold and aggressive fellow … unquestionably a hater of the white race … and evidently bent on mischief'. They would teach him a lesson in 'race etiquette'.[9]

Arriving at Williams' shack, they jumped off their horses and battered at the door, to be met by his wife and her terrified children. Sobbing and near hysteria, Rose Williams shouted that she didn't know where her husband was. She'd not seen him since early evening.

Denied their prize, the Ku Kluxers furiously stormed through the house, smashing it up and beating the cowering children. Amid all the din and mess, they discovered loose planks which they pried up to find Williams cowering beneath the shack. They dragged him to the nearby woods and slung a rope over a suitable branch. At gunpoint, they made Williams climb the tree with the noose around his neck in order to get sufficient drop. In desperation, Williams clung to the branch, refusing to let go.

The Klansmen on the ground waved their guns and threatened to shoot the terrified Black man, shouting and cursing. However, they were reluctant to shoot, feeling a bullet would be too quick. Eventually, one of the Klansmen shinned up the tree and along the branch. Once over Williams, he drew his knife and sawed off the screaming freedman's clamped fingers – one by one. Williams dropped. The noose tightened. For several minutes he kicked and struggled, his feet vainly scrabbling for firm ground. Eventually he ceased moving.

After that another group of forty-odd Ku Kluxers led by ex-Confederate Major James W. Avery went on several days of rampage. They whipped and beat local freedmen. They raped and beat the freedmen's wives and daughters. Then they left, as suddenly as they arrived. Yorkville was quiet.[10]

Perhaps aided by that momentary chill between the local population and the Ku Kluxers the arrival of the federal troops had brought, Merrill was able to bring a congressional subcommittee to Yorkville in June 1871. Led by Senator John Scott of Pennsylvania, the committee uncovered the recent atrocities and made an urgent appeal to Grant to utilise the powers of the recently passed Third Enforcement, or Ku Klux Klan Act.[11]

Under this emergency legislation, Grant would be able to temporarily suspend *habeas corpus* in areas where Klan violence could be proved. The legislation denied due process of law to proven members of the Klan. So, when Klansmen were arrested by federal forces, there was no appeal to sympathetic or cowed local state courts. The legislation also required all jurors in federal Klan trials to swear that they were not Klansmen. And perhaps most importantly, it authorised federal troops to assist federal marshals in arresting suspected Klansmen. Essentially, for the only time in US history, the Klan was declared an illegal organisation.

It was a bold step, marking a clear change of heart in the federal government's attitude to the Ku Kluxers. There was no doubt that it was necessary. Governor Brownlow's repeated use of militia to battle the Klan in Tennessee had ended in disaster. Not only had virtual war ensued, but the freedmen's rights had been eroded to leave them virtually enslaved, and Brownlow had to abandon his office. Locally raised militias could always be intimidated, out-manoeuvred and ultimately defeated by co-ordinated and well-trained insurgents. Troops with military experience, commanded by determined and impartial leaders, were necessary to defeat such an insurgency.

Secondly, even when successful militia actions could be mounted, it was essential to have the means to prosecute those brought to justice. Governor William Woods Holden's aggressive militia campaign in May 1870 in Caswell County, North Carolina, had achieved its military goals. It had identified and arrested over 100 Klansmen. But when Holden tried to suspend *habeas corpus* in order to prosecute his prisoners he was accused by a hostile state judiciary of assuming dictatorial powers. Not only did the Klansmen walk free, but Holden was thrown out of office in the election in August 1870.

The move to a federal system of enforcement was generally welcomed by the local population's business and planter community. Given that these people often supported Ku Kluxers, it seems surprising, especially in a region with such a high population of freedmen who might be seen as a threat. But the outrages in York County had proved to be a turning point.

*The Chester Reporter* complained that 'the cessation of lawlessness is but temporary' and that victims of Klan attacks had 'no hope of protection from local tribunals'. The *Yorkville Enquirer* told its readers that 'the Ku-Klux have renewed their violence and crime, whipping influential men for no other cause than their political opinions and the color of their skin'.[12] Enough was enough.

This local hostility to the Ku Kluxers had national ramifications. For the first time since the re-enfranchisement of all-male Southerners local pressures would spark a proper congressional investigation and a well-publicised report. Audiences in the North would read a detailed and convincing narrative of the horrors inflicted on the freedmen by Ku Kluxers in this region. For a while at least, freedmen were given more than words and promises by government. The equality under the law they were promised would no longer be threatened by their old masters' deviousness and hostility. Their voices would be heard, they would be given protection, and it appeared – at last – that they would be genuinely empowered by Washington.

# CHAPTER 17

Major Merrill's sixty troopers of the 7th Cavalry arrived in Yorkville in March 1871. Initially he was sceptical about the reports of atrocities. Like most Northerners, he felt that the former rebel territories were an entirely different country, a place where violence was endemic. He thought that the tales of the Ku Klux Klan were largely exaggeration, channelled through the superstitions and ignorance of the ex-slaves.

For generations white Southerners had promoted a myth that African Americans were essentially childlike, justifying paternalistic white dominance. A parent, especially in the late nineteenth century, had the right to discipline a child. Also, if a slave, or a freedman, was a child, then surely, he or she would have childlike beliefs and superstitions. It was entirely feasible that the Klan was one such superstition. The Klan might be an overreaction to Southern hijinks.

Many in the North, having been fed this line of thought, had little reason to disbelieve it. As one Northerner, a proudly self-confessed carpetbagger, a man who'd experienced the Klan first hand, put it, 'I think the general disposition at that time in the North was to assign the KKK to the category of horse play.'[1] In the minds of many Northerners, blackface, minstrels and other portrayals of Southern Black people as comically ignorant mingled with the urge to end the cruelties of slavery.

But Merrill was a scholarly and principled man. He'd the 'head, face and spectacles of a German professor, and the frame of an athlete'.[2] Although he had been born in Pennsylvania, he knew the South. He had graduated from West Point and served in the Civil War in Missouri, Georgia and Alabama. Most of that service had been spent fighting guerrillas, so he also knew something of the support such irregulars had in the region.

His initial scepticism was allayed by General Alfred Terry, the last military governor of the Third Military District based in Atlanta. Terry had been a staunch opponent of the Klan since his arrival in the region in the autumn of 1869. He informed Merrill that he'd quickly 'find that half has not been told you' about the depravations and terrors in the region. And sure enough, by the end of July he told congressional investigators that he never 'conceived of such a state of social disorganization being possible in any civilized community as exists in this county now'.[3]

He'd had this change of heart largely as a result of an unprecedented level of information he uncovered about the Ku Kluxers. Patiently and slowly at first, Merrill had spent a great deal of time and money recruiting informers. He quietly made it clear that the purpose of K Troop was to dismantle the Klan and bring them to justice. As trust in him grew and news spread, victims of Klan violence sneaked into Merrill's office in the town's Rose Hotel and gave information on the movements of the Ku Kluxers. Within a short time, he'd established a network of informants that enabled him to track Klan movements, predict Klan raids and identify Klansmen.

Merrill himself oversaw interviews with his informants and kept extensive records, even cross-referencing them in a way much like modern forensics. Klansmen were held in a makeshift jail until they 'puked' information about the order. At the same time Merrill took testimonies from victims and witnesses of Klan crimes. Within months he had testimony of over 600 whippings and eleven murders in Yorkville and the surrounding county.[4]

But the task confronting him was by no means straightforward. The morale of his troopers was low. The local white population was overtly hostile and some of his men died as a result of boobytraps set where they were billeted in the Rose Hotel. Merrill was plagued by a high level of desertions and sympathy for the white supremacists amongst the local population. It seemed overwhelming. As one of Merrill's troopers put it, 'Go out and shoot every white man you meet, and you will hit a Ku-Klux every time.'[5]

Merrill's solution was unorthodox, imaginative and pragmatic: whisky, and plenty of it. He made sure there were always casks on hand for troopers not on active duty. It may have done nothing to improve their fighting fitness, but it worked wonders on their morale and their loyalty to Merrill. And to minimise the enmity of the local white population, Merrill used surprise.

Taking advantage of his mounted troopers, he would launch lightning raids to arrest suspects as quickly as possible. Usually, he timed them to take place at exactly the same time. Simultaneous raids reduced the ability of the insurgents to get warnings out and increased the element of surprise. He also launched these raids when the men were at work, which eliminated scenes of fathers and husbands being torn from their families before being hauled off. It also considerably reduced the likelihood of family members stealing away to notify others of imminent raids.

When the cases Merrill had accumulated were presented to the York County Court of Sessions in September 1871, the full extent and depth of the 'Ku Klux Conspiracy' in the region finally became apparent. In January 1872 Merrill presented the whole story to the US Senate's South Carolina subcommittee. He recounted a sorry tale of delay, obstruction, cover-ups and jury intimidation, as well as frequent attempts to discredit him. He called York County 'a carnival of crime, not paralleled in the history of any civilized community'.[6]

The intrepid and indomitable Major Merrill had one very staunch and powerful ally in the corridors of power, the US Attorney General. Thin and very serious-looking, Amos Tappan Akerman had been born a New Englander. But in the 1850s he had moved South to earn his law qualifications in Georgia. However, tempted by the fortunes to be made, he set up as a planter, buying and owning slaves. When war broke out, although he opposed secession, he joined the Confederate Army where he rose to the rank of colonel. After initially serving behind the lines as a quartermaster, he saw active combat opposing Sherman's devastating march through his adopted home of Georgia.

By 1865, like so many others, sickened by the devastation of four years of war, he had joined the Republican Party and in a complete about turn he emerged as a diehard, if rather unlikely, supporter of full citizens' rights for the freedmen. As he saw it, 'there would be strife as long as one part of this free people [the freedmen] were denied rights which the other part [the whites] enjoyed'.[7] However, his past caught up with him and since he had served in the Confederate forces, he was initially barred from assuming his position as district attorney for Georgia in 1868. But in 1869, President Grant sensed his zeal and overruled the ban, allowing Akerman into office.

Once installed, Akerman lived up to Grant's leap of faith. He proved himself fully willing to use legal protections to help the freedmen begin to participate as equals in Southern society. By 1870 his efforts had once more come to the attention of Grant, who made him US Attorney General. Akerman went straight to work. Determined to counter what he called the 'systematic and organized depravity' in South Carolina, he used the full extent of the Third Enforcement Act, the so-called Ku Klux Klan Act, to counter Ku Klux activity in the Piedmont.[8]

With the information supplied by Merrill's intelligence, Akerman gave a series of lectures in the North, telling audiences of the nightly terrors that visited the freedman. Most importantly, Akerman never missed a chance to try to badger Grant into suspending *habeas corpus* in the region.

By November 1871 Akerman's relentless hectoring of the president paid off. Grant invoked the Ku Klux Klan Act, meaning *habeas corpus* and all attendant rights to legal representation were suspended.

Now Merrill would be able to make a series of mass arrests without the hazards associated with the normal legal process. Some 500 men surrendered immediately and by January 1872, when Merrill sent his report to the Senate, nearly 600 Ku Kluxers were in custody. Within a fortnight of the suspension of *habeas corpus* the first of the Ku Kluxers were on trial in the North Carolina state capital, Columbia.

For a brief period, the stenographers' transcripts of these crimes appeared in newspapers across the country. For the first time Americans read first-hand accounts of violence from the individuals who had suffered these horrors.

# CHAPTER 18

Merrill's investigations had been meticulous. Together with the wide-ranging powers the federal government assumed under the three Enforcement Acts, the prosecution was finally in with a fighting chance of convincing a court of the guilt of Ku Kluxers. But it would be trickier to establish the legal precedents that would allow these convictions to become the basis for full civil rights for the entire nation's freedmen.

The US District Court House on Richland Street, Columbia, was now the cockpit for a nation-changing fight over the powers of the federal government. The questions at stake were momentous. Should these hideous Ku Klux crimes, which under normal circumstances would fall under the remit of the state of South Carolina, be decided by the US Government? And decided by two judges in that state's federal court?

Wasn't states' rights just what the South had fought for – the right of each state to govern what was not *specifically* stated in the US Constitution? Where did the Constitution give the federal government the power over the individual state's judiciary to rule on issues normally vouchsafed to them – even if those issues included murder and rape? Might there be a workaround to protect the freedmen? And could prosecutions continue when *habeas corpus* was reinstated?

These were complex legal issues and the defence poured their efforts into dividing the rulings of the two judges. If that happened, the disputes would be sent to the US Supreme Court and become test cases for the validity of the Enforcement Acts. More importantly, they would test the Fourteenth Amendment, which gave full citizenship rights to the freedmen. In the process the court of public opinion would also rule – on whether Ku Kluxing was terrorism, or the legitimate protest of a group denied their own civil rights. It seems hard to grasp on the face of it that questions of law would become more decisive than the hideous actions of the Ku Kluxers.

The first case on trial demonstrated the painful challenges confronting the prosecution. The witness, a freedman named Amzi Rainey, told both Grand and Petit juries, on 1 February 1871, how he hid in his loft while his wife tried to reason with the large party of Ku Kluxers who had arrived at his farm. They wanted to know where Amzi was hiding, so they beat his wife and shouted in her face, threatening to kill her. The small girl Amzi's wife held in her arms began to howl and pleaded for her father's life. The noise infuriated one of the Ku Kluxers. Drawing his pistol, he shot the child in the forehead. Miraculously, the child survived.

While this was going on in the yard, members of the night-riding gang inside the house took turns in raping Amzi's oldest daughter in full view of the couple's two other children cowering in the corner. To spare his family further brutalisation, Amzi gave himself up. The Ku Kluxers beat and whipped him and then told him they would spare his life if he promised he would never vote Republican. After he did so they chased him into the woods anyway, shooting at him as he ran.[1]

There is no doubt that both juries would have been sympathetic to the plight of the Rainey family, especially since over two-thirds of the jurors were Black. But, as lawyers reminded them, the violence itself, who had perpetrated it and who had suffered from it were not the issues at stake. Those offences were the purview of the South Carolina courts, and they had already demonstrated that they were not interested.

What was to be decided in the *federal* courts was Constitutional Law, namely whether the Fourteenth and Fifteenth Amendments had been breached. But even if the juries decided these laws had indeed been breached, who would enforce them? The issue at hand was therefore: had the violence and intimidation violated Rainey's rights as a citizen?

The court found they had, and the other cases brought forward agreed with that assessment of Klan activity. But these were pyrrhic victories.

Separately, the Grant administration found itself rocked by an ever-widening ripple of scandals and corruption, and the Attorney General himself became embroiled in one. In December 1871, Akerman resigned. His successor George Williams initially showed a great deal of enthusiasm for the continuation of the trials of Ku Kluxers. These trials would carry on for the next two years.

But in spite of the scope and meticulousness of accounts, the victims' courage and the obvious lack of remorse in the defendants, the tally of the courts was poor. Over the whole period some 3,000 men were indicted by Grand Juries. Most were from South Carolina but many were also from other states. About 600 of those men who went to trial were convicted.

Most got light sentences – a year or less. Others were let off with fines. Some sixty-five were given more serious sentences of up to five years, ending up in the federal penitentiary in Albany, New York. Few of them served the full term. The vast majority of others, about 2,000, saw the charges against them dropped. Such was the pressure on the court system.[2]

In December 1872, about a year after taking office, Williams began to draw back from prioritising federal prosecutions of the Klan. He had watched the horrific violence subside. He began to grumble that the Fourteenth and Fifteenth Amendments were too expensive, too controversial. The US legal system shouldn't be burdened with enforcing them. Instead, he relied on an assurance:

> that the Ku Klux Klan and similar combinations of persons shall be abandoned and the rights of persons be respected, and when this is done obviously there will be little need for proceeding any further with criminal prosecutions under said acts.[3]

It was supremely naïve, but Klan prosecutions dried up in 1873 and the freedmen found themselves cast adrift, unable to claim or assert their legal rights. Finally, the US Supreme Court effectively neutered any real chance of federal enforcement of these rights in the 1876 ruling *US v. Cruikshank* – of which, more later.

Even before he left office, Akerman had sensed his fellow countrymen north of the Mason–Dixon line would soon lose interest for, 'Even such atrocities as Ku Kluxing do not hold their attention as long and as earnestly as we should expect. The Northern mind being full of what is called progress, runs away from the past.'[4]

He was right. Whatever his personal feelings might have been, George Williams almost certainly changed course for the very same reasons Akerman highlighted: the Enforcement Acts and the so-called 'Reconstruction Amendments' were at odds with the mood of the nation. And the situation in the South over the next six years would bear out Akerman's predictions.

To those battling them, the Klan was fighting for the past – they were trying to halt progress. To those within the Klans, they were fighting for the future of the South and the progress of the white race. But these were the years of the temptation of unlimited wealth in the resources of the West and the unfettered capitalism of industrialisation. For most Northerners these held far more promise than forever replaying the squalid brutality of the past, still raging in the backward South. Better, they thought, to leave the Klan and its allies to do as they wished. But it would take a shockingly violent act to turn the white supremacists' increasingly likely victory into a legal reality.

# CHAPTER 19

In a cemetery in northern Louisiana's Piney Woods region, there used to be a monument dedicated to three victims of the racial violence of the 1870s. The site is at Colfax, Grant County's county seat. Erected in 1921, it commemorated James West Hadnot, Stephen Decatur Parish and Sidney Harris. It says all were killed on Easter Sunday in 1873. Their names arched across the base of a 12ft marble obelisk commemorating the massacre followed by the words, 'Who fell in the Colfax riot fighting for white supremacy, April 13, 1873.'

Outside the courthouse, not that far away from the cemetery, there is another sign. It is a less flamboyant, brown metal plaque. It was erected in 1951 and reads, 'On this site occurred the Colfax Riot in which three white men and 150 negroes were slain. This event on April 13, 1873 marked the end of carpetbag misrule in the South.' It mentions no names. It was removed in May 2021.[1]

The scale of the infamous Colfax Massacre dwarfs any other act of white supremacist terrorism in the 1870s' South, and ranks it as one of the most significant racial massacres in a shamefully crowded field in US history. It was an orgy of violence. Figures are imprecise because the Black victims were simply rolled into an unmarked grave and forgotten. But it is currently estimated that up to 165 Black people were killed. And there they still lie, in the shadow of the monument erected some fifty years later to honour three white supremacists.

The subtext of the two monuments is clear and very informative. In the 1921 monument, the dead freedmen were simply erased. They were either unimportant, or 'the enemy'. In the 1951 plaque the subtext is equally clear. They were collateral damage, the necessary casualties of Louisiana's war against 'carpetbag misrule'.

The events that led to the atrocity were relatively simple. Like many other Southern states, in Louisiana the 1872 elections were seen as a chance for white supremacists to shut down the freedmen's hopes for equality. They were 'marked by rampant violence and pervasive fraud'.[2] There was ballot stuffing, voter intimidation and obstruction, particularly of Black voter registration. The results were so muddled, the electorates so polarised, that Louisiana ended up with two governors. Both held inauguration ceremonies, both appointed state and parish appointments. It was a stalemate.

In February 1873 a federal judge declared in favour of the Republican governor. In Grant Parish the Republican candidates took up their offices in the Colfax courthouse and they were 'radicals', sympathetic to the freedmen. There were reports that 'rapine, riot and outrage held high sway in Colfax' driving the white population of the city out of their homes.[3] Outraged white supremacists from all over Louisiana descended on Colfax. Their aim was to make a show of evicting the Republican office holders and imposing Democrats on the city and they were going to use force.

Armed with modern firearms and even a small cannon, several hundred white supremacists descended on Colfax in early April. They were out for blood. Outnumbered, outgunned and outmanoeuvred, the local freedmen offered little effective resistance. Before long they were forced back to barricade themselves in the only brick building in Colfax, the courthouse.

But the freedmen could not even defend the courthouse against the onslaught and they soon raised a flag of truce. The white supremacists ignored it and showed no mercy. Instead, they set the building alight and shot all those freedmen who came out of it. Those who stayed in it were burnt alive, hence the confusion over numbers killed.[4]

It might have ended there. But it didn't. Most of the bodies of the massacred freedmen were burnt up in the courthouse. Others were thrown into the Red River and some shoved into mass graves. It would have been as if it never happened had it not been for the newly appointed Louisiana US Attorney James Roswell Beckwith. An idealistic and ambitious young lawyer, Beckwith launched a campaign to bring the perpetrators to justice. Using a detachment of federal troops, Beckwith managed to indict nearly 100 men for the crimes at Colfax using the Enforcement Acts.

As usual, arresting these men was another matter.

Beckwith's pleas for horses and other resources failed. By the court date he was only able to produce nine men. Witnesses refused to testify and disappeared. In the March 1874 trial, the jury ruled one of the accused should be acquitted and could not reach a verdict for the other eight. The retrial was an even greater disaster for Beckwith. The presiding judge claimed the indictments unsound and said the murders could not be proven to be hate crimes. Therefore, they did not fall under the Civil Rights Amendments so they weren't subject to federal law.

The ultra-conservative *New Orleans Bulletin* delightedly published the presiding judge's entire summation on its front page, telling its readership that the 'negro will ... understand that if he violates the rights of the white man, he ... can no longer expect to invoke the strong arm of the Federal Government to protect him'.[5]

Sadly, that was to prove to be all too accurate. In March 1876 in the case of *The United States v. Cruikshank*, the tragedy of the massacre reached its final act. The Supreme Court ruled that the provisions of the so-called 'Ku Klux Klan Act' – the prohibitions on assembly, the right to bear arms and recognition of the rights of freedmen under the Fourteenth Amendment – were all unconstitutional.[6]

There is some evidence to suggest that at least some of those men who carried out the murders at Colfax were members of the Klan. Contemporary accounts, local and national, reported some of them as Ku Kluxers. Those who later detailed their actions sometimes talked of 'Ku Kluxing'. But they wore no outlandish costumes and adopted no disguises. They did not strike at night, or ride away. As far as surviving reports tell us, they had no connections with Grand Dragons, dens or oaths of loyalty.

It was now unimportant if its commander disbanded it or not: the Klan was so purely about the values that fuelled white-on-Black violence that it didn't matter if the whites assembled had sworn its oaths, wore its costumes or even saw themselves as members. Its agenda transcended any one physical or political group. Yet even in that state they had achieved results way beyond those of its past more physical manifestations.

From 1873 onwards, the fate of the freedmen was sealed. Individual states had full responsibility for policing Ku Kluxers. Local judiciaries, law enforcers and state legislatures in Tennessee, South Carolina and now Louisiana were already proving themselves unlikely to act on behalf of the freedmen. White supremacists in the South were essentially free to act as they wished. The massacre at Colfax and the acquittal of the perpetrators sent a message to would-be imitators. Go right ahead.

# CHAPTER 20

The position of the freedmen in the former Confederate states did not seem to improve as the 1870s wore on. The militia were under huge pressure. State funds simply couldn't sustain the huge demands placed on them. Democrat regimes just sliced their budgets. Republican states muddled on as best they could.

This was apparent in all areas of government, but perhaps it was most starkly obvious for those charged with physically protecting the freedmen. Militia-men had virtually no weapons. Many had not been paid for months, if at all. They felt abandoned. A desperate Arkansas Republican begged President Grant for money to support his Black militia-men: 'Where sir, is the money to come from to pay and support these betrayed poor negroes who leave their crops and families?'[1]

Things just got worse for the freedmen in the South. As the crucial election of 1876 approached it appeared that they had been terrified into an acceptance that they would in future be free in name only. They felt that the federal government was not willing to back up the fine words of the 'Reconstruction Amendments' and the 1875 Civil Rights Act with genuine, useful aid – let alone action. The situation was succinctly summed up by a letter from a Mississippi Republican magistrate to the abolitionist and civil rights activist James Redpath, some three months before the fateful election of 1876:

> The Negroes are now almost ready to take to the swamps, and unless the Government sends troops here at least a month before the Election, the Negroes will not go to the polls. We look to the Government to stand by us and if it does not … the Southern men will clean them up like Sitting Bull and Custer.[2]

He knew what he was talking about. The Mississippi elections of 1875 had been a bloodbath, even by the violent standards of the time.

Typical of the systematic and targeted violence of the election was a report from a local Black magistrate and candidate for the post of sheriff of Lowndes County. He told of heavily armed young white men 'very much like an army', which in many ways they were. Led by military men, and composed of large numbers of veterans, they forced 'most of the colored people' out of their houses and burnt many of those houses down. As their homes burnt, the terrorists threatened the occupants with instant death if they returned after the fires had gone out. In neighbouring Clay County, a freedman and teacher told of voters being intimidated with cannon and Black voters being warned that the so-called 'white liners' would 'carry the county or kill every nigger. They would carry it if they had to wade in blood.'[3]

In another part of the state a former slave, now a state senator, told of cannon being loaded with chains and then used to 'whip the niggers and run them out'. He said that in one incident in the city of Raymond in Hinds County, 150 potential Black voters were killed. While this death toll is probably exaggerated, the violence was real enough.

In the city of Clinton, about 15 miles from Jackson, the white suprema-cists had been sadistically creative. Armed gangs of white men patrolled the Black areas at night, taking down the names of all residents. They paid particular attention to any activists, ostentatiously noting down their names in what they called 'Dead Books'. They paraded through the streets with coffins printed with their names and inscriptions like 'Dead, Damned and Delivered'.[4] These were not idle threats. One Black state representative told how:

> They [the white supremacists] just hunted the whole county clean out. Every man they could see they were shooting at him just the same as birds. I mean colored men, of course. A good many they killed and a good many got away. The men came into Jackson, two or three thousand of them. They were running in all day Sunday, coming in as rapidly as they could. We could hear the firing all the time.[5]

The shocking levels of violence in 1875 excited a heartfelt rebuke from Grant, who would later condemn them as 'cruel, blood-thirsty, wanton, unprovoked and uncalled for'. He said that such mayhem was 'sure to lead to revolution, bloody revolution' but, as usual, he sent no federal troops.[6]

Grant did, however, sanction a Senate Select Committee to inves-tigate the atrocities in Mississippi and similar events in South Carolina.

Yet, predictably, this response did very little to dampen the brutality of those who wanted to disenfranchise the freedmen. Quite the opposite: Mississippi's white supremacists, like those of Tennessee and Louisiana, seemed to feel more empowered by the ineffectual response from Washington.

The difference was that Mississippi's white liners were preparing a far more sophisticated campaign to remove even the last vestiges of political power from the state's freedmen. Combining rabble-rousing editorial comment in newspapers, intimidation of freedmen, constant pressure on Democrat politicians at all levels and unrelenting, zero-tolerance, violence, Mississippi created a terrifyingly effective model which they could, and did, export. This so-called 'Mississippi Plan' would prove devastatingly effective across the whole South in 1876.

In the build-up to the General Election of 1876, the white supremacists put the Mississippi Plan into action in South Carolina. On 4 July 1876, after a parading Black militia squad failed to show enough deference to whites in Hamburg, South Carolina, a brutal massacre followed. Five militia-men were killed. Their bodies were hacked up and mutilated, then left to putrefy and rot for days, swelling up, stinking and obscene in the July sun in full view of the local population. The victims' friends, loved ones and relatives were simply too terrified to claim and bury them.

Yet even this inhumane level of brutality failed to bring any real federal response, let alone relief for the tormented freedmen. In what was now becoming a familiar pattern, the federal authorities blustered about the terrible consequences the terrorists' actions would elicit. Yet they failed to react, in spite of repeated and desperate pleas from South Carolina's fraught Republican governor.

In September, another South Carolina city, Ellenton, near Hamburg, was the scene of even worse brutality. Here, federal troops did arrive, but too late for the seventeen or more freedmen who had been killed and mutilated, let alone the unnumbered others who had been whipped, wounded or beaten by the local Red Shirts of the 'Rifle Club' in a week-long spree of inhumanly bloody violence.

There was a different mix of the elements for the Mississippi Plan when it was used in Florida. In essence, there was less murder, but more intimidation. Here, bands of heavily armed 'Regulators' rode around Black districts extracting promises from freedmen that they would vote the Democrat ticket. Those who went back on that promise would later find themselves 'starved out' when they lost their jobs, their loans and mortgages were called in, or their houses were set alight. Some Republican administrations authorised small bands of militia to guard the polling stations and ensure the freedmen access and ensure that the November election was free. However, 'Regulators' simply called in reinforcements from Georgia and neutralised the militias by sheer force of numbers.

In Louisiana the situation was similar. Democrat terrorists openly and violently intimidated freedmen at the polls. When the federal forces allocated to track down the thugs eventually got sufficient evidence to proceed against those involved, they found the perpetrators had disappeared. They'd simply slipped over county lines and state borders to hide out with sympathisers in neighbouring regions. Here they would be unknown, or the authorities wouldn't be granted jurisdiction to pursue them.

The Mississippi Plan, or at least the organisational principles behind it, essentially made it immaterial whether the terrorists themselves, the press or even the government – state or federal – called them Ku Kluxers, Klansmen or the KKK. Arguably, it was this unified strategy that eliminated the Reconstruction Klan, not the decree of Nathan Bedford Forrest. It was simply no longer needed. With the victory of the white liners, the Regulators, the Bulldozers, Red Shirts or whatever they now came to call themselves, Reconstruction – or at least the racial integration inherent in it – was doomed.

One by one the Republican governors and Republican legislatures, dedicated to integrating the former slave population into Southern society, fell to conservative regimes. The freedman was subjected during Reconstruction to the physical violence of the Klansmen and their successors, followed by the disenfranchisement of the Mississippi System. The Cruikshank decision of 1876 essentially made this exclusion into law and, as the 1870s closed and the 1880s opened, other legislation followed.

The effects of the removal of this legal protection were compounded by the withdrawal of the last overt signs of federal protection for the freedmen of the South in 1877. The path to this final indignity for the freedmen is instructive not least because it shows how little real support they had in Washington, in spite of the protestations to the opposite.

# CHAPTER 21

On 17 February 1877 *Harper's Weekly* published what would become a very famous cartoon by the German immigrant and social critic of the Grant administration, Thomas Nast. It showed a revolver acting like a paperweight on a pile of papers. A hand reaches out for the pistol and another hand presses down on it, preventing the weapon from being moved. The headline on the top paper, clearly visible in large print, shouts, 'Tilden or Blood'. The caption reads, 'A truce – not a compromise, but a chance for high-toned gentlemen to retire gracefully from their very civil declarations of war'.

It is one of the most famous cartoons of the time, and its cryptic message refers to one of the most important moments in the history of the post-Civil War South, the notorious Compromise of 1877, a political deal that was to change the USA's perception of the Klan for generations to come.

The election of 1876 was so close, it proved inconclusive. The Democrat candidate Samuel J. Tilden of New York cleaned up across the region. But there were serious anomalies. In South Carolina, the terrorist techniques were blatant, as was the ballot stuffing, with an absurd *101 per cent* of the eligible population magically turning out to vote. Louisiana and Florida showed equally suspicious returns and the subsequent investigations nullified Tilden's victories. For a while, at least, it appeared that neither party had a clear mandate for government.

To resolve this impasse some sort of trade-off had to be brokered. This became the Compromise of 1877.[1] Tilden agreed to back down in favour of the Republican candidate, Rutherford B. Hayes of Ohio. The freedman's protectors ought, then, to have held at least a few levers of power, but in reality the compromise negated any federal protection. To secure office, Hayes had to agree to the withdrawal of any remaining federal troops stationed in all former Confederate states.

Grant, in one of his final acts as president, had withdrawn federal troops from Florida already. Now, under the terms of the agreement many would later call 'The Great Betrayal', Hayes allowed the remaining 3,000-odd troops in the region to be withdrawn. Despite the fact that 3,000 men were not enough to really afford much protection to the freedman, the withdrawal was still a blow.

As we have seen, the government's ability to protect the freedman had a pretty poor track record during the Reconstruction years. The rhetoric was impressive but federal troops, support and equipment were unreliable and frequently non-existent. It is arguable that the troops permanently stationed there were only effective when the federal government was willing to augment their numbers during moments of crisis and armed conflict.[2]

Sadly, by the end of Reconstruction white supremacists and Southern elites could cry that the 'Redemption' of the 'Old South' had been achieved. The region had been returned to the old white elites. This had two seemingly contradictory effects on the Klan, as demonstrated in the actions of a former member, John Thomas Gaston.

Gaston was a Freemason, deacon of his local Baptist church and probate judge for Richland County. He was also the Grand Mogul of the South Carolina KKK. Looking back on the days at the close of Reconstruction, Gaston recounted how fellow Klan members 'came to our house and burnt their regalia after the Reconstruction Days and buried the ashes in our back yard at night. ... Our Negro servants were scared to death nearly.'[3]

This little ceremony illustrates some interesting assumptions about the South after 1867. To Gaston it was obvious the Klan had been active and important in the 1870s. When Nathan Bedford Forrest had ordered the Klan to disband in 1869 Gaston and his fellow knights had not burnt their 'regalia'. They only did so with the Compromise of 1877, when the 'Carpetbagger Rule' was finally toppled. Gaston's words also hint at the incipient rise to power of the former elites who would enjoy the 'New South' after Reconstruction.

Gaston's 1911 obituary describes the judge as a pillar of local society. Gaston's words are also loaded with another meaning: outspoken contempt for the former slaves. This was as unambiguous as the view of slaves voiced in the pre-war Plantation South. The only difference was Gaston's discretion, a tone of amusement that the ignorant 'servants' were so traumatised by the Klan and their emblems of hatred, oppression and murder that they might literally die of fear.

It is significant also that Gaston's words have a finality to them, a certainty that the Klan's task was finally complete, and they were no longer necessary. The solemnity of the burning and burial feels like a rite of departure, a pride in having been a part of the Klan, an elegy for the cama-raderie of shared strife and struggles. This elevated nostalgia would grow over the coming decades. In the collective memory of the white 'true-born Southerner', the brutality, cruelty and inhumanity of the Klan was sanitised and made sacred. The beatings, rapes, arson, lynchings, mutilations and murders were all forgotten, or at least rationalised, in the minds of those who felt white supremacy was the South's God-given destiny.

The Civil Rights Laws underpinning the ideals of Reconstruction were dismantled, making way for the early years of the 'Jim Crow Era'. Based on a recurring folk character popularised in nineteenth-century travelling theatre, Jim Crow became the symbol of a racist stereotype – the feckless, ignorant and obsequious Southern Black man. His name became syn-onymous with the oppressive measure taken piecemeal across the South to allow whites to dominate society. In the decades leading up to the twentieth century, these bullying tactics crystallised into law, creating a segregated state of apartheid across much of the USA, most notably in the South.

As this apartheid was put in place, the history of the Reconstruction changed to justify this transformation. Central to this change was the his-tory of the Klan itself. The Klan was eulogised and mythologised. Gone were its divisions and defeats. Gone was its relish for bloody murder and the blatant self-interest of many Klansmen. It would emerge as a chival-rous, patriotic and benevolent organisation united in a common goal to establish 'Home Rule'. It was an organisation of true Southerners, united against the corrupting influences of carpetbagger misrule and Republican stupidity that would lower the white race to the soulless greed of the North and the bestial impulses of the freedman.

For the next six or seven decades, this view of the Klan had signifi-cant traction across the nation. Government had not provided the backing needed to truly provide equality for the Black community. It became easier for the rest of the country to believe in inherently racist notions about Black people than to see the failures of its own government in Reconstruction. A myth took hold of Southern whites as oppressed, heroic and triumphant. This was racism.

For more than two generations after Reconstruction, Home Rule *for* the South and Redemption *of* the South would be seen as the Klan's ultimate and positive achievement. Over the next fifty years or so, the Klansmen of Reconstruction would become as instantly recognisable a symbol of Southern pride as Jeb Stuart, Robert E. Lee or Nathan Bedford Forrest themselves.

## PART IV

# KLAN RESURGENT 1877–1921

The spirit and method of the Ku Klux Klan has once more triumphed in Georgia. Once more Southern 'gentility' and 'chivalry' have revealed their true character in murder, secession and anarchy. For the same bestial spirit that lashed and ravished the helpless slave, the same Southern spirit that even today is celebrated in the blood-lust of the Ku Klux Klan as a virtue is living in the persecution and murder of Leo Frank.

Julius F. Taylor, *The South at the Bar*, 1915[1]

# CHAPTER 22

When Southern historian Hilary Herbert reflected on the Reconstruction period a mere thirteen years after it ended, he called it 'the darkest' period of US history. He was talking about the situation for whites in the South. That Herbert could say this about the freedman's post-Bellum struggles for equality without apology or argument reveals the utter hopelessness of the status quo that had taken root for Black Americans. Once there had been violent struggle – but at least there had been hope.

We might well expect Hilary Herbert to make this comment. He'd seen active service as an officer in the Army of Confederate States. He had represented Alabama in the House of Representatives as a conservative Democrat and he was, according to at least one specialist in the history of the period, 'a leading apologist for the ultra-conservative Redeemer regime[s]' of the South.[1]

Yet, by the prevailing thinking of the times, Herbert was no extremist. His comments appeared in a collection of essays written by respected Southern historians as well as leading politicians of the time – and they all sang a similar tune. It was a period of corruption and misrule, in which Republican regimes across the South had demeaned the white population and ripped off the Black.

One of the essays in the book characterised military rule in Virginia under Brigadier General John Schofield (1867–69) as having been 'absolute despotism'. Another pointed out how the local white population in Reconstruction-Era Mississippi had been tyrannised by 'the negro and the carpetbagger'. And a writer on the Freedmen's Bureau in Texas roundly condemned those working for it as 'unmitigated rascals', men who lived to con both Black and white Texans alike.[2]

It is tempting to think these scholars were attempting to justify the actions of the South during Reconstruction and, perhaps more significantly, attempting to justify their own repressive moment in time. But not only

Southern academics held these views, and not only academics of that time period. In universities across the country, negative views of Reconstruction prevailed – of the Radical Republicans, their agencies in the field and their ambitions for the future of the freedmen. This view was prevalent in the majority of respected contemporary commentators and was represented in the most important and influential texts on the period.[3]

The best-known advocate was a professor of history at Columbia University named William Archibald Dunning. Dunning was a figure so influential that his name has become synonymous with this version of events: the Dunning School of Thought.

Born and raised in New Jersey, Dunning spent no significant time in the South. He authored forty-three scholarly articles and five books and was a leading light in both the American Historical Association and the American Political Science Association. But he is perhaps best remembered for his major contribution to the image of the Southern 'Redeemers'. He cemented their image as heroic white supremacist Democrats whose commitment to Southern patriotism had essentially ended the so-called 'Tragic Era' of carpetbagger rule.[4]

From the completion of his PhD in 1885 until his death in 1922, Dunning expanded on this thesis, arguing that Reconstruction was a failure because the freedman was wholly unsuited to the role Reconstruction offered him. This was because to Dunning, Southern plantation slavery was a *modus vivendi* by which both white and Black people benefited. Although sometimes admitting that slavery was a greedy, cruel and inhumane system, he still saw it as an effective method by which the two races could co-exist in the South. He felt any replacement would need to observe the 'fact of racial inequality' which had existed in chattel slavery. *That* had patently not been one of the aims of Reconstruction. Reconstruction was, therefore, a set of policies that had been doomed to disaster from the start.[5]

Dunning also blamed the advocates of racial equality for crushing Southern whites in the process. The federal government was also to blame. Washington was made up of idealistic and out-of-touch people, or those too weak, feckless and corrupt to stand up to the folly of Reconstruction. To Dunning and his scholarly admirers, the only option left for Southern whites to effectively stop the madness of Reconstruction policies was violence.

His most important ideological mentor was the highly influential Columbia professor (and former slave-holder) John W. Burgess. Burgess gave his acolytes the view of a pre-Bellum South filled with 'intelligent, proud and courageous slave barons'.[6] He saw the Ku Kluxing of Reconstruction as the logical response to existential threats to Southern values. While admitting that some Klansmen were 'hotspurs and desperados', he called the Klan a 'natural, if not praiseworthy' group rallying in response to laws imposed by Congress during Reconstruction which clearly had 'overstepped its constitutional powers'.

Burgess maintained that 'the mere suggestion of employing the blacks alone in such service [as militia] turned every white into ... a sympathizer with the Ku Klux'. He argued that Reconstruction 'was a punishment [on the South] so far in excess of the crime [of secession] that it extinguished every sense of culpability upon the part of those whom it sought to convict and convert'. To him it was simply logic that if the law in such circumstances 'would not yield' to the logic of white supremacy 'it had to be broken'.[7]

This view formed the basis of scholarly belief until the Depression and the Second World War. From the 1890s to the 1930s advocates of the Dunning School of Thought skimmed over the murderous excesses of Ku Kluxing. They played down the gradual peeling back of the Fourteenth and Fifteenth Amendments. And they found justifications for the nation's Black population being kept in a position of justified inferiority.

It took the deep shock of the Depression and, later, the horrors of the Second World War and the atrocities of the Nazi regime to dent that faith in white supremacy. Only after these dreadful events would academics across the country reconsider who *was* and who *could be* considered worthy of playing a full role in US democracy and the need for a greater scope and role for the federal government.

The foremost contemporary historian of the era, Eric Foner, argues that the Dunning School's interpretation of Reconstruction saw:

> vindictive Radical Republicans fasten black supremacy upon the defeated South, unleashing an orgy of corruption presided over by unscrupulous carpetbaggers, traitorous scalawags, and ignorant freedmen. ... The heroes of the story were President Andrew Johnson, whose lenient Reconstruction plans were foiled by the Radicals, and the self-styled 'Redeemers', who restored honest government.[8]

The Dunning School's logic gave historical justification for the rise of the institutional racism of Jim Crow and led to its codification into national segregation. To these academics, the restoration of the *status quo ante* South – albeit without the legally sanctioned institution of slavery – was a return to the natural order of the USA.

To the majority of academics of the turn of the century, Reconstruction was simply a detour on the path of US progress and this view importantly laid the foundation for a resurrected Klan, at first on celluloid – and then in the tortured flesh.

# CHAPTER 23

On 26 April 1913, a 13-year-old girl disappeared in Atlanta, Georgia. The last time Mary Phagan was seen alive was when she took the short tram ride from her home in the suburb of East Point to collect her pay cheque from the Atlanta-based National Pencil Factory.

At 3 a.m. on the 27th, a Black night watchman and janitor named Newt Lee discovered her body in the basement of the factory. Her underwear was around her ankles, she'd been beaten, strangled and most probably raped. Initially, Newt was the lead suspect, but within days the evidence seemed to point to the manager of the factory, Leo Frank.

Frank was a thin, sallow, bespectacled man in his 20s. He wasn't an appealing character. With his fastidious clothing and nervous manner, he looked every inch the junior manager. Moving with a peculiar series of birdlike, jerky, sudden convulsions, Frank blurted out responses to the detectives' questions. His answers ranged from the callous to the eerily disengaged. Frank only truly became animated when he was asked about his double entry accounting system. It was all too easy for the investigators of Mary Phagan's brutal death to imagine this oddball outsider as a sex criminal. It seemed to many of those who interviewed him that he was simply too weird to be innocent.

Charged with Mary's murder, inherent suspicions of Frank's perversions were confirmed in the courtroom. Early in the case the prosecution produced eleven young girls who worked for him. In turn each 'went upon the stand and swore to [his] lascivious character'.[1] Frank's guilt seemed to be confirmed when one of these girls went on to claim he had been in his office at the probable time of the murder. Later in the trial the defence produced several other young women who contradicted those assertions. But the damage was done.

Leo Frank had been born in Texas, but moved to Brooklyn when he was only 3 years old and lived there for most of his life. He had studied mechanical engineering at Cornell and gone on to work in New York as a talented draftsman and engineer. His accent was that of a Yankee. But the most damning fact about Leo Frank to observers at the time was undoubtedly his religion.

Eastern European Jews made up a considerable proportion of the 'New Immigration' which swept into the USA in the early years of the twentieth century. Driven by economic hardships, exclusion from society, religious persecution and frequent outbursts of staggering violence, many left their homes in the near-medieval conditions of the shtetls of the Pale of Settlement. Whatever the cause, antisemitism had a long history in the USA as well as Europe. Being Jewish in the USA at the turn of the twentieth century meant being subjected to suspicion and prejudice.

Antisemites levelled a wide range of accusations against American Jews. Many of these charges had been imported from Europe. In the Old World, Jews were regularly seen as capable of doing anything for money. They looked different. They spoke Yiddish. They had different customs. They tended to group together for protection and society, which made them appear clannish. This antisemitism was usually limited to name-calling with occasional physical abuse and it led to exclusion from clubs, hotels, bars and other venues. But still Jews often prospered in the USA.

Yet the success of Jewish businessmen like Frank led to accusations that they'd only got there through corruption and impropriety. Jews were often accused of lechery and debauchery as well. After all, many argued, a person obsessed by profit and wealth would have little time for the niceties of virtue or decency. Leo Frank found this argument turned against him as he stood trial for the murder of young Mary Phagan.

Frank was accused of committing 'an act of perversion': oral sex with a variety of his young female staff. This penchant for 'oral sodomy', a 'crime of effete Orientalism', was seen as resulting from 'a physical abnormality' that precluded 'normal' sexual relations: circumcision. At the time this was a rare procedure for US-born, gentile men – especially in the South.[2]

The accusation was one of the main arguments for Frank's conviction. The prosecution left it to the press and the jury to draw the conclusion that the 'foreigner' Frank had forced himself in a perverted fashion on the innocent young Southern girl. It was a potent argument backed by simple prejudice and long-established precedent, redolent of the Klan's original justification for racial violence.

Some leapt on this connection, not least Georgia editor, lawyer, historian and populist politician Edward Thomas (Tom) Watson. Leading the charges against Frank, Watson condemned the factory owner as one of the 'Jewish libertines who run down gentile girls'. In Watson's eyes Jews like Frank were 'thick lipped rakes [who] glut their eyes on handsome gentile women'.[3]

Watson also condemned Frank for the clannishness of his 'race' and pointed out that Frank had brought in New York 'Jew-bought lawyers' to defend himself. He told his readers that these Yankee intruders, like their precursors, the carpetbaggers, were responsible for giving 'our Constitution a vicious stab'. Luckily their malicious efforts 'did not kill it'. When it emerged that 'greedy capitalists of the North and East' had successfully petitioned the state governor, John M. Slaton, to commute Frank's death sentence to life imprisonment Watson's anger rose to a fever pitch. To him, they had used their financial muscle to 'nullify the decree of all the courts'.

Watson's opposition to these Yankees tapped into a very live issue. The year 1915 was the fiftieth anniversary of the end of the Civil War. All over the South there were veterans' reunions. Old men who had fought each other as young men at Bull Run, Gettysburg and Shiloh now barbecued and drank with each other on the hallowed battlegrounds. Grandfathers shared stories of their bravery and luck with their grandchildren. Union veterans who'd charged the Confederate forces regardless of the danger of putting their backs out tried to appear spry and Confederates lost their dentures imitating their old Rebel Yell. But the scars were there. The war and the peace were at the forefront of their minds. So, when Watson spoke of Yankees and carpetbaggers, it struck a nerve.

Watson's characterisation of Frank as a foreigner in 1915 came at the apex of US xenophobia when the worst horrors of the First World War were being revealed. It was in 1915 that poison gas was first used on the Western Front. It was also the year that the war spread to the Middle East, to Africa and to Asia. In this, the second year of war, the British Royal Navy stepped up its efforts to starve German women and children into submission through blockade. The Germans responded by using U-boats to indiscriminately sink not only Allied-flagged shipping, but also those suspected of carrying goods for the Allies – without giving any warning. This culminated in the sinking of SS *Lusitania* with the loss of 140 American lives.

But from the country's safe distance, Americans found a new patriotism and a sense of common superiority for abstaining from these horrifying events. As is so often true in US history, when wars threatened, isolationism had to be converted into a moral position. When the evil 'foreigner' Frank brutalised one of their own, the parochial South naturally called for revenge. And if the legal system failed to deliver, it was incumbent on the community to take issues into their own hands.

Like many of the citizens of Georgia, when Tom Watson heard of what took place on that hot August night in 1915, he publicly, and in print, supported the actions of 'vigilantes'. These heroic figures had formed a posse and driven multiple cars across the state to Atlanta. There, unopposed, they broke Leo Frank out of his prison cell, drove to Mary Phagan's hometown of Marietta and lynched him. Early the next morning, Frank's body was found hanging from a tree.[4]

Soon after, in *The Jeffersonian*, Watson praised the actions of the murders. More importantly, he tried to elevate their actions by invoking the sacred memory of another group: the Klan during Reconstruction. The noble Georgian lynch mob of 1915 had stood up to the 'torrents of abuse poured upon the South' in the Frank trial much like the Klan had stood up to the impositions of Reconstruction. Now, as then, the ordinary Southern working man was portrayed in the Northern press as ignorant, bigoted and spiteful. But Watson proclaimed this lynching a patriotic act for the South, for the state of Georgia and another 'Ku Klux Klan may be organized to restore HOME RULE'.[5]

Unsurprisingly in the North the lynching was seen differently, although it still evoked images of Reconstruction and the Klan. But both North and South agreed the Klan had become a mythological force, with all the power a myth can have. The Klan, mercurial and opaque and malleable, could be just the answer for the USA – a USA in divisive transition from the tradition, certainty and security of Victorian values into the rationalism, insecurity and excitement of modernity. A time when someone, like Frank, needed to be blamed for those changes.

# CHAPTER 24

The second catalyst for the Klan's recreation was a film. To see the importance of this, just imagine the Klan and how they look. The vision that most probably appears is one of white-robed men, with matching pointed hoods. You might see uniformed Klansmen mounted on white-robed horses night-riding, raiding Black houses and forming menacing circles around terrified African Americans, all by the light of burning crosses.

Although these images are over 100 years old, they are enduring, and they largely draw on one source: a stuttering black-and-white film. Not just *a* film, but one that, like Leni Riefenstahl's 1935 Nazi propaganda film *Triumph of the Will*, in spite of its moral failure is nevertheless recognised by film historians as one of the greatest cinematic masterpieces of all time – *The Birth of a Nation*.

The story was taken from the work of Thomas Dixon. His series of three bestselling novels recorded the trials of Reconstruction from a romantic Southern, white supremacist, perspective. According to one biographer, his inspiration came in 1872, when the 8-year-old Dixon was taken to the South Carolina state legislature by his uncle. Watching the raucous proceedings, his uncle sourly pointed out that the legislature – in what had only seven years earlier been one of the leading slave states – comprised nearly 100 Black representatives, and only thirty whites.

Reconstructed South Carolina's 1868 Constitution was based on that of Ohio. It gave priority to the promotion of equality and public education and adopted some truly radical policies. Property and colour qualifications for voting were removed, welfare programmes were introduced, local government was given more autonomy, including the creation of budgets and increased taxes. Women were given rights to own property in their own names and divorce was made easier.

Many of these progressive reforms bordered on the criminal to most of the white population of a state that had seen over 20 per cent of its young men perish for the preservation of slavery. Accusations of corruption swirled about the Reconstruction regimes. Rumours spread that land would be appropriated and miscegenation encouraged. Violence broke out and white supremacist regimes were reinstated. South Carolina's nineteenth-century flirtation with representative democracy was all too brief.

But the young Dixon saw the proceedings in South Carolina's legislature through his uncle's eyes. In the laughter of the ex-slaves, he saw drunkenness. In their scruffy clothing, eating habits and bare feet, he saw not poverty, but disrespect for the solemn chamber of law. Yet while Dixon's uncle condescendingly judged the ex-slaves as ignorant, he reserved his true fury for the white representatives – the obsequious scalawags and carpetbaggers, whom Dixon himself would later call 'the prostitutes of the masses'. And his characterisation of them, in literature, on the stage and eventually in film, would influence millions of Americans.[1]

Thomas Dixon was an overachiever in a variety of careers. After starting his working life as a minister in his native North Carolina, the articulate, charismatic and supremely ambitious young Dixon charmed and fascinated his congregation. From the rural South, he soon went to greener pastures with more lucrative ministries in Boston and New York.

But Dixon had a parallel career. In May 1905, at the age of 42, he published his second novel in his 'Klan Trilogy', *The Clansman*. Dixon had already made an impressive name for himself with the first book, *The Leopard's Spots*, but *The Clansman's* success was of an altogether different magnitude. He worked quickly. It was only thirty days from first pen stroke to full manuscript and within months the book had sold more than a million copies. *The Clansman* made Dixon a national celebrity. Within weeks he turned the two books into a play, also called *The Clansman*. By the end of 1905, after a huge box-office success on Broadway, it began touring the country.[2]

The stage version of *The Clansman* had action, a good storyline. One reviewer called the play 'a runaway car loaded with dynamite'.[3] Quasi-historical scenes of heroism were offset by romance, appealing to men, women, Northerner and Southerner alike. But Dixon felt his work could reach an even wider audience through a new and increasingly popular medium: cinema.

Producing a film required screenwriters, production crews, a director, an agent and, most importantly, money. By September 1911 Dixon had formed a corporation and funded it with $10,000 to produce a screen version, hiring the European film company Kinemacolor. But his seemingly bullet-proof luck finally seemed to have deserted him. The shareholders could not agree with him on the most basic ideas behind the production and, perhaps more importantly, worried that the fashion for period drama that had propelled his earlier successes appeared to be dying out.

But then in 1913 Dixon was introduced to the director David Wark Griffith. Griffith had started his career as mediocre actor, moved on to screenwriting and then, in 1907, took on the role of director with his first film for the company Biograph. He would remain at Biograph for over five years, directing dozens of films, growing ever more frustrated with the increasingly formulaic and repetitive output. In 1913 Griffith began scouting around for a theme for his first independent film, noticing the massive successes in Europe of films like *Dante's Inferno* and *Quo Vadis*, both of a new genre not yet fully formed in the USA, the 'historical–spectacle' film.

Within hours of their meeting Griffith felt he could already 'see these Klansmen in a movie with their white robes flying'.[4] Dixon started with a suitably ambitious demand of $25,000 for the film rights, eventually settling on $2,000. It was less than 10 per cent of the original asking price, but he did manage to secure a quarter of the film's potential profits. This was a real bargain for Griffith, but when the film became the first real blockbuster in the USA, it still made Dixon a millionaire.

In film, time has always meant money, and Griffith worked quickly. He hired Dixon's Kinemacolor scriptwriter Frank E. Woods and the pair refashioned Dixon's three books and the play into a working scenario. Next came the casting of the all-white cast, followed by location scouting, props and recruitment of the Black and white extras. When this was completed, the film went into production.

In an unconventional move for the time, Griffith filmed out of order, filming the expensive epic battle scenes first. It was a canny move, ensuring these scenes were completed before his film went over budget, which, of course, it did, to the tune of $20,000. By some estimates, that amount rose to more like $60,000. Griffith balanced his books using his skills as a Hollywood hustler. He replenished his budget by trading meals for stock in the film. Griffith also stole the wages of the Black extras to purchase costumes for the film, a stark indicator of the status of African Americans even in the far West half a century after Reconstruction.

At roughly $100,000 the production cost of Griffith's film was huge by the standards of the time. Griffith took this seeming liability and turned it to his favour, embellishing the cost even more in order to promote the film. Publicists would later claim that $500,000 had been spent on production to bring together 18,000 people and 3,000 horses in the 'mightiest spectacle ever produced'.[5] All of these claims were gross exaggerations but it didn't matter: it was clear from the moment of the film's release that *The Birth of a Nation* was going to be a huge success.

Based on ticket sales alone, *The Birth of a Nation* changed movie history. In Boston, newspapers reported an estimated 185,000 had seen it. In Kansas City and New Orleans, upwards of 100,000; in Baltimore, 200,000. One Los Angeles paper put the total audience for the year at 5 million nationwide, but the *Brooklyn Eagle* argued it would reach nearly twice that amount.[6] Whatever the actual numbers, there was no disputing it was watched by more Americans than any other film before it.

It was also a new kind of film, over three hours long, far beyond the average thirty-minute films of that time. And it cost double the price of a regular movie ticket, nearly the same as going to see a highbrow play in the theatre. But for most audiences Griffith's new film was an event and worth the cost. Full orchestras played rousing Wagnerian themes when the Klan rode forth to rescue its besieged allies and dreamy romantic melodies when the innocent Southern girl, Flora Cameron, childishly skipped through the woods.

*The Birth of a Nation* was initially shown in huge, new, 'picture palaces' like the Strand on New York's Broadway or Clune's Auditorium in Los Angeles. These were a step up from the small, shabby, Nickelodeons in low-rent districts that preceded them. These were situated in the more prosperous and safer parts of town. With their plush seating, gilded mouldings and glossy paintwork, these new venues seemed as spectacular as the films. Going to these theatres was an experience, attracting middle-class audiences alongside the traditional working-class filmgoers.

In keeping with the pretensions of the new audiences, films began affecting a stance somewhere between entertainment and education. Now, in addition to operatic themes, melodrama and spectacle, films began to blur the line between fantasy and reality. The spectacular battle scenes in *The Birth of a Nation* drew on the well-known Civil War photographs and lithographs published which had accompanied serious newspaper reports and magazine articles about the war. There were instantly recognisable images, figures like Abraham Lincoln and John Wilkes Booth. Scenes like the South Carolina legislature in Reconstruction, where Dixon's uncle had been so shocked, elevated the film in the eyes of middle-class audiences. It was not mere sensation. This was, sadly, seen as 'educational'.

Perhaps the most important boost for *The Birth of a Nation* came from the incumbent president, Woodrow Wilson.

Wilson found himself both storyboarded into the film itself and used for the film's publicity. Wilson was respected not only for being president, but for having been a professor of political science at Princeton. A leading public academic, Wilson had written a recent and well-regarded constitutional history of the USA, *History of the American People*. And his was a very pro-South interpretation of Reconstruction. This text is quoted in *The Birth of a Nation* in three title cards, essentially lending the weight of scholarship and office to Griffith and Dixon's cinematic interpretation.

Wilson was also rumoured to have endorsed the film in 1915 at a private White House screening. After seeing the film, he allegedly quipped, 'It's like writing history with lightning.' This comment was uttered while sitting next to his old roommate and fellow Southerner, none other than Thomas Dixon. Less memorably, Wilson is said to have added the rider 'My only regret is that it is all so terribly true'.[7] To him, Reconstruction was the 'Tragic Era' with its carpetbagger corruption and treacherous scalawags.[8]

Whether he made those remarks or not, they have stuck, and at the end of the day it didn't really matter. 'It's like writing history with lightning' was great publicity and what other film could claim to have been endorsed by a sitting president? By 1915: none. Presidential endorsement or not, there is no doubt people were affected by the film. Women fainted. Confederate veterans gave the Rebel Yell. Audiences cheered, booed, shouted and broke into tears.

Incidents were reported of excited all-male audiences in the rural West and Deep South getting carried away, drawing their six-shooters and firing through the screen and up into the ceilings. 'No play ever produced has the gripping power of this picture. All the women were crying and not a few men.'[9] Promoting the film, Griffith played up its historical accuracy, while at the same time stressing how it had the potential to unite the nation. As he saw it:

> The Civil War was fought fifty years ago. But the real nation has only existed the last fifteen or twenty years, for there can exist no union without sympathy and oneness of sentiment. ... The birth of a nation began, according to an authority, with the Ku Klux Klans, and we have shown that.[10]

Playing to the emotions and sentiments of audiences, blurring the boundary between fact and fantasy, the film inspired hate. Newspapers across the country reported incidents of white men leaving the theatres and seeking out Black bystanders to attack. As the National Association for the Advancement of Colored People (NAACP) reported, one 'young man', on leaving the screening in New York, turned to his companion and said, 'I should like to kill every nigger I know.'[11]

Some were not content with merely acting like the Redeemers. They wanted to *be* Redeemers, and the film's publicity machine was only too happy to oblige. Men were hired to dress up as mounted Klansmen and parade outside theatres. At some theatres, ushers changed into Klan costumes for the second half of the film's screenings.[12]

In many regions of the South the film rapidly took on the status of 'a sacred epic'.[13] *The Birth of a Nation* reinforced a sentimental view of the pre-Bellum and Civil War South and the evils of Reconstruction. Many white families in North Carolina's Piedmont district took pride in the film. This was the region where the bloodthirsty depredations of the Ku Kluxers finally led an incensed President Grant to call in the 7th Cavalry and sanction the suspension of *habeas corpus*. Yet it was here that the population openly celebrated the film and their own real or imagined Klan associations.

At the film's premier in Spartanburg the audience was described in the local paper as 'near hysterical'.[14] They seemed to have forgotten the murders, whippings and beatings carried out by the night-riders. Instead, they accepted Dixon and Griffith's 'historical treatment of Reconstruction'. They felt the film vindicated their proud past, sending 'the message to the South, to the world then, and now, [and having] even greater value' than any previous interpretation.[15]

# CHAPTER 25

On Thanksgiving Day, 1915, nearly fifty years after the Pulaski Six met at Spofford House, sixteen men rented a sightseeing bus and drove to Stone Mountain, Georgia. Using only flashlights, they struggled along the path to the summit carrying heavy wooden planks bolted together in the shape of a cross.

When they reached the top of the odd, domed-shaped mountain, the men made an altar from boulders. Covering it with a US flag, they laid an unsheathed sword upon it. They lit the cross on fire and listened as their leader read passages from one of St Paul's letters to the Romans. Then they returned to the bus and drove back to Atlanta.

The tale of this 'symbolic rebirth' of the Ku Klux Klan had been masterminded by a tall, bespectacled, 35-year-old named William Joseph Simmons. The ceremony, Simmons later wrote, was intended to revive the Klan's 'spiritual purpose' in 'a different material form; the same soul in a new body'.[1]

For most of his life, Simmons had been a failure. He claimed to have been a medical student at Johns Hopkins but there are no records of this. He repeated the story often enough to earn himself the nickname 'Doc' with his cronies. After failing to follow his father into medicine, the 18-year-old Simmons joined the US Army as a private soldier fighting in the Spanish–American War. But before seeing any combat, Simmons suffered a 'nervous breakdown' and was medically discharged. This did not prevent him from later implying he had been a war hero and elevating his rank. After his breakdown he recuperated at his elderly parents' home, attempting careers as a Methodist minister, history teacher and garter salesman.

Simmons was a classic small-town character, striding around in an old-fashioned frock coat covered in lodge pins from the fifteen fraternities he'd joined. He was instantly recognisable, but a loner. The staff of the

*Atlanta Constitution* remembered him as a 'pious, prissy-walking, big man'. Charismatic, even sensitive, Simmons was seen as a fantasist with nothing but a nodding relationship to the truth. This was apparent in his own accounts of his life.

In addition to the nickname 'Doc', Simmons liked to call himself 'Colonel', a title one wag claimed had been 'conferred on him by the uniformed drill team of the Woodmen of the World'. In truth, Simmons had no close relationships outside his long-suffering wife and his local watering hole and lodge house – but he'd developed a close relationship with the bottle.[2]

By the time Simmons led the party up Stone Mountain, he was selling membership for the fraternity 'The Woodmen of the World'. This group had originally been founded in 1882 as a quasi-trade union for forestry workers. By 1915, the organisation had become a rapidly expanding life assurance company whose successes could be measured in the peculiar stump-like tombstones that marked where its members were buried. By 1915, the Woodmen were booming, and to such an extent that even the serial failure, Simmons, could succeed.

And Simmons did succeed. By 1915, he was bringing in $10,000 a year and was enjoying his job.

On 26 October 1915 Simmons created his own fraternity, registering it as the reborn Knights of the Ku Klux Klan.[3] Thirty-three men gathered with Simmons to sign the application to the state of Georgia. Some of these were original KKK members. Some had even participated in the lynching of Leo Frank.

In keeping with his own character and the confused history of the Klan, Simmons created his own myths. In later years, he would tell many different stories about how he was inspired to revive the Klan. Some involved romantic visions of clouds shaped as white-robed men mounted on white-robed horses. Others incorporated tales Simmons heard as a child in rural Alabama from his Black nanny and Klansman father. Still others focused on visions he'd had while recuperating from being hit by a car in 1911. All involved quasi-religious experiences and ended with reverence for the Klan's mission: to recreate a mythical brotherhood united by the chivalry of the Old South.

Simmons was probably just inspired by *The Birth of a Nation*. Like many across Georgia and the South, he was obsessed with the film. He pestered one of his few friends – a local theatre owner – for free tickets, watching the movie over and over.[4] But for all of Simmons' spiritual blather, his fixation with the Klan was also financial. There are plenty of accounts of Simmons attempting to dream up a new fraternity as a money-making venture. The trouble was he was simply not practical enough to make it pay.

Simmons was aware of this failing, so he took on a business partner, another fraternal salesman, named Jonathan P. Frost. In a 1924 exposé of the Klan written by federal agent Frank N. Littlejohn, the author claims that it was actually Frost who got the idea after seeing *The Birth of a Nation* in Atlanta. Littlejohn claims Frost met Simmons at a Woodmen of the World convention and shared his idea. Simmons immediately proposed himself as an organiser. The two men formed a legal business partnership, and the charismatic and scheming Simmons quickly forced Frost into the background.[5]

# CHAPTER 26

Simmons' Klan had a burst of recruitment in its first weeks. Appointing himself 'Imperial Wizard,' he arranged for men in bed sheets and pointed hoods to ride around on white-clad horses as theatregoers left *The Birth of a Nation*. The Klansmen paraded in front of the colonial mansions on Atlanta's famous Peachtree Street, firing rifles in the air and giving the Rebel Yell. After a fortnight Simmons had signed up nearly 100 members.

During this burst of action, Simmons also contracted a local manufacturing company to make standardised robes and hoods. Based on the costumes in *The Birth of a Nation*, they featured the trademark tall point. Although the design seemed identical to those worn by penitents in Spanish Semana Santa (Holy Week) since the days of the Inquisition, that similarity is probably simple coincidence.[1] The striking design was most likely chosen because the mix of rigid and flowing materials involved made it more difficult to knock up a homemade copy.

But, ruled by his sentimental streak, Simmons ignored the financial imperative and sold the robes at cost. At the same time, he took out adverts in local papers attempting to lure men to the 'classy order of the highest class'.[2] But Simmons' uncharacteristic salesmanship was always a bit hit or miss. It was Simmons' partner, Jonathan Frost, who was said to have given the Klan more concrete direction. For some time Frost had edited a local magazine dedicated to the ideas of racial purity and playing on fears of surges in immigration.

Across the nation, there was a sense that the pre-war emigration from Southern and Eastern Europe would explode once the restrictions of U-boats and Royal Navy blockades ended and peace was established in the Old World. Frost's Klan publications reflected this fear. Advertising was targeted to recruit only 'native-born American citizens', specifying that Klansmen must be Christians with no ties to 'foreign governments', 'sects' or even 'people'.[3]

Yet 1915 wasn't an easy year to recruit members. US anxiety about being drawn in to the First World War was yet to come. Only then could Tom Watson and his fellow rabble-rousers recruit new members with the spectre of a new Northern threat as earlier Klan members had done in early 1866. But the scope of that 'problem' could not approach the Northern 'aggressions' of the Civil War. So what was the purpose of Simmons' Klan? What should the Klan do?

In many ways Simmons was a throwback to the early Pulaski Six. Both Klan groups initially lacked a mission or rationale for being and both were apparently founded by people with a penchant for fantasy, playing dress-up, indulging in secret rituals and conducting themselves, paradoxically, as both the comic relief and knights in shining armour for their local communities. And both Klans found success using heroic, romantic images from the blockbusters of their time – Sir Walter Scott's novels and the film *The Birth of a Nation*.

There was another way in which the two Klans were similar in their larval stage: both were founded on pure, unadulterated silliness. The original Klan had covered its initiates in soot, given them donkey's ears and made them stumble over furniture blindfolded in a darkened room. But for sheer ridiculousness, however, Simmons would win the prize.

Simmons spent weeks putting together rituals in which 'Kludds' and 'Klexters' had scripted and meaningless, but deeply secret, 'Klonversations' with each other. He was no longer William Simmons: he made himself 'his majesty, the Imperial Wizard and Emperor of the Invisible Empire'. Eventually, when his work was completed on 4 July 1916, he unveiled the document, which he'd christened, in all seriousness, 'The Kloran'.[4]

Not surprisingly, there was only so much of this ridiculousness most of the new membership could take. Even Simmons knew the childish ceremonies and pointless meetings were failing. If he didn't find a purpose for the order it would gradually disappear – and with it the life savings he'd put into it.

By most accounts Frost tired of Simmons' grandstanding and ran off with the funds starting an alternative fraternity in Alabama.[5] The two men went to court and Simmons walked away in possession of the Klan. But it was a hollow victory. It forced Simmons into debt and seriously set him back in finding a solution for providing his Klan with a mission.

There was one slight swell in membership when the USA went to war in April 1917. In the national emergency, Simmons encouraged Klansmen to see themselves as quasi-auxiliaries to the Secret Service as ultra-patriotic volunteers of the American Protective League. He stressed the need for absolute secrecy, claiming that the Klan's 'secret service work made this imperative'.[6] Simmons made it plain that such vital – largely invented – war work meant members mustn't even tell families about their activities in the Klan. It was all very Simmons – very make-believe. However, it could also be spiteful.

Empowered by their Imperial Wizard, Klansmen snooped on their neighbours, reporting any suspicious and unpatriotic activities. They investigated those who had socialist tendencies, suspecting them of spying, subversion or sabotage. A suspiciously German-sounding name or an overtly German accent gave Klansmen the right to harass, bully or just march 'the traitor' to the authorities. 'Loose' women were another concern. They were a threat to the war effort: entrapping 'our boys', preventing them from serving their country and spreading unspeakable diseases.

It was all very cloak and dagger for these home-front heroes but, for Simmons and his goal of recruiting new members, it yielded remarkably little. By November 1918 Klan membership was faltering and its coffers nearly empty. Forced to find alternative sources of income, Simmons moonlighted. He was listed in the *Atlanta City Directory* that year as not only 'Imperial Wizard and Founder of the Knights of the Ku Klux Klan' but also as the 'State Manager, Heralds of Liberty'.[7] Even mortgaging his house failed. Simmons later wrote:

> For six long years [1915–21] ... I went through horrors of self-sacrifice, suffering and toil. Every dime I earned was earned to preserve its [the Klan's] life and promote its development.[8]

Maybe the Klan's mission was simply too sacred to Simmons. He was unwilling to sully its sacrosanct mission with the squalor of his financial needs. This is probably untrue. Simmons was willing to sell himself and the order when it was necessary. It is more probable that he was simply a terrible businessman. But his strange attitude did have one odd consequence.

A local photographer known as 'Matty' approached Simmons to do a photo story on the Klan. Matty was trying to get a scoop on a group of vigilantes operating in Athens, Georgia. Failing to find them, he settled for a story about Simmons. But Simmons flatly refused, not willing to 'prostitute' his order by posing for photographs. It was idiotic but to Simmons the sacred order's expansion would be by word of mouth. Yet, after five years, Simmons' Klan remained an obscure organisation with no more than 5,000 or 6,000 members in Georgia and Alabama.[9]

Undeterred, Matty hired out twenty local 'extras' to pose as Klan members and photographed them in bed sheets. He cut holes for their eyes and took their picture. Like any good capitalist, he sought out the cheapest labour he could find and paid his models a quarter a head. Legend has it those twenty hooded men were Black, but the first photograph of the Ku Klux Klan went viral all the same. Simmons and his Klansmen got nothing.[10]

# CHAPTER 27

According to Edward Young Clarke, he met Simmons through his business partner, Elizabeth Tyler. Her son-in-law, John Quincy Jett (universally known as JQ), had recently become a Klansman and thought Clarke was just the man to promote the Klan.[1]

Edward Young Clarke, 'EY' (ee-why) as he liked to be called, was small and hyperactive with a shock of black hair and serious-looking round glasses. He looked every inch the 1920s entrepreneurial wizard. Clarke came from privilege. His father had owned the city's foremost paper, *The Atlanta Constitution*, and his uncle had edited it. In the early twentieth century the *Constitution* was passed on to EY's brother who became the editor. EY was made marketing manager. But EY wasn't suited to newspaper work.

He was driven by ambition, not the search for the truth. He flourished in the emerging world of public relations, especially after teaming up with the irrepressible Elizabeth 'Bessie' Tyler. The two had met at Atlanta's Harvest Home Festival in 1915, where Tyler was running the 'Better Baby' parade. They immediately hit it off and pretty soon they'd created a new business and given it a rather grand, establishment-sounding name, 'The Southern Publicity Association' (SPA).

Tyler's upbringing could not have been more different than Clarke's. She was raised dirt poor, married at 14, and had become a mother and widow by age 15. By her late 30s Tyler was known for her intimidating, no-nonsense air, reinforced by her habit of dressing all in black. But she was intelligent, independent and determined. She needed to be.

As a single working mother making her way in the conservative South of the early twentieth century, Tyler's situation made her vulnerable to gossip. There is no evidence to support the tale she'd been a madam with her own brothel. But with her sassy affect, auburn hair and curvaceous body, Bessie Tyler attracted male attention – and female disapproval. Tyler learned to handle it, becoming thick-skinned and street smart, living off her wits and taking what jobs came her way while being distinctly flexible in her morals by the standards of the times. Women may have recently gained the vote, but they were certainly not equal – in any sphere.

By 1919 the SPA had made quite a name for itself. It represented the YMCA, the Salvation Army, the Red Cross and the Anti-Saloon League (ASL). But while these organisations were big players, they were certainly not big payers. And despite the founders' constant hype and grandiose claims, the SPA rarely made much money. Tyler's colourful background and Clarke's 'flexible' principles didn't help. Neither of them had much regard for everyday conformity.

When police raided an Atlanta hotel in October 1919, Clarke and Tyler were discovered in bed together. Unfortunately, both were married to others and adultery was a misdemeanour in Georgia. There was also evidence of a good deal of boozing and Georgia had been the first state in the South to go 'dry', meaning the 'production, transportation, and sale of alcohol' was illegal in the state.

They were arrested, held in jail cells overnight, and released on a $50 bond the next morning – still in their nightwear, according to some accounts. Each was fined $5 for disorderly conduct and a further $25 for possession of whiskey.[2]

The damage to the reputation of the SPA was considerable. Its main income stream was from charities. It didn't help that around that same time the SPA was in court trying to explain how $1,000 had migrated from the Theodore Roosevelt Memorial Fund's account to Clarke and Tyler's own personal accounts.[3] By the end of 1919 work had dried up, when along came Simmons.

Accounts of the negotiations vary. Some portray Clarke as running circles around the gullible Grand Wizard – who agreed to SPA's exorbitant 80 per cent commission fee. Clarke later stated that in order to get the financial ball rolling he initially put in $12,000 of his own money, while Tyler claimed she had stumped up $14,000.[4] But as the Klan grew, Clarke and Tyler were at pains to convince Simmons and others that they were not making a fortune. Their lifestyles showed another story.

There's no record of what Clarke did with his share of the profits, but Tyler flaunted her new-found wealth. In late 1920 she bought 20 acres of prime land on Atlanta's Howell Mill Road. Here she built an antebellum, plantation-style mansion, complete with veranda, columns, ample garages, a 300ft driveway and a caretaker's cottage. At a 1921 congressional hearing on the KKK, Simmons was asked if he felt Clarke's fee had been 'inordinate'. Simmons told the committee he'd consulted 'three gentlemen' who told him the fee seemed reasonable.[5] Clarke and Simmons signed the contract in June 1920, when the Klan had fewer than 3,000 members. By the autumn of 1921 the number of men joining the Klan had exploded.

# CHAPTER 28

When the anti-Klan *New York World* journalist Rowland Thomas appeared before the Committee on Rules in October 1921, he told them the KKK had about a half a million members. Clarke, boasting of the SPA's achievement, claimed the order had between 650,000 and 700,000.[1] For Clarke, the greater the number, the more money he and his associates would make – $8 for every $10 membership. By contrast 'Colonel' Simmons tried to show he was making nowhere near the money such membership numbers would imply, estimating the Klan had only 90,000 to 95,000 members.

It is never easy to know the numbers of the Klan at any given time – after all, it is a secret organisation. Estimates largely depend on who is making the guess and what motivates them. What is crucial is that the numbers in the autumn of 1921 were rising, very quickly. In fifteen months, Clarke and Tyler had turned the Klan around. So what were they doing that Simmons, with all his Kloran, titles and ceremonies, had not?[2]

Clarke had told Simmons that to get new members he was going to need salesmen – and that cost money. The problem was, neither Simmons nor the SPA had any. To get round this, Clarke came up with a scheme to pay his sales force by commission. The strategy was complicated and open to corruption, but it not only saved them the burden of having to raise cash ahead of hiring, it avoided the need to pay the administrative costs normally incurred by a large organisation.

Clarke's June 1920 contract created a mechanism for selling membership entirely on commission. All those employed by the newly minted Klan Propagation Department got a percentage of the $10 subscription fee.

This is not to say that the order had lost its penchant for the ridiculous. That $10 bought not only one's membership but a free title. As with most Klan-related designations, the name started with either 'K' and 'L' or indicated a specific role drawn from its pantheon of fantasy, myth and legend.

The fee itself was called the 'Klecktoken'. This one-off $10 charge was 'donated' by all those who joined the Klan. The money went directly to one of the recruitment agents known in the Klan's bizarre jargon as 'Kleagles'. Clarke had hired 1,100 of these salesmen to make 'things hum all over America'.[3] This sales force was essential to recruitment and to keep the flow of cash moving through the SPA and into the pockets of Clarke and Tyler.

It was complicated. For each recruit the Kleagles got $4 out of the $10. The Kleagle then sent the remaining $6 to the Grand Goblin, a 'Realm-' level Klan boss in charge of a large region of the country. The Grand Goblin would take 50¢ from the $6 he'd been given and send $1 to the state-level Klan boss, the Grand Dragon. The remaining $4.50 went straight on to Klan headquarters in Atlanta, where $2 was deposited into a 'central Klan fund'. It became the Imperial Wizard's cut. The rest went into the SPA's bank account, or the Klan propagation department. When all was said and done, Clarke and Tyler were in effect legally pocketing 25 per cent of *all* Klan subscription income.[4]

This is not to say that Clarke and Tyler had no overheads. In January 1921 they paid out one of their greatest expenses. They offered Simmons $25,000 in five instalments. The new contract also promised Simmons $100 a week (later raised to $1,000 a month).[5] The contract also promoted the Imperial Grand Wizard to the role of figurehead, essentially 'kicking him upstairs' to a purely titular role. This suited Simmons just fine. He would have his photograph taken posing in new star-spangled, purple robes. He would make rousing, long-winded speeches at Klan meetings to his heart's content. He could even adjust the ritual.

Underneath the rhetoric of the contract, there was a harsh reality: the real power in the Klan had now decidedly shifted. Clarke and Tyler now controlled the Klan. They made decisions on strategy. They issued press briefings. And they made most of the money – plenty of it. Many fraternities of this era were run for profit. But this one was on a different level.

The journalist Henry Fry's memory of being recruited in 1921 gives some idea of how the system operated. While working away from home, staying in a Chattanooga boarding house, Fry started chatting with a fellow boarder across the table and, over the course of several mornings, opened up to the stranger. Fry told the man, who it emerged was a Kleagle, of his disappointment that the First World War had ended before he could see battle. He also told of how he'd self-published a book on the 'Negro Problem'. The Kleagle realised he had a perfect Klansman on his hands.

Over the next few days the pair discussed how the USA's problems stemmed from the Reconstruction period when 'the Federal Government of Washington … was used as the agency for plunder, for unrestrained corruption, and for wanton disregard for all that is decent'. They examined 'the presence of the negro, as a constant danger and menace in our political and social life'. They looked into the Thirteenth Amendment, abolishing slavery, and agreed that the Fourteenth Amendment granting ex-slaves the right of citizenship and the Fifteenth, protecting the legal and political rights of the freedman, had been gross mistakes.[6]

Convincing Fry to join the Klan was shooting fish in a barrel, but as Fry himself said in 1921, Chattanooga was an unlikely place for the Klan to go recruiting. There weren't a lot of Black Americans left in the city. Unlike Chicago, New York or Detroit, Fry's recruitment Kleagle couldn't pin the town's social ills on hundreds of thousands of Black people fleeing the poverty and prejudice of the rural South.

Chattanooga's long-standing Jewish community was too small and self-contained to be scapegoated as it had been in Boston or New York. And compared with the unpatriotic, revolutionary-minded Catholics of New England, the Southern variety seemed docile. Indeed, according to Fry, the only Catholic church in eastern Tennessee was so poorly attended, it only held Mass once a year.

But Fry's recruiter was creative. Noticing the Masonic pins on his lapels, the Kleagle questioned him and discovered that Fry was – like the Grand Imperial Wizard himself – a serial fraternalist. In fact, Fry had 'brothers' in the Masons, Elks, Knights of Pythias and Odd Fellows.

Over the course of several conversations, the Kleagle began to see his 'prospect' as more than just an initiate: Fry, with his strong beliefs and lodge house contacts, was so well suited to the Klan that he ought to become a recruiter himself. The Kleagle shared with Fry that he needed to return to the local Klan HQ in Knoxville. Might Fry fancy trying to recruit new members in his absence?

Fry agreed. As the recruiter departed for the week, he gave Fry a piece of interesting advice on how he went about recruiting Klansmen in a new district:

> it is advisable to get the mayor, the sheriff and his deputies if they are eligible, and the police department. Also we want the telephone and telegraph people, and the better class of rail-roaders.[7]

Like insurgents seizing power in a *coup d'état*, Simmons' Klan first targeted the political leadership and the security forces. Having secured them, the Klan would then take control of the communications network and the transport system. As many African and South American leaders have found to their cost, this strategy cut off the opposition and rendered them powerless.

Fry was a rigidly ideological patriot as well as a white supremacist. The Kleagle's words may have struck him as too sinister, too Machiavellian. Soon Fry was to find the Klan's whole process undemocratic. For the moment, however, the temptation to join another fraternal group of like-minded white men was just too great. Habit, perhaps – and the prospect of a new lapel-pin – won out. Whatever his reasoning, convinced it was just another fraternity, Fry signed up.

# CHAPTER 29

Henry Fry was made a Kleagle and given his own district in April 1921. By the end of June, he'd resigned. He left the Klan and wrote a letter outlining his dissatisfactions sending it to Simmons himself. It criticised the Klan's relationship and told the Imperial Wizard that to him the Klan seemed like 'a secret political machine'. He went on to call it an organisation dedicated to the creation and perpetuation of hatred – directed at the USA's unique diversity of classes, races and religions. He ended his letter by accusing the Klan of being nothing but a 'money-making scheme' that the federal government should 'outlaw' and 'legislate out of existence'.[1]

Fry didn't just write to Simmons. He published his attacks on the Klan in nineteen newspapers across the nation. The articles were read by millions of people. And although he played it down in his early accounts, Fry had once been a journalist with the *Chattanooga Times*. He had also had freelance articles published in newspapers in New York and Philadelphia. It is possible, if not probable, that Fry had only joined the Klan in order to expose it, which would explain his uncannily perfect fit.[2]

There's evidence that Fry was working for the legendary New York editor Herbert Swope. Swope was the editor of Pulitzer's *New York World*, and was guided by a simple idea: 'Pick out the best story of the day and hammer the hell out of it'. And Swope saw the potential to do just that in Fry's exposé of the Klan.[3] In order to preserve Fry's credentials as an outraged patriot, Swope put his star reporter Rowland Thomas' name on the story. No one suspected it was actually Fry who was the one getting the scoop.

Throughout September 1921, the *World* ran a series of twenty-one Klan stories. The front page of the 6 September edition started them off, with a bang. Below pictures of Simmons, Tyler and Clarke, Swope ran a picture of a scrawled, unsigned postcard addressed to 'Mr Editor – The Evening

World'. The script was scrawled, but the message was clear. It called the editor and his staff 'nigger-lovers' and 'dirty yanks' and ended up by threatening that if they published their findings it 'will seal your death warrant'.[4] Swope no doubt calculated that this was bound to boost interest in the next three weeks of attacks on the order.

The paper ran banner headlines like 'Ku Klux Klan Wars on Catholics, Jews Reap Rich Rewards' and 'Ku Klux Made Jews and Negroes Target for Racial Hatreds' or 'Masonry Race Riots and Film Propaganda Used by Ku Klux Klan' and 'Talking in Millions. Klan Chief Gathers in Golden Shekels'. Inside, the paper told of tarring and feathering, financial fraud and Klan-sponsored vigilante violence.[5]

The effect was impressive. Swope claimed the *World*'s first article on 6 September had reached 2 million readers, and that over its three-week Klan coverage, daily readership was up by 65,000 to 100,000.[6] What was more, the *World*'s articles were syndicated in seventeen other papers.

From Galveston, Texas, to Columbus, Ohio, and New Orleans to Oklahoma City, over their breakfast tables Americans discussed the rising threat posed by the Klan. Then Pulitzer's main rival, William Randolph Hearst, joined in, setting his *New York American* on the Klan. This investigation was written by no less an authority than adventurer and pioneer aviator and ex-Klan King Kleagle C. Anderson Wright.

SPA's Edward Young Clarke had recruited Wright to put together the 'Knights of the Air', convincing Wright it would be a fraternity for airmen. Wright was installed in his own office in the new Hurt Building, one of the most modern and prestigious skyscrapers in downtown Atlanta. His new title was no less ostentatious: 'Chief of Staff of the Invisible Planet'.

Pretty soon Wright realised that Clarke would not provide the finances for the expansion of the Knights of the Air. Exasperated, the King Kleagle turned on his boss and gave his side of the story to Hearst. Pretty soon he saw it had morphed into another of Clarke's 'money-making plans'.[7]

It is uncertain what really motivated Wright's exposé. It could have been fury at his betrayal by Clarke. It may've been simple greed. But whatever it was, the effects on the Klan were devastating. The *American* ran its assault a little over a week after the *World*'s campaign started, claiming it had 'the inside story on the Ku Klux Klan'.[8]

Like Pulitzer's *World*, Hearst's paper announced its sources had received death threats from the Klan. From then onwards the *World* and the *American* tried to outdo one another. For the entire month of September, the two papers competed to publish the most shocking, violent and corrupt stories about the Klan.

On Saturday, 17 September the two papers really hit their stride. The *World* exposed the Klan's secret oaths and handshakes. The *American* told its readers the Klan brought in over $26.5 million in a single year. The next day the *World* focused on the Klan's 'recent beating and tarring of men and women'. The *American* ran with a picture of Simmons kissing the Stars and Stripes, while simultaneously concentrating on Klan threats to annihilate Catholic and Jewish fraternities.[9]

The following Monday, the *World* dredged up the steamy 'scoop' about Clarke and Tyler being caught in flagrante in 1919. The *American* countered with a claim that Clarke had been heard bragging he'd soon be the world's richest man. The paper backed this up with a claim that the Klan had earned $3.5 million from the sale of 'Holy Water' from the Chattahoochee River, at $10 a quart. The *American* said Clarke and Tyler had made $14.5 million in the last year.[10] And so it went on ...

# CHAPTER 30

From the very start of their coverage, both newspapers competed in another way – by sharing details about neutralising and possibly defeating the Klan. The *World* told its readers that the head of the Bureau of Investigation (later to become the FBI) was personally investigating Klan activities. And he was not alone. The Attorney General, Harry M. Daugherty, was responding to congressional 'demands for prompt action'.[1]

At Klan HQ in Atlanta, Clarke and Tyler denied all claims of Klan wrongdoing, issuing statement after statement as each accusation emerged. But by the end of September an investigation of Klan activities seemed unstoppable. The *World* claimed that by the end of its Klan series, the 'Invisible Empire lobbyists', congressional advocates paid by the Klan, had stopped concentrating on individual denials and moved to trying to prevent the apparently inevitable congressional investigation.[2] They failed, and by 21 September, two congressmen tabled a motion to conduct a full congressional investigation into the Klan.

Sensing that opposition was futile, Simmons abruptly changed course and had Klan HQ send each of the 530-odd sitting congressman a telegram calling for them to support an investigation into the Invisible Empire. The telegram stated that the Klan was confident that it 'will be fully exonerated from all charges, and slanders made against it'.[3] The tactic worked and the House Committee on Rules – the body responsible for assessing the necessity for legislation on a given issue – was convened to investigate the Klan.

The first witness was called on the morning of Tuesday, 11 October. Twelve committee members heard Rowland Thomas' testimony. The *World* journalist simply reiterated what had been said in 'his' Klan articles. Initially, the questions directed at him focused on Klan violence. His responses outlined beatings, tarring and featherings and other abuses carried

out by men in disguise. Motivation for these atrocities ranged from vigilantism to opposition to Catholics and Jews.

Central to Thomas' testimony was his overview of how greed motivated
the Klan. Claiming there were around 700,000 Klansmen, he explained
how these members generated at least $10 million. In closing, Thomas
pointed out that the Klan 'Emperor' (Simmons) was essentially an unelected
dictator, un-American and a threat to the nation.[4] In essence, Thomas was
pointing to the Klan being an unelected, undemocratic, money-making
machine. It was very similar to what Fry claimed in his letter to Simmons.

Before the lunchtime recess, the author of the *American*'s Klan series,
C. Anderson Wright, began his statement. At first the aviator seemed
flustered, uncertain of what month it was, but soon hit his stride. Wright
focused on the person he saw as 'the real power behind the Klan' – Elizabeth
Tyler. He argued that she controlled Clarke and both were dedicated to
making themselves very wealthy.

Wright told the court he felt he'd been duped by Clarke and Tyler, and
their ruthless, mercenary and un-American 'treason'. While his language
may have been hyperbolic, he had a point. The marketing duo had ousted
Simmons and they had certainly taken the Klan in a new and very different
direction where money replaced romance.

After lunch Wright really got going. He continued his character assassination of Elizabeth Tyler, telling how she made money off a brothel she
owned in Atlanta while preaching for the protection and elevation of US
womanhood. He revealed Tyler and Clarke, although unmarried, lived
openly together in a 'fine mansion' – with *peacocks*! He contrasted this with
the 'very sincere' 'Colonel' Simmons who 'was living in a little cottage with
his family, up a side street'.[5]

Next came Mr O.B. Williamson, 'a post office inspector'. He detailed
Clarke's dodgy property deals and siphoning of Klan funds into his personal
accounts. He highlighted Clarke's 'Imperial Palace' on Atlanta's prestigious Peachtree Road and his purchase of Lanier University – deals which
netted Clarke hundreds of thousands of dollars. He showed Klansmen
being fleeced when buying their robes at $6.50 when the manufacturers
charged $4. Manufacturing cost $1.50 and the company was owned by
Clarke himself.

Although damning, some of Williamson's testimony contradicted
Wright's. Williamson denied any knowledge of the Tyler mansion, calling it 'mythical' and rebuffed Wright's claims of impropriety between the
leaders of the propagation department. Williamson also disagreed about the
relative positions of Clarke and Taylor in the Klan. He was adamant that

'Mrs Tyler is not an officer of the order. She is merely a businesswoman working with Clarke.'[6]

On Wednesday, 12 October, Bureau of Investigation director William J. Burns made a brief statement, as did a leading Black rights activist, William M. Trotter. Trotter was the sole speaker at the hearings to challenge the consensus that the Reconstruction Klan had been a force for good.[7] Then the Supreme Attorney of the KKK, Paul Etheridge, spoke.

Etheridge began by dispelling Wright's assertions that Tyler lived in a palatial mansion and played a leading role in the Klan. He repeatedly called her home 'a very modest cottage' and attempted to convince the committee that, in spite of being 'one of the imperial officers' of the Klan, he hadn't met Tyler until 4 July 1921. He also explained in great detail how each of Wright's examples of Klan violence had actually been acts of self-defence.[8]

Then it was William J. Simmons' turn. He was introduced by disabled Georgian Prohibition Party congressman William David Upshaw, also known as 'Earnest Willie'. Upshaw stood up and gushed praise on Simmons. The 'Imperial Wizard' was 'one of the Knightliest, most patriotic men I have ever known'. He went on to say that he knew him to be as 'incapable of an unworthy, un-patriotic motive, word or deed, as the chairman of this committee, the Speaker of the House of Representatives, or the President of the United States'.[9]

His comments were met by sage nods from some around the table and in the closely packed chairs surrounding them. Others could barely conceal their smirks. But regardless of how his introduction was greeted, it was obvious to all in the crowded committee room that the fate of the Klan was now squarely in Simmons' hands.

# CHAPTER 31

William Joseph Simmons had been in Washington since the day before the hearings started. Getting off the train from Atlanta, he'd walked into a herd of reporters eager for comment and handled them well. Simmons appeared upbeat, composed and healthy. During the Wednesday sessions Simmons sat impassively as Rowland Thomas condemned the Klan. The Imperial Grand Wizard had 'smoked cigarettes incessantly and smiled often'.[1]

However, the seasoned PR man Clarke and his team had primed the Imperial Wizard well. When introducing himself to the committee, Simmons told them that for the last ten days he'd suffered from tonsillitis compounded by laryngitis and bronchitis. While looking healthy, he claimed this potentially lethal combination had resulted in coughing fits, frequently leading to vomiting. He asked the committee to consider his health when interviewing him.

Simmons then launched into a typically verbose and long-winded speech lasting until the end of the afternoon session – a good three hours – with no break. After an exhaustive lecture on the roots of the Klan and his role in its re-formation, he then detailed the suffering he'd endured. Next, Simmons started to refute the claims made by previous hostile witnesses. He denied their claims of Klan violence and explained how men dressed in stolen robes had harassed the public in Pensacola, Florida – while the genuine Klansmen had reported the imposters to the police.

He told a similar tale of how, in a South Carolina town, local Klansmen had offered a $500 reward for information on a group of fake Klansmen. He promised that any Klansmen who did misbehave were punished by Klan HQ – citing an instance in Mobile, Alabama, where inappropriate vigilante actions led the Imperial Wizard to withdraw the Klavern's charter.

Simmons flatly denied as 'lying slanders' and an 'outrage' the allegations of the beating and mutilation of a Mexican in Beaumont, Texas. And the

'Klan' beating of a Black man in Arkansas had happened when, Simmons claimed, there had been no Klansmen in that state. Simmons then digressed, telling the committee that he, personally, had no problem with Black people. To prove it he told them to go to his childhood town, Harpersville in Shelby County, Alabama, and 'ask those old Negroes something about Joe Simmons'.[2]

Simmons asserted it all stemmed from the malice and greed of news-papermen. He called Hearst 'a snake coiled in the American flag' and dismissed Pulitzer as a 'Jew'. To them every crime committed by a masked bandit and every act of group violence was reported as the action of Klansmen. Simmons argued, 'In their desperation to destroy the Klan those attacking us have charged us with everything from high prices to the spread of the [cotton-crop-destroying] boll weevil.'[3]

By Friday morning, the Imperial Wizard had found his pulpit and was at his preacherly best. The committee asked him whether or not he felt that, with his own 'imperial' title and legislative body – the 'Kloncilium' – the whole Klan thing might possibly represent a treasonous threat to American sovereign democracy. The sandy-haired Simmons countered, a little obscurely, with 'I am not a figurehead. The only head I have is a red head.' He also reassured the chairman in his habitual over-the-top language that 'ablaze in each Klansman's heart [burns] the sacred fire of a devoted patriotism to our country and its Government'.[4]

To back this up he read out the string of oaths, answers and rituals that kept the Klan flame alight. The chairman, obviously bored by Simmons' fatuous waffle, asked whether the seemingly endless Klonversations and extracts from the Kloran had not already been submitted as exhibits. When Simmons agreed that they had, the chairman banged his gavel – with obvious relief – and told the committee they could read the documents at their leisure.

But on this occasion Simmons was – for once – more lawyer than wind-bag. Aware he was probably speaking to a committee containing more than a few fraternalists, he adroitly sidestepped allegations of the Klan's supposed discrimination against Jews, Black people and Catholics. Instead, he argued that the criteria for eligibility in the Klan had not been created out of preju-dice but as a feature of the Klan as a fraternity, like any of the hundreds of others in US life.

He pointed out that the Knights of Columbus was open only to Catholics. The Ancient Order of Hibernians only admitted those of Irish ancestry. The Pope forbade Catholics from becoming Freemasons and aspiring African American Masons had to join a separate order, the Prince Hall. Why should the Klan be taken to task when it limited membership to only those who could prove white, Protestant and native-born US background?

As the committee drew its investigations to a close, Simmons took his theatrics to a whole new level. Confronted by a question on why the Klan needed to disguise themselves behind hoods, he told the chairman that to him and – by implication – other patriots, the hoods were simply part of the proud tradition of standing up for the oppressed white race, declaring, 'our mask and robe, I say before God, are *as innocent as the breath of an angel*'.[5]

Then, in a quivering voice, Simmons begged the Lord to be merciful to those he called 'persecutors of the Klan', using words mimicking Christ's last pleas – 'Father, forgive you, for you know not what you do.' He ended with, 'Mr Chairman, I am done.' With that, the Klan Messiah melodramatically collapsed from apparent exhaustion. The public gallery 'exploded with applause'.[6] The furious chairman banged his gavel, demanding decorum as the limp body of the Imperial Wizard was carried out of the chamber.

Irate, but ignored, the chairman was heard to hiss audibly under his breath, 'For cheap theatrical effect, damn such a faker!'[7] But Simmons' theatrics had worked.

The Klan was saved.

# PART V

# KLAN RAMPANT
# 1921–1924

But the Georgia grocer, the Boston dry goods man, the Oklahoma lawyer, the New Jersey dentist, all know this: that taxes are high, that even with Mr. Mellon's proposed reduction they will still be higher than they once were, that rents, clothes, coal, railroad fares, bread, butter, and eggs are high. … They mean to do something about it too. Their first step must be to organize with all the millions of others who feel as they do. They join the Ku Klux Klan.

Arthur Coming White, November 1924[1]

# CHAPTER 32

How can anyone estimate the membership of the Klan?

The Klan's enemies exaggerated the numbers to convey the order's threat to society. Its members exaggerated the numbers to demonstrate the Klan's reach, influence and power. Often Klan promoters, too, inflated membership estimates in order to impress would-be recruits. After all, who'd join an organisation with hardly any members? On the other hand, recruiters downplayed numbers when recruiting among the small-town and city elites – hoping to convey the Klan's selectivity, allowing only (to use Simmons' word) the 'classy' types. When the Klan was under fire, Klan spokespersons usually downplayed membership.

In the summer of 1921, before the meeting of the congressional committee, estimates veered wildly from 50,000 to over a million. Edward Young Clarke suggested the order had recruited 850,000 new members. Simmons said membership was fewer than 100,000. By the end of the committee's hearings, the accepted figure was closer to Simmons' estimate than Clarke's. Although we can't be certain, it is most likely the numbers were around 400,000 to 500,000 by 1922.[1]

But after the committee disbanded, those figures began to explode. As Simmons put it, 'Congress gave us the best advertising we ever got. Congress made us.' While this was true, it wasn't just Congress which had boosted Klan membership. With an uncharacteristic display of modesty, Simmons was leaving out his own crucial input.

It seems that the press also played a direct role. Awareness of the Klan had been simmering since D.W. Griffith's *The Birth of a Nation*. Now it burst onto front pages and into the daily life of readers all over the country. There were evn rumours that men were so keen to join that they even clipped out the facsimile of the blank Klan membership application on the front page of the *World*. They then filled it in and sent it to Klan HQ in Atlanta.[2]

Clarke was delighted. He bragged that over that period the Klan was recruiting 1,000 new members *per day*. Simmons had always played down the numbers. Now, he claimed the Klan's daily induction was closer to 3,500.[3]

Both estimates were tame next to the claims of one journalist. Stanley Frost, a reporter for the religiously minded weekly *The Outlook*, said that from late 1921 to early 1922, the Klan was recruiting 100,000 new members every week.[4] He could well have been right, at least for some weeks.

It was an unsettling time for those who remembered the excesses of Reconstruction, immigrants, Catholics, Jews and the last of the few aged ex-slaves, as well as those who thought that, by migrating from the South, they would have escaped the horrors of racism.

For no one reading the newspaper accounts could deny that the Klan was expanding in an unprecedented way. By the beginning of 1922, over 200 new Klaverns had been chartered. And these were no longer confined to Georgia and Alabama. Now the Klan had established itself in the former Confederate states of Texas, Louisiana and Arkansas and outside the South in Kansas, Missouri, California and Oregon.

The Klan was showing signs of becoming especially powerful in the non-Confederate states of Colorado, Indiana, Ohio and even Lincoln's home, Illinois. While not quite as successful, in the north-eastern states busy Kleagles had even made inroads into true Yankee territory in Pennsylvania, New York and New Jersey. In 1922, total national membership had reached 1 million Klansmen.[5]

How had this been achieved? In part it was the message, and partly the medium. Simmons' recruitment strategy had relied on a rather vague appeal to those he saw as being part of the 'highest class'. Clarke and Tyler now had Simmons focus his appeal on the values of religion, patriotism and fraternalism. These were ideals the USA could relate to – especially as the country emerged from the First World War.

Their fundamental message became 'back to basics': back to *American* ideals. For nearly three years before April 1917, Americans had watched the slaughter and suffering in Europe from a safe distance, understandably reluctant to join in. In fact, Woodrow Wilson won his second term in office with the slogan, 'He Kept Us Out of the War.'

But by spring 1917, Wilson was appealing to US citizens to reverse that decision. Changing a deeply ingrained public opinion about the war would be no easy task. Americans had little fear of invasion from the Germans and their allies. The job of reversing the prevailing attitude fell to the newly formed Committee on Public Information, as well as other propaganda bodies. They needed to come up with some vivid and compelling arguments as to why the USA should remain in conflict.

Using a mixture of patriotic appeal and constant reminders of German aggression, Wilson's propaganda machine sensitised the USA to all sorts of new enemies. Waste was one target. The government encouraged 'Meatless Mondays' in order to be able to supply the necessary food for US troops and their now dependent allies. The government introduced a wartime prohibition on alcohol so that grain could be diverted to food production. Most importantly, there was a barrage of information about the threat to the USA by both the 'unspeakable Hun' in Europe and his hidden supporters in the USA. There was the threat of nebulous saboteurs, fifth columnists and millions of so-called 'hyphenated Americans'.

The 'hyphen' referred to those US citizens who maintained a dual identity as both American and European. Among these were Austrian-Americans, Bulgarian-Americans, Turkish-Americans and of course German-Americans – those who were likely to have divided loyalties since their home and adopted countries were at war. These people could not be *true* Americans until they identified themselves simply as 'American'. Refusal to abandon the hyphen was considered treacherous, if not treasonous.[6]

By the end of the war it was not enough to claim you were American, you had to be able to prove it. Anyone who didn't conform to ideas of patriotism could easily become a target. Men, and it usually was men, were made to kiss the Stars and Stripes. They may well have found themselves beaten up, or worse, if it was felt they had behaved in any way less than the obligatory 'One Hundred Percent American'.

In May 1919 in Seattle, Washington, at the start of one of umpteen patriotic pageants, a uniformed sailor refused to stand when 'The Star-Spangled Banner' was played. A nearby spectator shouted at him to show respect. When the sailor refused, the man drew a pistol and shot the sailor three times. The crowd whooped and cheered the gunman. The sailor was seriously wounded but survived. In the subsequent trial the jury found the would-be murderer not guilty of assault. Outside the courtroom a band played a medley of patriotic tunes.[7] Clarke saw an opportunity for the Klan to capitalise on this patriotic wave.

Pure Americanism had another strand as well. From the 1870s until the start of the war in Europe, the USA had experienced an unprecedented boom in immigration. More immigrants arrived in the USA than in its entire history before 1870, peaking spectacularly between 1909 and 1914. Over 1 million immigrants per year entered the country, the equivalent of more than 1 per cent of the country's population arriving in a single year. By the start of the war, first-generation immigrants made up nearly 15 per cent of the entire population. This total had never been reached before and has never been reached since in the history of the USA.

In the 1890s Americans started seeing a change in the new immigrants. Their habits, language and appearance seemed much more foreign to Americans than the earlier waves of Germans, Irish, British and Swedish immigrants. These newcomers didn't look or act like 'true Americans'. In 1892, the massive immigration processing centre at Ellis Island had put in place new forms of data collection and analysis, including primitive punch-card 'computers' that were able to provide fast, accurate snapshots of arrivals – recording not only their countries of origin, but their age, religion, profession and something of their ancestry. The majority of these new immigrants were Italians, Poles, Greeks and Russians. To the insular US population, these people seemed so alien that many doubted they could ever really become Americans.

Then, in 1914 the war spread across Europe and the rest of the world. Immigration in the USA slowed drastically – the result of the Royal Navy's blockade of Europe, conscription, U-boats, mines and the fighting itself. From a surge of 1 million a year in the previous years, between 1914 and 1918 it had dropped to a little over 100,000 a year. But in 1919 there was good reason to worry: the USA's booming economy, the devastation in Europe, lack of food, employment, prospects and self-respect in the defeated nations, all drove fears of a new escalation of migrant numbers. And that was not all.

There was disease in Europe – the Spanish Flu pandemic, diphtheria, typhus and cholera. Most European states were in terrible debt and inflation was rising. Revolution emanating from Russia in 1917 threatened most of Eastern Europe and even Germany. There were renewed outbreaks of war in Russia, Poland, the Baltic States, Hungary and other European countries. Why would anyone want to stay in Europe? There was a real fear that the transatlantic migration was about to start again. But now Europeans were seen in a different light.

By the end of the war Americans had developed an idea of a European 'Old World' that was decadent, corrupt and immoral. Europeans had used poison gas, trenches, U-boats and starved each other to death, then they'd refused to commit to President Wilson's 'brave new world'. Could such people become Americans? Age-old ties that had linked Europe and the USA had been severed, physically and emotionally. Americans no longer saw Europeans as the cultural leaders of the world. The respect and emulation of Europeans that had long been the norm in the USA were gone.

US soldiers returning from the war told tales of the horrors of the Western Front. Family ties with Europe were weakened by the lack of contact the war had imposed. In short, the time was ripe to break those ties. Anti-immigrant feeling, patriotism and national identity in the USA had arguably never been more important to the US public. Even a fool could see that nationalism and all of its attendant prejudices had become *the* hot button issue of 1920, and Clarke and his team were not fools.

# CHAPTER 33

Throughout his appearance in front of the congressional committee, Simmons had doggedly insisted the Klan was a fraternity. He argued the movement was driven by a sense of belonging and the moral imperatives inherent in fraternalism. Mercenary as they were, the Klan Propagation Department, as Clarke, Tyler and their co-marketeers now called themselves, were not about to abandon that tie to fraternalism. They would alter it, manipulate it and pervert it, but they did not abandon it.

It was typical of Simmons' frustratingly unworldly character that his interest in fraternity focused largely on pageantry and romance. Simmons spent much of his time concocting rituals and sketching white-robed Klansmen on prancing horses. The canniness beneath his performance in front of Congress notwithstanding, Simmons was still a romantic. To him the fraternity that he had created was designed as a 'living memorial' to a proud past, not a means of securing a lucrative future.[1]

Meanwhile, Clarke and his propagation department were exploring interesting marketing possibilities of portraying the Klan as a fraternity. Fraternities were incredibly popular in 1920s USA. Nationally, estimates of fraternal membership ranged from 30 to 60 million, a vast figure when the USA's total population was just slightly over 100 million.[2]

An indication of just how important a part fraternities played in the life of everyday USA can be gathered for the small Kansas town of Drexel, just south of Kansas City. Home to some 500 residents, it boasted active lodges for the Knights of Pythias, the Woodmen of the World, the Odd Fellows, the Mystic Workers of the World and the Modern Woodmen, as well as one for the Eastern Star and the Free and Accepted Masons.[3] Drexel illustrated that aspirant small-town Americans loved fraternity, because, as one contemporary put it, the 'middle class simply adore[d] ritual, regalia and "hokum" … [it] constitute[d] the greatest social diversion'. And there weren't many others.[4]

Like Simmons, the propagation department saw that fraternity was a perfect vehicle for selling the Klan, but in states which didn't have a Confederate background, that was not always an easy task. In these cases, Clarke and his minions manipulated the past, right in keeping with the fraternal tradition. It was normal for fraternities to invent dubious pedigrees and massage history with elaborate origin myths. The vision that drove the Knights of Pythias derived from an ancient Greek myth exemplifying selfless friendship. The Freemasons went back even further for their inspiration. Masons liked to believe that their lineage went all the way back to the stone masons who built the Temple of Solomon.

Perhaps the best propagator of a myth is one who believes in it himself. This was Simmons, who repeatedly argued for the Klan's glorious cause. He linked the order to the Redeemers, who'd defeated the Radical Republican carpetbaggers, scalawags and their ex-slave minions. Simmons' Klansmen had seen *The Birth of a Nation* and they felt they personally could help restore the nation to its glorious past. Clarke's Klansmen could dress up as their heroes. If it sounds ridiculous, if it sounds like the Klavern was a massive 1920s Comic Con, that's because it was. And it would only cost them their $10 Klecktoken (plus $6.50 for the robes and hood).[5]

The USA in the 1920s was a mobile nation where over half of the population would die in a different city from the one in which they were born. The den, lodge, Klavern or fraternity was a place to escape family life, meet up with friends or perhaps make new ones. And the sociable element of fraternities was important. So was exclusion.

But if *everyone* could join a fraternity, why would *anyone* want to? When questioned in the congressional hearings about why the Klan would only allow native-born, Protestant, white Americans to become members, Simmons pointed out that the Knights of Columbus excluded non-Catholics. It was impossible for a gentile to join B'nai B'rith. But Simmons did more than assert that all fraternities excluded other groups – he downplayed the Klan's prejudice and exclusion and depicted it as perfectly natural behaviour practised by everyone.[6]

Clarke saw the Klan as an ally and competitor to the Masons. Early twentieth-century Freemasonry was regarded not only as mainstream and acceptable, but being invited to become a Mason was increasingly seen as a mark of success. Leading members of the business and professional communities saw being in a lodge as an essential part of their CV, albeit one they should only divulge to other Masons.[7] The lodge house became a hub for mutually beneficial deals between Masons. Masons traded contracts and advice with each other first. It was also the first place many strangers headed for when needing introductions or information.

When Clarke unleashed his thousand Kleagle-recruiters on the nation in 1920–21, Masons were one of his chief targets. They were Simmons' people of the 'highest class' – a cosy national coterie of local judges, lawyers, police chiefs, clergy and businessmen. In the lodge house problems could be thrashed out, deals cemented and contacts made. Mutual trust abounded. The logic went, 'if so and so is a Mason, he must be all right'.

What was more, the Master of any particular lodge usually had accurate and up-to-date rolls of members. And, as the lapels of Simmons' frock coat clearly showed, some fraternalists had a tendency to be 'serial joiners'. If a Kleagle could tap into Masonry, he had a good chance of recruiting members who controlled, or at least influenced, entire communities. What an opportunity.[8]

The propagation department thought big. They believed if the Klan could link themselves with the Craft, it would show that they were a force for the good of the nation. After all, the majority of presidents, leading generals, politicians and philanthropists had long been conspicuous Masons. Masonry held a prominent position in US society. Its members were important figures in US history.[9]

It is always a problem estimating how many and who joined the Klan, but it seems that Masons did join the Klan – in droves. One historian has estimated the total number of Klansmen in 1923 at 2.5 million and over 500,000 – or 20 per cent – of these Klansmen were also Freemasons.[10] One Oregon Mason said in the early 1920s, 'Klan-joining became contagious and ran epidemic' in Masonic lodges and that 60 per cent of Oregon's founding Klansmen were also Masons.[11] A Klan meeting at the Masonic Temple in Independence, Kansas, ended up with thirty-five out of forty Masons joining the Klan.[12] In Michigan's Newaygo County nearly two-thirds of Klansmen belonged to at least one other fraternity and nearly a quarter were Masons.[13]

But the enthusiasm was not universal. It was just as likely that Kleagles would meet with hostility in Masonic lodges. There were accusations that they only became Masons in order to recruit more Klansmen. What was more, political activity was strictly forbidden within the confines of the lodge, since it brought 'disharmony'. The Klan's portrayal of itself as the 'Fighting Fraternity' was, as one leading Mason put it, 'un-American, un-Masonic'. He added that 'no member of our fraternity should be associated with them in any manner whatever'.[14]

Unlike England, US Masonry has no central governing body. So responses to Klan activity were a matter for the state-level Masonic authorities. Some, like Tennessee, chose to ignore the Klan, as they did with all the activities of the 'profane' (non-Masons). Others, like the Freemasons of California and Texas, warned that Kleagles working within lodges would face expulsion. The Kansas Grand Master warned that it would end in disaster for the Masons.[15]

But the Propagation Department had positioned the Klan in the mainstream of US opinion. It also highlighted an internal friction: the point where the Clarke–Tyler 'Mad Men'-style absorption of the Masonic network rubbed up against the more traditional romantic visionary ideals of Simmons. It is tempting to see modern comparatives with the friendship networks which spurred the creation of social media and its current manipulation to rouse fear and anger.

It appears for every Simmons there is a Clarke. Clarke's strategy was generally to appeal to the existing prejudices and desires of the US public. He made a great show of how the Klan was 'all-American' and how it shared the concerns of the 'average Joe'. This might be a fear of immigrants, or the aspiration impulses apparent in the networking elements of existing fraternities. But there were also times when Clarke's team engaged in outright manipulation of the public, playing on the rising tides of anti-immigrant feeling.

Under his guidance, the Klan began hammering on a new, but related, alien threat to the US public: Roman Catholicism. It was to prove useful in all sorts of ways.

# CHAPTER 34

From the earliest days of white settlement in North America, there had been friction between Protestants and Catholics. The Pilgrim Fathers had braved an ocean to escape from what they saw as an increasingly 'Catholicised' High Church: the 'smells and bells'-style Church of England. The British monarchy's tolerance of Catholicism in Canada helped fuel the independence movement in the Thirteen Colonies. Even after the USA won their independence, their enemies to the north, south and south-west remained Catholic. Protestantism became one of the defining traits of Americanism.

Throughout the nineteenth century, anti-Catholicism festered in US identity. As the Indians were 'civilised', Protestant missionaries clashed with Jesuits and Catholic priests for the possession of their souls. Militant Protestantism flared up when the USA went to war with Catholic Mexico in 1846 and Catholic Spain in 1898. But it was in opposition to immigration that US anti-Catholicism took on its most visible and virulent form.

A defining moment of the early 1850s was the rise of the American Party. It emerged out of the secretive Order of the Star-Spangled Banner. They became better known as the 'Know-Nothings', for the response members invariably gave to information-seekers. The name stuck even as the party membership skyrocketed in almost all major US cities in the first years of the 1850s. Its platform was largely anti-immigrant. And because those immigrants were predominantly Irish and German Catholics, the Know-Nothings' mission and rhetoric took on a distinctly anti-Catholic flavour.

As increasing numbers of immigrants arrived, the party's appeal grew, especially in the increasingly immigrant-saturated cities of New England, where they won all but three of the 400 seats in the 1854 Massachusetts legislature. They dominated politics in Rhode Island and rabble-roused in Maine. They put up, very unsuccessfully, presidential candidates. Although they had large wins in Maryland and Louisiana, they held limited appeal in the South. Their stance on slavery issues had been neutral.

In the 1857 Dred Scott decision, the US Supreme Court excluded slaves from Constitutional rights. From that point on the battle lines were drawn. Know-Nothing party members jumped ship. Some became anti-slavery Republicans. Others joined the pro-slavery Constitutional Unionists. By 1860 the American Party no longer existed.[1]

But the Know-Nothing name would remain synonymous with anti-Catholicism. As the numbers of Catholic immigrants began to climb throughout the last decades of the nineteenth century and the early years of the twentieth, a variety of anti-Catholic parties echoed the message of the Know-Nothings. Some would prove more successful than others.

In the 1890s anti-Catholic voters flocked to Henry Bowers' American Protective Association (APA). With some 2 million members by the middle of the decade, the group ostensibly stood for religious freedom. This tolerance masked a virulent anti-Catholicism. The APA was fraternal in structure, with members taking an oath that they would use their 'utmost power to strike the shackles and chains of blind obedience to the Roman Catholic Church from the hampered and bound consciences of a priest-ridden and church-oppressed people'.[2] Their public pleas for 'free schools' and curbs on 'ecclesiastical power' were actually coded appeals for new laws limiting the expansion of the Catholic Church.[3]

In the crucial 1896 election, the APA aligned itself with the Republican Party, and set itself against the agrarian protest movement, the Populist Party. This unstable left-wing hotchpotch of currency reformers; disaffected and indebted farmers; women's rights campaigners; and advocates of electoral change became a dominant force on the Plains. When Republican candidate William McKinley defeated the Populists he quickly sensed the way the wind was blowing and disassociated himself from the APA. Almost instantly, the movement dissolved. The defeat of the Populists had unexpected consequences for anti-Catholicism when they absorbed yet another group: disaffected APA supporters and their vicious strain of anti-Catholicism.

This element of the Populist party was led by none other than Edward Thomas Watson, the Georgia politician who would, in 1913, condemn Leo Frank and praise the mob that murdered him. Every Populist presidential campaign Watson was a part of turned out to be a disaster. In 1892 Iowa congressman James B. Weaver had garnered almost 1 million votes in his presidential bid. But the 1896 campaign with William Jennings Bryan and Watson as VP was a flop. After this the Populist ticket haemorrhaged votes.

Watson stood as vice-president two more times, in 1904 and 1908. By his final bid in 1908, the Populist share of the popular vote had dropped to under 30,000. The party was dead but not Watson; under his toxic leadership, anti-Catholicism would live on.

Tom Watson trained as a lawyer. At the start of his career he won a number of cases for small farmers like his parents, quickly building a reputation for himself as one of Georgia's best trial lawyers. As he aged he became an increasingly nostalgic, vitriolic, uncompromising proponent of the Old South, building a career on his opposition to the reform ideas prevalent in the New South.

Although he stood up for the 'little man' in his battles against the wealthy, he objected to any change in the South's racial, political and religious foundations. For Watson, with his narrow-minded 'good ole boy' conservatism, shifting to anti-Catholicism was easy. And by the 1890s his transformation was complete.

He would publish a stream of anti-Catholic rants in *Tom Watson's Magazine* until his death in 1922. He ran headlines like 'The Roman Catholic Hierarchy: The Deadliest Menace' and 'Absolute Proof that Romanism Desired Death of Abraham Lincoln'. Circulation grew and imitators emerged. Aghast, the Catholic fraternity the Knights of Columbus said in 1914 it had counted over sixty national anti-Catholic weeklies with readerships ranging from 100,000 to 1.5 million subscribers.[4]

The runaway bestseller was Wilbur Phelps' Missouri-based weekly *The Menace*, a publication with an even more viciously anti-Catholic tone than *Watson's*. Started in a ramshackle old opera house in the Ozark town of Aurora, its first issue in 1911 reached twenty-two local readers. Three years later the paper was so nationally successful it was necessary for the local post office to set up a substation on the side of the railway solely to make sure the four-page weekly reached its huge readership every Saturday.

*The Menace* ran stories that were readable, current and shocking. It tapped into its readership's visceral fears of living in a two-nation USA, one rural and one urban. The rural side was traditional, pious, simple, righteous – and Protestant. The urban side was fast-living, progressive, immoral – and, of course, Catholic.

To prove Catholics were corrupting the morals of the nation, *The Menace* published salacious stories of 'virginal' nuns cavorting with lascivious 'celibate' priests. It exposed Catholic politicians at the very heart of big-city corruption. It was Catholics, working behind the scenes, who were responsible for the inexorable rise of big business.[5]

Wilbur Phelps' revamped Know-Nothing-ism, with its combination of anti-Catholic and anti-foreign sentiment, had found the zeitgeist of the nation and Clarke adopted it for his Klan. In a post-war moment demanding visible patriotism, the association of Catholicism with a foreign power became a potent recruiting tool for the Klan. Anti-Catholicism enabled the Klan to tap into the massive anti-immigrant sentiment. It could harness the fears spread by the anti-Catholic lobby that Catholics were disloyal. Their leader was the Pope, not the president, making them dangerously un-American.[6]

It didn't end there. The Kleagles used the argument that Catholic superstition and the position of the priest in the everyday lives of Catholics had kept the Roman Catholic masses in subservience and worked against democracy. For proof, one had only to look at Catholic countries like Italy, Ireland and Poland. In these places, regime change was a matter of revolution. No wonder Italy had produced so many leading anarchists and Ireland and Poland had given the world the most infamous nationalist terrorists. With such a legacy there could be only one conclusion: Rome was a breeding ground for revolution. And in the early 1920s, revolution was very much in the air in the USA.

For Clarke's much-vaunted 1,000 Kleagle-recruiters, particularly those operating in the overwhelmingly white rural regions, anti-Catholicism was a godsend. Oregon Kleagles presaged the arrival of the Klan with a lecture: 'Convent Cruelties', given by Helen Jackson, who claimed to be a nun who had escaped from a convent. 'Miss Jackson' told a horrific tale about how priests had repeatedly raped and impregnated her and then forced her to abort and bury the unborn babies.[7]

On the other side of the country, in the small textile towns of Maine, the Kleagles took full advantage of long-standing anti-Catholicism to ramp up their appeal to Protestant factory workers. The mills had long used seasonal French Canadian migrants to keep down wages.[8] In Texas and California anti-Catholicism became a dog-whistle phrase for anti-Mexican sentiment. In all four states the Klan boomed.

The Klan's anti-Catholicism was equally effective in Boston, Philadelphia, Chicago and other major cities. It was particularly focused against Italian and Polish immigrants. These groups were condemned as superstitious, backward and ignorant. Unlike their Protestant neighbours, they were cowed by years of dominance by Rome. They were seen as dim, deferring to their priests in all matters and unable to think for themselves.

In New York, Kleagles took advantage of the long-held belief that Catholics were linked with political corruption, especially in the Irish-dominated inner-city Democrat Party. Anti-Catholic propaganda portrayed Irish–Catholic politicians as demagogues, obsessed with skimming funds from public works, corrupting elections and packing all levels of local government with their placemen. Klan recruiters in New York also pointed out how these 'agents of Rome' flouted Prohibition laws and were frequently associated with bootleggers, gangsters and other ne'er do wells.

It was a proudly Protestant message and it tied in with the prevailing religious puritanism and revivalism sweeping the USA. New churches were built. Huge crowds flocked to see charismatic celebrity preachers like Billy Sunday and Aimee Semple McPherson.[9] With their strategy of appealing to Protestants, Kleagles actively targeted clergy. They handed out free literature and often waived the $10 Klecktoken, or membership fee. Their recruiting was so effective that, at the Klan's peak in 1924, twenty-six of its thirty-nine Klockards, or lecturers, were also Protestant ministers.[10]

There were clear advantages in the strategy of tying in with clergy. Ministers had ready-made lists of their congregations, an invaluable resource for ambitious Kleagles. With ministers in the Klan, congregants would hear sermons extolling the Klan and people instinctively trusted messages from the pulpit. Further, if a church was amenable, Klan members would arrive in full costume at a service and silently line up in the back. Then, on cue, they'd proceed down the aisles to the altar and make announcements about a forthcoming Klan rally, or social event. At other times they might ostentatiously give a donation to the upkeep of the church or an associated charity.

The Klan's recruitment strategies often included drama, just as the best services did. At the Woodward Christian Church in Oklahoma, the Reverend Harney McGeree gave a sermon on the Second Coming. He built up the suspense, telling his congregation that Christ would appear when least expected and in the strangest of places. At that moment 150 robed Klansmen marched down the aisle. The effect was 'electrifying'.[11]

Klansmen were known to turn up in all their regalia at funerals to see off their comrades. Sometimes, they'd take this further. In order to imply a local dignitary or other well-known figure was a Klansman, they even stood, uniformed, by the graveside of people who'd had no connection whatever to the order.

But the Klan was not universally popular at Protestant churches. One Southern Methodist condemned it as a 'leprous social disease'. In 1922 about twenty Protestant ministers in New York City gave anti-Klan sermons.[12] Ministers in liberal churches condemned the Klan for its racism, its commercialism and its clandestine habits. They saw the order as un-American and against the fundamental tenets of Christianity.

But Klan members argued they were '100 per cent American'. The wartime patriotism fostered by the federal government had not been satisfied.

Americans had been stirred up by Woodrow Wilson's idealism and rhetoric: his talk of the USA's sacred duty to 'make the world safe for democracy' and his dreams of international co-operation. At the war's end this patriotic fervour needed a new outlet.

Even though they had rejected Wilson's party and legacy in the 1920 election, people wanted to make the USA a beacon of civilised modernity for the rest of the world. And a major part of this urge came in the form of support for the prohibition of alcohol. To many Americans Prohibition was a rational and logical expression of the USA's moral superiority. It was, as President Herbert Hoover would later call it, 'The Noble Experiment', and Clarke and his Kleagles jumped on this bandwagon with enthusiasm.

# CHAPTER 35

On 17 January 1920, it became illegal to produce, sell or even transport alcohol in the USA. Americans largely supported the measure, although with varying degrees of enthusiasm. Many harboured the private thought that, if the experiment didn't work, Prohibition could always be repealed. A significant minority, however, felt the measure was vital to the moral health of the nation. The two leading 'dry' pressure groups – the ASL and the Women's Christian Temperance Union (WCTU) comprised Methodists, Baptists and many of the fundamentalist churches. It just so happened that two of these groups were the new Klan's biggest supporters.

This didn't escape Clarke and his Kleagles. The Klan adopted a strong Prohibition stance in order to lure members from the ASL and the WCTU. It didn't hurt that Catholics and Italians Irish and Polish immigrants were among the most outspoken anti-Prohibition groups and often caught breaking its laws. Newspapers portrayed these groups as the main producers, sellers and consumers of illegal booze.

In Texas, a pro-Klan newspaper linked Jewish immigrants to bootlegging, seeing a connection between 'homebrew and the Hebrew'. In *The Kourier*, the Klan weekly, Imperial Wizard Hiram Wesley Evans wrote, 'A scan of the names of bootleggers arrested each day in our large cities [and] one immediately realizes that the bootlegging industry is receiving its greatest impetus from persons who are not Americans.'[1] It seemed there were bootleggers and there were Americans.

The Klan's anti-bootlegging campaign did not just appeal to anti-immigration sentiment. As Americans began to see that Prohibition was not working, the Klan's Prohibition stance seemed clear-sighted and practical. One of the problems was the cost. In a time when direct federal taxes brought in only a small part of the national budget, duties and tariffs on 'luxuries' made up a large part of the federal income – and alcohol was a large portion of this income.

One estimate put the annual loss to the economy at $11 billion. State governments reported huge losses, too, with New York claiming losses of almost three-quarters of its revenue every year. In hindsight, the costs had not been exaggerated: in its first ten years (1920–30) Prohibition cost the federal government a frightening sum of nearly $250 million to enforce, and those costs grew, significantly, year after year.[2]

That huge expense didn't buy them very effective enforcement. In the early years, the Prohibition Unit of the Bureau of Internal Revenue was woefully understaffed and chaotic. Even General Lincoln C. Andrews, the assistant secretary of Customs, Coastguard and Prohibition, was unsure of the number of employees working for the unit. His best estimate for 1926 was 'about 3,600 to 3,800'. To put this in perspective, the continental US has a landmass of about 3.8 million square miles, meaning there was roughly one Prohibition agent for every 1,000 square miles.

Prohibition Agency morale was abysmal. The job was seen as increasingly futile. Agents were untrained and miserably underpaid. Staff turnover was extremely high. By 1926, 100,000 men had served as one of the nation's 4,000-odd 'Prohos'. Yet the demand for alcohol seemed unstoppable, and the profits made by bootleggers continued to grow. So, many of those who remained in the service simply 'went on the take'.

Throughout its history, 10 per cent of the entire Prohibition service was sacked for 'crookedness or incompetency' – and those were just the ones caught. The actual levels of corruption were certainly far higher. Kleagles pitched to recruits with the argument that Prohibition was poorly enforced and Klan membership, the solution. It would be cost effective. As the Oklahoma Kleagle put it, 'the people, taxed to the limit, are taking this method to put a stop to this cost on the town and country'.[3]

The Klan's mission had indeed coalesced around Prohibition and the reaffirmation of traditional Protestant US values. For the millions of families ravaged by drink, these seemingly abstract ideals offered tremendous comfort. In these households, drunk husbands squandered family budgets in saloons, beat their wives and children, then left them to scrape by. Children grew up hungry and without father figures while once loving family men found themselves alone and filled with regret. It is no small wonder that, to these Americans, abstinence became the beacon of hope that would restore their families and their belief in the nation's future.

Prohibition also linked back to the Klan's anti-urbanism. Recruits were sold on the Klan's historical belief of the city as the fount of corruption, rife with crooked politicians and immoral populations. Nowhere was this more apparent than in New York City. Flexing its political muscle at the 1924 Democrat Convention in New York, the Klan attacked and defeated the front runner, New York governor Al Smith, for his Catholicism, opposition to Prohibition and ties to corrupt political institutions.

Al Smith became the Klan's bête noire. From the Klan's perspective he was a product of a cabal of powerful political bosses known as the 'Tammany Machine'. They perfected 'machine politics', a system for harvesting the votes of the newly enfranchised and impoverished denizens of the poorer districts of New York. It was unethical and blatant and tied firmly to the city's Democrat Party. Indeed, the city's Democratic Party HQ was housed in the building which gave the whole system its name – Tammany Hall. Tammany became a synonym for corrupt politics and in the early 1920s the Tammany organisation was still bribing, bullying and bunging to get its own way. And in Al Smith's case that was the destruction of Prohibition.

As governor of New York, Al Smith had openly opposed Prohibition. One of his first acts on entering the Governor's Mansion had been to repeal New York's so-called 'Little Volstead', the Mullan–Gage Law. Passed in the post-Volstead euphoria, this Act had made violations of the new Prohibition laws a state as well as federal offence. Ironically, the draconian-seeming Act clogged up the New York courts and made New York City into one of the easiest places in the Union to get a drink. It had also put Smith on the Klan's radar.

So, when Smith ran for Democrat presidential candidate in 1924, nearly 350 of the delegates in Madison Square Gardens' Democratic Convention were Klansmen. Sixty of them had travelled from Atlanta and stood in full robes, in the convention hall.[4] Their target was Smith. He was the perfect embodiment of all they opposed: he was wet; he was Catholic; he was supported by immigrant votes; and he was Tammany.

The Klan succeeded in their anti-Smith crusade. On the 103rd ballot, delegates chose John W. Davis – not Smith or his most real opponent, William Gibbs McAdoo. In some measure this was down to the Klan. Behind the scenes the Imperial Wizard, Hiram Wesley Evans, played king-maker. He promised Klan support here. He threatened to withdraw it there. It worked and the Klan trumpeted its influence. It was arguably one of the Klan's most impressive achievements and the Convention was known from then onwards as the 'Klanbake'. The Klan now regarded itself as a political force, and people continued to join. But there were other causes that made Americans flock to the Klan in the early 1920s.

# CHAPTER 36

The USA had actually been involved in the First World War long before its troops arrived on the Western Front. The Allied war effort needed the USA's weapons, ammunition, food and money. Since 1914, factories and farms across the USA had been working at full tilt to fulfil these orders for Britain, France and the other Allied nations. With its agricultural and manufacturing sectors working at capacity, the USA profited.

In fact, the First World War made the USA. Industrial expansion after the Civil War had gradually turned the USA into an economic superpower, but the First World War made it *the* economic superpower. This could not have happened without several major changes to labour relations in agriculture and industry. World war had stopped the flow of cheap, disposable labour from Europe. Bosses could no longer rely on workforce compliance resulting from the terror of being easily replaced.

With war raging in Europe, US workers were able to negotiate better contracts. If they felt obligations were not being met, they could withhold their labour. Lack of immigrant labour gave them confidence. In short, labour gained significant power. But the war's end put this in jeopardy. When the fighting ended in November 1918, demand for US goods began to dry up.

Europe no longer needed munitions, industrial goods and food. Suppliers for the military, shipbuilding and food-processing industries were the first to be hit. More distant but no less dependent suppliers soon found themselves struggling. The USA tumbled into recession. The gains workers had made during the war years evaporated. Unemployment began to rise. At the same time, desperate, disillusioned immigrants flooded into the USA from war-torn Europe seeking a better life. Bosses were once again able to sack employees at will.

It was the kind of moment to make the Klan and groups like it prosper. Klan rhetoric already condemned open immigration and railed against the undesirable element it was allowing into the country. Now their anti-immigration pitch had a new selling point: the threat of Bolshevism and world revolution.

The Russian Revolution of October 1917 altered the course of the war, the fate of Russia and the confidence of capitalism. Most of Europe had been torn apart by war and was undergoing terrible economic depression. In Central Europe, in particular, demobilised troops were defeated, dejected and destitute. They were often miles from home and exhausted. They'd been brutalised, desensitised and they were trained to use weapons. They were the perfect followers for revolutionary activists.

Hungary's bloody and successful revolution soon followed, and it seemed increasingly likely that Poland and the Baltic States would fall into the orbit of Bolshevism. Even Germany teetered on the precipice with street fighting and murder squads. In Europe there were signs of revolution. China had its squabbling warlords; Mexico had decades-long instability, and Argentina was on the verge of revolution. Everywhere the 'Bacillus of Bolshevism' threatened to upend the existing order. And it didn't take long for some of these radical groups to begin popping up in the USA.

Anarchists, revolutionary socialists, communists, anarcho-syndicalists – all talked of seizing power in the name of the oppressed workers. There were strikes and walkouts in the steel mills, in the coal mines, on railroads, on farms and even on remote forest logging trails. There was a riot on May Day in Cleveland, Ohio. Two people were killed and over forty injured. It took baton charges and tanks to put it down.

In Seattle, radical dockers, factory workers, shipbuilders, shop workers – even milkmen – called a general strike. Troops patrolled the streets, supported by machine-gun squads and armoured cars. For five days it looked like the threatened revolution might actually happen. Anarchists sent thirty-six letter bombs disguised as toys to prominent industrialists and high-ranking officials, including the oil baron John D. Rockefeller, the financier J.P. Morgan and the commissioner of immigration for the port of New York, Frederic Howe. A housemaid lost several fingers on one hand, but no one else was badly hurt.

Then US Attorney General A. Mitchell Palmer had the front wall blown clean off his Washington residence. The clumsy bomber tripped on a rail, detonated the bomb and killed himself. Badly shaken, Palmer narrowly escaped. His dinner guests, Franklin and Eleanor Roosevelt, had just left. It was one of nine bombs set off simultaneously in eight cities. Then, to cap it all, the police went on strike in Boston. It was all thoroughly un-American.

As the country seemed to be descending into chaos, the federal government responded. With the help of a young J. Edgar Hoover, Palmer compiled a list of nearly 60,000 radicals. Under the auspices of the 1917 Espionage Act – made to protect military operations – the so-called 'Palmer Raids' of late 1919 and early 1920 began. Authorities raided clubs, bars and political societies, rounding up thousands of suspected revolutionaries.

Authorities deported 246 men and three women aboard a rusting, 30-year-old troopship called the *Buford*. The press nicknamed it the 'Soviet Ark', but there was truth in the name. In laying it on, the authorities were telling revolutionary radicals: if they weren't happy in the USA, they should go to Russia. They were essentially public nuisances, but even their enemies in the press found difficulty linking them to a coherent threat of revolution. It seems they were being deported as either 'malignant conspirators and destructive revolutionists' or 'apostles of peace, preachers of the principle of non-resistance'.[1]

The *Buford* left New York on Sunday, 6 December 1919 with sixty-two army soldiers guarding the passengers on their voyage across the Atlantic. After urgent repairs to the boiler in the German port of Kiel, the ship went on to dump its cargo of 'undesirables' in Finland before returning home. The radicals, still under military escort, travelled on, by train, to the Russian border. There, under a flag of truce, they trudged through a blizzard into war-torn Russia. Many returned to the USA as soon as they could.[2]

The legality of the 'Soviet Ark' was dubious. Most of the 3,000 arrested in the Palmer Raids would be released without charge for lack of evidence. Roughly 200 of the 6,000 convictions were upheld on appeal. But the national press remained almost universally convinced a threat remained. They saw the radicals as un-American, and the response of the authorities as inadequate, especially when – in September 1920 – a bomb went off on Wall Street.

The huge bomb, concealed in a horse-drawn wagon, had been loaded with nuts, bolts and metal that would act as shrapnel. People were so badly mangled it was difficult to piece together the bodies, but the coroner settled on a figure of 200 injured and forty killed. The dead included a long list of office workers, pedestrians and bystanders, as well as John Pierpont Morgan Jr's son, Junius. Fearing a revolution, 100 US Army troopers with fixed bayonets were despatched to Wall Street. The bells of nearby Trinity Church tolled. No one was ever convicted.[3]

The Kleagles had no difficulty exploiting this situation. The Klan placed 'the radical' right up there with the Catholic, the bootlegger and the corrupt politician. Like the other two in the Klan's trinity of hate, the radical was associated with foreigners. Klan speakers argued it was foreigners, unfamiliar with democracy, who were most likely to fall sway to Bolshevism. Americans had been born and bred on democracy: it was in their DNA. The sacred ballot box, not revolution, was the way to lasting reform. They'd forgotten 1776.

# CHAPTER 37

Like anti-Catholicism, the Klan's antisemitic ideology had complex roots. In part it drew on religious ideals: the Jews as 'Christ-killers'. Then there was age-old secular prejudice. Under the legislation of many European states, since medieval times Jews were restricted as to where they could live and what trades they could practise. They were excluded from owning land and were frequently subjected to violent persecution.

The result was that European Jews tended to practise occupations which could be easily re-established in case they were forcibly relocated. For that reason, Jews tended to deal in portable commodities like jewellery and gold. They also increasingly went into banking and moneylending, at all levels of society.

Some in European Jewry prospered. Jews funded governments, they funded wars, they funded trade. Governments lost power; states lost wars and deals went south. Debts could not be repaid. It was always the Jew's fault, as so famously illustrated in *The Merchant of Venice*. It seems no one likes a banker, particularly when they owe them money.

In Europe's more recent history, the Jewish population had gained freedoms. In Britain, France, Germany, Austria and even Russia, many of the laws which had constrained European Jewry were liberalised in the nineteenth century. Jews prospered, often funding industrialisation, and spearheading the entrepreneurial culture that went with it. Jews became middle class. An age-old respect for education suited them for the professions. Jews became lawyers, they became doctors, they became academics: they became ambitious.

In spite of these changes, Jews found that the prejudices against them remained in place and a proportion of Jews saw revolution as the solution. Jews were portrayed as being particularly committed to Bolshevism. Not only was the main ideologue of communism, Karl Marx, Jewish, but it was argued that so were many of the actual revolutionary leaders, most notably Leon Trotsky.[1] Antisemites argued that Jews were prominent in the Communist Party, at all levels, and in all countries. They were the ideal revolutionaries since they had no real homeland: they owed no political allegiances – they were outsiders.[2]

In the USA Jews were well represented in the public's imagination of radicals. Perhaps the best known were the celebrity feminist–socialist– anarchist 'Red' Emma Goldman and her sometime lover Alexander Berkman. The pair had been jailed for their activities in high-profile cases, but regardless had continued to publish influential essays, pamphlets and books as well as hold rallies and give lecture tours. They had openly spoken out against not just capitalism, but the war, military conscription and organised religion.

Writing in the *Imperial Night-Hawk*, the Klan's national newspaper, one Kleagle bemoaned the fact that Jewish radicals could openly seek to 'tear down the Stars and Stripes and supplant it with a red rag', and get away with impunity. He condemned the way in which they went out of their way to 'agitate strikes, bloodshed and anarchy … and to make the United States a working-class republic … dominated by the central government in Moscow'. So, as that Klan spokesman put it, 'there is a very real need for a hundred percent American organization … [to fight] the foreign revolutionary swine'.[3] And he, like hundreds of thousands of others, thought that was the Klan.

The *Night-Hawk* was not alone in pointing out the dangers posed by 'International Jewry'. No lesser a figure than the engineer, and man of the people, Henry Ford had sponsored and published a series of aggressively antisemitic articles in his own newspaper, *The Dearborn Independent*. The series kicked off with a collection of headlining pieces under the title 'The International Jew: The World's Problem'. It ran from spring 1920 and was so successful Ford published another three series, running for another eighteen months.

Drawing ideas from a slanderous fabrication of White Russian antisemitism, *The Protocols of the Elders of Zion*, among others, dealt with the entire spectrum of antisemitism. Jews controlled the world's business and financial systems. They sponsored and ran Bolshevism. International Jewry sought the downfall of the West and the USA. Jewish machinations and greed had sparked the First World War. Jews lay behind the 'Moron Music', jazz. Jews even encouraged and supported the USA's first homegrown traitor, Benedict Arnold, in his treason.

While most of these claims were clearly unsustainable, they did come from one of the USA's most influential and, at that time, respected figures.

Given that, the Klan's antisemitic racism found fertile ground in the early 1920s. As one particularly foul-mouthed Oregon Klansmen put it, 'In some parts of America the Kikes are so thick that a white man can hardly find room to walk.'[4] And as immigrant numbers began to climb after the wartime lull, there were real fears that unassimilable, un-American and undesirable immigrants would once again pour in. And this was not the only migration that Americans feared.

# CHAPTER 38

By 1921 the Greenwood district of Tulsa was booming. Like the rest of Oklahoma, it had benefited from the discovery and exploitation of huge oil reserves. The district had grown by over 10 per cent in the previous decade and its bustling streets and impressive houses were home to some 10,000 residents. Since the 1890s Greenwood had been an area of thriving, small, entrepreneurial businesses.

Greenwood had billiard halls, smart dress shops, a handful of hotels and a movie theatre. It had its own hospital, library and two local newspapers. Professionals – doctors, lawyers and real estate agents – chose to live in the smart red-brick houses of this area of town. But in spite of the image this conjures up, this was not the average US city district. Tulsa was a segregated city, in a segregated state – and the population of Greenwood was entirely Black.

But Greenwood was an affluent area of a prosperous city. The African American activist and social reformer Booker T. Washington famously referred to the region as the 'Negro Wall Street'. The *Tulsa World*, a white-owned paper, told its readers that 'Residents in the Negro section of the city have proven themselves no less enterprising than the white people'.[1]

But these assessments were not shared by everyone in Tulsa. As the city had become more affluent, crime had increased and it appeared the Tulsa police department (PD) was not up to the job. The local population frequently resorted to vigilante justice. In August 1920 a teenager who had apparently evaded justice was taken from his police cell and publicly lynched. That anonymous teenager was the only white victim of a lynching in the region since 1911. The twenty-three other victims were all Black.

Less than eight months later the Tulsa police were found wanting again, although the details of the incident are murky and, if it were not for their tragic consequences, laughable. It appears that on 30 May 1921 a young Black shoe-shiner trod on the foot of a young, white, female elevator operator in the Drexel skyscraper. The girl screamed. By the time the elevator reached its destination, the rumours had started and the police had been called. The young man was arrested and charged with rape.

By the next evening the rumour mill had created chaos. White people heard of Black mobs. Black people recognised the signs and armed themselves. At least one Black man had been shot as throughout the night white vigilantes drove through the Greenwood district firing out of the windows of their cars. By the night of 31 May and morning of 1 June the violence had reached a crescendo. Thousands of heavily armed whites raged through the Greenwood district, shooting indiscriminately, looting and setting property alight. One eyewitness reported seeing Tulsa police deputising white citizens and then instructing them to 'get a gun and get a nigger'. By late morning the National Guard was called out.

That evening, seven National Guard aircraft flew over the city. Even through the billowing smoke, they could see flames. Most of Greenwood was alight. They could tell that all the landmarks of Greenwood had been destroyed, including the district's church and its school. On landing, they reported that thirty-five blocks had been entirely levelled. What they could not see and did not know was that nearly 300 Black residents had been killed and at least half of the district's population of 10,000 were now homeless.[2]

A week after the rioting was over, Walter White, the head of the NAACP, arrived in Tulsa to write a report. A veteran of racial violence, he was nevertheless horrified by the state of Greenwood and the stories he heard. White claimed it was the worst race riot in US history – which it probably was.

But the rioters and looters were not finished. Shortly after his visit, the Grand Goblin of the Western Realm of the Western Domain of Klandom, George Kimbro, and the Imperial Representative of the Realm of Missouri, Kansas and Nebraska, George McCarron, also arrived in Tulsa from Houston, Texas. They were there to capitalise on the hatred. And the Klansmen were effective.

Within a week they had recruited twelve Kleagles throughout Oklahoma. The Klan recruiters were as opportunistic and crass as ever – but they found a willing audience. In August 1921, more than 2,000 would attend a public lecture given by a Baptist minister from Atlanta. The minister was also a top Klan rabble-rouser. The anonymous speaker declared, 'The riot was the best thing that ever happened to Tulsa … [but] judging from the way strange Negroes were coming to Tulsa we might have to do it all over again.'[3]

By the end of the month 300 white, Protestant Americans were inducted into the Klan in a ceremony on the outskirts of Tulsa. And then it took off. By the end of the year the Tulsa Klan was claiming 3,000 members.[4] Across the state, they were equally successful. At its peak, the Oklahoma Klan had anywhere between 100,000 and 300,000 members. It would become renowned as the most violent Klan in the nation.

# CHAPTER 39

The Oklahoma Klan was not alone in using race as a recruitment tool. All over the nation white supremacy was perhaps the most important unifying element of Klan ideology. In major cities where immigrants tended to congregate, white supremacy tended to be largely a matter of *how* 'white' those immigrants were. There were elements of white supremacy in antisemitism. Jews were often referred to, without particular hostility, in official and other sources as members of the 'Hebrew Race', inferring they were not members of the 'Aryan Race' and the early twentieth century defined races clearly.

The racial hierarchy of the late nineteenth and early twentieth centuries was complex. Not only were racial types defined by obvious physical traits, but there were also more subtle traits that distinguished the different 'races'. So 'race scientists', as they liked to call themselves, used facial features to differentiate, say, African or Asian origin from those of European or Native American stock. Other races were more defined by a process of reverse-engineering which used religion, geography, culture and history to essentially create a 'race'.

One striking example is provided by the economist and anthropologist William Z. Ripley. Although the benevolent and scholarly Ripley wrote his book to pay for his children's education, it went on to become one of the most influential race science texts of all time.[1] Ripley distinguished three European races: the Teutons, the Alpines and the Mediterraneans.

The Teutons came from the northern European regions of Scandinavia, Britain, Germany and the Netherlands. The Alpines were from France, Austria, northern Italy, Switzerland and so on. The Mediterraneans came from southern Italy, Greece and Spain. The traits Ripley attributed to these races were drawn from a medley of physical features, largely dictated by the shape of the skull.

However, over the early twentieth century, other 'racial anthropologists' added a raft of cultural prejudices. The most notable of these was the amateur historian, founder of New York Zoo and super-connected socialite Madison Grant. With Grant, as with most other 'race scientists', his views were largely drawn from his own interpretation of history and his own 'racial' background. Like Grant, these were almost universally, proudly, middle-class Anglo-Saxon.[2]

They also fused observable, quantifiable physical characteristics with elements of cultural and national stereotypes. So, to Grant the Teutons, whom he re-named Nordics, were fair-skinned, pale-eyed, tall and 'long-headed'. They were also intelligent, courageous, logical, sensitive and creative. The Alpines were shorter, darker-skinned, round-headed. But in addition, they were creative and fairly intelligent, but given to outbursts of melancholy and self-destructive violence.

The final group, the Mediterranean race, was again long-headed, but stocky and dark-skinned. They were also written off as emotional, cunning and far less intelligent than those who originated further north. On the borders of Europe lurked the Slavs, the Semites, the Magyars, the Bulgars and all sorts of other exotic-sounding races who periodically posed existential threats to the Western European races and so they were given racial characteristics reflected that menace.

Debates took place within the community of these race scientists which verged from the academic to the plain ridiculous, but the consequences for many Europeans were serious. These racial categories could be used to explain the desirability of various nationalities and informed the swingeing, race-based, quota-based immigration controls in the early 1920s. These signalled huge changes for the ability of Eastern and Southern Europeans to emigrate and settle in the USA – changes the Klan backed with enthusiasm.

In 1923, as the second of the decade's restrictive immigration quota Acts was being drawn up, the Imperial Wizard of the KKK, Hiram Wesley Evans, gave a lecture on the 'Klan Day' of the State Fair of Texas in Dallas. The title was 'The Menace of Modern Immigration', and it went down as probably the most important Klan speech of the 1920s.

Standing on the podium, fully robed with a sash pulled tight on his well-rounded belly, the dumpy ex-dentist was hardly the model of the Nordic race's much-vaunted superiority. Nevertheless, he gave a rousing speech on his version of the Klan's racially based immigration policy. He used statisticians to describe how it was clear that the Mediterranean, Slavic, Magyar and Semitic races supplied the lowest levels of literacy, the highest levels of criminality and the greatest instances of 'mental deficiency' of those residing in the nation. He used criminologists to show how they made up the overwhelming number of law-breakers. And he drew on population experts to show that 'the present United States is much less than half, perhaps little more than a third, of native Anglo-Saxon stock'.[3]

And the Klan also railed against what they saw as another equally damaging migration which was taking place, this time within the nation. The First World War had interrupted immigration, just as demand for US industrial and agricultural goods was taking off. One of the solutions industrialists in the North reached for was the virtually untapped labour source in the South – African Americans.

Black industrial workers promised many of the benefits that supposedly came from European immigrants: they were cheap, plentiful and – perhaps most importantly – desperate. The years since 1865 had not given the Black population of the South many of the benefits promised by freedom. The imposition of Jim Crow and then segregation had been accompanied by a variety of restrictions – on their ability to vote, their legal protections and their freedom of movement.

What was more, the cotton crop, still the region's primary industry, was devastated by the appearance of the boll-weevil. This insect lays its eggs on the cotton bud. Within weeks its emerging young devastate the crop, destroying almost all of the plant. Native to Central America, the boll-weevil spread north through Mexico in the late nineteenth century. By the second decade of the twentieth century it was creating economic havoc in almost all cotton production throughout the South. Those who could leave the plantations and small farms often sought a new life elsewhere.[4]

In many ways this exodus was self-perpetuating. As Black, rural Southerners made a better life in the North and Midwest, so they wrote to relatives, sweethearts and friends in the South, perhaps sending money, but also encouraging them to join them. Black newspapers also played a major role, especially *The Chicago Defender*.

The *Defender* ran stories of successful Black migrants. It was also the main source of job adverts offering reliable work for Southern labour and had a circulation of old editions way in excess of its subscription levels. In Atlanta, Georgia, the *Defender* was available in all Black-owned barbers' shops. In Savannah, one preacher regularly sold twenty-five to fifty copies to his congregation each Sunday.[5]

That is not to say that leaving the South was easy. Landowners and other employers fought hard to prevent the exodus. In Macon, Georgia, a local by-law required $25,000 ($400,000 in today's figures) for a licence to recruit labour.[6] In Jacksonville, Florida, labour recruiters faced a $600 fine and sixty days in jail.[7] Nevertheless recruiters did tempt hundreds of thousands to 'run any risk to get where they could breathe freer', as W.E.B. DuBois put it.[8]

All this meant that from 1905 it is possible to detect an exodus of dejected but ambitious African Americans from the rural South, moving North. It is estimated that some 400,000 Black migrants left the South between 1915 and 1920, and that a further million would go north in the 1920s. Over these years the number of Black residents in Chicago went up by 600 per cent. But it was Motor City, Detroit, where this exodus was most apparent. Drawn by the promise of plentiful, well-paid jobs in the wartime heavy industries, the city's Black population exploded by some 2,000 per cent.

What was more, after the war, the booming car industry provided alternative jobs. The figures tell the story. The city's Black population went from a pre-war figure of under 6,000 to more than 120,000 by the end of the 1920s. And it is here that we see one of the most explicit examples of the Klan's stirring up of anti-Black racial hatred.[9]

# CHAPTER 40

It all started on a steaming hot afternoon in late July 1919. A group of Black teenagers went swimming in the segregated water of Lake Michigan. Although they were unaware they had crossed into a 'whites-only' area, white beachgoers noticed and started pelting them with rocks. It seems one found its mark; sometime later, the body of 17-year-old Eugene Williams washed up on the beach. Tensions rose, culminating in a week-long orgy of bloody clashes, arson and looting. By the end, fifteen white and twenty-five Black people had been killed.[1]

Riots also broke out in Washington DC; Knoxville, Tennessee; Longview, Texas; Phillips County, Arkansas; and Omaha, Nebraska. The sparks that ignited each of these riots were unique – but the underlying tinder of race-hate was universal. There was a sense that the Black population was getting above itself.

There was a terror that the Black population would incrementally shift the racial boundaries. It might start with Black neighbourhoods seeping into white areas. Having done that, Black workers would compete for white jobs. Once in those jobs they would want to send their children to white schools. And, educated with white people, they might even aspire to marry white women.

To truly understand the nature and depth of the hatred this provoked and its consequences and uses to the Klan, it is necessary to jump forward to 1925. It is also necessary to move north to the urban, industrial heartland of the country.

In the engineering heart of the country, in Detroit, the Black population had been corralled into a segregated ghetto centred around three small wards on the east side, known locally as 'Black Bottom'. Overcrowded, unsanitary and squalid, it was nevertheless extremely difficult for the new and growing population of successful professionals and small business owners to leave. As the number of residents grew, so did the pressure to expand – or control – the neighbourhood's boundaries.

A brave few tried to buy outside the Black Bottom ghetto but met with concerted opposition. Through intimidation and mob violence, residents of the white-zoned neighbourhoods drove out those who tried. But the number of Black residents attempting to expand beyond Black Bottom continued to rise.

On 11 July 1925, the Klan organised a huge public meeting, complete with a backdrop of fiery crosses. The *Detroit Free Press* claimed as many as 10,000 robed Klansmen paraded in front of a large flaming cross. A robed lecturer goaded the crowd into a frenzy with demands that the informal neighbourhood segregation be backed by law. The audience loved it.[2] And it wasn't long before the Klan had an opportunity to put their rabble-rousing rhetoric into practice.

In September, Dr Ossian Sweet, a successful doctor, bought his family a bungalow home at 2905 Garland Avenue, in the all-white Charlevoix district. Pretty soon word had spread about the home's new residents being a Black family. Local men warned each other about the safety of their wives and daughters, planting fears that one Black family would just be the beginning. Eventually, they murmured, Charlevoix would become part of the encroaching sprawl of Black Bottom. The crime rate would rise, while house prices would plummet.

On 9 September, Garland Avenue residents congregated on the street outside Dr Sweet's bungalow. Children ran about, sensing excitement while adults strained to get a view of their unwelcome new neighbours. It looked like the little house was empty. Curtains were drawn, lights were off. Nevertheless, more and more people wandered past.

Within a few hours a gaggle of about thirty people stood on the street outside the neat little bungalow, a crowd largely made up of women and children. Initially the crowd had a party-like atmosphere. But as the police kept the gawkers from standing on the pavement in front of the 'Negroes' House', the mood became a bit less friendly. Someone grumbled that the police weren't doing their job properly – they ought to 'go in there and drag those niggers out'.[3]

Inside, Dr Sweet sat in the dark and peered out of the window at the growing crowd. Unlike most of his white neighbours, Sweet was a high achiever. Grandson of a slave and the eldest of ten children of a Florida sharecropper, against many odds, he had graduated from college. He'd obtained a medical degree and was a highly respected doctor at one the most prestigious Black hospitals in Detroit, Dunbar Memorial. Sweet and his wife Gladys, herself from a prominent middle-class Black family from

Pittsburgh, had spent the previous year travelling around Europe, visiting Paris, Vienna and other cultural capitals. Sweet was a man of the world, at least in his own estimation.

Also, unlike his working-class white neighbours, Sweet was dapper, dressing the part of a man who had made it. He was always turned out in understated, well-cut suits with crisply starched white shirts and tonal silk ties. He wore the round tortoiseshell glasses of the intellectual elite and kept a neatly trimmed moustache and fashionably short, cropped hair. Sweet wanted to live in an area where his achievements could be recognised. He had earned that bungalow – and had paid over the going rate for it. Still, he was grateful to be allowed the chance to buy the home.[4]

Sweet was undoubtedly aware that his white neighbours were not likely to feel the same. He would have read about the lynchings, torture and murder of similarly successful Black men in recent years. Sweet knew about the 1923 obliteration of the Black town of Rosewood, Florida, and the elimination of its population. Rosewood was a kind of Black pogrom where many of the town's Black citizens were killed and dumped into a mass grave. Survivors were forced to flee for their lives.[5] It is also likely that he knew about the Klan gathering in July, and the threats its members had made.

Sweet would have taken little comfort in the sight of seventeen policemen holding back the crowd on the pavement in front of his house. He knew they'd do nothing if the mood turned angry. Five times in that summer alone, Black people who'd settled in all-white areas had sparked riots. Each time, under the watchful eye of the police, they had been forced to move out of their new homes.

So why, then, had Dr Sweet taken the risk? The answer lies with one of those five families.

Dr Alexander Turner was chief surgeon at Dunbar Memorial Hospital and a colleague of Sweet's. Within hours of moving to the swanky Spokane Avenue neighbourhood, a mob had formed outside Dr Turner's home. Initially the crowd kept their distance, simply milling around. Then men began swarming over the garden fence and clambering onto the house, smashing windows, ripping slates from the roof, tearing out power lines and telephone wires.

When Turner opened the door to see what was happening the mob rushed past him and into the house, destroying his furniture and looting his possessions. Turner managed to escape by hiding on the floor of his expensive new car, the chauffeur driving him through the mob as they banged on the sides of the car. That night, a terrified Turner did as the mob demanded and signed over the deeds of his house to the Klan-backed Neighbourhood Improvement Society – some accounts say, at gunpoint.[6]

Despite his own terrifying experience, Dr Turner became convinced that Black people needed to stand up to the mob and establish their right to live in whites-only neighbourhoods. Dr Sweet, perhaps inspired by his colleague, decided that, when the mob turned on him, he would stand his ground.

Then, on the night of 9 September 1925, they came. Sweet, along with two of his brothers and several friends, were prepared to resist. The men had a rifle, two shotguns and seven handguns. But their armoury wasn't large enough for the enormous crowd, estimated at over 1,000 strong. Very quickly, the mob began hurling rocks, bottles and whatever else they could find at the house.

Sweet and the others retaliated. Shots rang out. One white man was killed, another wounded. The police, who'd been standing back, sprang into action, burst through the door and arrested all nine occupants on the charge of murder. The men were held in Wayne County Jail for two days until, finally, the NAACP was able to get them legal representation. Surprisingly – or perhaps not, given the men inside – when that representation did arrive, it was spectacular.

For $5,000, the NAACP secured the most famous US defence attorney of all time, Clarence Darrow. In court, Darrow spun the case to make it less about defending the Sweets, than about the actions of the police. Citing numerous instances of recent police negligence, Darrow gave an impassioned argument.

Though he was only able to secure a hung jury, in a subsequent trial Darrow famously acquitted Sweet's brother, Henry. It took the jury less than two hours to reach their verdict – this, in spite of Henry's admission that he had fired the fatal shot. In this one incident, time would prove that Sweet's colleague, Dr Turner, had been correct. Ossian Sweet and his family remained in the Garland Avenue house for more than thirty years.[7]

Sweet's vindication was encouraging, but it also revealed how far race hatred had spread beyond the Klan's traditional Southern strongholds. As Sweet himself poignantly put it during his trial, 'I realized I was facing the same mob that had hounded my people throughout our entire history. I was filled with a fear that only one could experience who knows the history and strivings of my race.'[8]

The Sweet case polarised opinion in Detroit. The morning after the mob attacked the Sweet house, Detroit's Mayor John W. Smith argued the Klan had ramped up racial tensions, leading to the death of a white man. But Smith also blamed the local Black population. He said that 'any colored person who endangers life and property, simply to gratify his personal pride, is an enemy of his race as well as an inciter of riot and murder'.[9]

For those drawn to the Klan, Henry Sweet's acquittal provided a clear example of how the nation pandered to the Black population. The Klan would argue that a Black man with a good lawyer could get away with murder and responded to the mayor's condemnation by distributing leaflets. These argued that Mayor Smith himself had created 'negro agitation' with his liberal messages of racial equality. Only a few days after Henry Sweet was acquitted, the Klan called the first meeting of the innocently titled 'Waterworks Association', a cover organisation founded to stop Black migration to white areas.

After its inaugural meeting, the Waterworks Association's first order of business was to organise a mass Klan rally. At this rally, the speaker admonished the crowd. Unless someone stood up to the Black population, he argued, they would continue to flood into Detroit from the South, eventually spilling over from the Black Bottom ghetto into white areas with dire social and economic consequences, spreading crime.

In the summer and autumn of 1925, the Detroit Klan reached its peak, with well over 100,000 members. It had become one of the most powerful chapters in the country.[10]

# CHAPTER 41

New targets, new marketing, new times — all these contributed to the phenomenal growth of the Klan in the early 1920s, but equally important was new leadership. Simmons' stellar performance in Congress definitely kick-started a revival in Klan fortunes. Clarke and Tyler's marketing strategy, their pyramid sales techniques and their grab bag of hate capitalised on the divisions of US society. But the final piece of the jigsaw that explained the rise of the Klan came in a far more prosaic shape.

In 1920, Hiram Wesley Evans became a Klansman. By 1922 he was the Imperial Wizard instructing the opinions and morals and commanding the actions of anywhere up to 6 million Klansmen nationwide. Although he was an unexceptional, short, rather pot-bellied, 39-year-old dentist from Dallas, his appearance was deceptive. Evans was an autocrat. Evans commanded the Klan. He was not the benevolent spiritual guide that Simmons had been. He was not content to pontificate. Evans wanted to forge the Klan into a political force.

There can be little doubt that Evans had plotted his rise to power for some time before he made his first move in December 1921. The coup started with details of financial irregularities exposed in the congressional hearings. During the hearings there was an accusation that Clarke's Propagation Department had received nearly $250,000 since its creation. Clarke testified that the true figure was less than $20,000. Few in the know believed Clarke, and his enemies started to spread damaging stories about his relations with Bessie Tyler, and her role in the leadership.

The Klan stood for clean politics, respect for family values and basic Christian morality, so the accusations against Clarke had the potential to do serious damage. They were also, ironically, even more dangerous to the leadership when the Klan's membership was expanding. Those in subordinate positions could smell blood. In December 1921 they moved. Fred

W. Atkins, the Grand Goblin of the Atlantic Domain, Clarke's immediate subordinate in the propagation department, went to the press.

On 3 December, *The New York Times* splashed the headline 'Deposed Goblins Say Klan is Broken'. Atkins told of how on 30 November, four 'Domain Chiefs' tried to oust Clarke and Tyler.[1] They claimed 'the whole crowd is rotten' and that Clarke's venality 'will break up the Klan forever'. He claimed that, in spite of rising numbers overall, the Klan was losing large numbers of its older members. The article pointed to in-fighting, with a claim that Simmons had told Atkins and his fellow Goblins that he felt 'everything you are saying [about Clarke] is true'. He reassured them that if Clarke had not resigned, 'William Joseph Simmons will'. He made the promise in front of about twenty people.

But he did not keep it. Instead, Clarke fired the four Goblins and Simmons, apparently on the advice of his physician, took the opportunity to 'go away for a short period of rest and recuperation' on the North Carolina shore. He promoted Clarke to Imperial Wizard in his absence. The dynamics of the Klan were shifting.

Power had moved from Simmons – the philosopher prince – to the kleptocracy of Clarke while behind the scenes lurked Evans.

Evans quickly proved to be ruthless and ambitious. One enthusiastic Klan supporter gushed about Evans claiming he had 'the determined convictions of Martin Luther, the kindness of Lincoln and the strategy and generalship of Napoleon'.[2] He might have also mentioned that the Dallas dentist had the cunning and scheming nature of Machiavelli. Within weeks of joining, he was essential to the running of the powerful Dallas Klan 66 and then made that Klavern an influential force in Texas politics and society. By 1922, Evans was its Exalted Cyclops, or chapter president.

Klan 66 was popular: it claimed a membership of around one in every three of the male, white, Protestant, native-born residents of Dallas, giving it around 13,000 Klansmen. Most ambitious Dallas lawmen were in this Klavern, as were many of the city's leading businessmen, clergy and professionals. But this middle-class basis belied its active and vicious racism, and Evans himself participated in one notorious incident. On 1 April 1921, Evans had led a band of Klansmen, who, in an action reminiscent of the Reconstruction Era, abducted a Black bellhop from the Adolphus Hotel. Alex Johnson was accused of having sex with a white woman in the hotel. They put a rope around his neck and bundled him into a car, which they drove to woodland 6 miles outside the city.

It is indicative of the level of racism in Texas that Klansmen also drove a *Dallas Times Herald* journalist in another car to the spot where they bundled Johnson out and tied him to a tree. After thirty or so lashes, the masked vigilantes cut him down. They then etched the letters 'KKK' on his forehead with silver nitrate. Satisfied with their work, they then trussed Johnson in chains, securing them with a padlock and ostentatiously threw the key away. Once back in the city, they dumped him, semi-conscious, shirtless and bleeding, on the steps of the Adolphus Hotel.[3]

No one was charged with any associated crime and the incident certainly did not harm Evans' career as a Klansman. Early in 1922, when the Klan 'Realm of Texas' was organised, Evans was promoted to Grand Titan of Texas Province 2. By the spring he'd been headhunted to become Imperial Kligrapp, or secretary to Imperial Wizard Clarke.

In part, this meteoric rise was the result of Evans' own efforts at self-promotion. The ambitious Texan had cultivated his relationship with Clarke and Tyler. For their part, Tyler and Clarke needed someone with solid Klan credentials to mollify the growing discontent stirred up by the congressional disclosures, and the actions of the rebellious Goblins. It seemed that this golden boy of the Texas Klan, Evans, was their man.

Over the next months, things continued to go Evans' way. In July 1922, furious at having lost his job to Evans, former Imperial Kligrapp David L. Wade went to the press. He renewed the accusations of corruption against Clarke and Tyler. He claimed Clarke 'kept W.J. Simmons drunk' to make sure no one uncovered his plot to 'become rich on ill-gotten gains'.

Wade detailed the ways in which Clarke skimmed money from the sale of robes, pocketing $2.10 on every robe sold by a manufacturing company he himself owned. He outlined how Clarke Realty bought land in the Klan's name, selling off the most valuable pieces to himself and leaving the Klan with the valueless real estate remaining. He explained how those who, like himself, opposed Clarke were simply dismissed and replaced with yes men. All this, he said, meant the rank-and-file Klansmen were beginning to lose faith in the temporary Imperial Wizard.[4] Clarke was getting increasingly isolated.

Then Clarke received another blow. In the autumn of 1922, his only real ally, Bessie Tyler, resigned. She did this, apparently, because of ill-health: she would die in September 1924. But it was probable that she went because the rumours of her long-standing affair with Clarke were once again circulating. Already a very wealthy woman, it is likely she calculated that the disruption caused to her life by remaining in the Klan probably far outweighed any benefits she might get by remaining. What was more, in August 1922 she'd married – for the fourth time. Without Bessie, Clarke knew that he was even more isolated, and sure enough, his misfortunes were just about to get worse.

By November 1922, Klan membership topped 1 million, and seemed to demonstrate almost limitless potential to expand further. Ambitious

Klansmen saw a great future for those bold enough to grasp it. They also saw their moment. That month Klansmen flocked from all over the nation to Atlanta. The order was holding its first national convention or, as they liked to call it, 'Klonvokation'. It was now that the dissident Klansmen made their move.

Meeting in the prestigious Piedmont Hotel on the evening of 26 November, the plotters were Klansmen of the very highest rank. There was Fred L. Savage, a sleazy, hard-nosed former New York strike-breaker/detective and Imperial Night Hawk – head of the Klan's own investigative department. Also there were two Grand Dragons, or state-level bosses, one of whom was the supremely ambitious Indiana boss, David Curtis Stephenson – of whom, more later.

Stephenson was as Machiavellian as Evans, with a subtle understanding of voters and politicians, and a ruthless ability to exploit both for his own ends. Alongside him was Arkansas boss James Comer, another shrewd political player. Like Evans, the three conspirators – Savage, Stephenson and Comer – saw Simmons as a liability to the future expansion of the Klan. He needed to go. Not only did he lack ambition, but he also lacked drive.

These men saw the Klan as a political force – a force capable of taking them out of state-level politics, and onto the national political scene. The trouble was that all three were so ambitious each could not allow the other to take power. The solution appeared simple. Why not back the unremarkable, rather shadowy, rather colourless, supreme apparatchik, Hiram Wesley Evans?

But there was also another problem. To many of the most ardent Klansmen, Simmons *was* the Klan. Simmons was the benevolent father of the Klan. What the plotters needed to do was get Simmons out of the way, to neutralise him.

They settled on a scheme that both recognised Simmons' exalted status in the Klan and, at the same time, relieved him of any real authority. The following morning, the day before the Klonvocation was due to start, Savage and Stephenson walked to Klankrest, Simmons' palatial home. Having just woken, and probably hungover, Simmons was confused when they told him that they'd discovered a plot to assassinate him and 'there will be armed men stationed round the floor to protect your honour'.

Terrified, Simmons later claimed he had dreams of 'a bloody shambles' as he stood before the ranks of Klansmen at the Klonvocation the following morning. He claimed he could face the constant threats to his life and in a hoarse voice he told the delegates he backed Evans as his successor. The delegates duly voted the Texas dentist in. The coup was complete.[5]

Evans now set about cleaning up and tightening up his Klan. He removed the last vestiges of Clarke's power, cancelling the Klan's contract with the

SPA. He did away with Simmons' cronyism, banning the old leader's pals from using the Imperial Palace as 'a loafing place'. Most importantly, he rewrote Simmons' Kloran, or Klan manifesto. The second section of the first article showed how he meant the Klan to go forward. It simply read: 'The government of this Order shall ever be military in character, especially in its executive management and control.'[6]

# PART VI

# HUBRIS
# 1922–1925

They paid ten dollars to hate somebody … and they were determined to get their money's worth.

Denver Juvenile Court Judge
Ben Lindsey on the Colorado Klan in 1923[1]

# CHAPTER 42

It was a hot 4 July 1923 in the 185 acres of Kokomo's Malfalya Park in Indiana. Thousands of robed Klansmen from Indiana, Illinois and Ohio squinted into the bright Midwestern summer sky. They watched as a tiny speck grew larger. Soon they heard the thrum of an engine. A small golden aircraft glinted, reflecting the bright sun and swooped around the park, the letters 'KKK' clearly visible under its wings. The crowd cheered as the plane came in for a bumpy landing.

Mounted Klansmen in full regalia galloped alongside a car driving towards the plane. A chubby figure in a purple Klan costume and pointed hood levered himself out of the open passenger cockpit, jumped down and got in the car. The white-robed horsemen flanked the vehicle once more as it traced the perimeter of the park and arrived at a large stage draped with red, white and blue bunting.

The audience roared as the figure in purple mounted the rostrum. He wore the Klan's trademark pointed hood. But his roundish, fleshy face was not covered. With a solemn expression, he leaned towards the microphone and shouted a coded greeting, 'Kigy!'

His voice still echoed in the public address system as he theatrically stepped back from the microphone. Thousands of excited Klansmen chorused back their allegiance in unison, 'Itsub.'[1]

He raised his hands, silencing the crowd. He spoke quietly, as if taking the assembled group into his confidence. His voice was clear and practised, his tone, apologetic: 'It grieves me to be late. The President of the United States kept me unduly long counselling on vital matters of state.'

As a murmur ran through the crowd, he grew louder:

Here in this uplifted hand, where all can see, I bear an official document addressed to the Grand Dragon, Hydra, Great Titans, Furies, Giants,

Kleagles, King Kleagles, Exalted Cyclops, Terrors and All Citizens of the Invisible Empire of the Realm of Indiana.

Shouting into the microphone, he read the words of the Imperial Wizard himself, Hiram Wesley Evans. It reinforced his role as Grand Dragon of the Invisible Empire for the Realm of Indiana: 'It so proclaims me by virtue of God's Unchanging Grace. So be it!'

The man in purple urged his ecstatic audience to practise the Klan's principles of 'One Hundred Percent Americanism' and whipped them into a final frenzy with the injunction to be on their guard against 'foreign elements'.

The crowd went wild. The dignitaries on the podium stood up as the Grand Dragon, with his retinue of officials, left the rostrum.

The crowd showered the stage with coins, jewellery and other valuables. His minions swarmed onto the stage and stooped to gather them as the man in purple and his entourage marched to a nearby pavilion.[2] Gradually, people began to disperse.

That was certainly not the end of the entertainment. Throughout the park, children took part in games and competitions. The plane performed loops and 'wing-walking' in great displays of aerial daring. Speeches continued throughout the day on rousing Klan topics. There were parades, boxing matches, bands, pie-eating contests, choirs singing and circus performers. The day ended with a huge firework display and the burning of twenty-five crosses. There was a lottery, in which a brand-new car was the prize. Klansman Victor Simmons won it with ticket 7705.[3]

In newspapers the next day in tones ranging from enthusiastic to appalled, journalists described the gathering – a real family day out, with robes and hoods.

Estimates put the number of Klansmen there at around 200,000. Records showed some 50,000 cars arriving in the days leading up to the event from all over the nation, swamping the little city of Kokomo and its 30,000 residents. As *The Fiery Cross* bragged before the 'Mammoth Meet', 'All roads used to lead to Rome. But those days are gone and July Fourth, under the starry banner of a free America, all roads will lead to Kokomo!'[4]

Like a swarm of locusts, the white-robed visitors stripped Kokomo of all resources, blocking the roads and emptying the shops. But the Klan had organised the event meticulously. They laid on food at the park; by their own count they had provided 6 tonnes of beef, 2,500 pies and 55,000 hamburger buns. True to their Prohibitionist creed, they had also provided 5,000 cases of soda and 'near-beer', as well as 250lb of coffee.[5]

The visitors had also put Kokomo on the map as a Klan town. Most Kokomo citizens felt it had been great publicity and gave their little city a sense of pride. As the Klan had grown and spread across the nation there had been competition to see which state, which region and which town could hold the largest rally. Throughout 1922 and 1923 crowds had grown at Klan rallies in Denver, Dallas and Cleveland. But Kokomo had topped them all.

This was no coincidence, for Kokomo really *was* a Klan town. With its two 'K's, it echoed those alliterations the Klan so loved. Roughly half of the city's estimated 10,000 eligible men belonged to the Klan's Nathan Hale den and a further 2,500 belonged to other dens. There was also a Women's KKK with 2,500 members. Some 400 boys under the age of 18 belonged to a junior KKK and there was even a 'Tri-K-Klub' for younger girls, although membership numbers were not recorded.[6]

With such a high number of Klan-sympathetic people together in one place, Kokomo resembled a mixture of religious pilgrimage, rock concert and political rally. But above all it was a Klan event. This was the Klan at play. An event where no one needed to be discreet or on their guard. Here hooded Klansmen strolled the park with their families. Here, they could be sure all their neighbours held their views. Here placards ranged from the simple demand of 'America for Americans' to 'The Pope will sit in the White House when Hell freezes over'.[7]

# CHAPTER 43

The man in purple was David Curtis Stephenson.

While some of the details about Stephenson's appearance on 4 July in Kokomo have been disputed, there are two absolute certainties. Firstly, that from that day forward, Stephenson became the Klan's poster boy. Secondly, that he was well on his way to turning Indiana into the Klan's most powerful state. Within months of the Klonvocation at Kokomo, Stephenson had attracted 350,000 Hoosiers (as Indiana residents were known) to join the Invisible Empire.

Steve, as he liked to be called, thrived on misinformation about himself. At the peak of his power, he once told a reporter, 'It's no one's business where I was born or who my folks were' and it remains difficult to piece together his background.[1] There were good reasons why he liked things that way, including his chequered career.

Historians tend to agree Stephenson was born in Houston, Texas, but as a child Stephenson's family moved to Marysville, Oklahoma. He left school at 16 and soon became a printer's apprentice. But Stephenson was ambitious – 'I'm a nobody from nowhere, really – but I've got the biggest brains,' he later boasted, adding, 'I'm going to be the biggest man in the United States!'[2] And in 1915, it seemed it might just be true. That year Stephenson moved to Madill, Oklahoma, married a wealthy beauty queen named Nettie Hamilton and talked his way into a post as editor of the local paper.

In what would become a pattern repeated throughout Stephenson's life, his employers – in this case the paper's owners – began to realise the smooth-talking editor lacked the necessary skills to do his job and sacked him. Hearing of this, his father-in-law stopped funding the young couple, even though his daughter was now pregnant. Stephenson was forced to move around looking for work, abandoning his now troublesome, and potentially costly, wife. He didn't attend the birth of his first child.

In fact, as his daughter, Florence Elizabeth, was being born, 'Steve' had wrangled a job as press officer for the mayor of Oklahoma City. For the moment, Stephenson had secured a high-profile job in the seat of power. But just as his career seemed to be taking off, Steve's dubious morality and relaxed relationship with the truth led to another firing when it emerged he'd been having an affair with a well-connected young woman, lying that he was single.

It was all going well when his wife Nettie, with Florence, had appeared out of the blue looking for Stephenson. He tried talking his way out of the situation, bluffing to both his wife and girlfriend, but it was too much – even for a liar of his skills. Stephenson was compelled to make a midnight flit to Miami and lay low. It was enough: Nettie divorced him.

Once again Stephenson took on short-lived jobs. He worked as a printer in Iowa, then in Texas and then back in Oklahoma where he also began to write speeches for the local Socialist Party. After war broke out, Stephenson joined the National Guard in Iowa and soon developed the leadership traits that were to take him to the top of the Klan. Impressing his superiors, he was transferred to the officer training camp at Fort Snelling, Minnesota.

Despite persistent rumours of heavy drinking, Stephenson was commissioned as a second lieutenant. He was assigned to active duty in November 1917, but according to his military record, he never saw service abroad. He was honourably discharged in February 1919 in Massachusetts, although even this detail of Stephenson's life is questionable.

Later, Stephenson would claim he had seen active service with the famous 42nd Infantry Division on the Western Front. The 42nd, known as the Rainbow Division, was one of the most celebrated American combat units sent to France, always in the thick of the fighting. The 42nd saw action in most of the major engagements, most notably the brutal Meuse–Argonne offensive, the deadliest battle in US history. Stephenson repeatedly claimed to be a part of the Rainbow Division, even though its storied veterans said they'd never heard of him.

After leaving the army, Stephenson drifted around, working as a salesman for a printing company in Akron, Ohio, newspaperman and stockbroker in Evansville, Indiana, and eventually a salesman for the Citizens Coal Company. One Indiana historian later described Stephenson: 'a squat, powerfully built, master salesman who exuded charm and good fellowship.'[3] He had the patter, the bonhomie and wasn't unduly troubled by little issues – like the truth.

But people liked Steve. He gelled with veterans, claiming he'd been 'there' – although his 'there' was a far cry from what they probably thought it was. He could talk to the working man – he knew the problems they faced making ends meet. Steve was a 'man's man' with a story that appealed to others like him. He tailored it to the get-rich-quick craze embraced by these types and claimed that while he'd been fighting on the Western Front the value of the shares he'd bought in the Citizens Coal Company had exploded. Almost accidentally, he told them, he had become a millionaire. With this story, Steve sold record numbers of shares in the company and rose very quickly in Citizens Coal, soon becoming a partner.

A respectable figure at last, Stephenson now fancied running for office. He put himself up for the Indiana Legislature. He was unsuccessful, but in the process he met and became an agent for city mayor and state Democratic chairman Benjamin Bosse.

In one version of Stephenson's life story, the ambitious Bosse sent him to Atlanta to encourage the Klan to move north into Indiana. Mayor Bosse felt an Indiana Klan based in Evanstown would be profitable, both politically and financially. Bosse sent his silver-tongued envoy, Steve, to persuade the Klan leaders of his scheme and to cut a deal.

Other versions say Steve joined the Klan after having been recruited by a very pushy Texan Kleagle named Joe Huffington. It is interesting that in both versions Stephenson said he was initially reluctant to become a Klansman, telling the New York World some years later that he had not joined until he was entirely convinced that the Klan 'was not an organization which took Negroes out, cut off their noses and threw them in the fire'.[4] Huffington seems to have managed to do just that.

Claiming he was convinced that the Klan was not a violent organisation, Steve joined and had applied his considerable talents as a salesman to drawing in new recruits. The citizens of Indiana had lapped up his message and joined the Klan by the thousands each week. The Klan offered an exciting new distraction. The salesman, the shop clerk, the farmhand – all could become part of an organisation which had 'redeemed' the South and would transform the nation again. The Hoosier would be a part of something great and he would be a Klansman. Heck, one day he might become a Terror, a Lictor, a Kleagle or even a Giant, a Dragon or a Cyclops. To those who bought into the Klan's ideals, life instantly became a little less humdrum and a lot more exciting.

According to an audit of Stephenson's recruitment campaign for the year from July 1922 to July 1923, Stephenson's Kleagles recruited nearly 118,000 new Klansmen in Indiana, with nearly 10,000 joining in a single week in June 1923.[5] The Klan didn't have anything like that uptake anywhere else in the entire nation.

Indiana was a phenomenon.

# CHAPTER 44

The organisation Stephenson established in Indiana relied on more than his charisma. As British Prime Minister Margaret Thatcher so explicitly put it in 1985, modern mass organisations require 'the oxygen of publicity' to survive.[1] Mass recruitment required mass media, and the Klan leadership of the 1920s understood this. It should come as no surprise, then, that the Klan's all-time peak in the 1920s coincided with the advent of modern consumer culture in the USA.

Central to this consumer revolution was the mass circulation press made possible by a new type of printing technology called linotype. Before the 1870s, newspapers required skilled labourers to set the typeface letter by letter, a time-consuming and expensive process which severely limited newspaper size and circulation.

But in the late 1880s a German immigrant watchmaker named Ottmar Mergenthaler invented the linotype machine. Instead of relying on the laborious, expensive and highly skilled old-fashioned typesetting, the linotype machine enabled type to be set by a single operative via a key-board. As revolutionary for the late nineteenth century as the personal computer would be for the late twentieth century, the linotype machine set newspapers free in the late 1800s.[2] Newspaper circulations soared and modern mass media was born.

But it was in the 1920s that newspapers became a part of US middle-class daily life – flung onto doorsteps in the cities, suburbs and countryside, retrieved by sleepy inhabitants and the juicy bits read aloud at the break-fast table. It has been estimated that in 1920 some 27 million Americans regularly read a daily newspaper. By 1930 that figure had jumped to almost 40 million.[3] The Klan took full advantage of this eruption of interest by Americans in the world around them.

Overseen by HQ in Atlanta, the Klan used a variety of strategies to secure its readership. Some Klan chapters bought up the newspapers of sister organisations, such as the Junior Order of United American Mechanics (JOUAM). The JOUAM was a Protestant, white supremacist fraternity with its own weekly paper, started in Atlanta in 1919. By 1921, the leading shareholder in the *Searchlight* was none other than Elizabeth Tyler, SPA co-owner and partner in the Klan's all-powerful propagation department.

Under Tyler's ownership of *Searchlight*, the Klan adopted the banner 'Free Speech. Free Press. White Supremacy' – although the only one of those ideals held in abundance was the third. Editor J.O. Wood epitomised these values. He claimed to advocate Prohibition, but teased 'Inspector Snoop of the Likker Squad'. He accused Jews of trying to 'destroy the government'. When he stood for election as a member of the Georgia Legislature he told voters, 'I am the original Klansman and proud of it. I belong to everything anti-Catholic I know of.'[4] He was elected, amazingly, and *Searchlight*'s readership continued to grow.

By 1922, *Searchlight* had more than 60,000 readers a week and boasted that for a mere 5¢ it was possible to buy the newspaper as 'far north as Atlanta and as far west as Butte, Montana'. However, not everyone was enticed by its claim to be 'Not a Moulder, But a Chronicler of Public Opinion'.[5] The Black-owned and operated *Chicago Defender* complained it would have been difficult 'to find a duller paper' and *The New York Times* argued it was useless to readers 'if they wanted anything in the way of world or local news'.[6] But if they wanted Klan propaganda it was fascinating.

To promote the Klan in Indiana, in 1922 Stephenson also bought the anti-Catholic weekly *Fact!* and transformed it into the Klan's influential eight-page weekly, *The Fiery Cross*. By March 1923, Stephenson was boasting the paper had 100,000 readers.[7] Klansmen from all walks of life were buying newspapers all around the country. Some newspapers, like two in Illinois, the *Herrin Semi-Weekly* and the *Pekin Daily Times*, kept their names but became vehemently pro-Klan. Sometimes it was more cynical. In Little Rock, Arkansas, the *Arkansas Traveler* was founded in April 1923 by two experienced newsmen who branched out on their own. They saw a good readership with Klansmen by publishing articles largely related to immigration restriction and anti-Catholicism.

Other papers changed their names to something more obvious – signalling that they were now a Klan paper. One of the easier ways to do this was to change a 'C' to a 'K' – so the *Michigan Courier* in Flint became the *Michigan Kourier*. By 1924 two newspapers formed, emulating Stephenson's *Indiana Fiery Cross* – the *Illinois Fiery Cross* and the *Minnesota Fiery Cross*.

These names were downright subdued next to one Dallas Texas paper, the *Texas 100 Per Cent American*.

Local presses carried stirring hometown tales of selfless acts of Klannishness. Some papers were more nostalgic, harkening back to Reconstruction's 'good old days' or advertising screenings of *The Birth of a Nation* and other Klan films and books. Papers promoted the order's fundraising barbecues or offered details on upcoming parades. Articles appeared against Catholics and other local enemies of the organisation.

Klan-owned and Klan-friendly businesses took out adverts in the newspapers hoping to attract customers. They displayed TWK ('Trade With the Klan') stickers in their windows. They offered discounts to those who replied 'AKIA' (A Klansman I Am) to their question, 'AYAK?' (Are You A Klansman?).

Many papers called for boycotts, publishing the names of Catholic or Jewish businesses particularly in the Klan heartland of Indiana. Here, one Jewish businessman suddenly found himself boycotted, even though he'd done all he could to integrate, even attending a local church. A Catholic grocery store owner was boycotted, even though the local Klan met in a room he rented to them above his store. A Greek-owned business saw its daily turnover drop from a peak of $1,000 to a low of $25 after negative press in *The Fiery Cross*.[8] Klan newspapers were also known to shame their 'fellow Americans' for a lack of patriotism, for not showing the proper deference, or support for the organisation.

HQ in Atlanta exerted a certain level of editorial control over Klan newspapers. Clarke and Tyler's propagation department sent 'boilerplate' articles that could be easily tailored to suit a specific locality. These might be anything from ready-made responses to Klan detractors to suggestions that certain 'Aliens' were involved in bootlegging.

By 1923 the Simmons and Evans factions of the Klan began to drift towards open conflict. In March, *Searchlight* nailed its colours firmly to Simmons' mast, declaring, 'There is only one Klan and Simmons is its head.'[9] In retaliation Evans came up with the idea of bringing the whole media apparatus 'in-house' and founded the *Imperial Night-Hawk*. Unlike *Searchlight*, the *Night-Hawk* was free to all Klansmen, and carried no advertising. It instructed Klansmen that when they finished reading it, 'Don't throw it away. Give it away. Put it where it will do most good for Klankraft.' Under the motto 'By the Klan, For the Klan' the *Night-Hawk* told its readers its mission would be to 'keep Klansmen informed of the activities at the Imperial Palace' – where Evans now resided.[10]

By November 1923 Evans had wrested control of *Searchlight* from Simmons. He ousted Clarke and Tyler. As editor of the *Imperial Night-Hawk*

Evans appointed an unassuming but staggeringly creative Klansman named Milton Elrod, a former editor of Stephenson's *Fiery Cross*. Under Elrod's editorship, the Klan's news presence became national.[11] Although the paper only lasted from March 1923 until November 1924, the twelve-page weekly covered nearly 2,700 Klan events in 1,285 venues across the entire USA. Only four years earlier the Klan's activities had been limited to, at most, twenty venues in just two Southern states.[12]

The Klan was one of the first organisations of that time to genuinely realise the potential of a national press presence. While retaining regional differences, it was capable of unifying Klansmen across 3,000 miles, coast to coast. This is clear from the membership. After Indiana the states with the highest Klan memberships included Texas, Oregon, Colorado, Pennsylvania, and Oklahoma. It is tempting to see this as the result of Evans' centralised Klan, but this was only in part true. As would be demonstrated by the Klan's experiences in Indiana, Arkansas and Colorado, that uniformity of purpose was often illusory. The reasons for peak memberships in many states would turn out to be very different.

# CHAPTER 45

By 1925, Edward Young Clarke and Bessie Tyler's pyramid recruitment scheme had led to Klan presence in every state in the Union. No other state would match Indiana's membership of 300,000 but there were some competitors. Given the Klan's Southern origins, it is a bit curious that the largest membership numbers were to be found in the North and West, with Ohio and Oklahoma peaking at around 240,000, Pennsylvania at 150,000 and Minnesota at 65,000. The state in the South with the largest number was Texas, with 200,000 members.

By contrast, New Mexico barely had any Klan presence at all, with less than 1,000 members. Others just flared and faded. The initially promising numbers in the Dakotas quickly declined to the extent that the two states were amalgamated with Minnesota.[1]

But, as we have seen before, it was often in the Klan's interest to exaggerate or underestimate membership. The more popular the Klan appeared, both locally and nationally, the more members it hoped to attract. People aspire to join an organisation they've heard of and be part of a movement their friends are in. Yet some Kleagles reported lower than actual recruitment numbers to HQ in Atlanta. This enabled them to pocket the entire $10 Klecktokens and leave out the cut due to the Grand Goblins, Grand Dragons and Imperial Kleagles.

It's also important to note that some states had relatively low Klan numbers except in some regions or cities. The Colorado Klan had a membership of 60,000, but 30,000 of those members were in Denver alone. This was nearly a third of the city's white adult population – including about 11,000 women.

The power of a Klan group often depended on regional management. The Denver Klansmen had tremendous influence on the rest of the state. Their leader, Grand Dragon of the Realm of Colorado, was a short, stocky homeopathic doctor with a luxuriant goatee named John Galen Locke. His friendly, open face belied a sharp mind and ruthless ambition.

Nicknamed 'The Toad', Locke ran Denver like a Tammany Hall boss, controlling the fire service, police, schools, courts and nearly all of the city's institutions. In 1924, Klan candidates were elected to six out of the nine top political offices in Denver including the mayor. A self-declared Klansman was elected Colorado governor. Openly Klan candidates ran for election as US senators and most elected state offices as well as for the state legislature.[2]

Locke was a particularly unusual Grand Dragon. His wife was a practising Roman Catholic, as was his secretary. His personal lawyer was Jewish. But like Stephenson in Indiana, Locke was less concerned about Klan ideology than what controlling the Klan would bring him personally. His success showed the Klan's rise often owed remarkably little to its stated ideologies, and far more to marketing.

This was especially true in Oregon. Since its earliest settlement, the state had had a noticeable anti-Catholic streak, and didn't have large numbers of new immigrants or African Americans moving there. Only 3 per cent of the population was Catholic, but it didn't matter: the 'threat of Rome' platform was recruitment gold.

Oregon Kleagles started their campaign on a town by slipping anti-Catholic pamphlets under doors, through letter boxes and into cars. These pamphlets told tales of arms caches stored safely away for the time when 'The Tyrant on the Tiber' (as they called the Pope) was ready to mobilise his army, the Catholic fraternity the Knights of Columbus.[3] Then they would soften up the population by screening *The Birth of a Nation*.

Now they were ready to play their trump card. Hiring a local theatre, they'd have Miss Helen Jackson deliver her 'Convent Cruelties' routine. In this, Jackson, an 'escaped nun', would tell how she'd fled a convent after being repeatedly raped and impregnated by priests and then forced to abort the babies. It was all total fabrication. Helen Jackson was not her real name, and far from being a nun, she was actually a former prostitute. Miss Jackson's tales of Catholic debauchery and cruelty were especially effective for mobilising potential recruits because they would be followed by an evangelist preacher's fire-and-brimstone sermon.[4] And the technique worked.

In Oregon, with a population of almost entirely native-born, white Protestant citizens, over 50,000 people joined the Klan. Members rose to positions of power in government. Among others, Klansman George Baker was elected mayor of Portland and the strikingly named Kaspar Kap Kubli – a proud, if inevitable, Klansman – became speaker of the Oregon House of Representatives.[5]

But their real coup came when Klan-backed candidate Walter M. Pierce beat incumbent Governor Ben Olcott. Olcott was so thoroughly out-manoeuvred by the Klan that at the 1922 National Governors' Conference he moaned, 'We woke up one morning and found the Klan had about gained political control of the state. Practically not a word had been raised against them.'[6]

With the Klan's dominance in Oregon politics, it became the only state to successfully outlaw parochial schools, calling them a means of indoctrination for successive generations of young Americans. The Klan whipped up enthusiasm for the measure by arguing that if parochial schools were allowed to remain open it would lead to the overthrow of Protestant democracy and the installation of the Pope as the ruler of the USA.[7] The Klan's message was, essentially, Protestantism is patriotism.

One of the interesting things about the Oregon Klan was the amount of activity in Klaverns outside of the major cities. While there was a powerful Klan leadership in Portland, Klaverns were also strong in smaller cities and towns like Eugene, Tillamook, Astoria, La Grande, Salem and Medford. Oregon Klaverns were also unusual in the way they dialled down violence. Aside from an instance of 'practice lynching' in Medford and a Tillamook Klavern running a Black piano tuner out of town for unspecified 'immorality', there are no records of Klan vigilantism in Oregon.[8]

By contrast, the Oklahoma Klan seemed to thrive on violence, perhaps a legacy of the 'frontier justice' that had long reigned there. Over 2,500 incidents of Klan violence were reported in the state in 1922 alone. Floggings were reported nightly. On just one night, nine people were killed by the Oklahoma Klan – one man was castrated, three were tarred and feathered and one was burnt to death.[9] It seemed Oklahoma men liked 'the rough stuff', as Edward Young Clarke called it, because the state's Klan was second in size only to Indiana.[10]

In Pennsylvania it was an act of violence *against* the Klan which led to a rise in membership, giving Kleagles an unusual opportunity to portray Klansmen as victims. The event took place in the summer of 1923 in Carnegie, an industrial town east of Pittsburgh. When a Klan rally morphed into a riot, a Klansman named Thomas Abbot was shot dead.

Imperial Wizard Evans quickly told Pennsylvania Grand Dragon Sam Rich that Abbot's death was worth 25,000 recruits and they should promote further riots whenever possible. The *Imperial Night-Hawk* ran headlines, 'Carnegie Mob Martyrs Klan Hero and Violates All Rights of Americanism' and 'Pennsylvanians are flocking to the Klan'.[11] Evans was right, by the end of 1923 the Pennsylvania Realm had some 150,000 Klansmen.[12]

In Texas attitudes towards violence were more ambiguous. The largest Klan membership in the South, it was the third highest in the country – peaking in 1922 with around 200,000 members. As membership grew in the first few years of the 1920s, violence began to escalate. Not surprisingly, given Texas' Southern roots, most of the victims were Black. The violence was commonplace and very public. Sixty-eight people were flogged in the spring of 1922 in the Dallas Klavern's own well-known 'whipping meadow' outside the city. Sometimes those carrying out the whippings were even badged as sheriff's deputies.[13]

As we shall see, in Oklahoma, Klan violence nearly led to a civil war. Eventually, throughout the state, popular support for the Klan began to wane. Texas seemed to be heading in the same direction. With increasing reports of violence, respect for the Klan turned to fear, then to disgust and, finally, to anger.

By mid-1923 new Klan membership had peaked nationally. The early years of the 1920s had seen spectacular growth. It would soon become apparent that the bonanza was over. The Klan's central leadership was trying to find new members or, more to the point, new income streams. They saw two alternatives: find a new source of new members in the USA, or try their hand in a new and untapped market: the rest of the world. The Klan chose to do both.

# CHAPTER 46

There was one obvious way in which the Klan could increase membership: admit women into its ranks. The Klan was very much a fraternity and thus by definition all male, but most of the large fraternities in the USA had created female 'side orders'. The Freemasons had the Order of the Eastern Star. The Odd Fellows had the Daughters of Rebekah. And women had been involved in the Klan since its inception, helping to formulate the order's ideology and develop its various practices.

The protection of 'white womanhood' had always been central to the Klan's mission. One of the prime drivers for violence during the Reconstruction period was the idea that white women needed protection from Black men. Black males were depicted as childlike in terms of mental abilities but with very adult appetites. The post-war South was rife with tales of freedmen lusting after white women and forcing them to 'give up their virtue'.

The Civil War-era South created the Southern Belle. She was the flower of the South and represented everything that was pure and kind and worth fighting for. One lovestruck Southerner gushed: 'Her diadem is the social affections; her sceptre love; her robe chastity, pure as the driven snow, enveloping her form, so that the imagination can find nought to blush at' and so on ...[1]

Rhetoric like that had sent troops off to fight the Yankees with an enduringly soft-focused home-and-hearth view of wives, daughters, sweethearts and mothers. Confederate soldiers were fighting to protect these pure, innocent and trusting women from marauding Yankees and, even more worryingly, their uniformed Black allies.

The end of the war and the beginning of Reconstruction made those threats loom even larger. Defeated Confederate soldiers brooded over this. What was to stop armed Black militia from indulging their lusts at gunpoint? Vindictive carpetbagger governments seemed to positively encourage racial mixing. The Freedmen's Bureau had established schools where grown ex-slaves would be taught by white Yankee women, violating racial boundaries held as sacrosanct for generations. This situation felt extremely threatening to many Southern whites and nothing illustrates this more clearly than the storyline of *The Birth of a Nation*.

D.W. Griffith's screenplay was adapted from Thomas Dixon's trilogy of novels about the Reconstruction. Griffith's plot is centred on the budding romance between two seemingly incompatible central figures, Confederate war hero Ben Cameron and Elsie Stoneman, daughter of a Radical Republican leader. Virulently racist, the screenplay dramatises the difference between the Confederate and the Radical camps when Cameron's little sister, Flora, is pursued by the lustful freedman and Union captain, Gus. Rather than allow herself to be despoiled by her attacker, Flora throws herself off a bluff.

A parallel plot point involves the promotion of inter-racial marriage by Republican Party members, including Elsie's father, the misguided Radical Austin Stoneman. Stoneman has placed his trust in the evil bi-racial tyrant, Silas Lynch. Lynch is installed as lieutenant governor and promptly tries to force through legislation legalising inter-racial marriage. This looming racial calamity and his sister's tragic end finally awakens Cameron to the inherent dangers posed to his beloved South by the Yankee occupation. Leading the Klan, Cameron goes on to redeem the 'Southlands' and win the heart of Elsie.

The helpless, vulnerable Southern Belle became a useful theme in the popular culture of the post-Civil War South. But in reality, the women of the Reconstruction Klan were often some of the fiercest keepers and preservers of Southern heritage – and myth. It was women who were responsible for instilling the ideology of the South into the next generation. And it was women who kept photo albums, genealogical records, trunks with medals, uniforms and other artefacts, tended gravesites and held memorial and commemorative ceremonies for their fallen Confederate ancestors – fathers, husbands, sons, brothers and even sweethearts.

Organisations like the United Daughters of the Confederacy preserved the myth of the righteous and genuine 'Lost Cause' of the South. And it was these same women who also helped to preserve the memory of the Ku Klux Klan itself. A memory which had nearly faded, and which had been inactive for two generations. Over those years these groups held fundraisers, sponsored textbooks, raised monuments and published memoirs about the Klan. Across the South, they held essay competitions for schoolchildren, encouraging the younger generations to engage with such issues as 'The Right of Secession' and 'The Origin of the Ku Klux Klan'.[2]

Southern women were also finding their feet politically and were prime movers in two of the most powerful lobby groups of the early twentieth century. The Women's Christian Temperance Union (WCTU) had been the driving force behind Prohibition, sponsoring Carrie Nation's direct actions, her brutal and widely publicised bar smashings. And under the leadership of Matilda Bradley Carse, the WCTU held huge fundraising drives, published large amounts of literature and lobbied both locally and nationally proving women could organise extremely effectively.

If the Eighteenth Amendment introducing Prohibition was largely the work of women, it was the Nineteenth Amendment – giving women the vote – that showed how they could change the country. Suffragettes had proved that women could be politically active. These newly empowered and educated women weren't just a political force; they were a huge economic power. The war effort, increasing mechanisation and the evolution of retail and office work put millions of US women into the workplace.

These shop girls, factory workers, secretaries and receptionists were becoming increasingly important consumers in their own right – and more self-confident in all aspects of US society. One symbol of the new woman was the 'flapper', a sexually adventurous and independent woman with bobbed hair, a raised hemline and strong opinions. It didn't matter that such women were a relatively scarce phenomenon, limited to metropolitan areas. The flapper had become a US archetype.

But this growing female assertiveness did not necessarily fit with *all* Americans. A significant part of the Klan's appeal came from its stance *against* the changes taking place in society and the prevailing craze for modernity. The Klan stood for old-fashioned virtues. The ideal Klansman was traditional, churchgoing, righteous and respectful, with his wife standing four-square at his side. When it came to the family and anything that threatened the sanctity of marriage, the Klan was especially adamant.

There are instances where Klansmen whipped promiscuous men and beat, tarred and feathered and otherwise tortured promiscuous women. The Klan was against divorce. A Klansman in Kansas found himself ostracised because he'd left his wife.

Klansmen also enforced their own ideas of sexual morality.

One of the most notorious of these incidents was featured in Colorado newspaper headlines, emblazoned with the story of a Denver hotelier's teenage son kidnapped by the Klan after it learned he'd made his girlfriend pregnant. Hooded Klansmen broke into the boy's house and took him to Grand Dragon Locke's office where a makeshift operating theatre had been constructed. Confronted by the surgical instruments, bright lights and a masked-up 'Doctor' Locke, the terrified boy was told to marry the girl or face castration. He agreed to marry the girl, but his father later brought a highly publicised prosecution against Locke.[3]

The Klan leadership in Atlanta took note of women's essential role in Protestant Middle America. It is no coincidence that the majority of regular churchgoers in the USA have always been women. Women were the bastion of respectable, small-town neighbourhoods. Attracting a constituency of women was not just logical, it could be very profitable. This was an opportunity not likely to be lost on the scheming Imperial Wizard, Hiram Wesley Evans.

# CHAPTER 47

In June 1923 Evans created the Women of the Ku Klux Klan (WKKK). In part, his hand had been forced; since 1920, many Klan-like sororities had been founded.

Evans worried about two sororities in particular, the Queens of the Golden Mask, founded by Stephenson, and the Kamelia, founded by Simmons. The pedigrees and track records of these two men had the potential to draw a significant number of prospective members away from women's organisations loyal to the Atlanta Klan. With his classic decisiveness, Evans simply incorporated Stephenson's Queens of the Golden Mask into the WKKK and then, in 1924, absorbed the Kamelia by buying it off Simmons.

Within six months of its founding, the WKKK had Klaverns in thirty-six states and claimed 250,000 members. Then it simply grew and grew, becoming most successful in states where the Klan was already powerful: Arkansas, Ohio and Pennsylvania. But it was Indiana that had the most Klan members and, now, the most WKKK recruits as well. Stephenson's WKKK in Indiana had about a quarter of a million members – effectively doubling the already record-high levels of Klan membership in that state.

Like other Realms of the WKKK, the Indiana Klan made much of its gender 'equality', arguing that the goal of achieving a 'One Hundred Percent American' nation would be impossible without women. The Indiana Klan's newspaper *The Fiery Cross* pompously declared, 'Woman is now called to put her splendid efforts and abilities behind a movement for 100 percent American'.[1]

Many of those women who joined the WKKK were the wives, daughters, sisters and sweethearts of Klansmen. Some had even persuaded their own husbands to join the Klan, then joined themselves when they were presented with the chance. One of the clearest examples of such family connections is that of the Grand Dragon of Arkansas, the formidable Judge James Comer. He was the person who appointed the first and the second heads (Imperial Commanders) of the WKKK. The first was his friend, Lulu A. Markwell; the second, his wife, Robbie Gill. He also appointed as first vice-president the wife of Fred Gifford, Grand Dragon of Oregon.[2]

That is not to say that these women were appointed solely through nepotism. The leader of the WKKK in Indiana and seven other states was an energetic, articulate and persistent woman named Daisy Douglas Barr. Ordained as a minister at 18, she'd been active in the Republican Party and the WCTU. By the 1920s she was a bespectacled, matronly figure whose appearance belied her ambition. 'Mother' Barr, as most churchgoers in Indiana knew her, had also been the Imperial Empress of Stephenson's Queens of the Golden Mask, the order that became Evans' no-brainer choice to lead the Indiana WKKK.[3]

Yet WKKK leadership would prove as varied as the men's leadership and just as riven by ambition. Where Barr used her considerable intellect and rhetoric to steer the Indiana WKKK, her leading rival in Indiana, Mary Barnadum, was more of a brawler. Despite being a schoolteacher for over a decade and a long-standing activist, Barnadum was far more combative and feisty than Barr. Prone to speaking first and thinking later, Barnadum accused Barr of embezzling WKKK funds. When that failed, she claimed Barr had slandered her. Later, she was forced to retract both accusations.

Barnadum didn't limit her attacks to court actions. She was arrested in Ohio for instigating a street brawl with what she saw as a rival faction of the WKKK. Among the ranks of the WKKK, too, were some brawlers. George Dale, the editor of the anti-Klan Muncie (Indiana) *Post-Democrat*, believed the women of the WKKK were far worse than the Klansmen, 'sister Amazons of Hate … bob-haired Amazons [who] demanded my death'.[4]

The WKKK was proudly concerned with 'women's' issues. Home, marriage, family and child-rearing were all centre stage at the WKKK's rallies. The female order aimed to make the Klanswoman 'a better house-keeper, a better seamstress, a better cook, a better wife, a better mother, a better woman – which makes a better citizen'.[5] But as the Imperial Commander of the WKKK, Robbie Gill Comer, put it, 'I make bold to assert that it has never been the purpose of God that women should be the slave of men' but that they would still 'vote with our men for right men, right programs and right government'.[6]

That said, the WKKK took on the same fundamental issues as those of the KKK itself. The women's order was as racist and bigoted as its male counterpart. The WKKK's agenda focused on Black migration and foreign immigration, with a prominent focus on 'women's safety', threats to white neighbourhoods and the impact on 'American' communities.

Debates at the 1927 WKKK Klonvocation in St Louis, Missouri, focused on uniform national marriage laws, Prohibition and 'threats to the sanctity of the home'.[7] The WKKK's anti-Catholicism was slightly different from that of the KKK, largely centring on the 'unnatural' demands of celibacy and the impact of the pent-up lusts on women and children. Klanswomen were dedicated to Prohibition, but unlike their male counterparts, the women's rhetoric centred less on the ethnicity and politics of the law-breakers and more on the moral evils of booze.

Klanswomen became especially interested in education and the dangers facing their children. Like their menfolk, they argued that true Americanism was endangered by the parochial school and any non-Protestant religious education. Bestial appetites of 'inferior' races had given Catholics a leg-up in what Theodore Roosevelt had memorably called the demographic 'War of the Cradle'.

One reason was the tendency of Irish, Italians, Poles and Mexicans to have larger families than those of 'true', native-born Americans. Parochial schools would then stuff these youths with foreign ways, inculcating blind obedience to the Pope, his bishops and priests in the USA. As one Indiana Klanswoman complained, 'The Pope was dictating what was being taught to the children, and therefore they were being impressed with the wrong things.'[8]

Earlier, a pre-WKKK women's chapter of the Oregon Klan named Ladies of the Invisible Empire (LOTIE) dedicated itself to outlawing parochial schools, pressuring the state of Oregon into passing the 1922 School Bill. This legislation essentially forced children between the ages of 8 and 16 to attend public school, making it illegal for their parents to send them to religious or privately funded institutions or private military colleges.

Oregon's Klans for both sexes set up a textbook commission and passed measures requiring that all religious instruction and reading be from the (Protestant) King James Bible. They forbade teachers from wearing nuns' habits or any other religious garb. And they required teachers to have all been trained and accredited by state, not private, organisations.

The Klan interceded in the lives of children not just indirectly, through legislation, but through recruitment to the Junior Ku Klux Klan. From 1923, if you paid $3 and were a white, Protestant, native-born boy between 12 and 17 years old, you, too, could join in the Klan craze. The Junior KKK had its own rituals, its own rules and even its own magazine, the *Junior Klansman Weekly*.

The order mimicked the rituals of the adult Klan, holding its ceremonies in conjunction with the parent organisation. At a meeting in Lykens,
Pennsylvania, the Juniors called their members to a meeting by blowing a
horn and burning a 'J'-shaped symbol next to the cross lit to summon the
adult Klansmen.

By 1924 the Junior Klan boasted members in fifteen states, largely in
the Midwest and leading to a girl's version, the Tri-K Klub. This was
based on, and run by, the WKKK. Those too young to join either of these
groups were installed in the Ku Klux Kiddies groups, where children as
young as 3 could be inducted into the 'Klankraft'. As one Klan-supporting
journal put it, 'parents were happy to be able to have whole families of
100 percenters'.[9]

Though the numbers are difficult to determine, it is likely that Ohio
and Indiana had the highest uptake in 'Juniors', with South Bend, Indiana,
reporting 200 children joining alongside their fathers' 4,500-member strong
chapter. To the South, in Kokomo (the scene of Stephenson's triumphant
ordination) 400 juniors joined 7,500 Klansmen and 2,500 WKKK.[10]

The 1920s family-oriented Klan did not identify itself with the brutal
night-riding Klan of the Reconstruction. Junior Klansmen and Tri-Ks
formed marching bands and paraded through the streets with their parents.
There were 'Miss Hundred Percent' contests for Nordic girls and even Klan
resorts where families could holiday together with other Klan families.

One such resort, the Kool Koast Kamp, was established by the Grand
Dragon of Texas in 1924 in Rockport on the Gulf Coast. Marketed as
the perfect family holiday retreat, its advertising wasn't subtle. Klan members could enjoy 'sandy shallow beaches for babes' and 'deep blue surf for
grown-ups'. For 'wonderful mothers' it was sold on the idea of restfulness,
providing 'No work whatsoever. No drudgery. No worry.' To the 'beautiful daughters' the curiously modern-sounding strapline was that the Kool
Koast Kamp was 'Kool in every way'. The whole site was billed as safe in
the somewhat unreassuring declaration, 'The Fiery Cross guards you at
night and an officer of the law, with the same Christian sentiment, guards
carefully all portals.'

All this was available to Klansmen, Klanswomen, Klan-teens and Klan
Kiddies for a mere $10 per family for ten days.[11]

# CHAPTER 48

By the end of 1923, it seemed the rise of the KKK was unstoppable. And yet those at its helm – Evans, Clarke and regional leaders – wanted more: more members, more power and, of course, more money. But with US-born men, women and children in the Klan reaching saturation point, where could the order turn to for new recruits? The answer came from the Pacific Northwest. Rather than emphasising US citizenship, the Washington State Klan made white supremacy its central tenet, creating an auxiliary movement, the 'not quite' Klansmen.

Formed by Luther Powell, King Kleagle for the north-west domain, the spinoff group defined itself as 'an organization for foreign-born US citizens who hold this country and its flag above all others in the world'. The 'Royal Riders of the Red Robe' soon boasted chapters in every state, although it remained strongest on the Pacific coast where its 'Grand Ragon' (Dragon minus the 'D') was based. This was Dr M.W. Rose, whose programme, as he put it, was for 'a real patriotic organization' for all 'Canadians, Englishmen and other white, gentile, Protestants ... who, except for accident of foreign birth, would be members of the Ku Klux Klan'.[1]

In advertisements the Royal Riders proclaimed many of the same values in much of the same coded language as the Klan. They called for 'the protection of our homes'; 'the supremacy of the white race'; 'the separation of church and state'; and 'participation in our public schools'. But Rose's Royal Riders took a more expansive view on what constituted Americanism. These 'loyal, patriotic', non-citizen, recruits became a robust income stream for the state- and national-level Kleagles, Grand Dragons, Goblins and Wizards.[2]

The Northwest's Royal Riders were not the only Klan group open to admitting foreign-born nationals. In Little Rock, Arkansas, the supremely ambitious Judge James Comer was known for collecting Klan-based auxiliaries like the WKKK and Tri-K. So, when Grand Rogan Rose and the Grand Dragons of Texas and Oregon proposed a charter for the 'American Krusaders', Comer not only accepted – he made the Krusaders' 18th Street HQ in Little Rock his own office.

Like the Royal Riders, the American Krusaders were open to 'Protestant Christians ... Caucasians' who 'would receive the spirit of chivalry ... men and women who are clean, honest and desirable citizens'. Kleagles tried to encourage Klan members to see these recruits, not as foreigners or second-class members, but as their own brothers. As one Michigan Kleagle put it, 'while we are Americans by birth, they are Americans by choice'.[3] Perhaps more importantly to the Kleagles, the Royal Riders and Krusaders, like all Klansmen, paid a $10 initiation fee, percentages of which would flow up and trickle down to Klan officials.[4]

But there were limits to who could join Klan auxiliaries. Both the Royal Riders and the Krusaders excluded from membership all Jews and Catholics and immigrants from Southern and Eastern Europe, including Greeks, Italians, Yugoslavs and Poles. But of course, given the vitriol these groups so frequently received from Klansmen, there were few hopeful members to reject.

There were also rumours that 'Protestant Negroes' would be allowed 'the rights of membership' in a special auxiliary movement – a Black Klan – but I've never found a single account of any Klan chapter or its auxiliaries ever actually deliberately recruiting African American members.[5]

But the Klan did briefly manage to expand outside of the USA when, in 1924, two Americans and a Canadian citizen incorporated the Knights of Ku Klux Klan of Canada. The object of the order was ostensibly to restore Canada's 'Britishness', but also attempted to distance itself from what it saw as the American Klan's violence. Not surprisingly, because there was nothing in it for them, Evans and the Klan hierarchy refused to endorse the Canadian upstart.

The Klansmen in Canada did take part in beatings, kidnappings and at least one tarring and feathering. But they managed to stop short of lynching, shooting or bludgeoning anyone to death. Much like its neighbour to the South, the motive of the Canadian Klan of the 1920s was largely financial. But unlike their US neighbour, the Canadian Klan was not particularly successful until the second half of the 1920s.

In 1926, after several years of dormancy, the Canadian Klan had a bit of success when two Indiana Klansmen burnt crosses and 'Kluxed' the prairies. At least 100 Klaverns formed in the province of Saskatchewan, claiming up to 40,000 members and achieving considerable success in local politics. Canadian and American Kleagles also 'Kluxed' Ontario, Nova

Scotia, New Brunswick, British Columbia and Newfoundland, even managing to establish itself in Francophone Quebec.

As in the USA, local grievances helped the Canadian Klan to recruit. The western provinces focused on pressuring for the exclusion of the relatively large Asian immigrant population. On the prairies of Saskatchewan, the targets tended to be the incumbent Liberal Party. In other regions, the Klan teamed up with anti-Catholic Orange Orders to become a mouthpiece for anti-Catholic immigration and opposition to the French Canadians. By 1928, the Klan's efforts had led to the outlawing of bilingual teaching and textbooks in state-funded schools.[6]

Other than Canada, the Klan didn't really transplant well, with one brief exception: Germany's Weimar Republic. Conditions at that time were, in many ways, similar to those of Reconstruction in the USA. Germany had undergone a catastrophic military defeat. Its citizens felt they were being exploited by the victors and their German collaborators. It's not hard to see parallels: substitute the Allies for the Radical Republicans and the carpetbaggers; the Jews for the scalawags; and loathing for the Treaty of Versailles for the hatred of the Thirteenth and Fourteenth Amendments, and for a moment Weimar Germany should have made fertile ground for the Ku Klux Klan.

Founded in 1925 by three Americans, Germany's Klan called themselves the Knights of the Fiery Cross. From the obviously derivative name to the initiation ceremonies, the German Klan drew heavily on traditional Klan symbolism. Oaths were taken on a Bible placed on the Stars and Stripes. Both orders were dedicated to white supremacy and both were viciously antisemitic.

The three founders were not known to have connections to Evans or any other Klansmen in the United States. Nevertheless, their cause was very similar. The order collected some 350 members in Berlin, and perhaps more elsewhere, selling a message of ultra-nationalism. These Americans were as bigoted, power hungry and exploitative of Berliners as their US counterparts were of their regional recruits. Within a year the Americans were expelled from their own order for financial impropriety. The order swiftly imploded, but it would not be the last flirtation between German nationalists and the Klan.[7]

# CHAPTER 49

The date of 8 August 1925 arguably marked the high-water mark of the Ku Klux Klan. In the sticky 90°F heat of a Washington DC summer afternoon an estimated 30,000 to 100,000 hooded and robed Klansmen closed off the Capitol District. They marched in well-disciplined formations, rank after rank. Even *The Washington Post* was struck by the event: 'Phantom-like hosts of the Ku Klux Klan spread their white robe over the most historic thoroughfare yesterday in one of the greatest demonstrations the city has ever seen.'[1]

It was an impressive and colourful event. There were the Klansmen, the 'rank and file of the Invisible Empire', white from pointed hood to the hem of their robes. Alongside them were 'kleagles, dragons, and other dignitaries of the organization in green silken robes and hoods, flaming red, bright yellow and red, white and blue'. There were also 'companies of Klans guards in snappy uniforms, white caps, black Sam Browne belts, and black puttees'.[2]

Even its most adamant enemies were forced to say that the parade that day was a success. The scathingly witty H.L. Mencken, who'd made a career out of attacking the Klan, was forced to acknowledge:

> The Klan put it all over its enemies. The parade was grander and gaudier, by far than anything the wizards had prophesied. It was longer, it was thicker, it was higher in tone. I stood in front of the Treasury for two hours and watched the legions pass. They marched in lines of eighteen or twenty, solidly shoulder to shoulder. I retired for refreshment and was gone an hour.
>
> When I got back Pennsylvania Avenue was still a mass of white from Pennsylvania Avenue to the foot of Capitol Hill – a full mile of Klansmen and their ladies.[3]

It was impressive, and it was meant to be. The Klansmen had been trained for this. Klansmen paraded all the time. But before they set off up Pennsylvania Avenue a loudspeaker reminded them, 'Regardless of what happens, what is said to you from the sidewalk, keep your eyes on the man in front of you. Never falter!'[4] They marched sixteen to twenty abreast, without masks (a condition of their permit to march), with their arms folded on their chests, rank after rank. They were serious and solemn.

Not all of it was solemn. Somewhere in the middle of the parade was Virginia's all-girl 'Kluxette' marching band. They tapped out rhythms on snare drums as they marched along, flanked by two vast Stars and Stripes flags. There was a glee club from Akron, Ohio, who boomed patriotic songs. There were Klan bands – some admittedly better than others. Some Klansmen carried banners. One read, 'KEEP KONGRESS KLEAN.'[5] It was all good natured. It was all impressive.

Yet, impressive as it was, some of it was illusion. In order to disguise the fact that only 30,000 of the anticipated 60,000 had turned up, the experienced organisers turned to theatrics. The Klansmen were cleverly distributed. Each man or woman (an estimated half of those parading were women) was an arm's length from the person in front, behind and to their sides. This had the effect of making them look far more numerous and contributed to the, perhaps deliberate, confusion over how many Klansmen took part.

But whatever smoke and mirrors were used, the parade impressed even cynics like Mencken. Yet, perhaps even more impressive was that it was estimated that 150,000 spectators came out to cheer on the white-robed ranks as they marched down Pennsylvania Avenue. The mood was generally upbeat. The overall effect was one of carnival and spectacle. Judging by the response, the Klan was popular. The Klan was acceptable. The Klan was mainstream. The Klan was American.

Or so it seemed.

In fact, the authorities had not been so sure. They had taken precautions. US Marines had been stationed at strategic points, including the doors to the Treasury building. And they seemed to take pains to distance themselves. The president, Calvin Coolidge, who had given an address to a Catholic parade only weeks before, was contacted to see if he would speak to the assembled Klansmen and -women. Realising the position in which he might find himself – whether agreeing or disagreeing to the Klan's request – the famously taciturn 'Silent Cal' Coolidge arranged to be out of the capital when the parade took place.

Similarly, the capital's Black population made themselves scarce. DC was a segregated city; it had suffered race riots at the start of the 1920s and the night before the parade the Klan had burnt a cross at Arlington. Washington's Black pastors urged their congregations to stay away.[6]

On the other hand, there had been those who thought the parade would lead to the 'city being bathed in blood'. One of the most vocal critics was an ex-Klansman, Thomas L. Avaunt. It seems his main objection was that the vast numbers taking part in the Klan parade dwarfed his own fraternity, the Protestant Knights of America. Yet, what's interesting about Avaunt is that he attracted more criticism than support in the press for his killjoy attitude.

The Memphis *Commercial Appeal* asked Avaunt and other objectors to 'let the Ku Klux parade!' The *Washington News* told them that 'There isn't going to be the slightest disorder' and the *Washington Evening Star* advised him, 'there's no occasion for alarm'. The New York-based *Literary Review*, which collated the week's news into a digest, said this was the 'prevailing view'.[7] None of these papers were Klan affiliated.

But what was the point of the Klan's March on Washington?

There is no doubt that Imperial Wizard Evans saw the event as a show of Klan strength. Evans had ambitions for his Klan. Evans saw the Klan as a political tool. To Evans moulding the Klan into a powerbase would turn him, as Imperial Wizard, into a kingmaker. The Klan had Middle America in its grasp. He'd had a taste of what could be achieved when the Klan's voting strength had scuppered New York's Catholic and anti-Prohibition Democrat presidential candidate, Al Smith's, chances in the 1924 primaries. He knew it could be done, and he knew how to do it. What was necessary was a reminder of the Klan's power, and the Washington March was meant to be that.

The reality was, however, that the Klan's power was slipping. Of those Klansmen and -women present, over half had come from two states, Pennsylvania and Ohio, and only half the 60,000 anticipated Klansmen had actually turned up. The costs of the event to the Klan leadership made it debatable whether it had actually been worthwhile, and that debate was apparent to others too. It was visible. Since the marchers in Washington were grouped together under banners denoting their states, it was obvious that the contingents from the huge Indiana and Texas Klans were noticeably small.

In its final analysis, *The New York Times* was almost certainly right when it said that 'the purpose of the march was a mixture of trying to "impress the Government" and show that the Klan was a power to be reckoned with, while "counteracting the reported tendency [of the order] toward disintegration"'.[8]

Both would prove to be hopeless tasks. The Klan's disintegration would prove unstoppable.

## PART VII

# NEMESIS
# 1922–1927

I saw girls and young married women dancing all but unclothed, their dress torn from them, ripped into rags and tatters, amid wild shrieks of glee and maudlin attempts at song. … Along toward three in the morning, I saw a certain high federal official, barely able to stand, making his way slowly and painstakingly across the hall. He was weeping the maudlin tears of a drunken man. 'Because,' he said, sobbing, 'I am growing old and soon will be unable to come to any more of Steve's wonderful parties.'

Court testimony about one of Grand Dragon
Stephenson's private parties given by one of his 'lieutenants',
Court Asher, November 1925[1]

# CHAPTER 50

There was no love lost between the Klansmen of Bastrop and the residents of Mer Rouge, two neighbouring towns in north-eastern Louisiana's Morehouse Parish. To the Klansmen of industrial Bastrop, the small planter community of Mer Rouge was a 'den of iniquity', a 'perpetual Halloween'. One Bastrop Klansman alleged that Mer Rouge residents were permanently hopped up on 'white lightning' and willing to 'pay a dollar any day for five minutes in a trollop's arms'. The thoroughly Baptist Klan of Bastrop saw the 'immorality' of the heavily Catholic Mer Rouge as being 'religion approved and sanctified'.[1]

Many in Bastrop's Klan believed one man was to blame, Watt Daniel, the handsome, swaggering son of a wealthy local planter. They were convinced that Daniel was fuelling the town's iniquity with hooch from his bootlegging operation. In November 1921, they sent Daniel a warning: shut down his still … or else.

It turned out they were tangling with the wrong man. Watt Daniel was a tough and rowdy war veteran. After the Bastrop Klan's threat, Daniel seized every opportunity to voice his contempt. In the winter of 1921–22, together with a young local garage owner, Harry Neelis, and a friend named W.C. Andrews, Daniel turned the tables on the Klan. All three men had been harassed by the Klan's 'Vigilance Committee', and they had had enough. They began tailing well-known Klansmen when they went out at night, tracking the activities of vigilantes and then broadcasting their findings to anyone who would listen.

One night, in the spring of 1922, the three friends followed a car full of hooded Klansmen to the shack of a poor Black Mer Rouge tenant farmer. In order to hear the conversation, they had crept recklessly close and found themselves surrounded by Klansmen with pistols, threatening to flog them. It was only when one Klansman recognised Daniel and pointed out his father's standing in the community that the Klan backed off and the young men were saved from a beating. The three friends were warned to keep silent, or they would be hunted down and made to suffer.

But Daniel didn't keep silent or abandon his counter-vigilance. In the summer of 1922, he tracked Klansmen to one of their secret meetings in a woodland clearing outside Mer Rouge. He crouched in the trees surrounding the glade and listened in. But Daniel was not a patient man, and halfway through the meeting he got bored. He stood up and crept away from his hiding place. Although he had served in the trenches, Daniel wasn't stealthy. He was quickly caught and dragged into the clearing, where once again he was recognised and reprimanded. The furious Klansmen warned him 'to keep his mouth shut or he'd suffer the consequences'.

Soon, a leading figure in the local Klan named Dr B.M. McCoin got involved, and that spelled trouble. Although he was a physician, McCoin was not a humane character. Scheming, cold and hard as nails, McCoin held no position in the hierarchy of the Morehouse Klan. And yet, McCoin was the undisputed moral compass of the Klavern, pointing 'due Confederate'. For McCoin and his followers, the moral high ground lay in the purity of the small-town South. To enforce these Southern ideals, McCoin frequently led night-riding raids like those that terrorised the freedmen fifty years earlier. But in addition to 'uppity' Black people, his victims now included suspected bootleggers and 'immoral' women.

In January 1922, McCoin and his party dragged a 16-year-old Mer Rouge girl down the high street to the local train station. They gave her $7 and told her never to come back to Mer Rouge. They offered no reason to the girl's distraught mother as she pleaded with them along the way. It was several months before the terrified teenager returned. McCoin's night-riders also intimidated local Catholics, flogged local Black farmers 'to keep them in their place' and threatened bootleggers and anyone standing in the way of their attempt to 'clean up' Mer Rouge.[2]

It was only a question of time before McCoin and Daniel came to blows. And it happened in August 1922. As the crowd dispersed after a baseball game in Mer Rouge, drivers found the road blocked by a broken-down car. Traffic began to back up along the wooded roadside and aggravated drivers sat sweating in their cars. After a while, fully garbed Klansmen emerged from between the trees clad in black 'raiding hoods', carrying hunting rifles, shotguns and pistols. They walked alongside the line of vehicles, peering in through the windows. Then they stopped at the car belonging to Daniel's father, 'J.L.'.

A Klansman called to his colleagues, 'Here's one we want.'

They dragged the old man out, bound him and roughly tied a blindfold over his eyes. Next, they found W.C. Andrews, 'Tot' Davenport and Thomas Richards – all known enemies of the Klan and friends of Watt Daniel. Eventually they came across Watt Daniel himself. Bound, blindfolded and gagged, three of the men were loaded into a truck while the other two, Watt Daniel and Thomas Richards, were stuffed into a car. Finally, the Klansmen removed the 'broken-down' car and drove off down the road.

Andrews, Davenport and J.L. Daniel turned up the next day. Two of them showed the signs of having been beaten. None of them knew where the younger Daniel and Richards had been taken, or what had happened to them.

The kidnappings divided the small town of Mer Rouge. Many thought Klan vigilantism was hypocritical and brutal – and wrong. Others felt if the police wouldn't do their job, let the Klan do it. As the editor of a local pro-Klan paper put it, 'When thieves and bootleggers make their open boasts and cannot be reached by the strong arm of the law then the community must protect itself and fight fire with fire.'[3]

The Klan claimed to have merely threatened the missing men, so frightening the two that they wouldn't return – for some time. But most people in Mer Rouge suspected much worse and feared the two friends had been murdered. In a letter to Louisiana governor John M. Parker, the kidnapped Thomas Richards' wife wrote:

> And just because he was not afraid of the Klan they have done this and they are now trying to make out it was not the Klan, but it was the Klan, as otherwise they would have been willing and ready to help me find my husband. I believe he is dead because he would have written if he is alive.[4]

Tales circulated that known Klansmen were regularly making death threats to anyone who even spoke of the kidnappings, saying they'd get the same as Daniel and Richards. But the Bastrop Klan knew the mood had turned against them and that they could not enforce those threats. They put great faith in a four-day inquest by a Morehouse Parish Grand Jury which failed to find sufficient evidence to prosecute. The success of this staged, mock investigation led the Klan to believe the matter was closed.

Many in Morehouse Parish had lost faith in the Klan as a force for 'American values' and instead saw Klan Number Thirty-Four as using their power simply to settle their own scores. The chapter's Exalted Cyclops was a Confederate veteran named Captain J. Killian 'Old Skip' Skipwith. To Skipwith, the Klan was the same organisation it had been during Reconstruction. He was in charge of 'a gang of night-riders, who were only too eager to carry out his orders, perhaps to go even farther than he directed'.[5] To him 'the flogging of citizens, their deportation and banishment and other kindred offences were but mere pastimes'.[6]

At his side was the sanctimonious Dr McCoin. This Klan bully-boy's hectoring and moralising of the locals had made him universally unpopular where he lived, in Mer Rouge. By the time of the kidnappings McCoin had fallen out with most of the town's prominent residents – so much so that one evening shortly before the kidnappings in early August 1922, McCoin was shot at.

Most in Morehouse Parish believed the Klan was behind the kidnappings. Very few people bought the Klan's incessant mantra that the two missing victims had 'just kept on going' and were running away from looming vigilante justice. Even fewer residents thought the two missing men would ever be found alive.[7] It was also widely known in the area that the Grand Jury inquest had been a put-up job. They were convinced it was designed by the Klan to exonerate themselves, especially when it emerged that not only was the Morehouse district attorney, David M. Garret, a Klansman but so were nine of the twelve-man jury.[8]

The backlash of the kidnapping was a collapse of Klan activity in Bastrop. As one prominent Morehouse Klansman said with only slight exaggeration, 'I *was* a Klansman. [But] Every member of the Klan here has resigned. I know of no exceptions.'[9] In addition, the Klan faced this reckoning without the support of Louisiana governor John Milliken Parker.

While the Klan, to a great extent, controlled local law enforcement in Morehouse Parish, Baton Rouge was a different story. Both Governor Parker and his Roman Catholic Attorney General, Judge Adolphe Valery Coco, saw fighting the Klan as essential to their own political survival. The Klan was only 50,000 strong in Louisiana but it had hefty political clout in both state government and law enforcement.

In an open letter in early September, Parker declared war: 'Neither mob violence nor the Ku Klux Klan shall run this state. The law must and shall prevail!'[10] But the Morehouse Grand Jury's whitewash meant that, in order to be effective, Parker would have to use federal investigators and federal courts. Local law enforcement and judicial processes simply would not convict Klansmen. This was not only Parker's problem: since Reconstruction, almost all investigations into Klan atrocities were covered by state law. Their crimes were not under federal jurisdiction.

Murder, rape, lynching, assault and, until the 1932 Lindbergh Law, kidnapping, were crimes under the jurisdiction of state law. Only abuses of the postal system, treason, piracy, sex trafficking, narcotics, abuses of Prohibition and car theft were considered federal crimes. To try the Bastrop Klan for the kidnappings, Parker needed to provide evidence that federal laws had been broken. Agents from the Bureau of Investigation and a postal investigator were sent down to Morehouse to investigate.

Bureau agents went to Morehouse and, sure enough, on the morning of 23 December 1922, they uncovered the badly decomposed bodies of Daniel and Richards. They had been tortured and shot, their bodies attached by wire to weights and thrown in the bayou. But even this gruesome discovery didn't finish the Klan in Morehouse. Federal agents could find no evidence of a federal crime; kidnapping, murder and even torture were all crimes tried by state courts.

On 5 March 1923, the Morehouse Parish Grand Jury was empanelled again. Few had any hopes that it would bring justice. The futility of the exercise was summed up by Exalted Cylops Skipwith. Seeing the names on the jury list, he turned to a friend and said, 'This is the last you will hear of it. There will be no indictments.'[11]

Some 125 witnesses gave highly damning testimony in open hearings. Large numbers of out-of-towners sat in the Public Gallery and some 4,000 people packed the courthouse in Bastrop. They heard details that seemed to seal the fate of the Klansmen. One witness told the Jury, 'If it had been my brother held in that car, Skipwith and [another prominent Bastrop Klansman] Stevenson would have been the first men I would have looked for.' Another claimed that if Daniel and Richards 'hadn't been so smart we intended to give them a trial for shooting at Dr McCoin, but they got so smart … that the boys decided they knew too much'.[12]

And yet, Skipwith's prediction came true. The Jury reached the conclusion that 'the evidence furnished was not sufficient to warrant the finding of true bills against any particular party'.[13] Furious, Coco decided to bring further prosecutions. In April, McCoin, Skipwith and sixteen other presumed Klansmen were tried for a variety of minor crimes – from firearms possession to stopping traffic. All walked from the court, free, having paid small fines.

It was a victory for the local Klan. Some of them even felt confident enough to go on the offensive, once more taking up their old line of condemning Mer Rouge as a hotbed of vice. Klansmen blustered that 'It was either surrender to the cut throats and lawless element or take strenuous steps to clean house'.[14] But it was more than a simple one-off victory.

The order's ability to intimidate and close ranks in places like Morehouse Parish plagued efforts to control the Klan. The repeated inability to use federal measures meant that, time after time, the Klan escaped prosecution – even for its most heinous crimes. But though they had slipped the law, this indication of the Klan's violence and hypocrisy made a critical mass of Americans regard it with increasing scepticism, if not hatred.

# CHAPTER 51

Look back to September 1922. Even as Simmons delivered his psalm to the innocence and honour of the Klan in Congress, in the heartlands of the country the order's brutality was all too apparent. The *World*'s investigation had listed 152 separate incidents of Klan violence that contributed to the congressional investigation. In the time between Simmons' defence of the Klan as being 'as innocent as the breath of an angel' and the kidnapping of Daniel and Richards in Louisiana, Klan violence was reported in Indiana, Texas, Oklahoma, Colorado, Arkansas, California, Alabama, New York and Mississippi. It ranged from violent threats, beatings, mutilations and whippings, to lynchings and murders.

While the Klan had escaped punishment for its crimes at Mer Rouge, it hadn't escape unscathed. Although the violence at Mer Rouge was nothing unusual, it was on a different level. It had attracted levels of national attention that the Klan hadn't seen since Simmons' performance in Congress and it had involved the federal government. Only this time that publicity was not positive. It was perhaps best summed up in an article published in the week the final Morehouse verdict came out. As one commentator saw it:

> To the mob the Ku Klux Klan offers as effective an instrument as could be contrived to satisfy, in the name of virtue and with the approbation of the evangelical church, its meanest and most brutal desires. There is the moral of the Morehouse unpleasantness. And a clear understanding of that would mean more than the hanging of every hooded ruffian in the parish.[1]

The trouble was that, in spite of Imperial Wizard Evans' attempts to move the Klan towards a more mainstream position in US society, the organisation was constantly showing its violent side. And the press loved to report it. To Evans' fury, they linked the Klan back directly to the excesses of the South in Reconstruction, especially in Texas and Florida.

Established in 1920, Texas was the first self-governing Realm within the Invisible Empire. Its motives were almost always racial. In February and March 1921 alone, Houston Klansmen whipped, tarred and feathered and castrated white people for helping Black people and Black people for helping themselves. By 1922, Texas had recorded 1,500 separate acts of violence.[2] But the violence in Florida was equally troubling.

In Florida, violent outbreaks started to be attributed to the Klan as early as December 1920. Florida Klansmen were far more wide-ranging in choice of victims than their Texas or Louisiana counterparts. Within a month of the Florida Klan being granted its charter, a white Jacksonville real estate agent was tarred and feathered for complaining about the coverage of Germans in a local paper. He was dumped from a moving car in the middle of town with a sign across his chest reading 'Herr John Bischoff, a Hun'.[3]

Later that month the son of a Daytona Beach man was fatally shot when eight Klansmen burst into a house looking for his father. They alleged his father had been 'intimate' with his own daughter. In Pensacola, a Greek immigrant was threatened with violence for bootlegging while the chief of the local PD looked on. Another (unmarried) man was beaten for abusing his 'wife' and his brother was beaten up as well, just because he happened to be with him. Death threats were sent to an anti-Klan newspaper editor.

Local papers reported the attacks as they happened, but the national press also took a keen interest. The *Omaha Bee* reported all these incidents and many more under the headline 'Death Dealt in Name of Klan in Florida'.[4] Under the banner headline 'State is Terrorized', the *Cincinnati Post* detailed the outrages in Texas, describing how 'men are kidnapped from city's crowded streets' in Fort Worth. It told readers how 'masked terror reigned supreme' in Childress and listed twenty-three separate Klan atrocities in the state from March to July 1921.[5]

Contrary to the superior fraternity Simmons had envisaged, the papers seemed to be reporting that Evans' Klan was rapidly turning into an organisation for thugs, violent low-lifes and bigots. Far from being seen as an organisation upholding law and order, it was increasingly portrayed as criminally intolerant. In Columbus, Georgia, the *Enquirer-Sun* lumped together 'Ku Kluxism, bootleggers, gangsters and terrorists'. The response appeared to justify that judgement. For that and other anti-Klan comments the Klan gave a show of local strength, marching past the paper's offices in full regalia. They organised a boycott which cut the paper's sales by over a quarter and they sent the editor, Julian Harris, a letter postmarked Atlanta advising him that 'Dead Men Tell No Tales'.[6]

On the other hand, there had always been a policy in the Klan to deny any knowledge of violence. Ever since Simmons' virtuoso performance in front of the Rules Committee in September 1921, the Klan almost always denied any part in acts of violence, as a matter of course. This tactic was taken up and used by both Edward Young Clarke and Hiram Wesley Evans when they ran Klan propaganda. On most occasions, when hooded lynch mobs or vigilantes struck and the Klan's name was mentioned, the Klan's leadership simply claimed they were men in disguise as Klansmen. They called them 'night-riders' to distinguish them from 'legitimate' Klansmen.

In fact, in numerous cases, the Klan even offered rewards for the capture and prosecution of night-riders. The Indiana Klan weekly, *The Fiery Cross*, summed up the Klan's attitude, claiming that even when the victims of violence were branded with the tell-tale 'KKK' it was not their work. This was usually the work of enemies of the Klan with 'a twofold purpose; first, to take suspicion from themselves, and secondly to try and harm the Klan'.[7]

This technique didn't always work. Doubting Americans asked why the Klan couldn't bring the imposters to justice, since they were always claiming they were more effective at crime fighting than elected law enforcers. It is a good question, especially given that it was Klan practice to recruit law enforcement officers when 'Kluxing' a new area. The result was that many of the police and courts tended to be lenient on, if not supportive of, Klan vigilantism, especially in 1922 and 1923, before the Klan's lustre tarnished.

A good example of this can be seen in 1922, in the Ozark region of Arkansas, when striking railroad workers crippled the local economy. Klansmen played a prominent part in establishing 'Citizens' Committees' that settled scores with strikers. They set up kangaroo courts and sentenced strikers to punishments that included flogging, expulsion and even, in one case, lynching. Black-hooded bands went out at night and carried out the sentences.

It all smelled of the Klan, although the name was not mentioned as such. By 1923, the situation was on the verge of getting out of control; the Arkansas legislature appointed a committee to hear weeks of testimony. In spite of the tales of astounding violence that emerged from the witnesses, the committee made no recommendations and apportioned no blame. It seemed the legislature backed the Klan's position. But the fact that the investigation had been convened at all showed that the public wasn't so sure Klan violence was always a good thing.[8]

But in terms of violence, the most outrageous Klans were to be found in Oklahoma. The state had a history of vigilante justice and the Klan fitted straight into this tradition. The mayor of the city of Enid told an investigator for the American Civil Liberties Union that they had a total of ten policemen, but nearly 1,500 Klansmen. He went on to tell him, 'You might condemn the method, but the results were entirely satisfactory to our city of twenty thousand.'[9]

As far as the Klan was concerned it was a virtuous circle. The more the Klan 'cleaned up' Oklahoma, the more the people of Oklahoma joined. As one Klansman said, 'I joined the Klan because it was doing things that needed to be done.'[10] And so it went on. Until, gradually, it didn't.

Having made itself the law in Oklahoma, the Klan soon saw itself as *above* the law in Oklahoma. Klansmen began to be seen as more interested in policing the behaviour of communities than in controlling crime as such. They gained a reputation for hypocrisy, enforced by totally disproportionate violence. Teenagers making out in cars would find themselves hauled out and beaten by hooded moralists. Personal vendettas were settled by 'whipping squads'. But who would rein them in? When their excesses were disclosed, juries of Klansmen refused to convict fellow Klansmen.

The Klan killed nine people in 1922 in Oklahoma. It was simply too much. The Klan had to be stopped, or so the governor said.

Governor John Calloway 'Jack' Walton was a Midwesterner. Born in Indiana, his family had later moved to Nebraska. He'd arrived and settled in Oklahoma as a young foreman overseeing railroad gangs. After setting up an engineering firm in Oklahoma City, he progressed, via labour activism, to elected politics. He was made commissioner of public works, then elected Democrat mayor of Oklahoma City. A populist to his ornate cowboy boots, when Walton was elected governor in 1922, after his inauguration on New Year's Day, 1923, legend has it he held a barbecue for an estimated 125,000 guests.[11]

Walton's election coincided with the coalescing of opinions in Oklahoma over the Klan. His electorate was all groups alienated and targeted by the Klan. This mix of Union men, socialists and radical Democrats with a smattering of Catholics wanted to curb Klan vigilantism and Walton was willing to do just that.

His opportunity presented itself with the trial of a Klansman for the murder of a policeman outside the small town of Wilson. The policeman, C.G. Simms, had been found dead outside the house of a known bootlegger. He'd taken part in a Klan raid on the house. He was found with blood seeping through his black 'raiding hood'. He died on the way to hospital. The bootlegger and one of his gang were also killed. Given the nature and circumstances of the raid, an inquest indicted eleven Klansmen for murder. This was odd, since it clearly showed how Klansmen had operated on either side, both as bootleggers and vigilantes.

The Klan demonstrated its true strength in the subsequent trial. Ten of those indicted were released. Only one was tried and, in spring 1922, the jury failed to reach a verdict in his case. Walton decided to make a show of that Klansman. A retrial placed him in the dock again. Again the Klansman was acquitted. It was stalemate.

But the governor was not going to back down. He ordered a ban on Klan parades and forbade the wearing of masks in public. He demanded the resignation of known Klansmen in county and city offices in Tulsa, including the sheriff and police commissioner. Although they looked impressive, these decrees were generally disregarded. Many Klansmen still paraded. The officers indicted refused to leave their posts and very few Klansmen abandoned their masks. The stalemate deepened.

By August 1923, Walton realised he'd have to either extend his war against the Klan, or back off. He chose to escalate his measures. He went nuclear. He declared martial law across the state. He suspended *habeas corpus*. He called out the National Guard. He established a midnight curfew in Tulsa. He also established a military court which heard testimony from over 140 victims of Klan violence.

But Walton's powerbase was fragile, marginal and generally unpopular with the rest of Oklahoma. Businesses feared union upheaval. Radicals saw him as a dictator. Uncertain about the future, farmers were cautious. The undecided fled from him, feeling that the governor's measures would simply escalate an already bad situation. A majority of Oklahoma residents agreed with the *Tulsa Tribune* and wanted 'Neither Klan nor King'. They were convinced that Walton was acting in 'as arbitrary and illegal a manner as ever the Klan did'.[12] By October they'd impeached Walton by close to a three-to-one majority.

Walton may have lost his battle with the Klan, but it did put Klan violence up there and into headlines. Newspapers across the nation told of civil war. The press lapped up gruesome stories – 'Mob Cuts Man's Ear Off: Masked Klansmen would Force Helpless Victim to Eat His Own Bloody Flesh'. The Oklahoma Klan became the symbol for bloody gun battles, floggings, beatings and other aspects of Klan terrorism. Newspapers began to portray the Klan itself as less than 'One Hundred Percent American', asking questions like 'Are you for the American Republic or the Invisible Empire?'[13]

The other problem the Klan had created was that it *inspired* violence – against itself. In April 1923 in Chicago, a bomb destroyed the offices of the Klan weekly, *Dawn*. A month later an angry mob in New Jersey penned up 500 robed Klansmen in a church, forcing police to break up the crowds and rescue the shaken and self-righteous Klansmen. Over the summer

Klansmen were attacked and beaten up in Ohio, Wisconsin and Delaware. In Pennsylvania two were killed in one incident and another killed in a different one, and in southern Illinois a virtual war broke out which would eventually leave twenty Klansmen and their opponents dead.[14]

In Atlanta, Imperial Wizard Hiram Wesley Evans had already realised the damage Klan violence could do. He told a meeting of Grand Dragons that 'The first time one of your Klansmen violates the law … let the judge and jury and the penitentiary take care of them. When we do that this thing will fade like the morning dew.'[15] But it was too late. As Governor Walton put it, 'With the American flag that it [the Klan] desecrated wrapped around its Dragons, Cyclops, Goblins and Wizards, it holds aloft the constitution while calling upon all the people to witness that it represents the only Americanism in the land.'[16]

# CHAPTER 52

By the mid-1920s there was growing discontent with the Klan, both inside and outside the organisation. And it was not simply highly publicised acts of violence which changed the view of the order. In many cases the perception of the Klan suffered just as much from doing too little as it did from doing too much. To many Klansmen and -women, the order appeared to be impotent and immaterial. More of a whining irrelevance than a sadistic bully.

To many of its longer-term, core members at the grass-roots level, the Klan simply didn't seem to do enough. What it actually did, didn't live up to what it promised it would do and that perception was self-fulfilling. Klan 'failure' led to declining numbers because the Klan wasn't doing enough. Declining numbers led to declining influence. Declining influence led to declining numbers. And so it went round until it eventually imploded.

Under Evans and Stephenson, there had been an attempt to turn the Klan into a political force. At its most simplistic, both had hoped to drag the Klan away from Simmons' dreamy visions of the ultimate chivalric fraternity and towards being a truly powerful force in US politics. And for a while – when they successfully derailed the presidential ambitions of Catholic, anti-Prohibition and Tammany-sleazy Al Smith – it looked like they just might be able to do just that. But as the 1920s progressed the issues changed.

The programme of racist anti-immigration, anti-radicalism, anti-modernism, anti-sleaze and Protestant 'Hundred Percentism' had frequently proved unattainable or largely irrelevant. The Klan's simple answers to complex problems, so compelling to those who joined in the early years of the decade, lost their appeal. To a great many Americans, the 1920s was a revolutionary decade. They lived vastly different lives at the end of the decade from those they'd had at the beginning.

Countless Americans had more money than ever before and they were encouraged to spend it in new ways, on new goods. By 1930 they were consumers in ways they could have barely imagined in 1920. They had radios and cinemas which kept them informed and entertained and encouraged them to spend still more. Electric light and power and running hot water became regarded as normal for the American home. And that home acquired labour-saving devices from vacuum cleaners to refrigerators to washing machines. Thanks to the automobile and better roads, they had greater mobilit, which that increased the diversity and availability of goods they could buy.

The 1920s had opened with the very real threat of revolution and palp-able economic decline. By the middle of the decade the USA seemed to be holding out the promise of perpetual growth and ever-improving prosper-ity. By 1924, the Klan's rants about the monstrous spectre of Bolshevism seemed just plain silly. The massive level of strikes that fuelled fear of socialism and divided the workers into 'us and them' in 1920 had subsided. Labour unions became increasingly conservative and compliant throughout the 1920s and their membership dropped from 5 million to 3. Court deci-sions seemed to be rolling back union powers, making the re-emergence of radicalism that much less likely as the decade progressed. The Klan's anti-radicalism seemed outdated and irrelevant.

Nor was this the only thing that had changed. At the Texas State Fair in October 1923, Imperial Wizard Evans had called immigration 'the one outstanding problem beside which all other national difficulties are transient and trivial'.[1] He'd rallied loyal Klansmen to brace themselves for a titanic struggle. But he was wrong. To most Americans that threat had largely diminished, if not evaporated, and it had certainly lost its sting as an issue.

The terror that immigrant numbers might climb back to their pre-war million a year had largely been neutralised. The Emergency Quota Act of 1921 had set an annual maximum of a little over 350,000 immigrants and that would be cut to a limit of 150,000 in 1924 by the National Origins Act. Equally importantly, these two milestones in immigration control had imposed visas which controlled how many could arrive and from which countries. The more 'threatening' Eastern and Southern Europeans and Asians had been targeted for massive reductions. Numbers for desirable 'Nordics' had been preserved. Although Evans unsuccessfully tried to put the Klan behind the attempts to impose further restrictions, he couldn't rouse sufficient enthusiasm. The issue was largely yesterday's news.

But the massive immigration of the early twentieth century was having a longer-term effect. It had substantially changed the US electorate. Some 14 per cent of the entire US was now foreign-born and a considerable propor-tion of them were Jewish, Catholic or otherwise at odds with the Klan. They were increasingly becoming naturalised and able to vote. Pursuing them as a group was not a good strategy. It could create a powerful anti-Klan lobby.[2]

While the Klan had traction in its anti-Mexican stance, particularly in Texas, California and Florida, it also failed to get this group banned. Again, it seemed the nation had moved on, and with the economy hotting up, the need to replace European labour was still enormous – until the Depression struck. The lobbies demanding open borders with Mexico proved to be far more powerful than the Klan.[3] This meant that, for all their anti-Catholic, racist bluster, it seemed the Klan was essentially impotent to do anything about Mexican immigration. For, while the debate had changed, the Klan's arguments had not moved on.

The Klan was equally bad at reading the public mood over Prohibition. In the early 1920s, when the Volstead Act was freshly minted, the mood of the country was in favour of banning the demon booze. Americans were on a crusade. A couple of years later it appeared those ruling the nation still drank. It was equally apparent that Prohibition just enabled criminals to make fortunes with impunity and pay the cops, the judges and the politicians handsomely to look the other way. It looked like everyone was on the take. And everyone was still drinking.

While the diehards of the temperance movement remained committed to the benefits of Prohibition, much of the population had lost what enthusiasm they initially had. The Eighteenth Amendment outlawing booze was the result of a coalition. It was led by the religious and moral zealots of the ASL and the WCTU. Alongside them were big business, who had bought into the dream of a sober workforce being a more compliant and productive workforce. Finally, sensing the votes in it, the politicians signed up.

What the coalition seemed to ignore was that alcohol revenues had to be replaced, and that business would bear the brunt of these new demands for income. Supporters, like the chemicals giant DuPont, visibly began to get cold feet as their profit margins showed little of the expected improvements. Then there were the politicians who simply followed the public. As the cowboy–philosopher Will Rogers put it, 'Why not settle this Prohibition fifty-fifty. Let the Prohibitionists quit drinking. ... Look at Congress; it voted dry, and drinks wet.'[4]

It is safe to assume that by the mid-1920s Prohibition was not popular with the majority of Americans. And this was true of the Klan membership. Many Klansmen paid lip service to the dry laws while merrily drinking away, especially at the highest levels. It was widely argued that William Simmons, the founder of the order, was a lush. David Stephenson, the charismatic leader of the biggest Klan in the nation, would be exposed as a violent alcoholic. And although none of the top Klansmen would actively speak out against the dry laws, few were strict in their observance of them.

To many it appeared that the Klan leadership's outspoken support for Prohibition was misguided, unrealistic or hypocritical – or all of the above.

What was more, even some of those who actively, and genuinely, supported the Klan's crusade against booze and bootleggers found the Klan's violent methods to be either an overreaction or an excuse for their own immoral behaviour. As the head of the ASL, the steely Wayne B. Wheeler, put it, they 'attempted to do enforcement by [the] wrong methods and have hurt rather than helped the cause' of Prohibition.[5]

Stories circulated of Klan raids that were far worse than the crimes for which the bootleggers were accused. Perhaps most notorious was the night of April 1922, when armed Klansmen raided the house of brothers Fidel and Matias Elduayen in Inglewood, California. They made the men's teenage daughters strip naked. The Klansmen remained in the bedroom with them for half an hour, probably gang-raping the two girls while their fathers, uncles and mothers were tied to chairs in earshot in the room next door.

As if that wasn't enough, it emerged that, when the city sheriff and his deputies arrived to investigate the break-in, the Klansmen opened fire and fought a gunfight with them. One Klansman was shot dead, and his son and another Klansman were wounded. All that simply to check whether the Mexicans were selling wine – of which they found no evidence.[6]

More successful, but just as violent and controversial, were the antics of Klansmen in southern Illinois. By the end of 1923, the Klan dominated the Prohibition effort in many regions of the nation. Nowhere was this clearer than in Williamson County, Illinois. Here, the local Law and Order League had had little difficulty persuading former Prohibition agent and the Grand Cyclops of the Herrin Buckhorn Klan den, Glenn Young, to lead their planned purge of bootleggers in the region.

From December 1923 until early January 1924, Young's Klansmen assisted by federal officers conducted a purge of hundreds of local gin joints. They raided roadhouses and illegal stills. They got fifty-five men jailed for running illicit liquor joints and levied over $55,000 in fines. Targeting those speakeasies owned by foreigners in particular, they frequently planted booze if the necessary evidence wasn't there. They smashed up premises and the owners before robbing their homes. All this upset the two local booze-lords who retaliated – violently.

Williamson County became the Wild West as Prohibition gunmen battled it out with bootleggers. The National Guard were called out eight times over the next four years. The violence was so extreme and the publicity so bad that Young was expelled from the Klan. The death toll for the unsuccessful Prohibition enforcement of 'Bloody Williamson' was twenty – many of whom were simply bystanders.[7]

But it was not just the causes the Klan espoused which were losing it support. The Klan was proving unable to introduce new measures. It has been estimated that in 1922 the Klan was behind the election of at least seventy-five national congressmen and senators.[8] More than that, in one way or another the Klan would end up dominating Texas, Indiana, Oregon and Colorado politics for the first half of the 1920s. But these electoral victories didn't translate into rafts of legislation.

The only really dramatic legislative achievement of these electoral triumphs was the Oregon School Bill. And that was struck down by a Supreme Court judgement in 1925. What was more, attempts to replicate that brief success in states like Kansas and Washington failed. The problem was that the Klan itself was divided politically. In the North and in the West, it was aligned with the Republican Party, traditionally the party of the US working man. In the South it was solidly Democrat, linked as it was with white supremacy since before the Civil War. This division severely blunted the Klan's political influence and it curbed Evans' national political ambitions.

What the Klan did achieve, politically, was to unite its enemies. Catholics, Jews, African Americans, Asians, immigrants, disaffected ex-Klansmen, as well as libertarians, internationalists, liberals and radicals – all had an instinctive hatred of the order. As the Klan gradually lost support, sensing blood, its enemies rallied and went into attack mode. The Vigilance Association supported the passage of anti-mask laws and measures to curb mob violence in all states, aimed solely at the Klan.[9] By 1924 they'd managed to get legislation to ban the wearing of masks in public in ten states, across the South from Louisiana to Oklahoma and as far north as New York and North Dakota, and many areas in between.

In 1923 in New York, the playboy, Tammany Hall, Democrat, Catholic, anti-Volstead Mayor 'Gentleman' Jimmy Walker, and the Klan bête noire, Al Smith, managed to push through legislation that forced Klan lodges to declare the names of all members. The Klan fought hard to try to prevent the passage of the bill and took it all the way to the US Supreme Court. There it failed. In 1928, the court ruled that Klan 'members disguised by hoods and gowns [were] doing things calculated to strike terror into the minds of the people ... [and] conducting a crusade against Catholics, Jews and Negroes, stimulating hurtful religious and race prejudices'.[10]

Quasi-political orders started to emerge, with a single aim: to bring down the Klan. In Texas the Dallas Citizens League got the ball rolling in April 1922 and soon anti-Klan organisations emerged all over the nation. Some imitated and ridiculed the Klan. Arkansas had the Order of Anti-Poke Noses. The Loyal Legion of Lincoln (Nebraska) burnt fiery 'L's when the Klan burnt its crosses. Fraternities like the veterans of the American Legion, the Irish descendants in the Ancient Order of Hibernians and the Freemasons made public statements about the Klan having 'no right or title to exist in a free country'. [11]

# CHAPTER 53

The 1920s Klan was something of a supernova: a powerful and impressive stellar event. It exploded on the scene in 1921. It burnt brightly for two, maybe even three years. Then it collapsed in on itself. Like a supernova, that implosion simply needed time and internal instability to come about. The 1920s Klan could have imploded all by itself. It didn't need sidelining from politics. Nor did it need the reports of violence, or even the indifference of its membership in order to collapse. It just needed the leadership it had because, like the proverbial fish, it rotted from the head.

The signs, the causes, of that implosion were there right from the start of Simmons' expansion of the order in 1920. When Simmons hooked up with Clarke and Tyler, the Klan became unstable. When Evans took over, that wobble became uncontrollable. The pyramid sales method lit the fuse. Kleagles, Goblins and Dragons in the field and the leadership in Atlanta, all became reliant on expansion – finding new recruits in new territories and within new groups. Because there had to be a limit to where and who those new Klans – men, women and children – could be found, expansion could not continue for ever. And when that limit was reached, and the income stopped pouring in – then what?

An organisation founded on profit had to find a new income source, or die. Having exploited female and juvenile Klans-people, an unscrupulous profit-addicted leadership would pretty soon turn to less obvious sources, less legal sources, of income. Allegations of corruption flew about and in many cases those claims were backed up by those in the know. As one minor New England Klan official said, 'I am convinced that the Ku Klux Klan is the greatest graft organization in history.'[1] But he was not only talking of his small New Jersey Klavern. He knew that it was higher up in the order that the real graft was taking place.

When Simmons appeared before the Rules Committee in October 1921, he was cross-examined about the Klan's vast income. He pleaded ignorance. It is generally argued that Simmons was not really in the loop when it came to the really big money being made. Yet from June 1920, when he teamed up with Clarke and Tyler, to when he sat in front of his inquisitors in Congress in October 1921, his personal income was around $170,000. That equates to a little under $2.5 million today.[2]

Given that income, there can be little doubt Simmons knew of the vast profits the order was making. And in spite of his claims to the contrary, he'd founded his Klan as a means of making money. He just wasn't very good at profitably exploiting it, but he was successful in playing down that side of his activities – at least in public. For, while Clarke and Tyler would make less, individually, than Simmons, it was them who were portrayed as the exploitative leaders whose greed threatened the integrity of the order.

As Evans ousted first Simmons and then Clarke, the rank-and-file Klansmen had been treated to this drama in the national press. They read daily accounts of their sacred order being dragged through the mud by self-serving, corrupt and over-ambitious leaders. Now they were to witness the Klan actually being condemned by those who had led it.

It started when an embittered Clarke sent the president, Calvin Coolidge, an open letter just after Christmas, 1923. In it he condemned the organisation he'd led as a 'real menace to law and order, individual rights and liberties and democratic political government'. He offered his services to the president to 'end the activities of an element of our citizenship … which is in control thereof'. The letter was published, in full, in The New York Times.[3]

Then things got worse. In March 1924, a year after his being charged under the sex-trafficking prohibitions of the Mann Act, Clarke eventually appeared in court on a white slavery charge. Caught between a hostile judge and a woman who seemed more than happy to give all the salacious details, Clarke tried desperately to save himself. In doing so he lashed out at the leaders of the Klan. In his defence, Clarke told the court that he'd been led astray by the immoral and drunken Simmons when they were staying in New Orleans. As details emerged about his past financial dealings, he claimed that Evans hadn't sacked him for corruption or immorality, but because he opposed the growing levels of violence in which the Klan was involved.

Clarke's final blow against the Klan came when he was asked by Judge Hutchinson if he didn't think it hypocritical to lecture Klansmen on moral-ity while paying young women for sex. He replied with uncharacteristic honesty, saying that he was involved with the Klan purely on a commercial basis.[4] Clarke was finished. In the eyes of the Klansmen and the general public there was no coming back.

But as all this played out, Evans still faced a threat from the charismatic leader of the Indiana Klan. David Stephenson had been chaffing at being controlled from Atlanta and he openly squabbled with Evans. The issue was one of Stephenson's pet projects, a Klan university. Steve had had his eye on converting Indiana's ailing, self-styled 'Poor Man's Harvard', Valparaiso College, into a national Klan university. It would teach a 'One Hundred Percent American' curriculum to Klan students, and in the process provide what he hoped was a lucrative sideline. Atlanta was to foot the bill.

However, Evans took no part in the planning stages and felt that the project would cement Stephenson as a powerful rival. But Evans allowed Stephenson to take negotiations to the final stage in the spring of 1923. Then at the last minute he refused to release the agreed funding. It was a calculated move, designed to humiliate Stephenson. Stephenson demanded a meeting. Evans agreed to meet, but refused to budge over payment, arguing he could not release national funds for what he claimed was an Indiana project. Stephenson was furious. He was forced to negotiate an expensive and demeaning retreat. Stephenson never forgave Evans and the Imperial Wizard knew he could no longer trust his most powerful Grand Dragon.

Evans' suspicions were right: Stephenson wasn't loyal to him and he made little secret of it. He told a colleague the Imperial Wizard was an 'ignorant, uneducated, uncouth individual who picks his nose at the table and eats peas with his knife'. He said that Evans had 'neither courage or culture'.[5] In June the two clashed over Klan violence in Ohio.[6] They disagreed over press strategy and the Klan's role in national politics. Evans thought Stephenson was skimming off Klan funds and getting far too powerful. He was also getting worrying reports of Steve's drinking and womanising from his team of investigators. The two leading Klan figures could not be reconciled.[7]

By the autumn of 1923 things had become so fraught that Stephenson 'agreed' to retire. His duties were taken over by the Grand Klaliff (Evans' vice-president), Walter Bossert. Ever the schemer and never one to remain idle, in May 1924, Stephenson appointed himself Grand Dragon of a new Indiana Klan. Bypassing Bossert, he carried on as if nothing had happened. The Klansmen, largely ignorant of the disputes at the highest level, accepted him. They knew no better.

In many ways this was because Evans had learned from the damage done by his public squabbles with Simmons and Clarke. He kept everything relating to his suspicions and the evidence he'd accumulated under the strictest secrecy. Very few Klansmen, and virtually none of the 'alien' public, knew of the spat. But by the end of 1924, Stephenson's behaviour would be making headlines across the world, accelerating, if not causing, the collapse of the entire Klan.

# CHAPTER 54

Madge Oberholtzer was an intelligent, pretty, brunette in her late 20s when she met the Grand Dragon of Indiana, David Stephenson. It was January 1925 and the event was a party to celebrate the inauguration of Ed Jackson, the state's new Klan-backed governor. Steve, as he liked to be known, was smitten but Madge was not sure. Despite repeated invitations, she refused to go on a date with him, until she eventually let him take her to dinner where he was charming, attentive, funny and flattering.

In the weeks after the date, Steve rang Madge several times pestering her for a second date. Madge was still unsure. She'd heard rumours about the Klan and their vigilante violence. Had she known more of Steve's history with women, she'd have run a mile. He'd regularly beaten both his wives, to the extent where they were hospitalised. In episodes of drunken lechery, he'd viciously attempted to rape at least two women who worked for him – one on the night of his triumphal inauguration as Grand Dragon in Kokomo.[1] But Madge knew nothing of this, and when Steve promised to secure funding for her Indiana Young People's Reading Circle, she agreed to the second dinner.

They saw each other regularly for several weeks until Madge abruptly and mysteriously ended the relationship in February. On the night of 15 March, Madge returned from an evening with friends. Her mother told her Steve had called several times, leaving a message to say he was heading for Chicago the following morning and wanted to see her about the Reading Circle before he left. He sent round his bodyguard, Earl Gentry, to walk her to his mansion, only a few blocks away. Madge complied.

The next two days were a nightmare for the young woman. On arriving at Stephenson's mansion two bodyguards and a very drunk Stephenson took her into the kitchen. Here they forced teetotal Madge to drink whiskey, forcing it down her until she was sick. She was then dragged out to a car and taken to the Chicago train. In his private sleeper, Stephenson pulled off the drunken Madge's dress and forced her onto the lower bunk. Holding her down, he repeatedly raped her, biting, chewing and mauling her face, breasts, thighs and buttocks, tearing out chunks of flesh and leaving her passed out in a pool of her own blood.

On reaching Hammond, close to the Illinois state line, Stephenson and the now visibly mutilated Madge left the train. They were met by a car and driven to a hotel, where they were booked into a shared room. Stephenson fell asleep, but, in pain and terrified, Madge found his pistol and contemplated shooting him and then herself. She rejected the idea when she thought of 'the disgrace it would bring on her family'.

Instead, when they left the hotel, on the excuse that she needed cosmetics to disguise the bruising and bite marks on her face, Madge went to a drug store. Here she bought a box of bichloride of mercury tablets. Popular as a household disinfectant, topical antiseptic and, in very small doses, as an all-too-often fatal treatment for syphilis, the compound is extremely toxic and very corrosive. For this very reason, it is very rarely used for domestic or medical purposes today.

Madge went back to the hotel. In the bathroom she swallowed six tablets. She'd aimed to take the entire eighteen tablets in the box, but retched so badly she couldn't get any more down. Soon, Stephenson discovered Madge in agony and vomiting blood. He made no effort to get her medical help. Instead, he forced her to drink milk and had his men bundle her off into the car for the lengthy and bumpy drive back to Indianapolis.

As they rattled along the rutted roads, Stephenson once more got drunk with one of the bodyguards in the front of the car. Madge vomited bile and blood all over the back of the car while writhing, groaning and begging for a doctor. The car rumbled on – Stephenson indifferent to Madge's pleas and pain.

When they arrived at Stephenson's mansion on the night of 16 March, Madge remembered him storming around the room in which she had been put. Drunk and panicking, he ranted at her as she drifted in and out of consciousness. In all the haze she clearly remembered him shouting, 'You will stay right here until you marry me. … You must forget this, what is done has been done, I am the law and the power.' Her condition was worsening by the hour, but still he made no effort to get her medical help.

In the morning Stephenson had his crony Earl Klinck drive her to her parents' house, carry her upstairs and lay her, groaning, on the bed, all the while carefully hiding his face from her mother, Mathilde. The distraught woman was simply told by the mysterious Klinck that Madge had been in a car crash. He instructed Mathilde to get her a doctor.

Dr John K. Kingsbury did his best for Madge, disinfecting and dressing her wounds, raising her critically low temperature and pumping her stomach. But it was too late to save her: the damage to her organs was too great. In mid-April, she died, but not before she'd spent an hour and a half dictating her ordeal over those awful two days in March.[2]

Less than a week after Madge's death Stephenson was arrested. He was indicted on 'first-degree murder on four counts': abduction; administration of a poison; assault; and refusal to give medical attention.[3] In spite of these grave charges, Steve appeared confident and in good spirits. When an *Indiana Times* reporter asked him to comment on the case against him, Stephenson told him, 'I refuse to discuss such trivial matters' and asked the reporter if he wouldn't rather be fishing than wasting his time in court.[4]

After all, as Stephenson had said to Madge back in March, he was 'the law' in Indiana. He controlled judges, mayors, legislators and even the governor. Further, the case against him relied on the deathbed confession of a very sick young woman. And her mental state would definitely be questioned, partly because of her physical state, but also due to the morphine she had been administered to deal with the agony of her condition. Perhaps more importantly, Madge stated herself that she had voluntarily taken the bichloride of mercury. It was suicide.

He believed the case against him was hardly compelling, but to be sure, Stephenson took on Ephraim 'Eph' Inman. This giant of a man, with a deep booming voice, was a real showman and the top criminal lawyer in Indiana. To be doubly sure, he also secured Marion County Criminal Court judge James Collins on his side. Their allegiance would be no mystery, as Collins had been exposed weeks before as a Klansman by the Chicago-based anti-Klan newspaper *Tolerance*.[5]

On the other hand, in Indianapolis, the mood of the city was increasingly unsympathetic to Stephenson and the Klan. The day after his arrest, the *Indianapolis Times* reported that Stephenson's glamorous mansion in the Irvington district had been set on fire. The paper's front-page sub-head ran: 'Incendiary Origin, Seen by Experts and Police'.[6] It could have been an act of hatred for Stephenson. But it might equally well have been arson *by* Stephenson to destroy any incriminating evidence.

Whatever the cause of the fire, it enabled Stephenson's legal team to shift the venue for the trial from what they felt was an increasingly 'hostile' Indianapolis, to the more supportive town of Noblesville. The county seat of Hamilton had been the scene of numerous Klan rallies in the past. They thought the change would win Stephenson's freedom. They were very wrong on all counts.

The evidence against him proved overwhelming. On 14 November 1925, Stephenson was convicted of the second-degree murder of Madge Oberholtzer. He was sentenced to life imprisonment. Although he blustered that he 'had just begun to fight', the conviction ruined the Klan in Indiana. Arguably, it was the most important of many scandals that turned many of the nation's most committed and long-standing Klansmen against the order.[7]

Stephenson was revealed as a blackmailer to those he'd 'helped', demanding they assist him in his relentless pursuit of money and power. He ensured their allegiance with what he called his 'little black boxes': archive boxes crammed with incriminating letters, receipts, cancelled cheques – essentially political IOUs. Evidence which could assuredly bring down any former ally, should they turn on him. In 1927, when the appeal against his sentence failed, he released these to the press, creating political mayhem in Indiana, bringing down figures including the mayor of Indianapolis, the state governor and several other leading politicians and law enforcers.[8]

It also emerged that Stephenson had used banks of telephonists to gather dirt on individuals and smear their reputations. He took bribes. He peddled influence. He assaulted and raped several women other than Madge. He drank perpetually and heavily. All the while leading an order which advocated high morals, temperance, family values and Protestant virtues.[9]

As if that wasn't bad enough, in July 1925, as Stephenson sat in jail awaiting the start of his trial, another shock buffeted the Klan. This time it came from the state where the order had started nearly sixty years before – Tennessee.

# CHAPTER 55

The Baptist legislator John W. Butler was the first person in the USA to pass a bill against evolution. The 'Butler Bill' made it a misdemeanour in the state of Tennessee to teach that 'man had descended from a lower order of animal' in any school funded by the Tennessee taxpayer. The crime carried a maximum fine of $500. Anti-evolutionists in Florida and North Carolina had tried in 1924 to get similar bills passed and, as with many other states, had failed.

In 1924, Tennessee was a solidly Christian, churchgoing state. Out of a population of around 1.25 million, over 1 million had been baptised as Protestants and, of these, nearly half a million were Baptists – conservative, traditional, family-oriented and evangelical.[1]

The bill easily passed, with over seventy votes to five. It became law without amendments. It took less than a week to go from its first reading to its appearance on the statute books. As Butler himself put it, 'I do not see the need for further talk, everyone understands what evolution means.'[2]

The Butler Act was not simply an attack on evolution; it was a defence of tradition, one of the hotbutton issues of 1920s USA, dividing citizens about the future of the nation. The evolution debate raised the now-familiar idea that the conventions of rural America were the backbone of the country. They were places of tradition, continuity and certainty in a changing world. Others believed in looking forward to the future and the shifting excitements and possibilities of urban life. Both sides of the growing debate on evolution centred around education. Should the USA's children be brought up on the scientific rationalism of Darwin or the doctrines of salvation (and damnation) preached by Calvinists and Lutherans?

Not surprisingly, the Klan's position was firmly in support of the Butler Act, against what they saw as the anti-Christian theory of evolution. Scientific reliance on empirical evidence over moral values and religious beliefs seemed fundamentally un-American. To some, it showed signs of a Jewish conspiracy. Others simply felt the theory of evolution was an attack on Genesis, the biblical creation story. Evolution was seen as a threat to undermine the Klan's entire project, demonstrating what one commentator called their 'provincial fear of all things foreign and its uncritical but loyal Americanism'.[3]

Opponents of the measure were equally committed to a fight. On 4 May 1925, the American Civil Liberties Union placed an advertisement in the *Chattanooga Daily Times* offering to finance a test case challenging the Butler Act. The civil rights group sought a public school teacher in the Tennessee system who was willing to come forward and admit to having taught evolution. By 9 May, the Dayton police had arrested 24-year-old John T. Scopes for breaching the Act.

Scopes was actually a maths teacher who occasionally taught physics and chemistry. He didn't teach biology, and later claimed he could not recall ever teaching evolution. But that was immaterial. He had been persuaded by an ambitious cabal of civil servants, teachers, businessmen and lawyers that it was his duty to put Dayton on the map.

On 25 May, *Tennessee v. John T. Scopes* was scheduled for court time and Dayton became the centre of an entirely new level of media circus. It was the perfect setting to test the new law. Even in rural Tennessee, it was a backwater, a town where most things came in twos: a population of less than 2,000 souls; two paved roads; two hotels; two drug stores; two blacksmiths; and two banks. It only had one theatre, one pool hall and 'one semi-professional distributor of *cawn* whisky' – as well as just one Catholic family, three garages and three Jews.[4] Dayton was just what the American Civil Liberties Union (ACLU) wanted.

But sleepy Dayton was about to become international news, largely due to the fame of the two leading advocates. The prosecution brought in William Jennings Bryan. Bryan had been a prominent figure in US politics since the 1890s. A superb public speaker, he was said to have spoken to an estimated 5 million people across the nation in his first unsuccessful presidential bid in 1896. On that tour he made one of the most famous speeches in US history, assuring his fame.

Bryan's 'Cross of Gold' speech, as it became known, was a rousing call for the rights of the 'little man' and protection of the weak. This would become the central theme of Bryan's unwaveringly Christian political ethos running as the Democratic presidential candidate – unsuccessfully – in 1900 and 1908. When the Democrats eventually got elected in 1912, he served as Woodrow Wilson's Secretary of State and, after resigning in 1915, he went on to become a leading light in the Prohibition Party.

Bryan was short and balding. Like Simmons, Bryan habitually dressed in an old-fashioned frock coat, starched collar and bow tie. Bryan was an evangelical Christian who gave radio sermons and held weekly Bible classes. His position on the issue was one of literal interpretation of the biblical creation story. To Bryan the word of the scripture was *fact*. He was deeply committed to exposing what he saw as the fallacy of evolution. It was a threat to morality and simply a wilful misinterpretation of the obvious and irrefutable truth. As he put it:

> while I do not accept the Darwinian theory I shall not quarrel with you about it: I only refer to it to remind you that [unlike the Bible] it does not solve the mystery of life or explain human progress.[5]

Bryan was essentially a figure from a bygone age. As the journalist and commentator Walter Lippmann put it ten years before he appeared in Dayton, 'Bryan is what America was, his critics are generally defenders of what America has become.'[6]

Ranged against him and sponsored by the ACLU was no lesser a celebrity. Clarence Seward Darrow looked the total opposite to Bryan. Darrow stood at 6ft tall and had a mane of thick black hair. He wore suits distinguished by a good range of cigar burns and whiskey stains. Darrow was a self-declared libertarian and agnostic who staunchly opposed Prohibition. He practised what he preached and drank and partied into his eighties, marrying twice. He found it difficult to be faithful to either woman. But he allowed and expected others to be less than perfect too.

As the leading criminal defence attorney of his generation, Darrow represented some of the most notorious criminals, frequently managing to convince hostile juries to see cold-blooded murderers as human and allowing the defendants to walk free. When Darrow took on Scopes' defence, he was fresh from representing Nathan Leopold and Richard Loeb.

These two wealthy Jewish teenagers from Chicago admitted bludgeoning to death 14-year-old Bobby Franks, shoving his battered body into a culvert and returning home as if nothing had happened. Just for the sheer hell of it. Undaunted, in a twelve-hour summation, Darrow argued the pair had come from such rarefied, loveless and amoral backgrounds that they'd lost touch with reality and, thus, morality. To the shock of much of the US public, and lasting hatred of many, Darrow was able to spare the two the death penalty. But it made him a hated figure for the Klan.

The case brought Darrow into the sights of the Klan. It had everything they hated: urban crime, Jewish immorality and the depraved consequences of modern relativism, tolerance and lack of faith. What was more, it showed the boozy and irreligious Darrow as a true enemy of US justice. Klansmen made no secret of their enmity. At the height of that spectacular trial the *Chicago Evening Post* received a note reading, 'I can tell you, that members of the organization are in the court every day. They are determined to see that justice is done.' It was signed 'KKK'. A human skull and bones were left outside Loeb's parents' house, with a note from the Klan threatening to lynch their son if 'justice was not done'.[7]

The two lawyers didn't let the US public down. Bryan pontificated on the truth of the scriptures. Darrow needled him and tied his logic up in knots. As Darrow rather gloatingly wrote to his friend, the journalist and fellow 'infidel' to Middle America, H.L. Mencken, 'I made up my mind to show the country what an ignoramus he [Bryan] was, and I succeeded.'[8]

Under Darrow's forensic cross-examination, the answers Bryan gave became more and more desperate. Typical of their exchanges was when Darrow asked him if he truly believed that Adam and Eve were the first humans.

'Yes,' Bryan answered.

Since they were the only humans, Darrow pursued, did Bryan believe Adam and Eve were entirely alone in the Garden of Eden?

'Yes,' Bryan answered again, as Darrow knew he would.

Where then, Darrow asked, had Adam and Eve's sons, Cain and Abel, managed to find their wives?

To this, Bryan could give no plausible answer. He said he didn't question the Bible. It was fact, even if he didn't understand everything in it.

With merciless precision, Darrow continued tripping Bryan up and taking him apart for two hours. Was Eve truly created from Adam's rib? Could Old Testament characters really have lived for hundreds of years as the Bible claimed? How many people lived in Ancient Egypt?

Darrow jabbed. Bryan floundered. Darrow went in for the kill. Bryan would lamely answer, 'I have been too busy on things that I thought were of more importance than that', or 'I have all the information I want to live by and to die by.'[9]

Bryan's replies didn't play well to journalists packed into the airless courtroom. They were seeking snappy responses. It was courtroom drama at its most engaging, or humiliating, depending on where you stood. To some, Darrow was putting a 'slur on the Bible'. To others Bryan was simply a 'foolish' old man who should step aside.[10]

Then, just as it was truly heating up – literally, the court moved outside to get out of the sweltering rooms – the trial came to an abrupt halt. It had lasted only seven days. It ended because, after having demolished Bryan on the witness stand, Darrow changed Scopes' plea to 'guilty', effectively denying Bryan the right to a grand summation. Scopes was fined

$100 for violating the Butler Act. And that was that. It all seemed a bit of an anticlimax. All the drama, all the media frenzy, all the passionate cross-examination – for a $100 fine?

The real impact was more subtle. Darrow's public annihilation of Bryan's literalist interpretation of the Bible made many Americans reassess their own beliefs. Those who sided with the 'Great Commoner' saw Darrow as having tricked a great, but sick, man into confusion. Five days after the trial ended, Bryan died of a stroke. While his diabetes and other underlying health issues certainly contributed, his death was generally seen as resulting from his humiliation in the courtroom.

In Dayton, Ohio (a larger town of the same name), Klansmen burnt a cross in honour of 'William Jennings Bryan, the greatest Klansman of our time'. Ohio Grand Dragon, Clyde Osborn declared, 'We will take up the torch as it fell from [his] hand, for America cannot remain half Christian and half agnostic.'[11] A year later, Osborn called for a meeting of the Grand Dragons with the stated aim of starting 'a drive to save America from pagan civilization' with Klan-backed legislation 'to bring about compulsory Bible education' in all US schools.[12]

Edward Young Clarke, ever the opportunist, promoted 'the teaching of evolution ... taken out of schools' as the main selling point for his new fraternity, the 'Supreme Kingdom'. He tried to raise the temperature of the debate by demanding the resignation of five Atlanta school teachers and a professor at the University of Georgia who'd all taught evolution.[13] Both the fraternity and the threat failed. The moment had passed, and many in the Klan saw this rejection as a sign of the times.

Bryan's supporters argued Darrow and his supporters had used logic to attack faith, exposing their shallow and mercenary lack of principles. It was the clearest illustration yet of how powerless 'good' men were to stop the onward march of atheism and moral relativism. To those who supported evolution, Darrow's merciless dissection of Bryan had been a virtuoso display of how to make the case for logic's triumph over super-stition. It showed them how backward the 'rubes' of rural America truly were. It reinforced their rather smug views of themselves as superior and more sophisticated.

But it was those who sat on the fence who were probably most affected. And this had a huge effect on the Klan. For those Klansmen and -women who had resisted the more or less constant bombardment by stories of violence, in-fighting and scandal, this was yet another humiliation. It was yet another challenge to their faith in the righteousness of their cause. Inevitably some must have fallen by the wayside. Some must have seen this attack on the religious underpinnings of their faith in the leadership of the

Klan as fundamental. Just too much. But few saw it as a call to arms. Most saw it as a call to quit.

The most lasting effect of the Scopes trial for the order would be the convergence of the US media, who had been circling like vultures over the Klan for years. It was in that sweltering, cramped courtroom in Dayton, Tennessee, that the media finally landed on the dying Klan and began picking.

# CHAPTER 56

Perhaps the most important result of the Scopes trial was the revelation that the Klan had lost control of the press. In Dayton, Bryan, his supporters – and, by implication, the Klan – came across as yokels and hicks. The most widely read columnist of the day, H.L. Mencken, held forth with an arsenal of brilliantly sardonic nicknames for Bryan's supporters including: 'Morons', 'Peasants', 'Hill-Billies', 'Yokels', 'The Lower Orders', 'Immortal Vermin' and 'Ku Klux Theologians'. Although using less provocative terms than Mencken, the majority of the nearly 200 journalists and radio broadcasters who descended on Dayton over the next seven days agreed.

The trial was covered in over 2,000 national newspapers, weeklies and magazines. The Klan did not come off well. By 1923, as one paper claimed, the situation had reached a point that 'scarcely a newspaper is printed that does not daily blaze with indignation over the iniquities of the Klan'.[1] Indeed, some papers had been founded with the sole purpose of attacking the Klan.

One of the most famous of these papers was the weekly *Tolerance*. Founded by an alliance of Chicago's Jewish and Roman Catholic activists calling themselves the American Unity League in 1922, it was dedicated to 'outing' Midwestern Klan members. The editor, a feisty Chicago criminal attorney called Patrick O'Donnell, stated his mission in simple terms. He promised he would 'smash the Invisible Empire' and he set about that aim by mixing public exposure with mockery. By January 1923 *Tolerance* had published the names of over 4,000 members of the Klan under headings like 'Who's Who in Nightgowns' or 'The Koo Koos'.

Although the titles were light-hearted, the effects of that exposure often turned out to be dramatic. In June 1923, *Tolerance* announced the exposure of over 12,000 Klan members in Marion County, Indiana, alone.[2] After his name was published, the president of Chicago's Washington Park National

Bank was forced to step down when large numbers of customers began withdrawing their savings. Similar stories abounded: an undertaker was left 'nearly ruined', a salesman found his client base had evaporated. But *Tolerance* collapsed when it mistakenly 'outed' the chewing-gum millionaire William Wrigley Jr as a Klansman. Wrigley won a court battle in which he sued the paper for $50,000. The verdict bankrupted the paper and *The New York Times* pronounced the opposition to the Klan to be 'leaderless'.[3]

But it soon emerged that *Tolerance* was not alone in seeing the power of exposure. Throughout the 1920s the Klan inspired some of the most celebrated and damning journalism of the decade. In 1923, two of the three Pulitzer Prizes in journalism were awarded for attacks on the Klan. In 1922, 1926 and 1928 prize-winning pieces were awarded to journalists and newspapers who exposed Klan misdeeds, each highlighting a different aspect of growing anti-Klan sentiment in different parts of the country, further diminishing the reputation of the order. But it was the final article that effectively dismantled the Klan.

In Kansas, William Allen White, editor of the *Emporia Gazette*, decimated the Klan in a uniquely inventive way. The 'Sage of Emporia', as he was called, had discovered that local Klansmen had rented rooms to hold a convention in the town's swanky new Broadview Hotel. Since the only other group staying at the hotel that weekend was an Italian barbershop choir, it was a cinch for White to go down the list and pick off every Protestant and Nordic name as Klansmen. Following *Tolerance*'s model, White published the list of names that Monday, complete with the Klansmen's addresses.

White's constant attacks certainly contributed to the Klan's demise in Kansas. Here, although the Kleagles claimed to have recruited an estimated 100,000 members by 1923, the Kansas Klan soon faced effective mask laws and extremely negative publicity, especially over the violence in neighbouring Oklahoma. In his failed gubernatorial run of 1924, White's mockery and pointed jibes continued to damage the Klan, contributing to its stagnation and collapse in Kansas.

In 1925, partly as a result of White's constant barrage of negative press, the Kansas Supreme Court ruled that the Klan was neither a fraternity nor a benevolent society but, in reality, a commercial venture, and one that was not chartered to operate in Kansas. It did untold damage to the Klan and, surrounded by an increasingly hostile population, it limped on until 1927, when the US Supreme Court backed up the earlier decision about its status.[4]

The most striking of the many investigative pieces about the Klan during these years was the coverage of election day of the 1923 Memphis city elections. On 8 November, the *Commercial Appeal* ran two editorial attacks on the Klan and six articles on Klan violence. The day's headlines included

'Claims Klan Leaders Demanded Flogging'; 'Victim and Slayer in Klan Blood Feud in Atlanta'; and 'Klan is Boastful'. A front-page advert asked 'WHICH? The Men Who Wear the Hood or the Men Who Wore the Uniform?' The incumbent and anti-Klan mayor was re-elected – along with his entire administration.[5]

Even newspaper editors once known for having supported the Reconstruction Klan began to take a stand against them, as with Julian LaRose Harris and his journalist wife in the Georgia paper, the *Columbus Enquirer-Sun*. Harris had once advocated the effort to 'prevent the Negro from prevailing at the polls'. By the 1920s Harris targeted the local reincarnation of the Klan and claimed it was nothing more than a venal, corrupt and misguided 'travesty' of the 'virtues' of the original order.

Many Southerners had parents and grandparents who had supported the order in Reconstruction and fought to 'free' the South from the carpetbaggers and Yankees. They found the 1920s' version of dues-paying Klansmen to be cynical, hypocritical and posturing. Like others in the region, Harris condemned the leadership as exploitative, labelling them 'grafters, blackmailers [and] spy-chiefs'.[6]

But when Harris tried to persuade other Georgia editors to follow his lead and attack the 'Cluck-Clucks', he had little success. Pretty soon his moral stance was costing both readers and advertisers, and the formerly healthy paper began to run into debt. Some 150 Klansmen staged a parade in Columbus, marching past Harris' offices in an effort to intimidate him. Instead, he stepped up his efforts.[7]

Something of a lone voice, Harris continued to expose Klan misdeeds in Georgia. He revealed how Klansmen forced the Atlanta School Board to sack Catholic teachers. He published instances of night-riding against the local Black population and every threat levelled by the Klan against anyone they saw as wrongdoers. He exposed police links at all levels within the Georgia Klan. And for two years, he vainly tried to encourage the population to back the new city manager's 'clean-up' campaign, only to be defeated by the well-entrenched Klansmen sniping at him from City Hall.[8] He did everything he could to shine light on the Klan as what he called 'the biggest and most senseless fraud ever put over on the American people'.[9]

Each time he launched a story, other Georgia papers, seemingly supportive of the Klan, would smear him, publishing contradictory accounts while condemning him as a Yankee, although he was actually born and raised in Georgia. The constant sniping took its toll. When asked to comment on the Klan in 1941, he recalled, 'I had such a long and bitter fight with the Klan … that I have rather lost [the] taste for any discussion of that infamous organization.'[10]

It took until 1924, with many false dawns, before Harris helped administer the *coup de grâce* to the Klan in Georgia. Having exposed the Georgia governor as having links to the KKK, he went on to reveal Klansmen at all levels of Georgia politics. His investigations were so relentless and meticulous that eventually even the Klan-sympathetic Georgia papers turned against the order. His exposures coincided with blistering headlines about Stephenson's corruption in Indiana, exponentially sealing the deal against the Klan. In 1926 the *Enquirer-Sun* won the Pulitzer for Public Service for its 'brave and energetic fight against the Ku Klux Klan'.[11]

Other papers, like the *Indianapolis Times*, *Star* and *News* attacked the Klan, as did the *Indiana Catholic and Record*. Edited by the Irish-born Joseph Patrick Mahoney, the *Record* exposed the cosy relationship between the Republicans and the Klan. Mahoney's articles managed to unify Catholic opposition in the state and rallied opposition to Klan-backed candidates, like gubernatorial candidate Ed Jackson.[12]

If the *Record* exposed and countered the Indiana Klan's political shenanigans, the *Muncie Post-Democrat* went for its moral lapses. With the indomitable George Dale as editor, the *Democrat* attacked the Klan with unconcealed glee, if not total reliability. He took pride in tormenting the Klan. On his balding, weather-beaten head he always wore a hat which had a Klan bullet hole in it. He had a face that always had a smirk, which made him appear like he was just about to tell a joke, but he was no joke to the Klan. He rooted out Klan hypocrisy, publishing the whereabouts of Klan-owned speakeasies and brothels. He fearlessly exposed lawmen and judges on the Klan's payroll, even getting himself jailed by one Klan judge.[13]

On the western border of Indiana, in Vincennes, the local paper, the *Commercial*, also boomed out against Stephenson's licentiousness and corruption. The editor, Thomas H. Adams, was unusual: he was a Republican critic of the Klan. Adams was compared with St Paul, in his conversion to the cause and the subsequent strength and the passion of his anti-Klan crusade. But like his fellow editors at the *Record* and the *Post-Democrat*, Adams was largely ignored in the Pulitzer panel's investigations into the press' role in the exposure of the Indiana Klan's corruption.

While those papers spoke out, the *Indianapolis Times* was reluctant to enter the fray. In Indiana in the early 1920s, the Klan was a powerful enemy, striking back hard at any whiff of opposition. For example, in September 1924, the *Times* published an editorial 'Stop the Klan' only to be slammed as 'anti-Protestant' and 'venomous' in the Klan's *Fiery Cross*.[14] For once, the *Times* didn't back down: its September headline read, 'No Secret Order Shall Rule Indiana', and from 1 November it began to carry out its sporadic, but relentless, exposure of Klan violence and corruption.

Following the investigations of Stephenson's Black Boxes, the *Indianapolis Times'* efforts led in 1926 to Governor Ed Jackson being charged with bribery and Indianapolis mayor John Duvall being tried for corruption. The rot went deep. The chairman of the Indiana Republican Party went to prison and Judge Clarence Dearth of Muncie was impeached. The entire city council of Indianapolis resigned and more than half the Indiana legislature were exposed as Klansmen.[15]

The fallout was dramatic. The Klan in Indiana had come to power on the promise to clean up politics and then systematically corrupted Indiana politics for its own power and profit. Voters had been persuaded that Catholics corrupted politics and threatened US values, only to discover it was actually the Klan itself that was the real threat to their way of life.

Stephenson had promised wholesome values, especially the protection of the family. Readers learned that Stephenson had mauled and chewed poor Madge Oberholtzer as he raped her. Stephenson had encouraged Klansmen to raid speakeasies and gin joints, smash up stills and tar and feather bootleggers. Yet he was exposed as a violent alcoholic who took kickbacks from bootleggers. But perhaps most unforgivably, Stephenson had placed great stock on 'Klannishness' and loyalty to fellow Klansmen, only to threaten and betray all those around him when he was under attack. As a fellow prisoner would later say of the ex-Grand Dragon of Indiana, he was 'the most arrogant arsehole I've ever met in my life'.[16]

At its peak, the Indiana Klan had boasted it had up to a half a million members. By 1926, it is estimated that there were fewer than 15,000 dues-paying Klan-folk in the state. By the end of 1927, even that figure had halved.[17]

# CHAPTER 57

In May 1927 a Klan handbill was slipped through letter boxes and doors in the Jamaica district of New York's Fourth Ward. It spoke of a riot in which 'Native-born Protestant Americans [are] clubbed and beaten when they exercise their rights'.[1] The 'riot' it described was actually a free-for-all brawl between 1,000 fully robed, hooded and masked Klansmen and 100 policemen in the Jamaica district of Queens on Memorial Day, 1927.

The violence broke out when the police tried to enforce a city-wide ban on 'extraneous' parades. NYPD police commissioner Joseph Warren considered the Klan's marches to be unnecessary and not, as he put it, 'to do with our wars'.

The police came off as the losers, with the Klan having 'worsted [police] detachments ... on four separate occasions during its four-mile march'. By the time they reached their destination only one Klansman had been seriously injured – the unfortunate Mr Losee, a spectator who had his foot run over by a police car. But several policemen were cut and bruised by their scuffles with the Klansmen. A reporter interviewing the Jamaica Station desk sergeant the following day noticed the cop had a 'cauliflower ear and a nasty gash' on his face. Seven 'berobed marchers' had been arrested.[2]

While this was a fairly minor incident when it comes to Klan violence, it does highlight some interesting points. Firstly, this was 1927, not 1922 or 1924. As the 1920s drew to a close, the Klan made the headlines less and less frequently, and when they did it tended to be about their own corruption. Klan numbers were in free-fall across the nation, about 300,000 in 1927, down from several million only two years before, and by the end of the decade they'd sunk to below 50,000.[3] Yet the order could occasionally manage to raise 1,000 men, as on this occasion, to parade in New York. And New York City was never a Klan stronghold.

Secondly, in this incident, the Klan was engaging in violence in broad daylight and against the forces of law and order. Although the marchers were masked, the violence was highly visible and easily attributable, something the Klan had traditionally shied away from, usually carrying out its violence in the shadows and under the power of secrecy. This open violence indicates a shift in the core nature of the Klan; a few years earlier, those policemen would have been allies of the Klan – if not fellow Klansmen. But in 1927 the Klan would declare that 'Americans [were] assaulted by [the] Roman Catholic Police of New York City', condemning the city police force for being brutal agents of the Catholic Church.[4]

The Memorial Day incident is remembered today for another reason: reports of the events list one of the 'seven berobed marchers' arrested on that Memorial Day Monday as none other than Fred Trump, President Donald Trump's father. Donald Trump has long denied any connection.[5] Later investigations proved the man arrested lived at the same address as Donald Trump's father.[6] But though he had most certainly been among those arrested, Fred Trump was never charged or required to put up bail and was dismissed on a charge of 'refusing to disperse from a parade when ordered to do so'.[7]

The vehemence of Donald Trump's denial of his father's involvement reveals just how toxic an association with the Klan had become, even at the time of the incident. To the vast majority of Americans in 1927, let alone 2015, the Klan was no longer an acceptable organisation with which to be associated. It was no longer even worthy of ridicule as it had been a few years earlier when writers like H.L. Mencken mocked the greedy and opportunistic Klansmen as 'Koo Koos' and 'Cluck Clucks'. The order was now seen as a violent, corrupt and wicked organisation for ignorant and bigoted thugs. Those who remained associated with it were considered deeply suspect.

In 1926 the Klan organised another Washington parade in an attempt to recreate its peak display of power in 1925. It was, in every respect, a shadow of the previous year's display, attracting fewer than 10,000 people. But while membership was greatly reduced, the order was more dangerous. As the Klan lost membership, the order cared less about image, profitability and expansion and more about its extremist mission. The organisation's rhetoric became more intense and offensive since those left were more hardcore and less compromising in their beliefs, and it would not be the last time in the Klan's long history that such a change would occur.

In the mid-1920s, the organisation became a refuge for a small and tightly knit group dedicated to vehement racism, xenophobia and other forms of hatred. As their mission edged back towards the extreme, the order's chance at gaining real political power became less and less likely – and they increasingly celebrated that.

Yet when the Klan attempted to defeat Al Smith again, despite mounting an increasingly vocal and strident campaign, the Klan's rhetoric failed to move voters or the press. Banging on about clean government and Prohibition, the Klan's rhetoric of moral indignation sat uneasily with newspapers flush with stories of the order's hypocrisy and greed. The Klan was increasingly characterised as noisy, bigoted and irrelevant.[8]

New members tended to be outsiders. Gone was the image of 'everyday Klansfolk' who'd comprised the order's millions in the early 1920s. Gone were the aspirant middle-class fraternalists looking to escape the humdrum existence of middle management in Middle America. Gone, too, were evangelical Christians seeking in the Klan a path to cleaner morals and Prohibition. The Klan was even too much for a group that had a few years earlier been a staple of its membership, the second-hand Ford-driving working-class nativists seeking refuge from the corrosive everyday acids of modernity.

The rabid anti-Catholic, hardline racist and anti-radical Klan members arrested on Memorial Day 1927 were fighting for causes that were no longer mainstream. Such people had always been in the Klan, but now they were less diluted, and as a result they felt less constrained. The overt violence and distinctly anti-establishment rhetoric of the Memorial Day riot in Jamaica is indicative of a shift in the Klan's position as it went into decline, and this fringe quality would become even more pronounced as the USA headed into the turbulence of the 1930s and 1940s.

## PART VIII

# LOOKING FOR A CAUSE 1927–1946

'Yes.' He leaned forward. 'There's nothing some of the boys would rather do than kill a goddamned Jew or nigger!'

William True 'Kike Killer' cited in
*The New Masses*, 25 August 1936[1]

# CHAPTER 58

In the years following the Civil War, the Klan was born as an insurgency, with very specific aims – to return the South to its system of government which preceded the Civil War. In the 1920s it became a mass movement, a pick-and-mix fraternity of hate. It flared up, prospered and imploded with spectacular speed. Its message of racism and intolerance, combined with its hypocrisy, violence and greed ensured that the Klan would never again be acceptable to the US public in general. The Klan would never again be able to make significant money for its leaders. The Klan would always have a minority constituency. Nothing made this clearer than the scene in a Pittsburgh courtroom in 1928.

The Klan's national boss – or Imperial Wizard – Hiram Wesley Evans was attempting to claim damages from a wayward group of local county-level Klan bosses, or Grand Cyclops. Evans lost and Judge W.H.S. Thompson took the opportunity to rule that the Klan was an 'unlawful organization … destructive of the rights and liberties of the people'. He added, 'they can get no assistance here' in his court.[1]

Judge Thompson was summing up prevailing opinion. From the mid-1920s onwards, the Klan was seen by most Americans as a pariah. By 1928 hatred and violent feeling towards the Klan were detectable everywhere. Rallies became ever more violent as opponents and spectators attacked Klansmen as they marched.

The day Fred Trump was arrested, Memorial Day 1927, an angry crowd grabbed the memorial wreath laid down by Klansmen in Queens, New York, and threw it from the memorial. It landed in the middle of a hostile crowd who shredded it and hurled the remnants at the retreating Klansmen. Some threw rocks and even tried to run Klansmen down.[2]

At a July Klan parade in Grand Prairie, Texas, one Klansman was stabbed and two others were arrested in a riot.[3] In the autumn another riot broke out at a Klan parade in Geneva, New York, with one Klansman clubbed on the head and another arrested.[4] From 1927 onwards, it became increasingly frequent for the Klan to find those they tried to intimidate were fighting back.

Klansmen who turned up at the house of a Greek–American in Alabama with the intent of whipping him – a second time – for marrying a 'pure' American woman were met by shotgun fire and forced to flee.[5] In Virginia, Klan members bent on intimidating a 60-year-old sharecropper were shocked when he forcefully defended his home, killing one night-rider and wounding others. Worse, this sharecropper was seen as defending his home – and never charged. It was a forceful contrast with Ossian Sweet's experience in Detroit, only two years earlier.[6]

In other instances, Klansmen were prosecuted in the *local* courts. The enemies of the Klan no longer had to rely on federal courts to overcome local support. Nowhere was this change clearer than in the Klan heartland of Alabama. In one instance Klansmen were prosecuted for whipping a mentally challenged orphan who'd jeered at them at a parade. In another they were successfully brought to justice for flogging an elderly Black woman so severely she later died of her injuries. For this horrific crime, Klansmen involved received prison terms of up to ten years.[7]

Throughout the Alabama justice system, prosecutors were showing a new level of hostility towards the Klan. As early as 1925, Alabama's Attorney General, Charles C. McCall, set up Grand Juries in five rural counties to investigate the upsurge in Klan floggings. McCall called 125 witnesses to bring ninety indictments against the Klan for violence. McCall was himself a Klansman, but, fed up with the corruption, violence and lack of purpose of Evans' Klan, he sought change and these Grand Juries were very hostile to the Klan.

In former Klan-ridden Crenshaw County, circuit judge A.E. Gamble summed up the new hostility, describing the Klan as 'a cancer eating into the firm flesh' of Alabama's body politic. He instructed the jury to 'use the knife' to surgically remove the thirty-six Klansmen indicted. They included the Grand Dragon (state boss), a former Grand Titan (county-level boss) and two Exalted Cylops (Klavern bosses).[8]

However, he found this was still the South and the residual strength of the Klan held firm. The Alabama Grand Dragon used his connections and the debts owed to him. He and his cronies successfully pressured Alabama Governor (and Montgomery Grand Cyclops) David Bibb Graves to cut the funding for the Grand Juries and the prosecutions withered away.[9] Yet the affair had some impact. The state Attorney General was outraged enough by Graves' action to resign his own Klan membership, claiming the Klan was 'in the hands of men who had no respect for the law'.[10]

In the most rural areas of Alabama, few Klansmen were prosecuted. One judge advised a Grand Jury, the Klan 'stand for what you and I stand for … the Constitution … white supremacy … the chastity of women … the public school and education … not for anything unlawful'.[11] And Alabama was by no means unique. As we shall see, support for the Klan retreated into its traditional Southern, ex-Confederate heartlands, and there it would remain long into the 1980s.

It was white supremacy, plain and simple, that allowed the Klan to retain its strength in the South. According to the Tuskegee Institute there were twenty-one lynchings in the USA in 1930. Only one out of those twenty-one murdered was white. All except three of the atrocities took place in the South, with half taking place in Mississippi and Georgia. Even at the end of the 1920s, when lynchings were supposedly in decline, being Black in the South was dangerous. And as the Depression began to bite, that danger became even greater.[12]

# CHAPTER 59

The Sixth World Congress of the Communist International (Comintern) signalled a stepping-up of the desire to spread the Bolshevik Revolution into the USA. In Moscow in 1928, the Comintern decided to address the 'Negro Question' in the USA. The party was already committed to 'the liberation of the Negro race from all white oppression'.[1] The great and the good of the communist world gathered that summer and came to the conclusion that the oppressed Black population of the Deep South was one of the most promising groups for spreading communist revolution throughout the USA.

A Black delegate named James W. Ford spoke of the 'revolutionary possibilities of the Negro toilers as the most exploited element in America'.[2] Ford knew what he was talking about. His parents had moved to Birmingham, Alabama when he was a young man. There his father worked as a miner and his mother became a domestic. It was a hard life, but it was certainly better than what they'd left behind when they'd been driven out of their native Georgia. Ford's grandfather had been tortured and burnt alive, lynched for 'getting fresh with a white woman'. Then his young family had been chased out of the Black community in Gainesville.[3]

Like so many other frustrated Southern Black people, after serving on the Western Front in the First World War, Ford became a part of the Great Migration. He moved north to Chicago, where he applied for a job as a radio operator. He was denied the position because of his colour. After a series of menial jobs, Ford ended up working for the US Postal Service, a job he was ultimately fired from as a result of his efforts to unite Black and white workers in a single postal union.

By 1925 Ford was working full time for the Communist Party of the USA (CPUSA). Over the next several years he was sent to Moscow to attend various Cominterns. He studied the ethnicity policies of the USSR, noting their contrast with the treatment of Black people in the American South by local, state and federal governments. Settling in Harlem, the political, artistic and intellectual centre of Black culture in the 1920s, Ford became a well-known figure on the left. He dedicated his time to travelling around the USA, making rousing speeches on the treatment of the Southern Black population and linking it to imperial oppression in Africa and the West Indies.

In 1932, Ford was chosen as the running mate for the Communist Party's presidential candidate, William Z. Foster. To him and other Black activists, communism seemed a viable alternative to the main parties. When it came to the South, even the radical solutions offered by the then presidential candidate Franklin Delano Roosevelt and his New Deal seemed too little, too late. In the midst of the Depression, communism appeared the one beacon of hope. And reports leaving Communist Russia suggested the situation there was improving as the capitalist states sunk deeper into depression.[4] So why not emulate their system?

Sadly for Ford, Foster's presidential bid polled only a little over 100,000 votes. But those votes had a deeper consequence. Ever after, white supremacists would view Black activists and their supporters as 'communists'.

In 1930, the CPUSA followed Ford's advice of two years earlier, establishing a Southern regional office in Birmingham, Alabama. Their messages of inter-racial collaboration and class agitation were greeted warily by many of the region's labourers. They rightly feared that organising and representing Black workers would be seen as a challenge to the position of white workers.

The Klan was quick to strike back, at first just circulating threatening leaflets reading, 'Negroes of Birmingham, the Klan is watching you'. They advised them to 'Tell the Communists to get out of town' and gave a PO box where they could anonymously report communist agitation.[5]

As the Great Depression really started to bite, conditions for those at the lowest end of society suffered most. Those employed in coal mines and industry were the victims of wage cuts and redundancies, especially below the Mason–Dixon line. In 1931, Tennessee Coal and Iron cut wages by 25 per cent, and a year later they sliced off a further 15 per cent. They also drastically cut back the scale of operations, laying off large numbers of low-paid workers.

Most industries opted to reduce the working week instead, hoping that when demand returned, they would still have a workforce. Many resorted to three-day weeks and there were reports of steel workers and miners working fewer than one or two days a month.[6] The situation was dire.

There was little that Black workers could do. They were politically impotent. As radical as FDR's New Deal policies of financial assistance and unionisation were, poor Black workers slipped through the cracks. With the highest levels of illiteracy, and lowest levels of political engagement, they did not represent an attractive constituency for FDR's Democrat Party.

FDR needed to keep the ultra-conservative, deeply racist, Southern Democrat establishment on his side. Year after year, Southern Democratic senators had been voted in and they controlled some of the key committees. It would have been political suicide for FDR to go to war with these grandees, especially over the plight of the disenfranchised Black Southerners. FDR knew these senators could freeze vital funding, delay reforms and obstruct relief. So FDR made wonderful speeches while, in reality, doing very little to resolve the dire problems of the region's poorest Black workers.

Unlike their white counterparts, Black workers could not even rely on the trade unions empowered by the New Deal. Existing mainstream trade unions would not represent them. Despite the National Industrial Recovery Act (NIRA) of 1933 instructing unions to open up to Black membership, Southern unions remained for white workers only. Any move to make them multi-racial would spell political disaster for any official who proposed it. As the president of the powerful Amalgamated Association of Iron, Steel and Tin Workers told his members, 'the union, of course, is not seeking to elevate the negro'.[7]

The communists were unimpressed. They held that 'Roosevelt compromises. He grants but small concessions to the working people, while making big concessions to [newspaper baron, William Randolph] Hearst, to Wall Street, to the reactionaries.'[8] As a result, many Black workers joined the CPUSA. It was one of the only organisations which would represent them, making communism a prime target for white supremacists. This was especially clear in Birmingham, Alabama.

Birmingham was the centre of the New South's drive for industrialisation. Its mines and steel works were meant to power the region's industrial revolution. Unsurprisingly, given its centrality to the region's economy, it was the first city to get a CPUSA office.

The hatred of communism ran so deep in white supremacist circles of the city, that in 1933, when orders came in banning the Birmingham PD from firing on unarmed CPUSA demonstrators, fifteen members of the department immediately resigned. It was not a coincidence that it also had a very active Klan, with probably the most powerful Klavern in the whole country. Klansmen from Robert E. Lee Klan No. 1 lit crosses outside the houses of known communists, beat up local communist activists and burnt effigies of CPUSA organisers. They swore that 'the Klan will either run communism out or will itself be run out' of Birmingham.[9]

All over the South, when communist activists agitated for Black rights, crosses were burnt and CPUSA organisers were beaten up and run out of town. In Dallas, Texas, masked Klansmen kidnapped and flogged two CPUSA activists who tried to represent local Black residents. But the true depth of the hatred and paranoia became apparent when a young Black theology student, Dennis Hubert, was shot dead in Atlanta. His 'crime' was that he'd observed and commented on three white women drunk in a park. Stories circulated that Hubert had been in local woods with the drunk white women, and had told a white eyewitness, 'You'd better take them women home.'

Hubert's 'uppity-ness' was blamed on local communists stirring up Atlanta's Black population and the Klan led efforts to bring them back into subservient compliance. They started with Hubert's family. His father, the Reverend Charles D. Hubert, had his house burnt to the ground. Tear gas bombs were thrown into a local Black church where the minister had given a sermon expressing solidarity with the Hubert family and an attempt was made to kidnap Hubert's father and his brother. Yet, in spite of the Klan's antics, a Georgia court convicted three white men for Hubert's killing.[10] Things had changed. The Klan could not always count on sympathetic courts.

The battleground was not limited to the city. Sharecroppers and tenant farmers suffered just as badly as the urban workers. Over-production; crashing commodity prices; natural disasters; the continued march of the boll-weevil – all combined to destroy Southern agriculture. Impoverished sharecroppers and tenants found themselves spiralling ever deeper into debt. Banks foreclosed. Mortgages were in arrears, or simply abandoned. Many were evicted, and their holdings sold. Others grimly struggled on. As one communist organiser put it, 'poverty, illiteracy, tuberculosis … malaria, starvation … that is the life story of the sharecropper'.[11]

Once again it was the communists who seemed to offer the only relief. While sharecroppers tried to unionise, they met with only regional success. The CPUSA backed campaigns to make sure the poor, illiterate tenants and sharecroppers were able to claim the subsidies offered by the federal government, as well representing them both locally and in Washington. They were militant. They fought evictions, used collective bargaining and organised strikes.[12]

As a result, they became targets for the Klan. A typical incident followed a meeting of some 200 Black sharecroppers in Camp Hill, Alabama. Police raided and dispersed under the white supremacist sheriff. Two days later the sheriff and his 'posse' shot a labour organiser. Lying mortally wounded in the road, the man still fought off his attackers, injuring the sheriff. The incensed deputies bundled the sheriff into a car and sped him to hospital, swearing to get revenge.

That night, Klansmen burst into the house of the organiser, placed a gun in the mouth of the barely living body in the bedroom and blew his brains out. Then they burnt down his house. Having mutilated his body, they took the mangled corpse and dragged it behind a car, before going on a spree of murder and arson. Local law enforcement arrested thirty-five of the Black sharecroppers. But the CPUSA and unions established local chapters all over rural Alabama with several hundred members. As was so often to prove the case, the Klan's brutality had served only to unite the sharecroppers.[13]

In Arkansas, CPUSA found that 'deputies, night-riders, vigilantes are the exploiters' answer to the croppers 'first move[s] to improve their living conditions'. Organisers were jailed with no charge for over a month in a flooded cell and beaten up upon their release. Two activists were dragged from a church service, pistol whipped by an armed gang carrying a rope and threatened with lynching. One activist was shot and another severely beaten by Klansmen. That same week a gang of forty Klansmen in full garb attacked the home of an elderly activist, the Reverend A.B. Brookins. They riddled his house with bullets, killing his sleeping daughter. The violence also spread to Mississippi where houses and churches were burnt down. Anyone associated with the CPUSA might receive death threats and beatings or be shot at and even killed.

Yet despite the violence, no one was prosecuted and no one, aside from the communists and their allies, defended the victims. As one activist saw it, 'The Federal government knows what is going on in Arkansas, and it wants nobody else to know about it, or to do anything about it.' But, 'Down in Arkansas we are fighters'.[14]

In Florida this battle between communists and unions and the Klan played out – with very different results. In 1935, the Klan went to war with Northern socialist agitators who'd come down to unionise immigrant workers in the citrus groves. In November 1935, three union leaders were then driven out to local woodlands where they were stripped, beaten with tyre chains, mutilated and tarred and feathered. Ten days later, one of the victims died. A Grand Jury indicted eleven men, including seven policemen.

The two surviving socialist activists claimed their tormenters were Klansmen, and newspapers in the urban North soon found evidence to back this theory, including the detail that the aggressors were in full Klan regalia as the beatings were carried out. The *Chicago Tribune* claimed that the four men indicted, who were not identified as policemen, were in fact Klansmen brought in from Orlando specifically for the planned attack.[15]

The *Boston Globe* claimed the police beat up the socialists because of their 'communist activities', not for the protection of white jobs but for their threat to expose an illegal gambling ring operated by high-up local politicians.[16] In other words, the Klansmen had been simply strong-arming it for the Tampa PD.[17] *The New York Times* took it even further, reporting that the presiding judge was in cahoots with the Tampa PD and insinuating that he was probably a Klansman.[18] Whether he was or not, five of the accused policemen were sentenced to four years. A year later they were acquitted by the Florida Supreme Court.

To those reading newspaper reports in the North, the Klan seemed increasingly associated with the Good Ole Boys of the South. To those reading newspaper accounts in the South, the Klan seemed connected with crime and corruption. North or South, most Americans simply saw the Klan as a violent, hypocritical, mercenary and outdated organisation.

That said, the clear and unequivocal connection between activists and communists had been made. In Klan circles the control and elimination of communism would remain one of their primary tasks.

# CHAPTER 60

The modern Klan emerged in the 1930s. It wasn't a mass movement. It couldn't attract millions of members. But Klansmen didn't seem to care about how their actions were perceived. Their language had few constraints. Having alienated most of their former supporters, by the 1930s the Klan was an extreme organisation and its priorities changed to suit its extremism.

Although anti-radicalism had been a strand of the 1920s Klan, its concentration on the eradication of communism would, from the 1930s onwards, develop into an obsession. It would bleed into, and feed off, the Klan's anti-Catholic and antisemitic beliefs. It would be central to their increasing militarism. It would lie behind their increasingly anti-establishment rhetoric. All of them were linked, and those links became strengthened by two events of the early 1930s.

The first of these was the election of FDR, in 1932. The Klan initially supported FDR, the Democrat, seeing him as a friend to the working man and perhaps the only feasible route out of the Depression. Klansmen even campaigned for FDR. But as the campaign reached its seemingly inevitable climax, and the true radicalism of FDR's New Deal began to emerge, the Klan turned hostile to FDR.

The problem seemed to centre around FDR's 'Brain Trust'. Assembled to create the policies which would become the centre of the New Deal, this group of three advisers – two Columbia University professors of law and one of economics – were all seen as linked with socialism, collectivisation and the USSR.

That stance had the effect of turning the Klan against FDR. As a Rhode Island Kleagle explained to his fellow Klansmen in 1933, he could no longer vote Democrat because he believed 'The New Deal has become communistic'. Klan speakers at a Virginia rally claimed FDR's administration had 'honeycombed Washington with Communists'.[1] Hiram Wesley Evans went even further. He called on the Klan to take part in a Redemption-style 'crusade', arguing they should lead it because of their 'record of heroic achievement'.[2] He also drew on the 1920s prejudices, pointing to FDR's campaign manager, the wily James Farley, as a Catholic, and warning Klansmen of 'Catholic control of American government and life'.[3]

Nor was it only communists and Catholics that were associated with FDR. A great deal was made of the appointment of 'the Jew [Henry] Morgenthau' to the Treasury. It was pointed out that the all-powerful Secretary of the Interior, Harold Ickes, had a Jewish background. Legally, the New Deal was protected by two dominant Jews, Felix Frankfurter and Louis Brandeis. When FDR recognised the USSR and appointed a Jew as the first US ambassador, Klan alarm bells rang. The New Deal turned into the 'Jew Deal' and even the blue-blooded archetypal WASP (a middle- or upper-class 'White Anglo-Saxon Protestant' American) FDR had his name morphed into the Jewish-sounding 'Rosenfeld'.[4]

At all levels of the New Deal bosses were accused of hiring Jewish lawyers and advisers. And no matter how tenuous the connections, the Klan and their allies made links to a plot revolving around Jewish–communist world revolution. The Klan-affiliated Knights of the Camelia condemned the Secretary of State, Cordell Hull, for his 'Jewess' wife. She was a Protestant, but had previously been married to the socialist journalist John Reed. Worse, they pointed out that, through her family connections to a Jewish bank, Hull promoted 'the Lenin–Trotsky Jewish–communistic revolution in Russia under which 30,000–60,000 Christians have been slaughtered'.[5]

This obsession with the 'Jewification' of government was linked to the second event that altered the Klan's trajectory in the Depression. It centred around nine Black teenagers in Alabama. The youngsters were 'riding the rails', jumping on and off moving freight trains, in Jackson County. Arriving in the rural town of Paint Rock on 25 March 1931, they were arrested on charges relating to a fight that had broken out between them and a group of white teenagers a couple of days before.

As the train was cleared by the local sheriff and his deputies, two young white girls also emerged. Ruby Bates and Victoria Price accused the youngsters of gang-raping them. There was little evidence other than the rather sketchy testimony of the two girls, but this was Alabama. The Black teenagers were charged with rape. They faced the death penalty. By April an all-white, all-male jury sentenced all except the youngest to death. He was 12 when the alleged incident took place and therefore a minor.

For the next five years, all-white Alabama juries repeatedly sentenced the teenagers to the death penalty, while the Supreme Court attacked Alabama's lack of adequate representation and the composition of its juries. Several of the teenagers were sentenced to death, reprieved, and re-sentenced to life-term sentences. One of the young men was killed by guards in prison. Another died in a prison brawl. Two had their charges dropped. The five remaining in prison were pardoned, individually, in the decades afterwards, until all of them were given posthumous pardons in 2013.

The Scottsboro Boys, as they became known, became a rallying point for both liberals and white supremacists in the 1930s. The communists sponsored their defence through their in-house International Labor Defense (ILD). A high-profile case, it had the power to further their cause in a way that no other case had. They organised marches. They held rallies with high-profile speakers. They organised letter-writing campaigns, inundating congressmen and government officials with information about the plight of the young men and pleas for clemency. They made sure the Scottsboro Boys became newsworthy and remained in the headlines.

The communists were not the only ones who fought for the young men. The NAACP hired Clarence Darrow, of Scopes fame. However, both the ILD and the NAACP secretly tried to cut out the other, while in public welcoming their contribution. The ILD wanted a cause which would help them gain popularity, and the NAACP did not want to be associated with communism. As one local paper put it, it was 'a nauseating struggle between the communist group and the negro society ... that selfish interests may be advanced through the capitalization of the episode'.[6] Disgusted by the NAACP's behaviour, Darrow backed out, leaving the ILD's legal team to fight the case all the way to the US Supreme Court, twice.[7]

On the other side opposition was united. White supremacists saw the issue as yet another instance of the bestial behaviour of the African American. The Scottsboro Boys proved white women all over the South were under threat. And no sooner had the nine been arrested than a lynch mob formed outside the Scottsboro jail. Although the Scottsboro sheriff called out the Alabama National Guard to defend the prisoners, the Klan continued to press for a simple, old-fashioned, lynching.

To the Klan there was no doubt the nine defendants were guilty of rape. They were Black, and two white women had made the accusations. To them, that was all the evidence any true Southerner would require. In May 1931, they sent a letter to the ILD's assistant secretary telling him that if he was just to:

> come on down to ... any Southern state and ask some white man to account to you why a rapist is under conviction and to be electrocuted and see the accounting you'll get. A necktie of hemp and your rotten carcass decorating a telephone pole or tree.[8]

But the Scottsboro case provided the Klan with another link to its traditions of hate. In a bizarre turn of events, the NAACP's white local attorney, Stephen Roddy, cracked under the pressure, killing his wife with an axe. It was indicative of the squabbles behind the defence team that the ILD had been sniping about Roddy's white supremacy connections for some time. They even claimed he was a dues-paying Klansman.[9]

Whether or not Roddy had been in the Klan, he was replaced by another local, white attorney. George W. Chamlee was described as a true Southern gentleman and, as befitted that tag, he was a mass of contradictions. The grandson of a decorated Confederate soldier, he'd spoken out in defence of lynching. At the same time, he was elected county solicitor by a coalition of African Americans and trade unionists. He was also notorious in his hometown of Chattanooga for being the only attorney willing to defend communist agitators on trumped-up charges of vagrancy.[10]

To Klansmen, for Chamlee to represent the Black 'rapists' made him a scalawag. He was a traitor to his Southern, white heritage. What was more, in court he worked with a Jewish communist, Northern ILD lawyer Joseph Brodsky. Klansmen insisted Brodsky was a carpetbagger. To those who wanted to read the situation this way, it was Reconstruction all over again. Even those who didn't necessarily agree with this interpretation warned that ILD and NAACP 'interference … would result in … organizations like the Ku Klux Klan … [indulging] in violent retaliation against the Negroes'.[11]

In fact, like the comparisons made with Reconstruction around the Frank lynching in 1915, the actual response was not terribly violent. In November 1932, after the conviction of the eight Scottsboro Boys, a CPUSA-organised protest was broken up with considerable violence by Klansmen. But other than that, the Klan largely blustered, leaflet dropped and threatened mayhem.

Nevertheless, the tragic fate of the young victims of Scottsboro polarised opinion in the South. Once again, the Klan had a constituency, however small, and however hated, that it could draw on. Yet, confirmed in its anticommunist, antisemitic and racist creed, the Klan could no longer claim to be national in its ambitions. It was now well and truly Southern, and it would remain predominantly in the South until the 1980s in spite of its attempts to break out.

# CHAPTER 61

In addition to the Depression, the rise of totalitarianism characterised the 1930s. The Klan used the threat of the Soviet Union and its expansive doctrine of world communism to recruit members. But this was only one side of the Klan's relationship with European dictatorships. If communism was the threat, fascism was the solution – and most especially Nazism. As early as 1930 a French commentator observed, 'The Ku Klux Klan are the fascists of America.' He had a good point. After the public relations train wreck of the late 1920s, fascism was one of the courses the Klan took as it struggled to recalibrate itself.[1]

When Hitler entered the German Chancellery in 1933, he did nothing to aid the revival of the Order of the Knights of the Fiery Cross, Germany's branch of the Klan. The Knights of the Fiery Cross had withered away in the late 1920s and its leaders had dissolved what remained in 1930.[2] Hitler probably saw the antisemitic, ultra-patriotic order as taking members away from the Nazi regime.

The Nazis had toyed with an alliance with the Klan in the 1920s, hoping to form what one fascist journal called a 'world-wide confederacy of Nordic races'. Or that was what the Klan mouthpiece *The Kourier* claimed in 1925.[3] At that time the Nazis were a paramilitary group of fewer than 30,000, dreaming of the overthrow of the German state. Friendship with the Klan meant the Nazis could tap into a membership in the millions. By 1934, when the positions were reversed, *The Kourier* was claiming the now only 10,000-strong Klan had put Hitler into power: 'The spark that fired Hitler and other German nationalists to build a new Germany may easily have been ignited by the example of the US Ku Klux Klan.'[4]

Unsurprisingly, as a major new player on the world stage, Hitler wanted little to do with an organisation that now had a putrid air about it – at least not in his early years in power. Nor was he particularly interested in establishing a support base in the USA, a nation he condemned as being 'half Judaised and the other half negrified'.[5] To Hitler, propagandising the USA seemed pointless.

This didn't mean Nazi supporters in the USA felt the same way. Within months of the Nazis coming to power, Americans joined the Swastika League, the Friends of Hitler, Teutonia and other pro-Nazi organisations. And most of them sought ties with the Klan. One prominent US Nazi, Leslie Fry, actually tried to *buy* the Klan from the cash-strapped Hiram Wesley Evans for $75,000. But before the deal could be struck, Fry fell foul of the US authorities on charges of sedition and had to skip the country.[6]

There was one organisation which had serious recruitment potential for the Klan: the Amerikadeutscher Volksbund. The Bund, as it was known, had been founded by Fritz Kuhn, a charismatic German-born devotee of Nazism. Kuhn was obsessed with Hitler, trying his best to *be* him. He closely studied and imitated the Führer's impassioned speaking style and wild hand gestures. He wore his hair in the same slicked-down side parting. For a while he even sported Hitler's trademark moustache. His image, however, was marred by thick-lensed, round-framed glasses, more reminiscent of Hitler's henchman, Heinrich Himmler.

A German veteran who'd won the Iron Cross in the First World War, 'Bundesführer' Kuhn somehow managed to rhyme his politics with the Klan's creed. In his thick German accent, he never tired of condemning 'Rosenveld's Jew Deal' and the damage it had done to the nation. He was rabidly anti-communist. He banged on about the problems the USA had as a result of its tolerance for race-mixing and the conspiracies of international Jewry.

Kuhn managed to fuse the hyper-German patriotism of the Nazis with the Americanism of the Klan. He celebrated Adolf Hitler alongside George Washington, lauding both as the founders of their nations. At rallies, goose-stepping, brown-shirted, paramilitary Bund members carried swastika banners next to the Stars and Stripes. The Bund had even domesticated the stiff-armed Nazi salute, replacing '*Sieg Heil*' with 'Free America'.

Many of the rising stars of the Bund and other pro-Nazi groups had actually been Klansmen in the 1920s. William Dudley Pelley, leader of the Silver Shirts, a powerful fascist paramilitary movement, had dabbled with the LA Klan. Georgia journalist Eugene Sanctuary, the editor of one of the leading pro-Nazi newspapers, *X-Ray*, had been a Kleagle in Indiana.

Given these connections, it is hardly surprising that there were persistent rumours that the Klan was planning a formal alliance with the Bund. The most informed of these rumours came from John C. Metcalfe, a reporter for the *Chicago Daily Times*. He and his brother James had gone undercover for most of 1937, becoming active members of the Bund and gaining the trust of the highest-ranking leadership of the group. The following year, John Metcalfe testified to Congress that 'the Bund was seeking to consolidate' with the Klan to create a 'Nazi-Fascist movement' all over the USA.[7]

Unusually for the Klan, in the 1930s the most enthusiastic reception came from the metropolitan areas of the North. In the heartlands of the South, the traditional Klansfolk could not overcome their mistrust of the Bund's foreign nature. However, in Chicago, Milwaukee and especially New York, with their large immigrant German populations, the amalgamation of the two orders was more welcome. This was especially apparent when the Nazis were at play.

In May 1937 on Long Island, the Bund opened a summer camp. It was based on a Nazi model that mixed Nazi propaganda, rigorous exercise and fresh air. Camp Siegfried offered German food, German beer and the chance for Bundfolk to socialise with people of their 'own race'. In July the Bund opened a second camp in New Jersey. The idea was the same, but the scale was far grander. Camp Nordland could host events for up to 10,000 and in August 1940 it was the venue for a joint summer rally of Klan and Bund members.

The event was organised by the New Jersey Grand Dragon Arthur Bell. In his welcome speech, Deputy Bundesführer August Klapprott eulogised the meeting's demonstration of 'the common bond' and argued that the 'principles of the Bund and the Klan are the same'. It was a spectacle. A Klan fiery cross was burnt next to a swastika. A couple were married in a Klan wedding. Nearly 3,500 hooded Klansmen mingled with brown-shirted Bundsmen, singing German marching songs. It all seemed very cosy. But it wasn't.[8]

While this celebration of Nordic America was going on, protesters along Nordland's perimeter fence chanted 'Put Hitler on the Cross', and sang the 'Star-Spangled Banner'. They jeered and heckled the uniformed fascists and hooded Klansmen. More importantly for the Klan, the event had been condemned by the national leadership before it even took place. Evans' replacement as Imperial Wizard, James Colescott, had denied official permission for the rally, and told Bell that the objectives of the Klan and the Bund could never align.

Colescott had never been enthusiastic about the Klan's ties with the Nazis and, by 1940, it was obvious that the tide was turning against the Nazis in the USA. He made press statements telling the press there was 'no common ground … on the part of the Bund and the Klan' and that there was 'absolutely no connection in any way, shape or form between the German–American Bund and the Klan'.[9] But the damage had already been done.

News of Nazi aggression, refugees coming from Europe and an openly hostile Democratic administration, as well as effective British propaganda, all contributed to an increasingly hostile US attitude to the Nazi regime. By 1937 the FBI had already investigated the Bund. At that time it stated the Bund was not in breach of federal laws, but the pressure was on. In October 1940, the House Un-American Activities Committee (HUAC) was investigating the putative Bund–Klan merger.

HUAC, or the Dies Committee, was chaired by the hardline, white supremacist, vehemently anti-communist Texas congressman Martin Dies. Dies and his cronies in HUAC had little interest in probing the Klan. They were far more enthusiastic about examining connections between communists and unions and having a bash at FDR supporters, so the Klan was able to walk out of the committee rooms pretty much unscathed. The Bund, however, was definitely tarnished and Colescott stepped up his efforts to distance the Klan from the Nazis. It was too late. The link was already in the public consciousness and it seemed no amount of press releases could break it.

The storm broke when Hitler declared war on the United States in December 1941. The Klan's enemies circled like vultures. Colescott desperately tried to break all ties with the Nazi regime, playing up the Klan's patriotism. HUAC called Colescott in to testify, but though the committee gave him an easy ride, the Klan's enemies relished the squirming sycophancy the Imperial Wizard was forced to adopt. They loved it when Colescott revealed that the organisation had fewer than 10,000 members and that in some states it had no members at all.

Many of the most influential members of the political establishment saw the Dies Committee's investigation as a whitewash. First Lady Eleanor Roosevelt compared both the Dies Committee and the Klan to the Gestapo. The Black newspaper *The Nation* agreed, arguing it would be 'as logical and just as fruitful to have the Klan investigate the [Dies] committee' as the other way around. Congress, it seemed, was as hostile to the Klan as its enemies in the press.[10]

The Klan seemed to have reached rock bottom, but things were about to get a great deal worse.

# CHAPTER 62

The year 1944 was a bad one for the Klan, so bad, that by the year's end it ceased to exist.

It all stemmed from 1 July 1916, when the Ku Klux Klan was made into a corporation in Georgia. This incorporation entitled the Klan to 'Legal Personhood', granting the organisation the same legal rights as a citizen of the USA. As a corporation, the Klan could sue and be sued. It could take out loans, mortgages, buy and own real estate and do almost anything a US citizen could do. But, of course, those rights came with obligations. Most importantly to the Klan in 1944, the obligation to pay taxes.

Under the terms of its 1916 incorporation in the state of Georgia, the Klan had claimed it was 'A Tax-Exempt Fraternal Beneficiary Society'. As a fraternal, benevolent order it wasn't subject to the Corporation Tax that had been introduced in 1909, nor to the 1915 Income Tax. To qualify for these exemptions all the Klan was asked to do was provide evidence to the commissioner of Internal Revenue that it had a right to exemption. Apparently, the Klan never did this. At the time, nobody seemed to take much notice.

Since its foundation in Pulaski, the Klan had been deliberately modelled on other fraternities, most especially the Freemasons. It had always claimed it was a fraternity. It granted charters to new Klaverns, just like a fraternity. It had the rituals of a fraternity; it had the hierarchies of a fraternity; and the costumes, oaths and ceremonies of a fraternity. For nearly ten years after its incorporation, it seemed to be accepted nationwide that the Klan *was* a fraternity.[1]

Then, in 1925, the Kansas Supreme Court ruled that, despite its protestations, the Klan was not a fraternal organisation, nor was it benevolent. The ruling was upheld by the US Supreme Court in 1927, rendering the Klan, legally, nothing more than a commercial venture. The Supreme

Court refused to grant the Klan a charter to operate in Kansas.[2] The Klan was not considered a fraternity in the eyes of the federal government, and more importantly the Internal Revenue. In 1944, this would have disastrous consequences for it.

Although the wartime Klan continued its anti-union activities – most notably in Birmingham, Alabama, and the fruit groves of Florida – it attempted to show its patriotism. But the order's inherent intolerance, bigotry and violent rhetoric sat very uncomfortably with the 'Four Freedoms' laid out by FDR in his January 1944 State of the Union Address.[3] How could the USA provide leadership for the brave new post-war world's civil and human rights when Klansmen were still lynching, rioting and threatening union organisers and Black activists? To the Roosevelt administration – they couldn't.

So, FDR drew on the experience of the Internal Revenue Service (IRS) and Al Capone. For years the authorities tried unsuccessfully to bring Capone to justice. Finally, a team of financial investigators had managed to convict Capone of Income Tax evasion and get him sentenced to eleven years in prison. It was a shrewd move. While some, including Capone, felt it would be oddly immoral for the IRS to collect legal taxes from illegal money, the team managed to convince both the jury and the US public that justice had been done. They simply asked, why should the average Joe pay his way when criminal braggards like Capone seemed untouchable?[4]

In April 1944, Imperial Wizard James Colescott received an unwelcome shock 'when the Revenuers knocked on my door and said they had come to collect three-quarters of a million dollars that the government just figured out the Klan owed as taxes earned during the 1920s'.[5]

The raid was the result of months of work by Marion Allen, the Bureau of Internal Revenue collector for Georgia. The Klan had not filed any tax returns, arguing it was exempt, so the investigation had used the distinctly unreliable records of the Kleagles. From these, Allen calculated that the 20 per cent tax rate would be due on the Klan's income between 1921 and 1926, leaving it liable to a tax bill of $685,305.[6]

Colescott called a secret meeting of all the Grand Dragons (state bosses) in Atlanta. They voted unanimously to accept a proposal that 'repealed all decrees, vacated all offices, voided all charters, and relieved every Klansman of any obligation whatever'.[7] What they agreed to was essentially the disbanding of the Ku Klux Klan, with Colescott ruefully adding, 'Maybe the Government can make something out of the Klan – I never could!'[8]

It was a momentous decision, but Colescott was at pains to say it did not mean the end of the Klan. As he told *The New York Times* that June, it was merely 'suspended ... and could reincarnate at any time'.[9] Colescott was right. The Klan would 'reincarnate' several times after 1944, and to many observers there seemed to be little difference whether it had officially disbanded or not.

In reality, the disbanding was nearly fatal. This was soon apparent. In October 1945, Dr Samuel Green, an Atlanta obstetrician, held a cross-lighting ceremony on Stone Mountain, announcing the rebirth of the Georgia Klan. In May 1946 he received the tax demand for $685,305, plus the interest which had accrued since 1944. The message was clear: anyone wanting to found a Klan would have to pay that bill first, with ever-increasing interest.

So how is it there is a Klan in existence today? Well, actually, there isn't. There is no 'Ku Klux Klan'. To use that name, the KKK, the founder(s) would need to clear the tax bill, with compound interest – which would amount to several million dollars. Unlike their wealthy 1920s ancestors, Klansmen nowadays don't tend to be rich. What they do have, and what Green was forced to utilise, is a legal loophole. He founded the Association of Georgia Klans (AGK) and so avoided the tax liability. Others followed his example. In nearby Florida, home to the most successful Klan of the 1930s and 1940s, state officials granted a charter to the Knights of the Ku Klux Klan of Florida (KKKKF).

So disparate, disjointed and fractured in spirit and in name, the Klan limped on.

But in 1944 the organisation known as the KKK ceased to exist.

## PART IX

# RETURN TO THE HEARTLAND 1944–1968

You know what the NAACP stands for? Niggers, Alligators, Apes, Coons, and Possums.

>Stump speech of Paul Johnson in his successful bid
>for the Governorship of Mississippi, 1962

# CHAPTER 63

In 1944 *The New York Times* ran a story asserting that in 1922 in Jackson County, Missouri, Grand Kleagle Harry Hoffman had sworn in a recently elected judge as a Klansman. The judge was an unusual Klansman. He was connected to the local political boss, 'Big Tom' Pendergast, and the Klan was the sworn enemy of political bossism and machine politics. Pendergast was also Catholic.[1] However, that's not the most interesting part of this story. The judge went on to hold much higher office and was running for vice-president of the USA when the story broke in 1944. In April 1945 he would become the 33rd president of the USA. His name was Harry S. Truman.

Truman's own comments illustrate how much the nation's views had changed over the twenty years since he joined the Klan. Truman's grandparents had been slave-holders and he admitted being brought up in 'a violently unreconstructed Southern family' of 'Lincoln haters'. In 1911 he wrote an infamous letter to his fiancée, Bess, telling her 'one man is just as good as another as long as he's honest and decent and not a nigger or a Chinaman. ... It is race prejudice, I guess.'[2]

Thirty-six years later, Truman assured the NAACP, 'There is no justifiable reason for discrimination because of ancestry, or religion. Or race, or color.'[3] Truman's actions as president show that he seemed to mean these words. A year after his speech to the NAACP, he sidestepped a hostile Congress to desegregate the military by Executive Order. He'd already established the Fair Employment Practices Commission in 1945 and appointed a Committee on Civil Rights. This committee produced a widely circulated report entitled *To Secure These Rights* which spelled out his administration's plan for ending what Truman saw as complacency towards civil rights.[4]

The executive branch was not alone in taking actions to move a civil rights agenda forward. In 1944 the Supreme Court ruled that all-white Southern primaries were unconstitutional, stipulating that the votes for a Democratic candidate in any state with white-only voters would not be counted. In 1948 it extended the remit of the Fourteenth Amendment to include the protection of individual rights from violation by non-elected individuals.

That decision effectively reversed the infamous Cruikshank ruling which had protected the perpetrators of the Colfax Massacre of 1873. Since then, it had proved to be one of the most important legal shields the Klan used to protect itself from federal prosecution for its atrocities. The court began making other landmark decisions, slowly dismantling the legal sanctions supporting Jim Crow and segregation. One of the most important actions the court took was to eliminate racially based exclusions from juries. State resources, including the studying of law, became available to non-whites. These decisions, in turn, led to a series of landmark civil rights cases that would shake the very essence of segregation.

These decisions garnered a good deal of opposition. Klans began to emerge in the South as the white elites found the basis of their dominance under threat. They were careful not to call themselves 'the Ku Klux Klan' and risk incurring the tax bill and rapidly escalating interest of the 1944 IRS decision.

Grand Dragon Samuel Green's tax loophole seemed to be a success. Through his Association of Georgia Klans, he gathered some 2,000 members on the hallowed ground of Stone Mountain. Under a burning cross, Green melodramatically announced, 'We are revived!' and, in the tradition of Klan exaggeration, claimed a membership in the tens of thousands.[5]

In June 1946 the Alabama Federated Knights of the KKK (FKKKK) was founded by roofing contractor and veteran Klansman William Hugh Morris. By September, they'd received a state charter. In Florida, the state granted a charter for a group known as the Knights of the Ku Klux Klan. In West Virginia an ambitious butcher, Robert Carlyle Byrd, wrote to Samuel Green telling him that, as a 'former kleagle of the Ku Klux Klan', he felt 'The Klan is needed today [1946] as never before and I am anxious to see its rebirth in West Virginia ... and in every state in the Union'.[6]

Compared with the numbers of the 1920s, the late 1940s Klan's were negligible. But like the Klan of the 1930s, they compensated in violence. In 1946 alone, the Georgia AGK held cross burnings, burnt down a Black church and carried out bombings, beatings, numerous floggings and at least four fatal shootings. They even mounted what the FBI called a 'well-organized plot' to kill the anti-Klan governor Ellis Arnall.[7]

In the years that followed, Alabama hosted various equally violent Klan groups that targeted union organisers and Black social organisations all over the state. In one notorious incident, they even raided a Black Girl Scout clubhouse. But in the summer of 1947, the Alabama Klan launched one of the most violent periods in US history. Hoping to preserve Birmingham's reputation as 'America's most segregated city', they committed over twenty racist bombings and arson attacks between 1947 and 1951, and thirty more between 1951 and 1964. The city was quickly dubbed 'Bombingham' in the national press.

In part, the Klan was still able to prosper in the Deep South because of a long-standing representation in both politics and law enforcement. One of the key figures was supremely racist Georgia governor Eugene Talmadge. In 1946 Grand Dragon Samuel Green bragged he had mobilised over 100,000 voters to get Talmadge re-elected for a third term. In return Talmadge appointed a well-known Klansman as the head of Georgia's Bureau of Investigation and pardoned a Klansmen convicted of whipping a Black union organiser to death. *Life* magazine reported that Governor Talmadge had also justified his *own* flogging of a Black man by saying, 'The Apostle Paul was a flogger in his life.' Unimpressed, *Life* compared Talmadge with the Gestapo and reported to its largely Northern readership that the governor 'deliberately stirs up racial hatred'.[8]

In 1946 'Ol Gene' lived up to that reputation, running his campaign on planks so deeply committed to segregation that he even promised to 'put inspectors at the state line to look into every sleeping car and see there's no mixing of the races'. On one infamous occasion, Talmadge riled up an audience so much that when he finished his speech they rushed off and burnt down a Black church. And when asked about his strategy for keeping the Black population away from the polls, he simply handed the questioner a note with 'pistols' scrawled on it.[9]

The police were just as racist. In Atlanta, Klavern No. 1 held a special meeting for a local police officer John 'Trigger' Nash. For killing his thirteenth Black man 'in the line of duty', Nash was given a standing ovation. He told the gathered Klansmen that he hoped he 'wouldn't have all the honour of killing all the niggers in the South and … [that] the people would do something about it themselves'.[10]

There is no doubt the epidemic of bombing in Birmingham, Alabama, could not have happened without the support of the police. Under the watchful eye of the Commissioner of Public Safety, the notorious Eugene 'Bull' Connor, segregation was brutally enforced.

On one occasion Connor ordered an audience listening to the then First Lady Eleanor Roosevelt to separate into white and Black areas. On another, he arrested a visiting US senator from Idaho because this future vice-presidential candidate attempted to address the local Southern Negro Youth Congress.[11] But more than this, Connor allowed the Klan bombings to occur by ignoring the actions of their leading bombmaker, the odious 'Dynamite Bob' Chambliss.

As a quarryman, Chambliss knew explosives. He was also a lifelong Klansman who had joined a variety of splinter Klans since the 1944 Klan disintegration. But most importantly Chambliss was a psychopath dedicated to destroying the town's growing Black population. Bombing an unspecified number of Black homes in Birmingham endeared him to Commissioner Connor. He was even given work servicing vehicles in the police motor pool. Most astonishingly, Connor had Chambliss, explosives and all, ferried to bomb sites *by his own squad cars*.[12]

While the Klan grew in some areas, the general trend in the decade after the Second World War was one of decline. The viciousness of the Klan in Georgia and Alabama over this period should be seen more as a desperate rearguard action than an organised campaign of terror. It was a response to power and influence slipping away from them, not growing.

The Klan lost a powerful ally in Eugene Talmadge when 'Ol Gene' died of liver disease in December 1946. The following year his successor Ellis Arnall revoked the charter of Green's AGK. Klans in New York, California, Kentucky, New Jersey and Wisconsin would suffer similar fates. FBI investigations into the Klan were taking place in Georgia, Alabama, Florida, Mississippi, Tennessee, Michigan, New York and California.

Even in Alabama, Klansmen were indicted in the late 1940s and early 1950s with increasing frequency. In 1949 seventeen Klansmen in Jefferson County were indicted on forty-four charges, including sexual assault, burglary and flogging. Three of the defendants were cops. Another was Dynamite Bob Chambliss. The charges couldn't be made to stick – but it was only a matter of time before that changed too.

It seemed the times were a-changing, even in the Deep South.

# CHAPTER 64

The year 1955 saw the killing of a 14-year-old boy from Chicago. It was an event so appalling, so vicious and so senselessly shocking, many would come to see it as one of the starting points of the US civil rights movement.

In August 1955, seventh-grader Emmett Till took his second trip south to Money, Mississippi, a small hamlet of cotton sharecroppers in the Delta region of the state. Till was visiting relatives – his great-uncle, aunt and a whole bunch of cousins of around his age.

Visiting his country cousins, Emmett played the sophisticated city boy. Full of youthful devilment, one evening Emmett and the boys skipped the preaching at the local church by his great-uncle, Moses Wright, and went to the local grocery store to buy sweets. The owners were a young white couple, Roy and Carolyn Bryant.

On the way there, Emmett teased his farm-boy cousins about their backwardness. He bragged that in Chicago he attended an integrated school. Pulling a photograph from a new wallet his mother had given him, Till showed them a picture of his classmates, who were indeed both Black and white. He pointed to one particularly pretty white girl and said she was his girlfriend. Emmett's cousins were amazed – and not a little horrified.

Fired up with teenage bravado, Emmett wolf-whistled Carolyn Bryant who was serving alone that day in the store. Bryant would later claim Till 'came in our store and puts his hands on me with no provocation'.[1] The boys left the store very fearful that first night, but several nights later they had forgotten it, until the small hours of the sticky Southern night of Sunday, 28 August, when Roy Bryant appeared at Emmett's great-uncle's house, where the teenager was staying.

With Bryant was his half-brother, 'J.W.' 'Big' John William Milam, who stood ar 6ft 2in and weighed 235lb. He'd served in Europe in the war and apparently specialised in brutal close-quarters hand-to-hand combat. After leaving the army, Milam had taken up work renting field hands to the local planters, a job that drew on his toughness, as well as his inherent racism.

On that fateful night, Milam stood outside Preacher Wright's door waving a pistol and demanding that Emmett be handed over to them. Faced with armed, white men in the dead of night, Emmett's relatives brought the boy out.

It would be the last time they saw him alive.

The 14-year-old was thrown into the back of Milam's Chevy and taken to a tool shed near Milam's house where he was tortured for several hours. The FBI released details of Emmett Till's autopsy in 2007. It revealed he'd suffered broken legs and wrists and skull fractures so serious the bone simply fell to bits during the examination.

As dawn broke, Bryant and Milam again bundled Till into the Chevy and drove him to a lonely spot on the bank of the Tallahatchie River. They forced him to strip. Milam calmly walked up and shot Till behind the ear. He was almost certainly dead before hitting the ground. Using barbed wire, they bound the boy's broken body to a 74lb metal fan they'd stolen. The two men rolled Emmett Till's weighted body into the river and returned to Milam's house. There, they destroyed Emmett's clothes and constructed alibis.

Three days later Emmett Till's mutilated body floated to the surface of the Tallahatchie River, 8 miles downstream from the scene of his execution.

Three weeks later, Bryant and Milam appeared in court facing charges of first-degree murder.

Some 400 people watched the trial in the historic red-brick, Romanesque courthouse in the county seat of Sumner. It was a media sensation. It had sex, it had violence, it had mystery and it was *pure* Southern bigotry. And it was the first trial in which the nation had the opportunity to view the state of justice in the 'Segregation-Era Deep South'.

According to John Herbers, who covered the trial for United Press Associated, the 'big, fat, obscene-talking' sheriff of Tallahatchie County, Clarence Strider, was less interested in seeking justice than making sure that his courtroom remained totally segregated. To this end, he tried to prevent Black Detroit congressman Charles Diggs from entering the courtroom. Strider segregated the Black press to a makeshift desk – a card table. Each morning, as he walked past, Strider greeted them with a cheery, 'Hello Niggers.'[2]

During this period when more white offenders were brought to trial in the South, variations on the court proceedings of the Till case became a stand-ard script. The state produced compelling evidence against the defendants.

Family members like Moses Wright, Emmett's great-uncle, would testify with quaking voices in spite of the obvious danger. Standing and pointing at Bryant and Milam, Wright swore with absolute conviction that they were the men who took Emmett from his house.

Willie Reed, a young, local, Black sharecropper, also showed tremendous courage, testifying in a barely audible voice that he'd heard screams and the sounds of beating coming from Milam's shed that night. He told of how Milam had come out of the shed strapping a .45 pistol to his hip and demanded if Reed had heard anything. Not surprisingly, Reed lied to Milam, saying, 'No.' Immediately after their testimonies, both Wright and Reed fled separately for Chicago. Wright left behind his home, his car and all of his unharvested cotton crops. In Chicago, Reed was hospitalised for a nervous breakdown.

Emmett's mother Mamie testified with complete confidence that the body pulled from the river was indeed her son. She would win national sympathy when she refused to allow her son's torture to be disguised by the undertakers. She insisted on an open coffin that displayed Till's hideous injuries. It is estimated some 7,000 mourners attended the funeral in Chicago. It was a moment that sparked such outrage, such horror, its role in the civil rights movement is difficult to exaggerate.

Yet back in the courtroom, the white defence attorneys called Mamie Till's certainty into question by putting the local embalmer on the stand. He claimed the body was too badly decomposed to be identified. Later it emerged he never saw Emmett Till – alive or dead. The undertaker who collected the body from the riverbank told the jury he'd removed a ring from the grossly swollen hand. It was later identified by Mamie Till as belonging to Emmett.

But the doubt planted by the embalmer was reinforced by a local doctor and Sheriff Strider, who both claimed the body was in such a bad state of decomposition it was impossible to tell the race of the victim, let alone identify it. Yet Strider had been certain enough at the time of discovery to write 'colored' on the death certificate and send the corpse to a Black funeral home, even mentioning Emmett's ring.[3]

Injustice was swift in Mississippi in 1955. The trial began on Monday, 19 September. By Friday, 23 September, after an hour's deliberation, the all-white, all-male jury returned a verdict of 'not guilty' on both men. Milam and Bryant never even took the stand. The jury later admitted they could have delivered their verdict quicker, but, aware of the publicity surrounding the trial, they wanted it to appear that they'd struggled to reach a decision, so they'd sent out for some Cokes.

Incredibly, only six months after the trial, Milam and Bryant tacitly admitted that they'd carried out the killing. The Iowa-based bi-weekly

*Look Magazine* paid $3,100, to be divided between themselves and Carolyn Bryant, for their side of the story. *Look* also guaranteed that their comments wouldn't be directly attributed. But in reality, anyone familiar with the trial could clearly see who'd said what and it appeared that Milam was only too keen to tell William Bradford Huie how he'd stood up for the sanctity of Southern womanhood.

As Milam saw it, 'When a nigger gets close to mentioning sex with a white woman, he's tired 'o livin'. Safe in the knowledge that the Constitution's 'Double Jeopardy' protection left them immune from prosecution for the murder, he added, 'I'm likely to kill him.' Then he went on to claim he'd asked the 14-year-old, 'You still "had" white women?' When Till defiantly answered 'Yes', Milam saw red. As Huie melodramatically reported, 'That big .45 jumped in Big Milam's hand. The youth turned to catch that big, expanding, bullet at his right ear.'

Huie was left with the feeling that 'the white people in Mississippi either approve [of] Big Milam's action or else they don't disapprove enough to risk giving their "enemies" the satisfaction of a conviction'.[4] And those 'white people of Mississippi' knew who the enemies were, and they were no longer isolated and terrified pockets of rural Southern Black people. With the horrific murder of a 14-year-old, the cruelty of the white supremacist South had over-reached itself. Till's murder and the travesty of the trial was about to spark a war against white supremacy in the South and, the year before, the US Supreme Court had drawn the battle lines. The conflict was going to be over the sacred Southern institution of the segregation of the races.

# CHAPTER 65

In 1896 the US Supreme Court had ruled in *Plessy v. Ferguson* that the racial segregation in seventeen US states did not violate the guarantee of 'equal protection of the law' established with the Fourteenth Amendment. With the *Plessy v. Ferguson* decision, a doctrine of 'separate but equal' had been enshrined in US law, allowing separate sections on public transportation, separate schools, sports facilities, colleges and hospitals. Businesses could refuse to serve Black customers, set up Black cinemas and whites-only restaurants. Walls were built to segregate cities – Black one side, white the other. Even public restrooms and drinking fountains were segregated.

But if one court decision could enshrine a principle, another could demolish it. On 17 May 1954, the US Supreme Court unanimously ruled that the segregation of schools in Kansas was 'neither separate nor equal'. With the landmark *Brown v. Board of Education* decision, the court ruled that segregation deprived children in Black schools 'of the equal protection of the laws guaranteed by the 14th Amendment'.

The *Brown* decision held within it the power to overturn white supremacy. New battle lines were drawn and the two sides made their positions clear. Segregationist Judge Brady bemoaned 'Black Monday' as 'Socialistic doctrine'. Integrationist Dr Frank Price, moderator of the Southern Presbyterians, condemned segregation as 'Godless' and declared the *Brown* decision 'a God-given opportunity' for mankind.[1]

In many parts of the South, the opposition began to formulate plans to oppose integration. Georgia's governor, Eugene Talmadge, warned the press, 'We're not going to secede from the Union, but the people of Georgia will not comply with the decision of the court.' In Louisiana the state senate approved a vote to continue segregation in public schools by a majority of thirty-two to one. In Indianola, Mississippi, the first of many Citizens' Councils was formed in July. Dedicated 'to oppose school integration by all lawful means', it would be followed by many across the South.[2] Predictably the Klan took more direct and fewer legal measures.

Emerging from a period of relative dormancy in the early 1950s, the Klan took the *Brown* decision as a starting gun. Days after the decision, a cross was burnt on the lawn of a Black Korean War veteran named Andrew Wade in Louisville, Kentucky. Wade had bought a house in a traditionally white area. Night after night drivers hurled rocks and fired shots at his house. A month later a bomb destroyed it. Luckily Wade's house was empty at the time. By the end of 1955 nearly 200 racially motivated bomb and arson attacks had rocked the South. There can be little doubt the Klan was behind most of them.[3]

Between 1955 and 1956, white supremacist violence ramped up. Civil rights activists were murdered in Texas, Mississippi and Georgia, as well as an entire family of nine in Alabama when the wrong house was bombed. White supremacists rioted in Alabama, South Carolina, Tennessee, Kentucky and West Virginia. Activists' houses were bombed in Alabama, South Carolina, Georgia and Tennessee. Churches were firebombed in South Carolina and Alabama. Crosses were burnt in Alabama, South Carolina, Florida, Tennessee, Virginia and Kentucky.

While not all these atrocities could be tied directly to the Klan, they were all instigated by white supremacists. Support for the Klan seemed to be growing. Most people stopped short of openly advocating Klan activities, but newspapers across the South offered indirect approval, frequently running stories about individual Klansmen's donations to churches and other 'good works'.

Local law enforcers regularly turned a blind eye to Klansmen, hid evidence and even supplied false testimony and alibis. When Black NAACP activist Reverend George Lee was killed in a drive-by shooting, the sheriff of Humphreys County, Mississippi, tried to distract investigators. He stalled the investigation, claiming he had evidence of 'some jealous nigger' who carried out the shooting. It took the intervention of US Attorney General Herbert Brownell to push the investigation through. Even then, no one came forward with any incriminating evidence.[4] Georgia was even more blatant in its support of the Klan, granting a charter to autoworker and long-time Klansman Eldon Lee Edwards for the new and powerful 'US Klans'.

In the early 1950s the Klan would have been happy to find 100 willing protesters to march against integration but now the numbers were climbing. In 1956, costumed Klansmen staged a drive-by shooting in Clinton, Tennessee, packing into 125 cars to protest the enrolment of twelve Black students at the local high school. Over the next two years, the formerly peaceful town would suffer white supremacist riots, intimidation and beatings, culminating in 1958 with the bombing of the high school. But the number of Klansmen involved in Clinton was modest compared with the 1,000 or more white-robed men who marched through Montgomery, Alabama, later that year or the 3,000 who had paraded through Atlanta, Georgia, earlier in the same year.[5]

The Klan may have enjoyed rebounding support in the South, but it was increasingly seen as an abomination by most in the North. As the country approached 1960, crosses were still occasionally reported to be burning on the lawns of Delaware, Pennsylvania and Illinois. But, for the most part, Klan activity was limited to its original Southern, Reconstruction heartland. The Southern Regional Council, an Atlanta-based agency devoted to racial integration, claimed that the Klan carried out 530 acts of violence in eleven Southern states, recording twenty-seven Klan bombings in 1959 alone.[6]

The Klan drew parallels between the 1950s and 1960s attempts to give Southern African Americans full civil rights and the efforts of Reconstruction almost a century earlier. Once again, the North was interfering in the South's affairs, imposing laws which took away the South's rights to govern themselves. It was the 1860s and 1870s all over again, and once again many whites turned to the Klan for help in preventing the disappearance of 'the Southern way of life'. As the historian C. Vann Woodward put it, for many white Southerners this was a 'historical flashback ... a flesh-and-blood materialization of ancestral nightmares that had troubled their sleep since childhood'.[7]

# CHAPTER 66

The late 1950s saw the emergence of some of the most violent Klans of all time, fulfilling predictions that desegregation would lead to an escalation of violence. To preserve the considerable investment dollars that had begun flowing into the South in 1941, local businessmen formed Southern White Citizens' Councils. In doing so, they hoped to prevent 'the need for any hot-headed bunch to start a Ku Klux Klan'.[1]

The Citizens' Councils made much of operating within the law, but they were also vehemently segregationist and determined to stop integration. Their playbook was 'more decorous, tidy and less conspicuous' than night-riding and tarring and feathering, but it was cruel.[2] They encouraged boycotts of integrated businesses. They published the names of Black activists, who were often then fired from their jobs. They encouraged bank managers to cancel loans and mortgages to integrationists of both colours. This indirect economic violence made the councils into a kind of country-club version of the Klan, with added hypocrisy and self-righteousness.[3]

The white Citizens' Councils essentially radicalised the Klans. These middle-class pressure groups attracted many of the professionals who had, in the 1920s, been forces of moderation within the Klan. By contrast, the Klans which emerged in the late 1950s and early 1960s consisted largely of unskilled, uneducated misfits who saw violence as the only answer to integration. By 1958, it was estimated that there were 40,000 Klansmen in some twenty-seven different factions.[4]

When the white Southern elites refused to implement the Supreme Court's rulings, the Black population organised in despair and disbelief. The NAACP formed new and more radical chapters. They were joined by organisations like the Southern Christian Leadership Conference (SCLC), the Student Nonviolent Coordinating Committee (SNCC) and the Congress of Racial Equality (CORE). Although these groups were avowedly non-violent, their methods made history. They engaged in bus boycotts, sit-ins, race-mixing in public spaces, encouraged Black voter registration and set up free Black schools. These activities prompted many enraged Klan members to lash out.

In January 1957 in Tallahassee, Florida, Black activists successfully boycotted a local bus company. Furious, Klansmen in that region singled out the vice-president of the local SCLC, Reverend Charles Kenzie Steele. They raked his house with gunfire and set up a burning cross outside the church where he preached, Bethel Missionary Baptist Church.

In Tennessee, Klansmen bombed the integrated Knoxville City Auditorium as well as an integrated school in Clinton and a home in Chattanooga which had recently been shown to Black buyers. In Georgia, they bombed an integrated roadside market in Americus.

That same January the publicity surrounding the success of the SCLC-led bus boycott in Montgomery was answered with sustained Klan violence. Four Black churches and the houses of two local civil rights leaders were bombed. Klansmen also shot up the front of a store owned by one of the boycott leaders. Hooded Klansmen mistook delivery driver Willie Edwards for a leading civil rights activist and made him jump to his death from a bridge. Klansmen bombed and set fire to the house of a local TV newsman who had reported on them unfavourably. They also bombed Black-owned homes and taxi ranks.

On 30 January 1956, Martin Luther King, the face of the bus boycott, was about to take a shower in his Montgomery home when he heard the thump of a bomb landing on his porch. It failed to go off. Within hours, 500 furious African Americans gathered outside the house. They said they wouldn't move until the police did something.[5]

King defused the situation and the Montgomery PD went through the motions. They knew the Klan was behind it: many of them were either Klansmen or close relatives of Klansmen. Under pressure, they had just arrested five men on similar bomb charges. Two of the five had already 'confessed' to being local Klan members. The judicial system carried on as usual: the all-white jury naturally freed the two Klansmen. But there were signs things were changing. Charges were dropped against civil rights workers for running an illegal boycott. But the other three bombers were never brought to trial.[6]

These ultra-violent Klans of the 1950s hardly needed the police to neutralise them. They were unpopular with businessmen because of their impact on the local economy. Klan chapters were short-lived and many that emerged fought with one another. To many, the local Klan groups seemed just plain silly. At the same time, they were *so* violent they outraged even those who previously supported them, including the police.

The perpetrators of the Montgomery atrocities belonged to the Alabama-based original Ku Klux Klan of the Confederacy. This ultra-violent order was founded by Asa 'Ace' Carter in 1956. Carter was not the average Klan leader. Intelligent and articulate, after the war he'd trained as a journalist at the University of Colorado under the GI Bill that enabled ex-servicemen to gain new qualifications and skills. In one way Carter did resemble some of the other memorable Klan leaders of this era: he was a psychopath.

In 1953, Carter worked as a broadcaster at Radio WILD in Birmingham. The station was sponsored by the American States Rights Association and the Alabama Citizens' Council. Carter's segregationist views were too much for his audience and he was sacked. The problem was his violent antisemitism which he'd picked up in the late 1940s while working for the right-wing political rabble-rouser Gerald L.K. Smith. By the mid-1950s Carter founded his own North Alabama Citizens' Council, which advocated revoking US citizenship from all Jews.

The Klan group Carter formed in November 1956 reflected these views. Drawing heavily on Nazi iconography, members of the order resembled stormtroopers as they strutted around Birmingham in brown shirts, Sam Browne belts and polished jackboots. Carter made himself Grand Marshal, favouring the khakis and paratrooper boots that would later become the go-to uniform of militant white supremacists.

While there were never more than thirty-six members, the Original Knights were frighteningly violent. They planted bombs on Black targets and attacked prominent Black figures. On one occasion Carter and three others stormed onto the stage of Birmingham's municipal auditorium where Nat King Cole, a Black man, was singing to a white audience. They threw punches at Cole and kicked him after they'd knocked him down, then attacked the SCLC leader Fred Shuttlesworth and stabbed his wife in the hip. Six men were arrested on riot charges. They got a maximum of six months.[7]

Then there was the time in the Klavern when Carter was questioned by other members about where the dues money had gone. Quietly, he drew his pistol and shot two of his own Klansmen. Most notoriously, on 2 September 1957, Carter bragged he was going to set his 'mad dogs on a retarded nigger'. He and members of the Original Knights kidnapped a Black handyman named Judge Edward Aaron, castrated him with a razor blade, poured turpentine on the open wounds and passed his testicles around in a paper cup. After this ritual was completed, they dumped his near-dead body on a highway with a note pinned to his chest warning Black 'trouble-makers'. Found by police officers and rushed to a local hospital, Aaron survived.

The extreme and very public nature of the Original Knights' violence garnered them unusual hostility from the Birmingham PD. Within weeks, the BPD had arrested several members of the Original Knights on bombing and other charges. By the end of 1957, four members of the group were sentenced to jail terms of twenty years each. Amazingly, Carter himself was never charged with any crimes, but his foot soldiers were so regularly jailed that the Original Knights were forced to disband in early 1958. They'd lasted a little over a year.[8]

Jesse B. Stoner, self-styled 'arch-leader' of the Christian Knights of the Ku Klux Klan, was only marginally less psychopathic than Carter. He was even more antisemitic, but not as bright. While Stoner qualified as an attorney, those meeting him would have no problem identifying his politics. Strutting around his hometown of Marietta, Georgia, Stoner wore a jewelled Confederate flag on his lapel and a pistol ostentatiously on his hip. He was the epitome of the kind of leader fuelling in-fighting between Klan factions in the South.

Stoner stated on record that Hitler was 'too moderate' in his hatred of Jews. He told a journalist he would make being Jewish 'a crime punishable by death'. He was so hysterical in his racial rantings that he was actually expelled from the Associated Klans of America. Later, Stoner would condemn US Klans as 'Jew dominated'. Even the supremely racist Bull Connor, Birmingham's Chief of Public Safety, hated Stoner. In 1958, Connor joined forces with William Morris of the Associated Klans and attempted to frame Stoner with a faked bomb plot.[9] It failed, but Stoner was imprisoned that year for a real bombing at Birmingham's Bethel Baptist Church.

If violence led to the downfall of many of the Klans over this period, sheer stupidity wrecked the ambitions of James 'Catfish' Cole. His North Carolina Knights of the KKK did not last even as long as Carter's Klan. Cole founded his group on 13 January 1958. He chose to target the local Native Americans in Robeson County, North Carolina. To announce his campaign against the Lumbees, he burnt several crosses and led a rally at the local town of Lumberton on 18 January. It would be the Carolina Knights' only outing.

Before the rally, Cole bragged that 500 of his Klansmen would attend. Only forty materialised. Unfortunately for him, plenty of photographers and journalists turned up – and over 1,000 Lumbees. Angry about the threats Catfish had made, the Lumbees smashed up all the PA equipment and chased the Klansmen off the field. *Life Magazine* summed it up: like Custer, 'the Klan had just taken on too many Indians'. To cap the disaster, Cole was charged with inciting a riot and sentenced to eighteen months in prison. The Carolina Knights were disbanded. They'd lasted less than a week.[10]

# CHAPTER 67

Like so many psychopaths, Original Knights founder Asa Carter went on to have a very successful, albeit odd, career. In the 1970s he transferred his journalistic skills to writing popular fiction, specialising in Westerns. He changed his name to Forrest Carter. I was more than a little surprised when I found out he'd written the storyline for one of my favourite movies, the 1976 Clint Eastwood film *The Outlaw Josey Wales*. But before his career shift, Carter continued to play a pivotal role in the white supremacist movement in Alabama.

By the early 1960s the slippery Carter managed to avoid the fate of his minions, reinventing himself as a speech writer and adviser for judge and Alabama governor George Wallace. Carter acted as a kind of go-between for Wallace, enabling the governor to consult with Klansmen and other violent white supremacists while still retaining a polite distance. It was Carter who wrote Wallace's infamous inaugural address with its resounding promise that Alabama would fight for 'Segregation now, segregation tomorrow, segregation forever'.

In his successful and vehemently racist campaigning for the Governor's Mansion in 1962, George Wallace made himself the focal point for Southern whites in their struggles against racial integration. He was well suited to the role. Son of a hard-drinking hardscrabble farmer with a ferocious temper, young George barely mourned when he died at 40. He was not much closer to his music-teaching mother. She tried her best to turn her son into a cultured Southern gentleman. Instead, she drove George into becoming a man who relished shocking and offending those who might consider themselves to be his betters.

After law college, Wallace tied himself to the progressive policies of his mentor, James Elisha 'Big Jim' Folsom. He was 6ft 8in and over 280lb and believed that 'as long as the Negroes are held down by depravation and lack of opportunity, the other poor people will be held down alongside them'.[1] He believed taxing the wealthy and improving education for all would bring a better day for Alabama. George seemed to agree. By the time of Big Jim's second inauguration in 1955, George Wallace, the 'Fighting Little Judge', was generally seen as his heir and successor.

Ambitious and calculating, Wallace saw better electoral potential in representing those who objected to integration. He had done the maths and reckoned they were the constituency who would get him into office. As Folsom himself put it:

> George wasn't no race bigot either back yonder. Me an' George was always close. We just disagreed on one thing. I never did want to take any credit for hangin' niggers. And he wasn't always like he is now. He just wanted to get elected to things, that's all.[2]

Wallace himself argued his gripe was not with the Black population, but with the federal government for forcing decisions on Alabama, as it had in Reconstruction. But whatever the source of his change of heart, the result for the Klan was the same: without directly admitting it, Wallace propagated, promoted and protected it.

Wallace used Asa Carter to discern and harness the extremes of segregationist thought. Wallace never addressed the Klan directly – Carter did that for him. As one Klansman put it, 'Carter got the crowds all churned up. He was really good at that … spoke to 'em and told 'em George Wallace was the white saviour … against no-good Communists on the Supreme Court and no-good scalawags on the local federal benches.'[3] In return Carter saw his racist creed put into action after Wallace managed to get four Klansmen, the men who'd been convicted in 1957, freed on bail. But Wallace's connections with the Klan went much deeper than this.

Wallace had close ties with another leading Klansman, Robert 'Bobby' Shelton. A lifelong Klansman, Shelton had defected from the US Klans in 1958 and founded his own Alabama Knights. In 1961, he merged his Alabama Knights with Klans from Georgia and South Carolina, founding the United Klans of America (UKA). According to the FBI, by 1962 he had probably recruited up to 10,000 dues-paying members, making them far and away the most important, and one of the most violent, Klan groups in the country.[4]

Unlike many other Klan leaders of the time, Shelton realised the benefit of close political ties. He and his UKA members worked hard to get Wallace elected, and few locals were in any doubt about the closeness of their relationship. Not that they minded. The majority of Alabama's opinion formers favoured segregation. To them, the Klan was 'just the shock troops, the guerrilla warriors for preservation of the order'.[5] Wallace's election proved that to be true.

The UKA argued that it favoured civil disobedience rather than violence, but two particularly brutal murders carried out by UKA members would play a central role in the collapse of the Klan in the 1960s. And they would happen with the apparent blessing of George Wallace.

# CHAPTER 68

On Sunday, 15 September 1963, at 10.22 a.m., the phone rang at the 16th Street Baptist Church, the leading Black church in Birmingham. A teenage girl walking past answered. The voice at the other end said simply, 'Three minutes' and the line went dead. The girl put down the receiver and walked on into the main body of the church. Just as she went through the door, there was a huge blast.

A bomb had gone off. The blast was so powerful it threw the driver of a passing car clean out of the vehicle. It tore down a good part of the building and left a vast crater. It killed 14-year-old Addie Mae Collins; Carol McNair (11); Carole Robertson (14); and Cynthia Wesley (14). Their bodies were so shattered they could only be identified by their jewellery and clothing. Around twenty others were injured, including Sarah Collins, Addie Mae's 10-year-old sister, who was left blind.

The following day, at the Birmingham Young Men's Business Club, a local attorney asked his audience:

> Four little girls were killed in Birmingham yesterday. A mad, remorseful worried community asks, 'Who did it? Who threw that bomb? Was it a Negro or a white?' The answer should be, 'We all did it.' Every last one of us is condemned for that crime and the bombing before it and a decade ago. We all did it.
>
> The 'who' is every little individual who talks about the 'niggers' and spreads the seeds of his hate to his neighbor and his son. The jokester, the crude oaf whose racial jokes rock the party with laughter. The 'who' is every governor who ever shouted for lawlessness and became a law violator. It is every senator and every representative who in the halls of Congress stands and with mock humility tells the world that things back home aren't really like they are. It is courts that move ever so slowly, and newspapers that timorously defend the law.

Charles Morgan Jr would never practise law in Birmingham again. He and his wife received death threats. He was ostracised by the city's white great and good.[1] But if his audience felt he was a traitor to his race, the rest of the nation felt very differently, not least the White House.

President John F. Kennedy immediately put the FBI on the case. With its vast resources and ability to remain above local prejudices and differences, the federal investigators managed to attract local informers – both Black and white. Pretty soon they had traced the bombing to none other than Klansman 'Dynamite Bob' Chambliss and at least two other accomplices.

All three were members of the ultra-violent Cahaba Bridge Boys, a splinter group of the Klan's local Eastview Klavern No. 13. But the FBI's suspicions yielded little. Chambliss and the two others were charged with illegally possessing dynamite. The state of Alabama fined them $100 each and they walked out of the court, free men.

Kennedy, the FBI and the local Black community knew that figures like Bull Connor and Al Lingo, the heads of Public Safety in Birmingham and Alabama respectively – had probably played a role in this miscarriage of justice. Connor had been elected to the post every year since 1936, with the mandate to keep the city 'safe'. That meant keeping the white population 'safe' from their Black neighbours, through segregation. And when he saw that safety threatened, he took measures to protect his electorate.

So when the Freedom Riders rode, white and Black people side by side, on inter-state Greyhound buses in 1961, Connor was sanctioning a Klan 'welcome committee'. They beat the Freedom Riders so badly that some of them would be permanently disabled. He 'protected' Birmingham from peaceful integrationist marchers by setting attack dogs on them and soaking them in freezing water from high-pressure hoses so powerful they could scalp a person. Connor protected Birmingham's whites by arresting over 3,000 legally sanctioned protesters including Martin Luther King Jr and 950 children. He even ordered sixty Birmingham parks to close to protect the public from the perils of integration.

Connor was associated with the KKK: he might have been a member. When he stood for Birmingham mayor in 1962, the Klan came out in force to support him. In what they grandly termed 'Operation Midnight Ride', Imperial Wizard Bobby Shelton appeared in Birmingham. A large group of his UKA stormtroopers intimidated Connor's political opponents and marched, chanting, for him. Asa Carter spoke and Dr Edward Fields of the National States Rights Party put in an appearance.[2]

Connor attended Klan meetings, supporting and protecting Klansmen and their activities. The police chief and Chambliss went back at least a decade. As early as 1950, when Chambliss was arrested for bombing the house of a

Black activist, Connor had protected him. The police commissioner refused to allow Birmingham detectives or state investigators to question him. Instead, Chambliss was released without charge after a matter of hours.[3]

As the FBI began to amass evidence against Dynamite Bob and his fellow Klansmen, it seemed the local police were doing their best to hide it. Although Connor had been voted out of office, his protection of Chambliss continued. Chambliss would later be convicted of the bombing and serve out the rest of his life in prison. While in prison he would regularly write to his niece, Flora Chambliss, giving his side of events. One 1979 letter claimed the mayor, Art Hames, and Bull Connor 'know all about the Bombing'.[4]

According to the official investigation, Chambliss escaped conviction for the bombing in 1963 because he was 'at home' at the time of bombing. This alibi was corroborated by 'interviews of relatives [his sister], a Birmingham police officer [most likely Chambliss' own nephew, Floyd Garrett, who claimed he called around to collect a shotgun], neighbours and [his] wife'. None of them could be considered impartial. And there is no doubt crucial evidence was hidden and statements 'lost' by the BPD.[5]

On the other hand, a witness claimed she saw a suspicious car in the early morning of the 15th. At 2 a.m., Gertrude Glenn, an African American, had just arrived in Birmingham from Detroit. She was looking for a parking space when she saw a white-on-turquoise 1957 Chevy DeSoto. The lights were on in the car and she could clearly see white men sitting in it, in a Black area of town. When she reported this to the BPD, they told her that she was 'mistaken'. She later identified to the FBI one of the three white men inside the car as Chambliss. The car turned out to belong to the brother of one of his accomplices, Tommy Blanton. Her evidence would prove pivotal to the conviction of Chambliss in 1977 and Blanton in 2001.[6]

The FBI mistrusted the local police all the way through the investigation. They'd had Bull Connor under surveillance since 1941 and embedded undercover agent Gary Thomas Rowe in the Eastview Klavern. Rowe gave the FBI valuable information about Klan meetings with City Hall, the BPD and the Alabama state troopers.

Rowe provided the FBI with evidence of the PD leaking back information to the Klan about police investigations and suspicions, and disposing of evidence that might prove detrimental to the Klansmen. The climate of mistrust worked both ways. Al Lingo arrested three FBI agents on spurious charges of possession of dynamite. In the meantime, the bombers went unpunished. Eventually, J. Edgar Hoover told his lead investigator that he felt they would never be able to solve the case and, in 1966, it was closed. By that time the FBI had investigated and prosecuted Klan activity in the states of Alabama and neighbouring Mississippi, with mixed results.

# CHAPTER 69

In 1961 one of the founders of the SNCC, Bob Moses, launched a voter registration drive in Mississippi. As he saw it, it was all very well to educate, integrate and protect the Black population of the South, but to make real change the laws that were in place guaranteeing rights, the Constitutional Amendments, had to be enforced. To achieve this in a democracy, those who ignored those laws had to be voted out.

As one activist put it, 'If you can't vote, you's willin' to be beaten. If you's willin' to be beaten, then you is a slave.' And nowhere was this more true than in Mississippi. Here, 85 per cent of the Black population lived below the poverty line, and only 7 per cent of African Americans entitled to vote were registered to vote. Most whites in the state clearly wanted to keep it that way.

To register to vote in Mississippi, it was necessary to pass a literacy test for which the county registrar was able to request that a potential voter read aloud from any of Mississippi's 285 statutes. If the would-be voter was successful, they might then be asked to interpret the legal gobbledegook to the satisfaction of the (usually hostile) registrar. Some counties demanded proof of residence in the form of the notorious Grandfather Clause. This meant you could only vote if your grandfather had been entitled to the franchise in 1861. This effectively ruled out almost all the Mississippi Black population. Virtually none were entitled to vote before the Civil War. They had been slaves.

In this environment Bob Moses' efforts were met with predictable hostility. He and other activists were arrested and fined for trying to register local African Americans to vote. The Klan threatened them, beat them, firebombed their meeting places and offices, and shot at them with an arsenal of shotguns, rifles and even machine guns. Moses and the others doggedly continued their efforts in the face of constant intimidation, beatings and some deaths. But the movement achieved little.

In rural Leflore County in Mississippi, for example, by the end of 1963 slightly over 250 Black residents had the vote. This was an improvement from no voters at all when they started in 1961, but hopeless when compared with the votes of over 10,000 whites. Yet the Black population made up 60 per cent of the residents of Leflore.[1] By 1964, it was clear they needed to try something different.

On 15 June, the first wave of what was promised would be when 1,000 mostly white volunteers arrived in Mississippi for a 'Freedom Summer' drive to register voters. Organised by the Council of Federated Organizations (COFO), the drive to register voters united CORE, SNCC, SCLC and NAACP volunteers. Their mission was well planned and the volunteers carefully chosen.[2]

The activists were given a crash course in the techniques of non-violence. The young Northern college students were chosen for their calm demeanours and, more cynically, for their middle-class backgrounds. It was felt, wrongly, that children of wealthier parents might be less likely to encounter violence and defuse it if they did. They might also be more likely to remain in contact with professional parents who would have the wherewithal and the means to counter problems on their children's behalf. They'd also have the money for bail.

Among that wave of volunteers were two New Yorkers. Mickey Schwerner was a 24-year-old sociology graduate student at Columbia. He had been involved in a variety of desegregation and other civil rights programmes for CORE when he was assigned to Meridian County, Mississippi, with his wife Rita in the summer of 1964. They were joined by Andrew Goodman. A college student at Queens College, 20-year-old Goodman was a friend of Paul Simon and had aspirations to become an actor. Importantly, both Schwerner and Goodman were Jewish.

They were met in Mississippi by James Chaney, a 21-year-old Black plasterer's apprentice, ex-Freedom Rider and NAACP and COFO activist. Within weeks of their arrival the three activists had become targets for members of Sam Bowers' White Knights of the Ku Klux Klan. *The New York Times* explained the logic:

The average [white] citizen [of rural Mississippi] has been led to believe that this [Freedom Summer] will be an 'invasion' to make Mississippi the battleground in [sic] behalf of Negro rights.[3]

To Klansmen these Northern, Jewish beatniks were communists. Worse still, they were carpetbaggers 'who try to tell us how to run things'.[4] Sam Bowers saw it as a war and outlined to his followers the existential threat the COFO 'agitators' posed to the Klan, Mississippi and the South as a whole:

> events which will occur in Mississippi this summer may well determine the fate of Christian Civilization for centuries to come ... our enemies offensive will consist of two basic salients which have been designed to envelop and destroy our small forces in a pincer movement of Agitation [sic], Force by Federal Troops and Communist Propaganda.[5]

After driving out to view the remains of a burnt-out local church where they were organising a voter registration drive, the three CORE workers were pulled over by Klan-affiliated Neshoba deputy sheriff Cecil Price. They were accused of speeding, arrested, held briefly in the county jail, fined and released. Upon their release they were followed by Klansmen – never to be seen alive again.

Under pressure from President Lyndon Johnson and Attorney General Bobby Kennedy, J. Edgar Hoover swamped Meridian County with FBI agents determined to find the COFO workers. With the help of 400 sailors they dragged the local swamps and bayous. They scoured the pine woods and scrub areas. They found the car the activists had used, but no sign of the three young men. Mississippi locals treated them with undisguised hostility.

Governor Paul Johnson went on the radio, telling the public the three COFO 'boys were in Cuba' and the FBI was wasting taxpayers' money. The Mississippi Bar Association told locals that they were under no legal obligation to aid or inform the FBI. And Imperial Wizard Sam Bowers said that Mississippi now had to decide if they wanted 'segregation, tranquillity and justice or bi-racism, chaos and death'. He was adamant that there was 'no disappearance'.[6] The whole incident was simply a plot by the 'Communist Revolutionaries' who'd come South as carpetbaggers.[7]

Yet within six weeks, thanks to anonymous information, the bodies of the three COFO workers were discovered at the base of an earthen dam. They'd all been shot, and Chaney, the only Black victim, had also been severely beaten. Twenty-one Klansmen were charged with the murders, including the Neshoba county sheriff and the deputy who'd fined and released the young men into the hands of the Klan.

The FBI's success was not matched by immediate success in the courts. The 'bristlingly segregationist' federal district judge, William Harold Cox, declared that 'The right of every person not to be deprived of his life and liberty without due process of law is merely guaranteed by the [Fifth and Fourteenth Amendments of the] Constitution of the United States'.[8]

It meant that once again the Klan would benefit from being tried in a state rather than federal court. And this was a state where one local attorney had told FBI agents that he considered the COFO workers had got what was coming and that the 'FBI only comes in on it when worthless Jews and nigger-lovers are killed'.[9]

Within a year the US Supreme Court had overruled Cox. A second trial took place in a Mississippi courtroom with the same Judge Cox presiding. Eighteen Klansmen were tried and seven of them found guilty. The sentences ranged from four to ten years. It was the first time in Mississippi's history that a prosecution for the murder of civil rights activists had resulted in convictions.

The world had changed. The Imperial Wizard of the White Knights must have been shocked. Sam Bowers got ten years. As he had walked into the courtroom, he'd been overheard telling a friend, 'Judge Cox will probably make the FBI take those bodies back and put them where they found them because they found the bodies on an illegal search warrant.'[10] Many saw the verdict as a new dawn. *The New York Times* announced the decision as 'a measure of the quiet revolution which is taking place in Southern attitudes'.

Judge Cox on his sentencing saw nothing revolutionary in his decisions. As he said, 'They killed one nigger, one Jew and a white man – I gave them all what I thought they deserved.'[11]

# CHAPTER 70

The FBI claimed that nearly 1,000 people came forward in their investigations of the COFO killings. Some 500 of them were Bowers' Klansmen. For all his talk of outright war and the preservation of civilisation, the FBI claimed most of Bowers' soldiers were easily bought. The alacrity with which these Klansmen turned informers was not unique to Mississippi. The Bureau had recruited them from all over the South. One of these was Gary Thomas Rowe, or Tommy as he was known in his hometown, Birmingham, Alabama.

Tommy Rowe was 26 when he was first asked to join the UKA in 1959. Powerfully built and short-tempered, Tommy was also something of a hell-raiser. He solved most of the problems he encountered with a stiff drink or his fists. He often drank at the Veterans of Foreign Wars (VFW) Club where he sometimes worked as a bouncer. The more Tommy drank, the more he complained about the uppishness of the local Black residents and their 'white nigger' allies. The Birmingham VFW was a well-known Klan hangout and Tommy was ideal Klan material. But when asked to join he said he wanted to think on it.

In 1960, Tommy paid his Klecktoken of $12.50 – it had gone up $2.50 since the 1920s – bought his robes and agreed to part with his $1.67 dues each month. The FBI now had someone inside the famously violent Eastview Klan No.13.[1]

Tommy Rowe was destined to become one of those characters who are present on the scene at pivotal moments in history, like Forrest Gump or Woody Allen's Zelig. Tommy was in there in 1963 when Chambliss' bomb killed the four little girls at the 16th Street Baptist Church. He was able to give Hoover's men essential information – much of which would not be used until Chambliss was brought to trial in 1977.

Tommy Rowe was also present on 25 March 1965 in Selma, Alabama, riding in the red-and-white Chevy Impala as it drew level with a blue Oldsmobile bearing Michigan plates. At the wheel was Viola Liuzzo, a 40-year-old white civil rights activist. She had been one of the 32,000 people who'd participated in the spectacular march from Selma to Montgomery and witnessed Martin Luther King addressing a crowd of 25,000 in front of the Alabama state capitol. After experiencing this 'shining moment in American history', Viola was now giving Leroy Moton, a Black man and fellow activist, a ride home.[2]

Tommy Rowe was in the back seat of the red-and-white Impala when his Klan companions fired fourteen shots into the Oldsmobile. Viola was shot in the head several times and died instantly. Moton survived.

Tommy found himself in a difficult position. He told the FBI he hadn't fired his .22, although he'd stuck it out of the window when the others did. When the FBI checked the pistol for residue, they agreed it hadn't been fired.[3] He was secretly granted immunity, but his name was read aloud on national television by President Lyndon Johnson, along with the other Klansmen involved in Viola's killing. The president told his audience she'd been 'murdered by the enemies of justice who for decades used the rope and the gun, the tar and the feather to terrorize their neighbours'.[4]

The Selma march had been the news event of the month. TV crews, journalists and radio presenters were swarming around the area. Johnson knew he had to react, and his genuine personal fury and reading out of suspects' names on prime-time television prompted an unprecedented reaction. FBI boss J. Edgar Hoover also knew this was a crucial event. He knew it would emerge that one of his operatives was in the car with the gunmen who'd killed Viola. So, with typical sneakiness, he tried to shift the emphasis onto the victim.

Hoover leaked that – contrary to the Alabama coroner's report – Viola had needle marks on her arms indicating drug use. He also said the coroner had found traces of semen on her body, even though she'd been away from her Detroit home and husband for some days. These claims were later proven false, but they gave the Alabama courts just what they needed to cast doubt on the FBI's case and return hung juries – twice. Myths of the Lost Cause resurfaced. Viola was painted as a carpetbagger and a disgrace to pure womanhood.

Once again, the justice department was forced to turn to the statutes of 1871 and the Klansmen were charged with intimidating African Americans under the Ku Klux Klan Act. In December 1965, three Klansmen were sentenced to ten years apiece by an all-white, all-male jury.

But the true impact of Viola's murder was felt in Washington, where President Johnson ordered Congress to launch a thorough investigation into the Klan. To this end, Johnson gave the HUAC $50,000. The 20,000 man-hours of investigations leading up to the committee's hearings were highly successful. They managed to convince HUAC that the Klan *was* un-American.

Before the hearings opened in October 1965, the committee had stolidly refused to investigate the Klan, arguing that it was fundamentally a patriotic organisation. By contrast, HUAC had subjected civil rights activists to nine separate investigations. But by the time of the hearings the consensus was: 'These [Klans]men are terrorists pure and simple. Their purpose is terror. Their work is terror. Their strength is terror.'[5]

The Klansmen called to give testimony were aware of that hostility. From the start, Bobby Shelton set a belligerent tone. The UKA's Imperial Wizard pleaded the Fifth Amendment – 158 times! For three weeks others followed Shelton's lead. Klansmen Sam Bowers and Jesse Stoner 'respectfully declined' to answer questions, as did Grand Dragons Bob Jones of North Carolina, Bob Scoggin of South Carolina and other sundry Klansmen from Georgia and Virginia.[6]

The proceedings dragged on. Towards the end, Charles Weltner, a liberal committee member from Georgia, confessed the investigations had not been 'as revealing and significant as we hoped'.[7] Shelton, Bowers and Jones all received prison sentences for obstructing the course of justice, but HUAC quickly left the Klan behind, moving on to pursue more fruitful subjects like anti-Vietnam War activists Abbie Hoffman and Jerry Rubin. Meanwhile, J. Edgar Hoover took over the Klan investigations, bringing his considerable talents for deviousness and inventiveness.

# CHAPTER 71

In September 1965, J. Edgar Hoover launched what was to become the FBI's most comprehensive attack on the Klan. COINTELPRO-WHITE HATE used covert, subversive and often suspect methods to disrupt the Klan's activities. It was a very *Hoover* operation, provoked by his obsession with communism. Under Hoover, white hate was intrinsically linked to the Cold War. He might have had a point: by many accounts, by May 1963 a quarter of Radio Moscow's broadcasts were about the brutality of Connor's BPD.[1]

In a report to President Eisenhower in 1958, Hoover's FBI had first presented the Klan as a 'Hate Group'. That same year the FBI started to help Southern law enforcement with investigations of bombings across the region. This continued into the early 1960s as violence exploded in Alabama, Georgia and Mississippi in 1963 and 1964; FBI involvement increased. When the violence culminated in the COFO murders, President Johnson issued specific orders for the FBI to infiltrate Klan groups. With Viola Liuzzo's murder, that infiltration morphed into COINTELPRO-WHITE HATE.

COINTELPRO's aim was to upset and unbalance Klansmen, to destroy their trust in each other and convince them they were under constant surveillance. Infiltrators constantly kept FBI agents aware of upcoming Klan events. COINTELPRO has been called a 'Hoover-hatched scheme of cheap psychological warfare and dirty tricks'.[2] That pretty neatly sums it up.

Out-of-town Klansmen would arrive at hotels to find their reservations cancelled, leaving them stranded. Klan foot soldiers found strange postcards in their mailboxes, frightening their families and inducing paranoid thoughts about their fellow Klansmen and leaders. Agents sent Klansmen anonymous greetings on birthdays and anniversaries, often unsettlingly bland but creepy or containing veiled threats. Klan leaders' names were published in local newspapers with insinuations about their financial or sexual misdemeanours. On an individual level, this was usually just irritating to Klansmen and their families but collectively it induced a culture of deep paranoia.[3]

Some Klansmen escaped unscathed. UKA boss Bobby Shelton proved to be remarkably clean living, dedicating almost all his time to Klan business. But in North Carolina the FBI had particular success, sending the rank-and-file Klansmen crudely illustrated cartoon postcards depicting the sexual shenanigans of their popular Grand Dragon, Bob Jones. Some Klansmen quit straight away while others just grumbled and remained surly Klansmen.[4]

As Hoover's programme hit its stride, it became more ambitious and creative. In 1970, the Miami FBI office gave Bobby Shelton's TV interviewers detailed, confidential information about the UKA, exposing their dodgy finances, ultra-secret passwords and details of Klan activities around a Nation of Islam farm in Alabama.

The usually controlled and steely Imperial Wizard squirmed on live TV. Over the following weeks the newspapers dug deeper, lapping up the Klan's discomfort. *The New York Times* even uncovered a plot in which the Klan would buy the Alabama ranch from the Nation of Islam. Likely this was just more COINTELPRO misinformation but, true or false, the result was more paranoia, discomfort and disillusion with the Klan, from within and without.[5]

Perhaps the FBI's greatest coup was to get control of Shelton's speechwriter, turning the Klan into an anti-communist mouthpiece. The speechwriter remains anonymous to history, but he achieved Hoover's desired effect. An analysis of the UKA's newspaper – unsurprisingly called *The Fiery Cross* – shows Shelton's rhetoric to be focused far more on communism than on race. Hoover must have felt he had turned the Klan into the FBI's own mouthpiece.[6]

Hoover's smugness would be short-lived. In March 1971, the activist group Citizens' Commission to Investigate the FBI burgled an FBI field office in Pennsylvania, taking away a good haul of files detailing the FBI's dirty tricks, illegal activities and questionable targets. The press was more than happy to expose the FBI's illegal surveillance programmes targeting an array of non-threatening organisations. A month later COINTELPRO-WHITE HATE was closed down.

# CHAPTER 72

The media played a central role in the downfall of the 1960s-era Klans just as it had in the 1920s. But from the outset of the Civil Rights Era (1954–68) the media across newspapers, radio, television and film was largely hostile to the Klan's message of hate. Most Americans were horrified when 'Big J.W.' Milam and Roy Bryant smirked at each other while being tried for the indescribably savage murder of Emmett Till. When viewers in New York and Boston saw TV footage of white men and women rabidly scream-ing and shaking their fists at young African American girls trying to go to school in Little Rock, they must have wondered if they lived in the same country. When the nation saw Bull Connor on television using his 'Nigger dogs' and high-pressure hoses on peaceful protesters, when they read about lead-filled baseball bats and firebombs being used on Freedom Riders trying to integrate buses, they probably realised they really did live in different countries.

To most of the USA, this was the time when the white hood and the burning cross became the visual representation of all bigotry, race hatred, violence and ignorance. One pivotal moment was when AGK's Grand Dragon Samuel Doc Green told Black journalist Roi Ottley, 'There ain't a nigger that's the equal of a white man. If God wanted us all equal, He would have made all people white men.' New York native Ottley summed up Green as 'a museum piece ... a primitive fanatic, without the slightest knowledge of affairs beyond his neighbourhood'.[1] He could have been talk-ing about most Klan spokesmen.

The Klan and its supporters failed to understand the media, and they certainly knew nothing of how to use it. But Klan opponents had a very good grasp of the power of the press – and they knew how to manipulate it. They appointed well-informed, presentable and on-message spokes-people. Civil rights activist organisations carefully chose their battles, and even more closely vetted their soldiers, finding spokespeople who understood that the cause took precedence over passion.

This is clear in the management of Rosa Parks' image. Rosa and her husband Raymond had been in the NAACP since their late 20s. They had worked closely with other activists. Rosa had fought hard to defend the rights of local Black victims of white rape. And she'd previously clashed with the very same bus driver who famously told her to give up her seat for a white man, over the same issue, more than a decade before. But her past activism was played down in favour of depicting the 42-year-old seamstress as the 'Black everywoman' who'd just reached the end of her patience.

Rosa's status as a Black activist was less appealing to all-important liberal whites. Depoliticising her past was also a way to make her more sympathetic to fellow African Americans, who still needed to be convinced things could change. So the NAACP played down her associations and activism and played up her working-class, middle-aged ordinariness. They also chose *not* to make 15-year-old Claudette Colvin the face of the boycott because, although Claudette had refused to give up her seat nearly a year before Rosa, she was unmarried and pregnant, and – after all – this was 1955.

The activists were also extremely careful to control the news agenda. When they organised a march, they informed the press, used easily identifiable and clearly worded banners, and gave press releases. They notified television stations and timed their activities to hit the prime time. They gave informative and intelligent interviews.

The clearest example of their media-savvy approach was their series of marches from Selma to Montgomery in March 1965. The press was informed of their purpose – to exercise their right to vote. They were encouraged to film the tens of thousands of racially integrated and peaceful marchers, and – perhaps more importantly – the violence they received from Alabama state troopers. They made sure that the media had pictures of 54-year-old Amelia Boynton tear-gassed, beaten and bloody, lying on the road by the Edmund Pettus Bridge on Bloody Sunday, 7 March 1965. Around the world, that image became synonymous with police violence.

But their media message was tinged with the threat of revolution. As a month before that bloodshed, Malcolm X warned the South, 'I think the people of this part of the world would do well to listen to Dr Martin Luther King and give him what he's asking for and give it to him fast, before some other factions come along and try to do it another way.'[2]

This lent even more power to Martin Luther King's measured rhetoric. It persuaded President Lyndon Johnson to throw all his weight behind the marchers and demonstrators in Selma. He even persuaded Alabama's segregationist governor, George Wallace, to use his troopers to protect rather than attack the marchers. Johnson would refer to the Selma marches as 'a turning point in man's unending search for freedom'.[3] The tide was truly turning.

Contrast that with the local Selma white supremacist Namon O'Neale 'Duck' Hoggle, who condemned actions of the activists, calling them 'self-appointed saints' and accusing them of meddling with Selma's 'nigras' and stirring them up.[4] His comments were comparable to those of George Wallace, who, only days before the notorious 16th Street bombing in 1963, called for 'a few first-class funerals'. Comments like Hoggle's stood in stark contrast to the soaring rhetoric of Martin Luther King, with his dreams of a world of love, forgiveness and equality.

Most Americans knew where they stood, and that was against the Klan.

# CHAPTER 73

In 1967, United Artists released a trailblazing film. *In the Heat of the Night* starred the African American actor Sidney Poitier as Philadelphia detective Virgil Tibbs. Tibbs is arrested in Sparta, Mississippi, for the murder of a rich industrialist. It pretty soon emerges that the only reason he is a suspect is that he's an out-of-town Black man with a wad of cash in his wallet. When the victim's wife discovers that Tibbs is a homicide detective, she foists him on the reluctant and racist police chief and the pair go on to solve the case together.

The plot may seem slightly corny to us today, but the film was truly groundbreaking in its day. Not only did it make Poitier Hollywood's first real Black star, but it signalled an acceptance by Hollywood of themes that would have been simply out of the question even at the beginning of the 1960s. Up to that point it would have been inconceivable to have Tibbs slapping the face of a white plantation owner after that man slapped him. It would have been unrealistic to have had Tibbs insisting on being present in the room for the interview with a white rape victim.

These scenes depicted a Black assertiveness that would have been viewed with horror by many Northern audiences, let alone white Southerners, only a couple of years before. To those impatient for change, it would have appeared wishful thinking. But that change in views *was* taking place in US society outside Hollywood. After all, even films were commercial ventures that could not afford to be out of sync with the views of their audiences.

And there was no doubt that African Americans *were* becoming increasingly assertive. Only a year before the release of the film, Huey Newton and Bobby Seale had founded the Black Panthers in Oakland, California. They openly carried weapons, dressed in paramilitary uniforms and confronted the all-white police – head-on. The ideologies of civil rights were changing. CORE and the SNCC had declared non-violent protest 'inappropriate' and would go on to exclude white members. One lead-ing SNCC member and former acolyte of Martin Luther King, Stokely Carmichael, preached militant 'Black Power' to a largely white audience at Berkeley, to the horror of the NAACP leadership.[1]

The disillusion and impatience felt by civil rights leadership fed onto the streets and into the ghettos. The summer months saw rioting explode in most major cities in the period from 1964 to 1968. In 1964 violence broke out in Harlem. Over the next days it spread to Rochester (NY) and three cities in New Jersey. When the situation calmed down one man was left dead, 144 had been injured and nearly 520 had been arrested.

The following year war broke out in LA's Watts district. As the African American rioters and looters sang 'Burn Baby, Burn', an area of 50 square miles was put under military control. Thirty-four were killed, 1,000 injured and 600 buildings destroyed. In 1967 violence exploded in over 160 US cities including Detroit, Tampa, Cincinnati, Atlanta and Newark, Plainfield, and New Brunswick in New Jersey. The 1967 National Advisory Commission on Civil Disorders identified specific instances of white racism; housing discrimination; disparity of opportunity; and most notably police mistreatment and violence as the most important causes of the disruption.

But it was the assassination of Martin Luther King on 4 April 1968 that triggered the most widespread violence. The so-called Holy Week Uprising broke out spontaneously in more than 110 US cities. The USA had never experienced anything like this. It took over 58,000 National Guardsmen and regular troops to bring the situation under control, by which time forty-three had died, 3,500 had been injured and over 27,000 arrested.[2]

Previous civil disturbances on this scale, especially those prompted by race and involving largely African Americans, would have sparked a resurgence of the Klan. After all, in 1920 riots like those in Tulsa, East St Louis and Washington DC had played a significant role in Klan recruitment. In the second half of the 1960s the opposite happened. Sam Bowers' Klan lashed out in Mississippi, killing NAACP activists, burning churches and synagogues, and bombing the homes, offices and cars of activists. But in general, although Klan numbers are difficult to pin down, the trend was definitely downward.

Non-governmental organisation the Anti-Defamation League (ADL) estimated the Klans reached a peak of around 55,000 members in total in 1967. The HUAC dropped that to a total of 16,000 active members in thirteen Klans, spread over eighteen states. The FBI gave a figure of 14,000 in 1968 and the leading Klan historian of the period, Wyn Craig Wade, saw a reduction to only 3,500 Klansmen in 1970. Whichever figure is true, the Klan was definitely declining. In fact, as the Klan entered its centenary, J. Edgar Hoover bragged it was now 'defunct'.[3]

## PART X

# WHITE SUPREMACY BECOMES WHITE POWER 1968–1995

Wake up and smell the tear gas. Freedom is calling its sons and daughters.
KKK Leader and Theorist Louis Beam[1]

# CHAPTER 74

In June and July 1946 on the Mutual network, the most popular children's radio programme in the nation broadcast a series called 'Clan of the Fiery Cross'. In the first episode a multi-ethnic kid's league baseball team in the city of 'Metropolis' takes on a star pitcher. Tommy Lee is Chinese, and unbeatable. The pitcher Tommy replaces, Chuck, is furious. Seeking revenge, he calls on his uncle, Matt, Grand Scorpion of the Clan of the Fiery Cross.

Matt and his hooded vigilantes promise to drive Tommy and his family out of Metropolis and rid the city of all non-white, non-Christian 'vermin and scum'. But they reckoned without the support of the local newspaper man, the *Daily Planet*'s Clark Kent. As you've probably guessed, Clark Kent's alter-ego, Superman, takes on the Clan and, over the next fifteen cliff-hanging episodes, battles the 'filthy weed of intolerance ... and the threat posed by these lunatics in nightshirts'.[1]

It proved to be one of the most popular radio shows of the decade. *Newsweek* called it 'the first children's program to develop a social consciousness'.[2] *The Washington Post* told its readers that 'of all the late afternoon little dramas for little people ... "Superman" had received the most comment and laurels – all in tribute to the battle against intolerance'.[3]

Legend has it that, throughout the series, the codewords, rituals and other secret details of the Clan were taken from the genuine ceremonies of Samuel Green's AGK. It was an obvious breach of security. The man who would claim the credit for this breach was a tall, slight, 30-year-old Florida journalist, William Stetson Kennedy.

Kennedy was a thoroughbred Southerner. Not just one but two of his ancestors had signed the Declaration of Independence. Another had founded the Stetson hat company. Others had been Confederates and Klansmen. He kicked against that background, proud to be labelled 'the renegade scion of a respected Southern family'.[4] To Kennedy, the situation at the end of the Second World War resembled the one at the end of the Civil War:

> the South [could] continue down the path of prejudice with poverty and privation for all but its exploiters. Or it can take the high road to democracy – political, economic, racial; for democracy is indivisible – and proceed full speed ahead to the promised land of liberty and justice for all.[5]

Kennedy's subversion of the Klan started slowly. In his 20s he worked for the New Deal on the WPA's Writers' Project exposing Klan attacks on labour activists. He joined the Klan as 'John Perkins', learning their secrets from the inside before allegedly exposing that information on the radio. He made the Klans look silly rather than threatening, their names idiotic, not menacing.

As Kennedy predicted, 'the millions of kids who had listened to Superman were not likely to grow up as Klansmen'.[6] He saw that the Klan was being forced to accept that white supremacy as a mass movement was a thing of the past. The aspirations of desegregation; the commitment to removing overt racial discrimination; increasingly colour-blind immigration policies – all these indicated that the federal government knew it could no longer accept that the USA was a white man's nation.

Kennedy saw the Klan's cohering around the idea that it was the *white* population that was oppressed and threatened. It was a movement for white power, an idea that drew upon the militant Black Power movement of the late 1960s. The Klan denied being motivated by the hatred of other races, but rather it claimed to be driven by love of the white race. They believed in a common white racial identity and white separatism. It was, of course, ridiculous – as Kennedy saw, not least because it was nearly impossible to bring about. But still, they tried.

The Klan's ultimate goal was to divide up the nation by race. The most extreme plans involved the creation of a physically separate white ethno-state. To its adherents, racial separation was God's will. Others saw it being brought about by a nuclear catastrophe or race war. It would involve a *Götterdämmerung* or Armageddon, a cataclysm so extreme it would exterminate the human race, except, of course, for the chosen white people.

In the coming decades Klansmen would become increasingly entangled with neo-Nazis; disaffected veterans from Vietnam; ultra-violent, anarchist, skinhead groups; and survivalist militias training for the forthcoming race war necessary to bring about the white homeland. They would turn to bank robberies, arms thefts, drug deals, counterfeiting and – occasionally – martyrdom to achieve their aims. They would become more and more linked with the fringe 'Christian Identity' sects of the 'chosen'. Some became involved with the 'victory or Valhalla' pagan Norse religions. Still others drew on pseudo-religious millenarian theories of the End of Days.

These extreme views marked a distinct shift within the Klan: a belief that they could no longer operate within the 'system'. From that point onwards, the Klan saw itself as an outlaw group, governed by racially based conspiracy theories of which the general population was ignorant. It fell to the *Klan* to train whites for the racial battles ahead. Klansmen would come to relish their outsider status: it was the Klan and their white power brothers against the world.

There was, however, one last brief interlude where the Klan tried to appeal to the doubts of an increasingly liberal mainstream USA.

# CHAPTER 75

At the age of 20, David Duke first made the headlines when he picketed the speech of a Jewish civil rights lawyer. William Kunstler had unsuccessfully defended the 'Chicago Seven', a group of activists accused of conspiracy and crossing state lines to commit a riot at the 1968 Democratic National Convention. Kunstler himself had been sentenced to four years in Cook County Jail for contempt of court, a sentence which was stayed until he won the appeal in 1972.

As Kunstler addressed students at Louisiana State University (LSU) in July 1970, Duke paraded around the campus in full Nazi regalia with placards reading, 'Kunstler is a Communist Jew' and 'Gas the Chicago Seven'. A month later he was invited to address the US Nazi Party in Washington DC.[1]

A less than stellar student at LSU, Duke saved his passion for the promotion of his antisemitic and white supremacist views. He hung a swastika in his dorm room and handed out Nazi propaganda on campus. In 1969 he made an impassioned speech on a local radio station arguing that Black people should be forcibly returned to Africa and Jews exterminated.

After his exploits with Kunstler, he joined the White Student Alliance and published a newsletter called *The Racialist*. In an argument he would use throughout his career, Duke claimed his belief in 'white pride' did not mean hatred of other races. Moving to New Orleans in 1972, he married a fellow white supremacist, Chloe Hardin. The following year he joined the New Orleans group Knights of the Ku Klux Klan (KKKK).

Led by real estate developer James Lindsay, the KKKK was closely linked with neo-Nazis. Within a year, the young and ambitious Duke had risen to the rank of Grand Wizard. By the time of Lindsay's murder in 1975, the KKKK had around 6,500 members, a significant improvement on its situation in the late 1960s.[2]

In an effort to raise the KKKK's profile and increase recruitment, Duke abandoned some of the Klan's usual ways of operating. He allowed Roman Catholics to join, encouraged women to participate as equal members and recruited on college campuses rather than focusing on police stations or bars. He also (publicly) professed non-violence and did away with the closed hood, making Klansmen's faces visible at all times. He hired rock bands for rallies.[3] Most importantly, he played the media game – very successfully.

At 6ft 2in, Duke was trim, boyishly handsome and articulate. He dressed in an elegant suit for interviews, reserving the Klan hood for ceremonies. He wore his hair fashionably long and spoke in a calm and eloquent tone. Even when he was advocating Holocaust denial or condemning African Americans as 'welfare scroungers', he was, as one female journalist put it, 'the Klan's answer to Robert Redford'.[4] To my mind, he looked more like David Hasselhoff.

Instead of Imperial Wizard, Duke called himself the Klan's 'National Director'. He appeared on national television talking about the unfairness of positive discrimination and his mission to level up the 'white race's' position in US society. He staged slick publicity stunts like 'Freedom Rides North', a protest against integrated school busing in Boston.

Nothing demonstrates Duke's media-savvy better than the 'Klan Border Patrol' event he staged in 1977 in southern California. Duke told the press that he had 230 armed Klansmen patrolling the 2,000-mile border to prevent Mexicans from entering the country illegally 'to take US jobs away'. In actuality, his border guard was outnumbered five to one by reporters – but the stunt worked. When no aliens appeared in the tiny section his men had briefly patrolled, Duke bragged, 'I think some Mexicans are afraid to enter the country because of the Klan.'[5]

Within a couple of years the KKKK expanded into Florida, Alabama, Texas, California, Connecticut and New York. When Klansmen failed to turn up at a California rally and press event, Grand Dragon Tom Metzger dressed spectators in Klan robes – and very likely paid them. As reporters arrived and saw the ten or so Klansmen milling around, Metzger said that each one was a delegate representing their local Klaverns. This strategy seemed to work: the next rally drew thirty Klansmen and, the next, eighty.[6]

For a while it looked like Duke was on his way to reviving the Klan and its triumphs of the 1920s. Even the notoriously publicity-shy Bobby Shelton grudgingly admitted, 'He comes on like a reasonable person, serious, sincere and conservatively dressed. No flaming, wild-eyed nut would go over half so well.'[7] Duke did not return the admiration, stating that 'freshmen, sophomores, juniors in college [had] never even heard of Shelton'.[8] By 1979 Duke had contributed to a rise in what a Gallup poll called 'favorable opinions of the Klan' among white populations, an increase from 6 per cent in 1965 to 11 per cent in 1979.[9]

But there were serious problems with Duke's leadership. Most importantly, he was unable to delegate power. As a result, the Klan lacked the state-level leadership so crucial to its survival. In 1975, Kentucky's Grand Dragon, Phillip Chopper, publicly called Duke 'a fraud' and accused him of embezzling thousands of dollars of Klan funds. Jerry Dutton, the Grand Dragon of Alabama, left the KKKK in 1977. The biggest blow was the 1980 resignation of Tom Metzger as Grand Dragon in California. Metzger couldn't deal with Duke's gentrification of the order and went off to found his own neo-Nazi skinhead group, White Aryan Resistance (WAR).[10]

In the summer of 1980 Duke himself abandoned the KKKK, telling a British newspaper he'd quit because he couldn't stop his Klansmen doing 'stupid or violent things'.[11] The reality was he'd tried to sell the organisation's 3,000-name mailing list to Bill Wilkinson. Louisiana-based Wilkinson's Invisible Empire Knights of the KKK (IEKKK) had broken away from the KKKK in 1975 and taken up to a third of Duke's Klansmen by 1979. Admitting defeat, Duke offered to hand over leadership in return for $35,000. Unfortunately for Duke, it turned out that Wilkinson had been an FBI informant for the last six years. He recorded their meeting and exposed Duke's offer, forcing the embarrassed National Director of the KKKK to promptly resign.[12]

Duke would always claim he'd left to create a new order which could show that white 'racialists' were not racists, but 'innocent victims and benevolent champions of equality and justice'. He provocatively called his organisation the National Association for the Advancement of White People (NAAWP). Its ideology was pretty standard racist-right fare. Claiming deep and sincere religious roots, Duke spoke of 'white pride' and 'positive discrimination'. He also attacked feminism, condemned alternative lifestyles and advocated strict law-and-order policies. He demanded protection of Constitutional rights – especially over the right to bear arms – and more stringent immigration policies.

The NAAWP never attracted more than 1,000 members, but Duke continued to try to make his message mainstream by running for state and national office. He unsuccessfully ran for the Louisiana state senate in 1979 and won a seat in the Louisiana House in 1989, standing as a low-tax, anti-busing, law-and-order Republican. He stood for the US Senate in 1990 and pulled in over half the white votes cast in Louisiana. The following year he was trounced in his attempt to gain the Governor's Mansion. He made rather half-hearted runs for US president in 1980 and 1988 and raised funds for Pat Buchanan's far-right Reform Party in 2000.

As the new millennium opened, with his face 'enhanced' by plastic surgery, his hair dyed and his body perma-tanned and ripped, Duke was probably the best known and most vocal advocate of the racist right. Echoing the trajectory of the Klan itself, his failure to gain a major office made his rhetoric ever more antisemitic. After a fifteen-month imprisonment for tax evasion and fraud, Duke travelled to Europe. He gave lectures in Germany, Austria, Russia, the Czech Republic and Italy, treating audiences to a mix of Holocaust denial, white supremacy and conspiracy theories revolving around Zionism.

With lecture titles like 'Open Letter to the World' and 'The White World's Future', Duke frequently found himself in trouble with the authorities. He was banned from the Czech Republic, Germany, Austria and Italy for Holocaust denial. In 2009 this ban was extended to cover all European Union states that participated in the free-travel zone created by the Schengen Treaty.

On his return to the USA, Duke renewed ties with Don Black, leader of the white supremacist Council of Conservative Citizens and, as it happens, his ex-wife's new husband. Black was now the administrator of the online bulletin board and hate site Stormfront.org. It had been founded in 1995 with the motto 'White Pride World Wide'. By 2008 it had grown to 130,000 members. Duke used it as a vehicle to get back into the mainstream of white hate.

In 2015 Duke was back in the headlines, giving interviews to CNN and Fox News, accepting the debate challenge of gravelly voiced far-right radio host Alex Jones, and discussing immigration, race and the 'Jewish Question'. The following year Duke came out in favour of Donald Trump, telling his supporters that voting for anyone other than Trump was 'treason to your heritage'. Trump tried to distance himself from Duke, publicly disavowing him on Facebook and Twitter and claiming three times during a CNN interview that he didn't even know Duke.

Even today the SPLC refers to Duke as 'the most recognizable figure of the American radical right'. And although Duke condemned his former fellow Klansmen as backward and violent, he's been careful to maintain his connections with the organisation. He became the go-to interviewee whenever white nationalists and white supremacists were in the headlines.

Articles and interviews almost always refer to him as 'David Duke, former Imperial Wizard of the KKK'. Journalists see him as a spokesman 'within the Klan' and, through these almost boilerplate references to Duke as former leader of 'the Klan', rather than the more accurate Knights of the KKK (KKKK), Duke not only gets an injection of publicity, but makes the Klan appear more powerful, unified and widespread than it actually is. The mistake reinforces the idea that Duke is part of an organisation with a history going back to 1865 and not the founder of an order he created in 1974, which expelled him less than six years later.[13]

# CHAPTER 76

David Duke should be seen as something of an anomaly in the modern Klan. His seemingly rational, media-savvy charisma was pretty well unique in white supremacist circles. The leaders of most Klan factions were as uncompromising in their speech as they were in their beliefs. They went back to the Klan's roots.

Sometimes this took the form of implicit violence, as in 1979 when a local Black citizens group requested that an Invisible Empire Klan motorcade driving through Decatur, Alabama, be unarmed, as local ordinances demanded. The Klan leader, Duke's nemesis, Bill Wilkinson, responded with a public, curt and threatening, 'If you want our guns, come and get them.' Four Black demonstrators were injured at the event, trying to do just that.[1]

Other leaders opted for arcane mysticism. Robert E. Miles, the self-proclaimed strategist of the 'Fifth Era' Klan, represented the organisation through numerology. Since 'K' was the eleventh number in the alphabet, 'KKK' became three times eleven – '33'. And '5' represented the fifth iteration of the Klan.[2] So, he advocated maintaining secrecy by signing messages '33/5'. Quite simple when you know how.

Both of these traits – violence and mystery – were to prove central to the post-1970s Klan, as they had to all Klans before Duke. The man who best personified these sides of the Klan during and after the 'Duke Era' was a man of action, a decorated Vietnam veteran. Louis Beam had served as a gunner on a UH-1 Huey helicopter with the 25th Aviation Battalion for eighteen months, returning from his extended tour of duty in 1968.

It was the most important experience of his life and he brought several things home to Texas with him. Along with the waking nightmares of PTSD, he would retain a lifelong hatred of the Viet Cong and communism.

What he left in Vietnam was his patriotism, at least patriotism as it related to obedience to the federal government.

Like many other Vietnam vets, Beam felt the government had betrayed him. He thought the government deceived and demeaned their sacrifices by pulling out and ignominiously surrendering to the Viet Cong. He condemned the government for leaving soldiers behind as prisoners of war in terrible conditions in North Vietnam. He felt the government allowed 'peaceniks', hippies and communists at home to spit on their service, ignore their sufferings and to openly criticise their actions while fighting for the Stars and Stripes.

Beam also came home with a hatred of African Americans. Like many other Southern GIs, Vietnam had been his first real experience of mixing with Black people. Although ostensibly desegregated, the races self-segregated with varying degrees of more or less disguised, mutual hostility and often violence. Beam condemned his fellow Black servicemen as stupid, dirty and un-American. And on his return to Texas, he railed against 'the unnatural caldron of black, brown, yellow and white' resulting from 'an alien political system that seeks to exalt the inferior, base, incompetent and unfit over the superior, creative, constructive and beautiful'.[3]

Beam had joined Shelton's UKA in 1968, pinning his medals onto his robe. But in 1976 he left to join Duke's KKKK, rising to become Grand Dragon of Texas. Yet, that same year he demonstrated the difference between his approach and that of Duke. At a public Klan rally the Texas Grand Dragon told assembled Klansmen – and the press – 'I've got news for you, nigger. I'm not going to be in front of my television set, I'm gonna be hunting you. ... I've got the Bible in one hand and a .38 in the other hand and I know what to do.'[4]

By 1980 Beam was publicly condemning Duke's attempts to change the system from within, by standing for office. He believed the Klan needed to abandon Duke's rational approach because, as he put it, 'Where ballots fail, bullets will prevail'. He sought armed conflict with the government and this was where he played a vital role in the evolution of the Klan. Beam believed the Klan's mission was to fight the federal government with its agenda of racial equality and integration. To Beam:

> although the battlefield has changed and the rules were different [to Vietnam], THE WAR CONTINUES. ... Once again the Klan must ride; it will face a governmental tyranny, unrestrained by moral bounds ... a government that while posing as a legal body, seeks unlawfully to exterminate the descendants of those who conceived it.[5]

From the outset, Beam not only advocated, but practised violence.

Initially, his targets generally related to his Vietnam experience. In 1971 he and four other Klansmen bombed a prominent left-wing radio station in Houston and machine-gunned the local Communist Party HQ. Some years later he was arrested for an attempted assault on the visiting Chinese leader, Deng Xiaoping.

Then in 1981 Beam hit the national headlines when he rallied Klansmen to 'aid' Galveston shrimp fishermen in their battle to exclude Vietnamese competition. The squabble had roots in the mid-1970s. The Vietnamese refugees had experience of shrimping and, with their extended families, co-operative practices and pooling of resources, they quickly started to undercut their white competitors and came to dominate the industry.

This brought accusations of illegal behaviour and unfair government subsidies from the local white fishermen. Tempers frayed. Beam charged in, portraying the dispute as a continuation of the war in Vietnam. He and other Klansmen made accusations that pets that disappeared and local vermin were being eaten by the Vietnamese. He argued that the Viet Cong were involved in supplying money and firearms to the Vietnamese shrimpers. There were sightings of robed Klansmen on the docks and mysterious arson attacks on Vietnamese boats.

Newspapers stoked up the conflict, marking it in terms of war. *The New York Times* referred to it as 'one of the last pitched battles of the Vietnam war'. The *Houston Chronicle* called the conflict the 'Viet-Klan proceedings' and the *LA Times* depicted it as the 'Texas-Asian Fishing War'. Yet, in spite of this, support for the Klan started to ease off. In May 1981, a Klan rally in Santa Fe was attended by fewer than 100, less than a third of those who'd attended a rally in February. A week later a young Black female judge granted an injunction prohibiting Klan robes, arming fishermen or burning crosses around Galveston Bay. Tensions subsided and, spitting threats at the judge, the government and non-whites, Beam and his Klansmen moved on.[6]

The 'shrimp war' was undoubtedly Beam's most high-profile action in the eyes of the press and the public. Like other 'racially aware' veteran Klansmen, Beam felt that the Klan needed to become a paramilitary force, capable of winning the imminent race war which must result from the government's integrationist policies. In 1983, Beam laid out his beliefs in his *Essays of a Klansman*, but he had already started to put those ideas into practice.[7]

In 1977 Beam had used the Veterans Land Board scheme to buy 50 acres in Double Bayou, an out-of-the-way, swampy backwater in Chambers County, Texas. He called it 'Camp Puller' and here, permanently armed, living in fatigues and brutalised by a violent brand of 'military' discipline, Beam sought to turn his Klansmen into paramilitaries. By the end of 1980, he had opened up Camp Puller to anyone willing to pay – including, on one notorious occasion, giving lessons in lethal armed and unarmed combat to (white) high-school-aged Civil Air Patrol and Boy Scouts.[8]

It was also at Camp Puller that Beam trained his elite Border Watch. While the original idea came from California's Tom Metzger in 1977, it was Beam who formalised and militarised the idea in 1983. As they both saw it, they were helping the overstretched and complacent US Border Patrol officers in their duty to patrol the land border with Mexico, looking for undocumented immigrants.[9] To Beam and others, the time to fight on behalf of the state, as he had done in Vietnam, was now gone. White power activists need to fight for the white race and a white homeland, and wage war on the enemies of that aspiration – the federal government.

To this end he dedicated his efforts to working out the best ways in which to achieve his revolutionary race war. In another 1983 essay, he popularised a theory of cell structure for his insurgency. The technique had already been used with considerable violence in the USA by a disparate group known collectively as the Posse Comitatus.

The name is derived from the Latin for 'the power of the county' and was inspired by the Posse Comitatus Act of 1878. This post-Reconstruction federal law expressly forbade the use of federal troops to enforce state legislation – 'except under circumstances expressly authorized by the Constitution or Act of Congress'. This protection of 'states' rights' had enabled the essential dismantling of the Fourteenth and Fifteenth Amendment protections for Black Southerners and the establishment of first Jim Crow and then the full-blown segregation of Southern society.[10]

The founder of the twentieth-century posse, William P. Gale, argued that the 1878 law neutralised and essentially invalidated all government at a higher level than the county sheriff. Alongside this belief, Gale was also committed to an 'organic' Constitution. He held that the original 1789 Constitution and the Bill of Rights formed the law of the USA. They were complete and unalterable. Subsequent amendments, like the Thirteenth, freeing slaves, or the Fourteenth, giving African Americans citizenship, were invalid. Given this, Gale and his followers did not recognise the power of any state or federal legislation, or their right to enforce those laws.

Gale's United Christian Posse Association was founded in 1969 in Glendale, California, and quickly spread to Portland, Oregon. By the 1980s Gale was broadcasting his religio-racial-political rants to Western states from a powerful country-and-western radio station KTTL in Dodge City, Kansas.[11]

The Posse Comitatus also attracted neo-Nazis and Klansmen, who in one of their publications called it 'a heartening sign of public determination to see law enforcement restored'. David Duke supported it and told *Newsweek*, 'We get their material and funnel it to our groups.'[12] And the ties to the Klan worked both ways. Gale usually wrote under a pseudonym – 'Colonel Ben Cameron' – a reference to the central hero of *The Birth of a Nation* and arguably one of the most important Klan figures of all time.

And it wasn't just Duke who was drawn to the posse. Beam felt the anarchic violence and disparate groups could provide valuable tactical lessons to the white power movement. Like his Klansmen in 1983, the dissimilar groups of the posse were frequently bound only by their violent response to the 'system'. In 1982, eight posse members in Colorado were jailed for bombing an IRS office and attempting to kill a federal judge. In 1983, Gordon Kahl, a North Dakota farmer and posse member, killed two federal marshals sent to arrest him. He then killed an Arkansas sheriff before he was killed in a shootout when his hideout was raided. That same year posse members claimed they'd murdered a sheriff in Kansas and engaged in a gun battle with a county SWAT team after a South Dakota farmer 'seceded' his farm from the USA.

While the success of these posse members was, at best, debatable, their martyrdom was not entirely in vain. It was no coincidence that 1983 was the year Beam announced his theory of Leaderless Resistance for the Klan, a command structure which the Tamil Tigers had been using with devastating effectiveness in their insurgency in Sri Lanka. He combined it with the lessons of the posse. As he saw it, the usual setting-up of a clear hierarchy of command within an insurgency made the organisation 'easy prey for government infiltration, entrapment, and destruction of the personnel involved'.[13]

In order to avoid the potential catastrophe of infiltration, Beam advocated the creation of 'phantom' cells – small, autonomous groups. Each would operate independently of the other. But they drew their strength from a clear, shared and unified set of objectives. Beam felt the key to achieving this seeming contradiction lay in having a public-facing leadership that was 'above ground', public and legitimate. Unlike Gale, Beam's leadership would break no laws and would promote and publish its objectives in plain sight – relying on being protected by the First Amendment's sanctification of free speech.

The active cells were, by contrast, invisible and underground – and committed to a violent struggle. But their actions would be informed and directed by the above-ground elements. To those investigating the organisation the two elements had no tangible or detectable connection, other than shared theoretical beliefs. His theorising made it look like those who carried out seemingly mindless acts of horrific violence – lone-wolf mass shootings, random lynchings, bombings and the like – could, by affiliation with groups like the Klan, have a greater impact than simply fulfilling their personal fantasies.

Beam's widely read – and largely impractical – theories would convince a new generation of homegrown terrorists that were struggling towards a higher goal than their frequently deranged minds originally conceived. They had the power to make these loners a part of something bigger than themselves. His encouragement of ultra-violent acts would definitely contribute to the evolution of modern Klan, white power and anti-state thinking. And nowhere is this more apparent than in the violent white power atrocities that culminated in the 1995 Oklahoma City bombing.

# CHAPTER 77

As in the 1930s, in the 1970s and 1980s the Klan was once again forced to look for new allies. There were plenty to choose from, including disaffected Vietnam veterans on remote compounds preparing for race or nuclear war; tax resisters agonising over the welfare state handouts to immigrants and minorities; fringe white supremacist religious groups; racist skinheads; neo-Nazis; and sometimes even pagans and women.

As Gale's posse and Beam's Leaderless Resistance demonstrated, there was potential in the apparently formless mass of discontent. What would unify these groups was far more mundane than the grand ideas their leaders preached. Groups such as those of Gale and Beam fell out and cohered for the same reasons as we make and lose friends and acquaintances in everyday life. Members would meet someone from another faction, start relationships, fall out with former comrades, marry, move back home, find religion or simply drift into another order.[1]

This took place on an organisational level as well. Klan and Nazis socialised together, frequently holding rallies in the same space. Ideologically, it made sense, and it is not surprising that the most notable white power atrocity of the 1970s took place at a jointly organised event.

In November 1979, around forty neo-Nazis and Klansmen descended for a motorcade parade through a Black housing project in Greensboro, North Carolina. Calling themselves 'The United Racist Front', they arrived heavily armed with guns, hunting weaponry and tear gas. Undaunted, members of the Communist Workers Party (CWP) provocatively called their rally 'Death to the Klan' and equipped themselves with handguns, police batons, hard hats and sturdy sticks.

Months earlier in the nearby city of China Grove, the CWP and local Black activists had descended upon the Klansmen in the city's community centre where they were enjoying a screening of *The Birth of a Nation*. Armed activists surrounded the building chanting 'Death to the Klan' and 'Decease the Rotten Beast'. The terrified and outnumbered Klansmen couldn't leave the building until their besiegers tired and dispersed. Vowing revenge, they spent the next months studying the well-publicised television footage of the event. They singled out the most prominent CWP activists and vowed these 'race traitors' and communists would suffer.

Things turned ugly in Greensboro that November afternoon. After shooting that lasted fewer than two minutes, four white men and a Black woman were dead. All except one were members of the CWP. Six more were seriously wounded – one Klansman and five CWP.

Although the Klan probably saw this massacre as some sort of victory, the aftermath proved to have far more impact than the shootings. A year after the killings, the state of North Carolina charged fourteen Klansmen and neo-Nazis with felony riot and first-degree murder. They had video footage of the shootings, eyewitnesses, weapons and FBI ballistic reports.

The defence pleaded self-defence and the all-white jury acquitted them. It was not portrayed as a victory for racism, but as a validation of US anti-communism. In North Carolina, in 1980, this was apparently grounds for shooting a man. As one Klansman put it as he left the court, 'People have been treating us like heroes. Anytime you defeat communism, it's a victory for America.'[2]

In 1984 the US Justice Department charged nine of the perpetrators with 'conspiracy to violate the civil rights' of the Greensboro victims. Once again, an all-white jury acquitted them, maintaining that the Klansmen were just defending themselves against 'political hatred'. Finally, in June 1985 the victims filed a $48 million lawsuit charging eighty-seven defendants with the 'wrongful death' of the five shooting victims. This time the defendants were not just Klansmen or neo-Nazis. They now included the city of Greensboro; the FBI; the state of North Carolina; and the US Justice Department. The civil jury found eight of the defendants liable and ordered five Klansmen and Nazi shooters and three policemen to settle the claim for $350,000. That sum went to the only non-CWP victim's widow. The relatives and dependants of the dead communists were not eligible for any compensation.

The message seemed to be that politically motivated killing was legitimate while racially motivated murder was not. Klansmen and neo-Nazis interpreted the decisions following Greensboro to mean there were many who, while stopping short of actual violence, seemed to tacitly support their views.[3]

The Klan–Nazi fusion seemed to be cemented and the Klan's fears calmed. In fact, the Klan became more like the Nazis. Like Beam's Texans,

Klansmen adopted fatigues and military-style dress. Swastikas blazed alongside crosses. Klansmen got SS runes tattooed on themselves. The white robes and the hood were reserved for ceremonies. As Gorrell Pierce, Georgia's Grand Dragon of the Federated Knights of the KKK, succinctly put it, 'You take a man who fought in the Second World War, it's hard for him to sit down in a room full of swastikas … But people realize that time is running out. We're going to *have* to get together.'[4]

Pierce was alluding to a change which had been apparent since the early 1970s. In an article in Bob Shelton's *Fiery Cross*, a neo-Nazi argued that the enemy was not the Black population, but the federal government, 'a corrupt, unnatural and degenerate monstrosity'.[5] In 1976, fellow neo-Nazi Eric Thompson (the pen-name for Eric Campbell) elaborated on his thinking.

In his article 'Welcome to ZOG-World', Thompson outlined the theory of a shadowy Jewish cabal controlling the federal government. ZOG was an acronym for 'Zionist Occupational Government'. Thompson's theory amalgamated a rich seam of international antisemitism and simple paranoia which drew on medieval, White Russian, Nazi and other sources to create what he called 'a picture of the enemy'. In his dystopian vision, the West was ignoring obvious signs that Jewish conspirators were gradually coming to control the economies and taking over the governments and media outlets all over the world. In order to fulfil their objective, they had to enslave gentiles, and the white race seemed largely oblivious to this threat. He warned that 'They Live, We Sleep'.[6]

From the early 1980s on, Thompson's ZOG theory would come to subtly dominate white power theorising and legitimise a 'revolutionary turn' in their thinking. For Nazis, racial–religious cults, skinheads, militiamen and, of course, Klansmen, fighting the mythical ZOG became their focus. It justified fighting the federal and state government. The overthrow of ZOG, with its evil objectives, legitimised criminal activity and 'direct action' including robbery, destruction of property, murder and even the overthrow of the federal government itself.

# CHAPTER 78

Born in Georgia, William Luther Pierce came from another of those prestigious Southern families with ancestors who'd played leading roles in the Confederacy but which had since fallen on hard times. But Pierce himself was successful. An academic child, he went on to become a professor of physics at Oregon State University. In 1965, in his 30s, he left academia and moved to Washington DC to become a senior researcher for the aerospace manufacturer Pratt and Whitney. He soon became involved in far-right politics.

Within months of arriving in the capital, he was editing *National Socialist World* for the charismatic US Nazi Party leader George Lincoln Rockwell. The job fitted well with Pierce's own politics, which were passionately white nationalist and rabidly antisemitic. By 1974, he'd founded his own neo-Nazi group, the National Alliance (NA), an order he hoped would act as the political storm troopers for a white nationalist revolution. It never happened. His efforts cost him his career.

His attempt to prevent US firms from selling munitions to Israel failed spectacularly. Pierce was put on federal watchlists for the association that episode flagged up with so-called terrorist groups like Hezbollah. Then in 1978, much like the Klan had been, the NA was hit with a massive bill for income tax arrears. Partly to dig himself out of that financial hole, Pierce published a book that would become, in the FBI's words, 'the Bible of the racist right'.[1]

*The Turner Diaries* was first published in 1974 in serial form in the neo-Nazi journal – *Attack!* It has been in print ever since, although it owes more to *Star Wars* than *The Birth of a Nation*. Pierce wrote it under the pseudonym Andrew MacDonald, telling the tale of the 'Organization', a white citizens' insurgency struggling to overthrow a racially inclusive, Jewish-controlled puppet federal government calling itself 'The System'. Although the book was written before Thompson's diatribe, it shares a great deal of his ZOG theorising.

But the appeal and importance of *The Turner Diaries* lies in the way Pierce lays out a blueprint for the violent overthrow of ZOG. The novel centres around the experience of Earl Turner, a young white Organization guerrilla who narrates the escalation of the Organization's resistance into full-scale nuclear war and his own crucial role in the culminating Kamikaze-style destruction of the Pentagon.

Pierce's political influence collapsed by the 1980s but *The Turner Diaries* had sold hundreds of thousands of copies and become required reading for white supremacists. For those who wanted simple solutions to 'the race problem' the book seemed to act as a handbook. Readers studied and imitated the Organization's methods, tactics and infrastructure.

One of the book's most enthusiastic fans was Odinist 'Bob' Mathews, tax-protesting, anti-communist, white nationalist militia-man and associate of Louis Beam. Blatantly imitating Pierce's fictional work, Mathews formed his own white power group, The Order. The name was taken directly from *The Turner Diaries*, as were its rituals, structure and strategies. In imitation of *The Turner Diaries*, The Order began with a crime spree.

They began by counterfeiting $50 bills, but were quickly caught and a member imprisoned. Next, they robbed an adult bookstore – netting less than $370. Their luck changed with a Seattle bank robbery that landed them $26,000. Further robberies and burglaries netted them nearly $45,000. Finally, in July 1984, they hit the jackpot. Robbing a Brinks armoured car in Ukiah, California, they hauled over $3.8 million.[2]

After the robbery, Mathews gave Louis Beam $100,000, illustrating The Order's close ties with the Klan. Frazier Glenn Miller of the Carolina Knights of the KKK got $200,000. Richard Miles of the UKA received $15,500 and the ex-KKKK Grand Dragon of California, Tom Metzger, was given $300,000.[3] These windfalls put them on the radar of the authorities. What was more, in spite of his close connections to Beam, Mathews did not seem to have absorbed the Texan Klansman's strategy of Leaderless Resistance. His mistake would have devastating results for himself and The Order.

In what became a legendary last stand in the white power movement's mythology, Mathews single-handedly held off 100 FBI agents and a helicopter in a remote hideaway in Washington state. Eventually the building caught fire and ignited Mathews' stockpile of explosives. His body was never recovered. With information given by member Tom Martinez in a plea deal, the FBI was soon able to round up the remaining members of The Order in Operation Clean Sweep. They received sentences of up to 250 years each. The movement was broken.[4]

But Mathews' death did very little to stop the crime sprees and violence. Legend has it that his dying words were, 'Should you die my friend, another friend will emerge from the shadows to take your place.' There was even a commemorative medal hawked around at white power rallies bearing these words.[5] Mathews' heroic death in battle stirred the Posse Comitatus into action. With great enthusiasm and little caution, they undertook assassinations, bombings and other crimes. But the FBI always seemed one step ahead.

By 1986, posse founder William Gale and seven of his members were jailed for tax evasion and sending death threats to IRS agents. Even without Gale, the posse continued the fight. That same year, one of his men would die in a shootout with the police and others after firing homemade mortars into the California courthouse where Gale was on trial. After this, the posse quickly haemorrhaged members.

Posse members were jailed in Arizona and Utah after being connected to real estate scams, robberies, hidden stockpiles of arms and explosives, and several bombings that included a synagogue, an IRS office and the Anti-Defamation League's offices. In 1990 Gale's successor James Wickstrom faded away after being jailed for three years on counterfeiting charges.[6]

A Klansman named Frazier Glenn Miller came to The Order's rescue, calling the prosecution of the remaining members of The Order nothing less than a 'declaration of war'. He renamed his Carolina Knights of the KKK the White Patriot Party (WPP), dressed them in full military gear and issued a rambling document in which he told his comrades they were 'honour bound and duty bound to pick up the sword and do battle with the forces of evil'.

In a bizarre alternative reality, Miller turned assassination into a game. He established a points system for – presumably – the murder of 'Niggers (1), White Race Traitors (10), Jews (10), Judges (50)' and his nemesis, 'Morris Seligman Dees (888)'. He ended his rant with 'Let the battle axes swing smoothly and the bullets whizz true. Glenn Miller, Loyal Member of "The Order".'[7]

Instead of going out in a blaze of glory, reality caught up with Miller and his gang. They were quickly arrested and put on probation for minor assaults. Miller himself broke the terms of his freedom and served a two-month sentence. Upon his release he went on to serve five years for conspiracy for trying to kill anti-Klan activist Morris Seligman Dees, founder of the Klan's new nemesis, the SPLC.

# CHAPTER 79

Klan threats. Klan bombs. Assassination attempts. Throughout the years, none have stopped the Southern Poverty Law Center (SPLC) in its mission to create 'racial justice in the South and beyond'.

Based in the heart of the Deep South in Montgomery, Alabama, the SPLC has represented some of the poorest, most vulnerable and abused populations in the USA. Throughout its fifty-odd years of existence, the SPLC has exposed and brought to justice extremist hate groups – above all, the Klan.

The SPLC was founded in 1971 by two graduates of the University of Alabama Law School. One of them, Morris Seligman Dees, had just sold his direct mail marketing company for about $6 million ($48 million today). With his new-found funds, Dees vowed to focus on civil rights work for those who could not afford legal representation. The Center quickly succeeded, expanding to five full-time lawyers and the necessary support staff. Clients initially brought death penalty appeals and cases of racial discrimination but by 1979 the SPLC, under Dees' leadership, was largely targeting the Klan.

Dees had an indomitable drive to improve himself. He had grown up poor, the son of a local tenant cotton farmer. A bright, good-looking and popular youth, he graduated law school in 1960 and set up a law office with Millard Fuller. It was successful, but not nearly as successful as a side business they had established at the same time.

The Fuller and Dees Marketing Group started off by selling customised birthday cakes. Well-priced and promptly delivered, they had trouble meeting the demand. They expanded into niche markets, offering items with a rural and domestic appeal like tractor seat cushions and cookbooks. They seemed to have the Midas touch.

Dees was handsome, showy and brash. He spoke with a salesman's patter tinged with the confidence of a self-made millionaire. He loved the lime-light and enjoyed playing the provocateur. Dees genuinely didn't care what Montgomery's Good Ole Boys, or the city's liberals, thought of him. Many of them called him 'the most hated man in the city'.

His father had been a friend of the progressive governor James 'Big Jim' Folsom, himself a mentor of future white supremacist George Wallace. Folsom and Dees' father were staunchly opposed to inequality as they saw it, the power of once elite men who threatened to rise on their families' past reputations. Young Morris would often eavesdrop as his father and his friend drank and argued politics late into the night in the Dees' small home. Folsom's future racist protégé notwithstanding, he was a man dedicated to equal opportunities for Black and white people. To Folsom, the Southern poor white's exploitation of African Americans demeaned themselves, and indeed was the result of their own exploitation – by the elites who had a vested interest in misdirecting their rage. The two friends felt they, too, were demeaned by it– and Morris inherited this view.

Dees was a wild teenager who largely ignored the colour line. He partied, danced and drank with the local Black population. He lived through the Montgomery Bus Boycott, heard Martin Luther King speak and witnessed first hand the day-to-day cruelties and sufferings of the segregated South. He was deeply affected by the horrific 16th Street Baptist bombings and the difficulties faced by Arthurine Lucy, a Black student trying to get a degree at the University of Alabama.

Yet in one of his first cases, Dees defended the UKA's chief liaison officer Claude Henley, who had been filmed beating up a civil rights activist during the attacks on the Freedom Riders in 1961. Dees managed to convince the jury what they were seeing was a 'personal brawl'. Henley got off with $100 fine and Dees earned a much-needed $5,000 and a lingering mistrust among civil rights activists.

But Dees became an activist after witnessing the increasing injustices of segregation. In 1971, 'all the pulls and tugs of my conscience' drove him to found the SPLC and eventually set his sights on the most egregious symbol of race-hate in the region – the Klan.[1]

In 1981 the SPLC founded Klanwatch with the aim of monitoring, exposing and fighting Klan activity across the USA. There were notable successes from the outset. In one of its first actions, it sued Louis Beam's Texas Knights, preventing them from further terrorising the Vietnamese fishermen in Galveston and closing down Beam's paramilitary training bases at Camp Puller and Double Bay.

In 1983, in retaliation for the SPLC's campaign, three KKKK members burnt down the SPLC's offices – the first of many fires to come. The SPLC was able to track the men down and provide evidence to prosecutors that helped convict the arsonists. In the mid-1980s, SPLC investigations and lawsuits closed down paramilitary groups of the Alabama Knights of the Invisible Empire and the (North) Carolina Knights. But it was in 1987 that the SPLC landed their most serious blow on the Klan.

It all began in March of that year at the weekly meeting of Klavern 900 of the UKA in Mobile, Alabama. The small group of Klansmen listened to their Grand Titan, Bennie Jack Hays, who was furious that a white jury had acquitted a Black youth charged with murdering a white policeman. Hays said the time had come to show their fellow white men how to instil fear into the Southern Black people. Fired up by this speech, two members, his son Henry Hays and James 'Tiger' Knowles, decided to do some 'missionary work' – or freelance violence.

Henry and Tiger began by burning a cross on the lawn of the Mobile County courthouse. Pumped up, they cruised around in Henry's black Buick looking for action. Around 11 p.m., they saw Michael Donald. The Black teenager was walking down a street to get cigarettes for his mother. The two forced Donald into the car at gunpoint and drove the terrified youth to a nearby wood. His death would be a ritual killing, a lesson. After all, as Bennie had told them in the Klavern meeting, 'If a nigger can get away with killing a white man, a white man should be able to get away with killing a nigger'.

Donald fought back – hard. No sooner was he out of the car than he charged at Knowles and knocked him to the ground. Knowles' gun went spinning. They used a carpet knife to overcome the young man, beating him until he passed out. Henry went to the Buick, grabbed a noose they'd made and slipped it over Donald's head. Still, Donald rose up and fought back with the noose hanging around his neck. Eventually, the pair beat him to death and, still full of rage, cut the dead man's throat. They later tied Donald's body to a tree in downtown Mobile in order to make it look like a lynching. Donald's blood-and-gore-stained hi-tops scraped the ground and the rope hung slack at his feet. It wasn't very convincing, but the message was clear.

The two murderers were eventually caught and SPLC attorneys went to work. Using the civil courts, Dees brought prosecution on behalf of Beulah Mae Donald, Michael's grieving mother. Instead of suing Henry Hays or Tiger Knowles, or even Bennie Hays, Dees went for the UKA itself. He sued them for 'conspiracy to interfere with the civil rights' of

Beulah Mae by espousing racist violence. It was a long shot, but it worked. In December 1987 the Southern District of Alabama awarded Beulah Mae $7 million.

It was a shock to the Klan. Just like the famous 1944 IRS ruling which cost the Klan its unity, this decision showed financial penalties sometimes did more damage than criminal ones. The way to defeat the Klan was to make them pay for their crimes, to make it too expensive to continue to spread their messages of hate.

The victories continued. In 1988 the SPLC won $1 million in damages against two Klan groups in Georgia. In 1989 they won a settlement for victims of Wilkinson's 1979 Klan violence in Decatur, Alabama. In 1990 they sued and won over $12 million in a case for the murder of an Ethiopian student in Portland, Oregon, by skinhead Klan members of WAR.

In the coming decades the SPLC would go on to win many, many more.

# CHAPTER 80

The effect of the SPLC's campaign on the Klan was seismic. In 2003 the UKA's previously indomitable Bobby Shelton was reported as telling *The New York Times*, 'The Klan is my belief, my religion. But it won't work anymore. The Klan is gone. Forever.'[1] In some ways Shelton was right. The Klan as it had been, *had* gone. Dees had made sure that high-profile actions with the Klan's signature violence – easily recognised and easily attributable – were a thing of the past.

It wasn't simply hyperbole when Shelton said the Klan was his religion. Distorted as their creed was, to the Klan, religion was one of their most binding features, differentiating members from the 'un-American' and providing a justification for violence. The Klan liked to see their made-up rituals and symbols as the sanctioned if arcane rites of Christianity. The burning cross warned their enemies and their badges included the image of Christ's blood within a cross. Even the Klansman's hood and robes had religious roots.[2]

The Old Testament had often been wheeled out to justify slavery and therefore white supremacy in the pre-Bellum- and the Reconstruction-Era South and it formed a critical part of the Klan's self-justification for its brutal mission. Protestantism had been central to Klansmen's Americanism in the 1920s. The Klansman or woman was not a superstitious foreigner who owed allegiance to a distant and corrupt Pope. They were Americans and, in their world-view, the USA was Protestant. Catholics were immigrants.[3]

Nor was a Klansman a venal, tribal, immoral Jew who sought the overthrow of the US state. Unlike Jews (so they felt), a Klansman was a native-born American. Jews hated Christians – they killed Christ. When the US Supreme Court legalised abortion with the *Roe v. Wade* decision of 1973, Klansmen framed it as a threat to the innocent, an attempt to annihilate the white race by means of a 'White Holocaust'. In this disgusting inversion of history, Jewish doctors aborted white US babies. The KKKK's former California Grand Dragon summed up the warped logic:

> Almost all abortion doctors are Jews. Abortion makes money for Jews … Jews would do anything for money, including the rape of innocent children followed by the ripping and tearing of the living child from the young mother's womb, while it is still forming.[4]

Also central to this white power creed was the equating of Jews with communism. Jews were a controlling cabal, a ZOG. It was from this fantastical antisemitic conspiracy that another strand of Klan 'spirituality' emerged.

Christian Identity was not new. The theology behind it had originated in Britain and crossed the Atlantic in time to play a role in the Klan's flowering in the 1920s. It drew on the work of Richard Brothers, John Hines and David Baron, theologists who based their religious world-view on a triumphalist analysis of the British Empire.

The British Israelite sect believed the 'English-speaking nations', as Winston Churchill would later call them, were the descendants of the mythical Lost Ten Tribes of Israel. They were God's chosen people, which explained why the Anglo-Saxons above all other 'races' were so successful – militarily, economically and, in the eyes of these believers, morally.

One of the leading lights of this sect in the USA was Reuben H. Sawyer, a Portland, Oregon, pastor who preached a potent brand of nativist theology that was perfectly matched to the Klan's messages of WASP white supremacy. Upon joining the Klan, Sawyer rose swiftly to become the north-west's King Kleagle, head of recruitment.

A very impressive speaker, Sawyer preached to thousands, appearing on a stage that was decorated with a sword, the Stars and Stripes, a Bible and the image of a burning cross. It was pure Klan theatre. In 1922 he told a crowd that 'in some parts of the USA the Kikes are so thick that a white man can hardly find room to walk on the sidewalk. And where they are so thick, it is Bolshevism they are talking: Bolshevism, and revolution.'[5]

The emergence of Christian Identity antisemitism was gradual but crucial. The movement had started out pro-Jewish and Sawyer even gave lectures on the British tribes to Jewish audiences. But as he got more involved with the Klan and antisemitic pseudo-scientific 'race theorising', Sawyer drew up a distinction between 'authentic Jews' and 'inauthentic Jews'. To Sawyer and most other British Israelites, the *real* Jews originated from the Saxons, Angles, Celts – or the Sephardic Jews.

The Sephardim were a branch of European Jewry associated with a more Europeanised and liberal lifestyle. Originating from Spain and Portugal, they had spread across Europe fleeing persecution in the early sixteenth century. To the British Israelites all other Jews were essentially imposters and, unlike the Celto-Anglo-Saxons, had no claim to Judaism or divine favour. And most Jews who'd immigrated to the USA in the huge wave of immigration at the turn of the twentieth century were not Sephardic.

By 1950 Klansman Wesley Swift had founded the LA-based Anglo-Saxon Christian Congregation and was running an Anglo-Israel Bible class. He taught that President Truman's Secretary of State was 'a stooge for Stalin' and ranted to his congregation that 'all Jews must be destroyed'. He prophesied that 'before November 1953 there will not be a Jew in the United States', adding, 'at least a Jew that would be able to walk and talk'.[6] It was pure ZOG conspiracy – twenty years before Eric Thompson would coin the term.

By Swift's death in 1970, his Church had been taken over by a far more militant leader, Richard G. Butler. Butler was a follower of William Gale and a supporter of the Posse Comitatus. He went on to found his own 'Christian Posse Comitatus'. Also influenced by Robert Mathews' Order, Butler changed the focus of the Church, and renamed it the Church of Jesus Christ Christian. While he kept up the antisemitic rants, his new Church was more committed to white power terrorism.

To realise his 'religious' message, Butler formed a Christian Identity political wing. Members of the Aryan Nations were heavily armed, dressed as paramilitaries and trained in a Louis Beam-style compound at Hayden Lake in Idaho. They also carried out Klan-style 'missionary work' – violent operations – while at the same time spreading their gospel of race-hate by preaching to other white power movements.

It started with inviting small groups of racist skinheads. Year on year it grew. By 1981, Butler had founded the ambitiously titled 'Aryan World Congress'. Dubbed by the SPLC as a 'twenty-four-hour orgy of hate', it has grown into the most important gathering of white power groups today. Held annually on Hitler's birthday – 20 April – up to 200 gathered to hear lectures, discuss tactics, buy memorabilia and eat, drink and hang out with like-minded racists.

Discussions ranged from deciding where the white homeland would be after the race war to theories on why the bridges over the Rio Grande were made strong enough to support invading Chinese tanks. As absurd and fantastical as they were, these meetings served a more important function. They reminded the disparate factions of white power that they shared common goals, holding out for the dream that, if they were to unify, they would become a serious threat. Not least, they saw the meetings as a forum where the deeds of 'heroes' in the struggle for white power were celebrated.

# CHAPTER 81

When the Alfred P. Murrah Federal Building was bombed on 19 April 1995, the immediate assumption was that it was the work of Middle Eastern terrorists. Three days later and some 80 miles away, an Oklahoma state trooper stopped a 1977 Mercury Marquis with no licence plate. The driver was a decorated Gulf War veteran, Timothy McVeigh. Two days later he would be charged with the bombing which led to the death of 168 people including nineteen children.

McVeigh pleaded guilty to the bombing. Six years later he was executed by lethal injection. McVeigh went to his death unrepentant, convinced of the righteousness of his cause. Hours before his execution he wrote to a boyhood friend:

> I know in my heart that I am right in my struggle, Steve. I have come to peace with myself, my God and my cause. Blood will flow in the streets, Steve. Good vs. Evil. Free Men vs. Socialist Wannabe Slaves. Pray it is not your blood, my friend.[1]

McVeigh could have come from white power central casting. He was a veteran of the 1991 Desert Storm campaign in Iraq. Like Louis Beam, he left the military with a growing mistrust of the federal government, claiming among other things that he'd been ordered to shoot surrendering Iraqi prisoners.[2]

Like the Posse Comitatus he saw taxation and federal intervention as central to the decline of the nation. As he saw it: 'Taxes are a joke. ... More taxes are always the answer to government mismanagement. ... Politicians are out of control.'[3] McVeigh was also deeply committed to protecting the Second Amendment and the 'right to bear arms'.

In the early 1990s McVeigh is estimated to have attended more than eighty gun shows in over forty states, handing out bumper stickers and pro-gun literature. He was particularly fond of talking about *The Turner Diaries*. At one gun show he echoed the plot of Pierce's novel when he told a reporter that the federal 'government is afraid of the guns people have because they have to have control of the people at all times'.[4]

What likely tipped McVeigh over the edge were two bloody and mismanaged clashes between the authorities and white power extremists, Ruby Ridge in northern Idaho and the Branch Davidians in Waco, Texas. These events were tragic, but the number of people killed was far fewer than the number of lives lost in McVeigh's bombing of Oklahoma City or those lost on 9/11.

But as one of the leading figures in the SPLC put it, in August 1992 the 'opening shot' was fired in 'a more or less open war between the American radical right and its government'. Ruby Ridge was where the 'white-hot anger at the federal government finally ignited' into war.[5]

Eight years earlier a Christian Fundamentalist and ex-Special Forces veteran named Randy Weaver moved his family from Iowa to Idaho to await Christ's return. They lived off the grid in a basic cabin at Ruby Ridge, not far from Richard Butler's Aryan Nations compound at Hayden Lake. Weaver's interpretation of the forthcoming apocalypse soon began to take on the racist, antisemitic and violently anti-establishment views of his neighbours.

In 1989, Weaver sold two illegal guns to an undercover federal Alcohol, Tobacco and Firearms (ATF) agent. When Weaver failed to appear at court federal marshals attempted to arrest him. On 24 August 1992 their failed attempts culminated in a botched siege at his cabin in which his wife Vicki, son and a federal marshal were killed, and Weaver and another white power activist were wounded.

At the subsequent trial, Weaver was acquitted of all charges except failure to appear in court, for which he served four months. By contrast, a 1995 Senate subcommittee found that the rules of engagement used by federal forces at Ruby Ridge were 'unconstitutional'.[6] The Weaver family settled their $200 million lawsuit out of court.[7]

Almost as soon as the anti-government feeling around Ruby Ridge died back, another siege seemed to replace it. In February 1993, ATF agents received reports from a UPS driver that the Branch Davidians were stockpiling munitions at their compound in Waco, Texas. After several weeks of surveillance, ATF agents attempted to arrest their leader, David Koresh. They were met by a hail of bullets.

The Millennialist sect had a history of conflict and things quickly escalated. The ATF called for support from the FBI, local law enforcement and US Army units, including tanks. On 19 April the buildings of the compound mysteriously caught fire and burnt to the ground. Later, the badly burnt bodies of seventy-six Branch Davidian adults and children were found in the compound's smoking ruins. To this day their cause of death remains a mystery and fuels conspiracy theories.

Authorities have argued that the fires were started by the Davidians themselves and the dead were the victims of a mass suicide. Gun-rights activists maintain that the siege was unlawful, since the Second Amendment allowed for gun ownership. Predictably, the Branch Davidians became martyrs for the white power movement and Koresh was set up as a kind of civil rights activist.

McVeigh drove to Waco and camped outside the compound, distributing Second Amendment literature and giving press briefings on the breach of rights suffered by the Davidians. From that point on McVeigh would do more for the white power movement than simply hand out leaflets. In the early 1990s he teamed up with an ex-army buddy, Terry Nichols. They lived on Nichols' farm in Michigan and trained themselves in the use of homemade explosives, tear gas and other weaponry. And they discussed possible targets, varying from the UN building in New York to the 'assassin' of Vicki Weaver.

While McVeigh's bombing of Oklahoma City was not attributable to the Klan, it was a clear expression of the white power cause. McVeigh had – albeit very briefly – been a member of a Klan group, probably Bill Wilkinson's Invisible Empire Knights of the KKK, and he was known to have attended Klan rallies and purchased Klan merchandise.[8] More important than his actual affiliations is the way his actions were perceived. McVeigh was seen as a martyr to the cause of white power and his actions revealed the danger of domestic terrorism to the country as a whole and led to a considerable tightening of security.

The SPLC estimated that in the ten years after the Oklahoma City bombing, the FBI and other law enforcement agencies were able to prevent over sixty acts of domestic terrorism. The *Intelligence Report* estimated that paramilitary white power militia membership declined from over 850 in 1996 to a little over 150 in 2005.[9]

Despite appearances, the terrorist acts of the white power movements and the Klan had not been broken, they had gone underground. The use of new technologies and an emphasis on covert action would prove far more nimble, disruptive and powerful.

## PART XI

# HATE IN A DIGITAL AGE 1995–2022

There aren't that many white separatists out there but there are a lot of people who are closeted racists. They don't like to call themselves racist but they wouldn't want their daughter to marry a black man.

Tom Metzger, 2016[1]

# CHAPTER 82

Timothy McVeigh has been described as a 'lone-wolf' terrorist, someone acting on Louis Beam's theories of Leaderless Resistance. But McVeigh did not act alone. His ex-army buddy Terry Nichols had helped him manufacture the bomb, for which he received a life sentence. There was Michael Fortier, who raised money for McVeigh and lied to the authorities on his behalf. He would serve eleven years. But the emphasis on McVeigh as a 'lone wolf' is important for what it says about the USA, technology and isolation in the twenty-first century. To those in the know, McVeigh and his co-conspirators had been 'red-pilled'.

The expression comes from a scene in the 1999 science-fiction film *The Matrix* where the protagonist Neo is offered a choice by his mentor Morpheus between taking a red pill or a blue pill. The blue pill would return Neo to a state of suspended ignorance like the rest of humanity. Instead, Neo chooses the red pill, which initiates him into a whole new world, allowing him to see the 'Matrix' through which reality can be controlled. McVeigh's red pill was the newly accessible internet and where it was able to take him. Through this technology he could access the paramilitary theories of Louis Beam and the Posse Comitatus. He could learn all about the Second Amendment activism and the elaborate conspiracies of William Pierce's *Turner Diaries*.

The white power movement, and particularly the Klan, had been quick to grasp the potential of the emerging information technologies and the internet. Louis Beam was ahead of his time, seeing the possibilities offered by linking desktop computers via dial-up modems. In 1984 this was a technology already being used by the military and universities, but it was far from being generally available. Beam created the Aryan Liberty Net, essentially pre-empting the social networks of today. This secure network initially united Klansmen and, soon after, other white power groups, via cyberspace.[1]

Liberty Net allowed 'patriots' to send out promotional and propaganda materials. As Beam put it, 'interested in knowing what you can do to help ensure the survival of the great race of men who gave you the Magna Carta and the Declaration of Independence? Through the net, you can ask an expert in the movement. … You are online with the Aryan Nations brain trust.'[2] As slow and unreliable as dial-up modems seem today, Beam's use of them enabled the unification of the white power movement. It was a game-changer.

No longer isolated geographically, white supremacists could recruit and spread their message online, without the authorities or anyone outside the network even realising it. To Beam the internet was the realisation of the dream of an 'Invisible Empire', the perfect embodiment of Leaderless Resistance. Expanding groups could use Liberty Net to take on 'missions' for the cause without the danger of face-to-face meetings, the mail or other less secure methods of communication.

Beam demonstrated the power of the internet by outlining a points-based assassination scheme at the 1983 Aryan Nations World Conference. His 'computer index on traitors' resembled a 'shoot 'em up' video game. Anti-Klan groups (like the SPLC), FBI agents, federal judges and inform-ants were all given a value. Points – and no doubt fame – accrued to those Klansmen who 'took them out'. It was a violently surreal world. The points system was immensely appealing to those who'd already been red-pilled and it motivated them to want to red-pill newbies.

Liberty Net's potential attracted Robert 'Pastor Bob' Miles, David Duke's KKKK Grand Dragon of Michigan. Another early enthusiast was Aryan Nation leader Richard Butler, who had hosted the initial discus-sions of the concept at his Hayden Lake compound. Butler gleefully mused that Liberty Net would put the white power movement on the 'edge of tremendous violence'.[3]

But in many ways the problems of getting Liberty Net off the ground were the same as those the Klan had always faced. Chief among these was money. For Beam's Klan, setting up the network itself wasn't that expen-sive – around $3,500 – but the costs to the individual members were high. It required a desktop computer and a modem, which in the late 1980s came to a prohibitive $2,000, the equivalent of nearly $5,000 in 2022. White supremacists were not renowned for their wealth.

The solution to this conundrum demonstrated how much more organ-ised the white power movement was than authorities realised. Robert Mathews of The Order donated a significant amount of his $4 million haul from robberies to finance 'a message operation center' for Liberty Net. He also channelled $300,000 through Pastor Bob Miles and gave Butler

$40,000 and Beam $100,000. Much of that, no doubt, went on to fund Liberty Net's expansion.

While Liberty Net was aimed at a membership that was already red-pilled, David Duke's KKKK successor Don Black had greater ambitions. In 1981 he took part in 'Operation Red Dog', an unauthorised paramilitary action dreamt up by the Klan and other white supremacist organisations. Black and other paid mercenaries invaded the Caribbean island of Dominica, hoping to reinstate its former prime minister.

The list of participants didn't exactly inspire confidence. Alongside the Klansmen, neo-Nazis and other white supremacists, there was a gay vigilante, a nurse connected to the Irish Republican Army and a mysterious gun-runner – not the most natural set of allies for Klansmen. The ten conspirators planned to take over an island with 80,000 residents and oust the Black prime minister and reinstate his white, Apartheid-era predecessor. Not surprisingly, the whole thing was a fiasco.

FBI agents in Louisiana uncovered the details of the plot and the conspirators were arrested before they even boarded their boats. The press nicknamed the whole disaster 'the Bayou of Pigs' after the abortive 1961 invasion of the Bay of Pigs in Cuba. Black was sentenced to three years for violation of the 1794 Neutrality Act which made it illegal for private US citizens to wage war against a state with which the USA was at peace. With echoes of ZOG, Black claimed, 'What we were doing was in the best interests of the United States and its security in the hemisphere, and we feel betrayed by our own government.'[4]

Yet the indomitable Black bounced back. In 1996 he founded Stormfront. org, with the objective of establishing 'White Pride Worldwide'. He advocated 'mainstreaming' the Klan and used the inclusivity of the website as a recruitment tool. Unlike Beam and Butler, Black's rhetoric was subtle, playing down violence and putting the emphasis on 'defending the white race'. He offered 'white scholarships' for college students and sent birthday greetings to members. It worked. By 2005 Stormfront had over 50,000 registered members, rising to over 300,000 in 2015.[5]

By the mid-1990s the Klan had realised the potential of the new digital media. Desktop software and consumer-grade printers could, with a minimum of training, produce attractive flyers and pamphlets in bulk at a fraction of the cost offered by commercial printers. And there was email, which, as Black had shown, was a relatively secure and safe method of internal communication. When combined with listserv programs, email could also be used to send mass newsletters and subscription invitations at a negligible cost.

Stormfront was an early proponent of computer bulletin boards and chat rooms: a cheaply created virtual space which allowed white power members to instigate discussion threads, arrange meetings and comment on each other's postings. By the late 1990s, white power activists had moved to a fundamentally online presence.[6]

Thom Robb of the Knights Party had produced the first Klan website. Like Black, Robb focused on recruitment and pushed the site as a 'kinder, gentler' version of the Klan. He stressed that he wanted to produce 'A message of love NOT hate'.[7] Others followed Robb's example. Most of these websites were not particularly sophisticated, just cut-and-pasted versions of existing material with primitive graphics and even worse copywriting.

But there were those who got it right. The most successful of these websites was probably one created by Duke's former California Grand Dragon, Tom Metzger, the White Aryan Resistance website, *The Insurgent*. Initially *The Insurgent* ran alongside the organisation's TV show *Race and Reason* and radio broadcasts, but soon WAR had an exclusively online presence. The internet was cheaper, less liable to censorship and had more diverse possibilities for marketing and recruitment.

By the early 2000s, *The Insurgent*'s secure website sold T-shirts, key fobs and caps branded with the distinctive WAR logo. The site also featured downloadable racist games like *Drive-By 2* and *Border Patrol*. These were pretty crude 'shoot 'em up' games in which players trawled suitable areas assassinating non-white victims. Along with these novelties came the usual stream of antisemitic, anti-immigrant, anti-gay, misogynistic materials.[8]

It seemed that, while the technology was novel, the content was predictable.

# CHAPTER 83

The digital age offered huge possibilities to the white power movement. Not only did it enable highly cost-effective tools for communication and recruitment, but it was also largely unpoliced and anonymous. This played to the last strength left to the Klan: the ability to disguise its diminishing physical numbers with a hyped online presence.

Its memorable name and instantly identifiable iconography – the hood with its menacing eyeholes, the white robe and the burning cross – were representative of the most recognisable white hate group in the world. If an individual searched for white power websites, the Klan would probably be the first to come up. In 1998 Klan websites made up the majority of the 350-odd hate sites on the internet and, until very recently, they continued to dominate.[1]

In the late 1990s it was still easy to appropriate and utilise a website's material. An unintended consequence of the 1944 tax demand was that the Klan's famous icons were not trademarked or subject to copyright laws. Anyone who wanted to cut and paste images from Klan websites could do so legally. It was difficult to find out who was behind a website or if their claims were real. The post-truth world was very useful to the Klan.

Just as the internet had enabled a huge new pornography industry, it enabled an explosion of hate. Individuals who would not want to be seen at a Klan rally or entering an adult bookstore, could, with a computer and a modem, find what they needed in the privacy of their own homes. There was minimal risk of neighbours, bosses, friends or spouses discovering their dark secret. The authorities could not track who was accessing what.

Lost, angry and usually male adolescents could easily be drawn into the organisation using techniques like Metzger's racist computer games. These websites fed teenagers outlandish conspiracy theories and hateful propaganda, sometimes with tragic results. FBI reports of the early 1990s estimate

60 per cent of US hate crimes were carried out by youths. Moreover, in a strong demonstration of the red-pill effect, these offenders were not formal members of hate groups.[2]

This is borne out some years later by Dylann Roof, the 21-year-old who killed nine Black parishioners of Charleston's Emanuel African Methodist Episcopal Church and wounded one in June 2015. At his trial, prosecutors revealed his internet history, a pick-and-mix grab bag of hate available on the web. It included Klan iconography, neo-Nazi propaganda and tales of soldiers of fortune. Attorneys showed the jury selfies of Roof in a Klan hood, raising his arm in a Nazi salute as he posed next to Confederate war graves.

Oddly, Roof also left a 'manifesto' in which, after ranting about Jews, Blacks, Hispanics, East Asians and patriots, he explained to investigators, 'We have no skinheads, no real KKK, no one doing anything but talking on the internet. Well, someone has to have the bravery to take it to the real world, and I guess that has to be me.'[3]

Roof's note points to the virtual world where the alienated, disaffected and politically impotent sought the catharsis the Klan had always promised, only now they didn't need to leave the house or show their faces. They could threaten elaborate forms of imagined violence with impunity with little chance of being traced. And they never had to come into physical contact with their online allies or victims.

Many of those who visited Klan websites did not go on to join the order. But the web enabled millions to be sensitised to the Klan's message. In a slickly worded announcement on his European–American Unity and Rights Organization website, David Duke announced his 2004 conference had attracted over 67,000 virtual attendees, a staggering figure proving that the internet was, for the white power movement, a reservoir of millions of potentially sympathetic activists.[4]

By the late 1990s the internet seemed to be not only a tool for attracting people to the white supremacist movement but, as Beam had predicted, a tool for uniting disparate groups. An article posted on one site could be replicated on hundreds of others, enabling cross-pollination of ideas as well as greater co-operation and fraternity. As historian Kathleen Belew observed, 'A suburban California skinhead might bear Klan tattoos, read Nazi tracts and attend meetings of a local Klan chapter, a National Socialist political party, the Militant Aryan Resistance – or all three.'[5]

Then came 11 September 2001 (9/11). The attack on the Twin Towers and the Pentagon had a devastating effect on the USA. Predictably, an atrocity of such magnitude generated the usual slew of conspiracy theories. There are those who say planes couldn't have brought down the Twin

Towers, or that a plane could not have hit the Pentagon at the angle alleged. There are others who report that the FBI detected suspicious activity by Israeli Mossad agents, equipped with surveillance gear, around the time of the jets hitting the World Trade Center. Still others deny the involvement of Al-Qaeda or any Islamist organisations. There are almost infinite variations on such themes. The only thing which seems to unite them is that they all question the 'official' version of events. They knew the truth of the events behind that dreadful day: they'd been red-pilled. They called themselves 'Truthers'.

The rise of violent jihadism fed ideas of evil, dark-skinned, foreigners carrying out atrocities on US soil. The Bush administration's response added further fuel to this hatred with the US-led War on Terror. The campaign not only cemented that idea of the evil foreigner, but it also distracted the intelligence services, leading their post-Oklahoma focus away from the domestic far-right brand of terrorism.

After 9/11 the far right leapt on the conspiracy theories of ZOG and Jewish world dominance. The return of soldiers wounded in Iraq and Afghanistan and the unprecedented number of refugees sparked growing anti-Muslim feelings and violence in Western Europe, Australia, New Zealand and the USA. All Muslim activists became 'potential terrorists' promoting holy war against the USA. Rumours spread that Muslims were infiltrating the US Government and would soon subject the USA to Sharia law.[6]

To the 'patriots' who emerged in this febrile atmosphere, any criticism of the Bush regime's tactics or the War on Terror was treason. Far-right news outlets began to emerge, condemning any criticism of their views as Orwellian 'newspeak'. The far-right pundits used all forms of online and broadcast media to get their messages across. The conspiracy theories, hate-mongering and intolerance which had been emerging in the 1980s and 1990s headed right into the mainstream of the USA's media, where it mainlined into the body politic. The emerging 'Alt-Right' was not going to be ignored.

# CHAPTER 84

While the impact of 9/11 on the far right may have been dramatic, the effect on the Klan itself was muted. According to most Klan websites, ZOG was behind the atrocity. About a month after the attacks Thom Robbs' Arkansas-based Knights Party posted a message at kukluxklan.org, a url which looked like *the* Klan website, telling visitors to 'PRAY for America!' because 'The terrorist attack on US soil indicates that once again US policy is putting American citizens at risk'.[1] The site was careful not to call for any reprisals or name Muslims or any other 'external' threat.

In fact, 2001 was a quiet year for the KKK. There were no notable Klan incidents in the headlines around 9/11. The number of cross burnings in 2001 dropped from the year before and no Klan took responsibility for anti-Muslim incidents. Oddly, most Klansmen seemed conciliatory. One went on record as saying, 'I've nothing against Jews, their [*sic*] pretty good allies.' Presumably, he was talking of the Israelis. He added, 'And I've nothing against Muslims and Blacks. Only thing is the races should not intermarry.'[2]

Most of the news relating to the Klan in the last months of 2001 centred around a Klansman confessing to 'cleaning up' after the notorious 1964 Mississippi Burning murders and the subsequent re-opening of the FBI's investigation. This is significant. It shows the changing attitude towards racial violence. In the first five years of the twenty-first century, the Klan was under pressure as Civil Rights-Era miscarriages of justice were corrected. In 2001 and 2002 Klansmen Thomas Blanton and Bobby Cherry both got life in prison for their part in the 1963 16th Street Baptist bombing. In 2005 Klansman Edgar Ray Killen was convicted of organising the murders of the three civil rights workers in Mississippi in 1964. The Mississippi court gave him sixty years.

The shift in mood was demonstrated earlier in a decision in 2003 when another Mississippi court found Klansman Ernest Avants guilty of the murder of Ben White. In 1966, White had been abducted and shot eighteen times and his body dumped in a ditch, purely because he was Black. A month later, remorseful, Avants' partner in the murder had confessed to the crime, incriminating Avants. Yet a Mississippi state court at the time still produced a hung jury and Avants had walked free. In 2003 the verdict was unanimous. Avants got life. The federal judge told the court, 'Times have changed since 1966. When Ernest Avants' generation is finally dead, I hope most of the hatred will have died with it.'[3]

It seemed the Klan was aware of this and was playing down overt, deeply ingrained racism. An incident in 2003 highlighted their new focus. As part of an FBI 'sting' operation, agents in Pennsylvania picked up David Wayne Hull, once a known member of the violent White Knights of the KKK, the faction which carried out the Mississippi Burning murders in 1964. Hull was picked up trying to buy five hand grenades from an undercover FBI agent to make pipe-bombs to destroy local abortion clinics. When asked if he wasn't worried there might be people in the buildings, he told the agent, 'If they're there, they are killers or a woman killing a foetus; either way, fuck 'em.'[4] He was convicted on seven charges and sentenced to twelve years.

Since the 1980s, the Klan's central belief had focused on the white power message of the survival of the white race. Anything which stood in the way of that mission was a fair target. Legislation on race equality in education, representation, employment, housing or social mobility was seen as unfairly favouring the non-white races. Welfare measures were seen as supporting those in ghettos and paying them to raise large families. Even gay rights and feminism were seen as disruptive to the white, nuclear family. But it was abortion which drew the most obvious hostility.

The Klan objected to abortion on racial grounds. To them, it was white babies being aborted, making way for the further expansion of the already soaring non-white birth rates. Since 1985 the Klan had produced 'Wanted' posters for prominent abortion providers. In 1994 Florida Klansmen organised a rally to show support for the killer of an abortionist, for as one Klansman told *The New York Times*, 'Some day we may all be in the trenches together in the fight against the slaughter of unborn children'.[5]

'Pro-Life' campaigning, even on the Klan's racial grounds, had mainstream appeal. When a Republican senator and congressman for the state of Alabama put forward their 'Human Life Protection Act' in 2018, the language within it could have come straight from the Klan playbook. As they put it:

more than 50 million babies have been aborted in the United States since the Roe decision in 1973, more than three times the number who were killed in German death camps, Chinese purges, Stalin's gulags, Cambodian killing fields, and the Rwandan genocide combined.[6]

The measure became law. Alabama refused to grant abortions, even where pregnancy resulted from rape. Nor was it just in Alabama. In Florida, a Republican state senator sought to implement similar measures. He argued that 'When you get a birth rate less than 2 percent', as he claimed was the case with Western Europe, 'that society is disappearing'. More worryingly still, from his perspective, 'it's being replaced by folks that come behind them and immigrate, don't wish to assimilate into that society and they do believe in having children'.[7]

The Klan seems to be regaining mainstream appeal on the issue of gun rights as well. The voice-over for a 2022 advert for Jerone Davison's US congressional campaign tells the audience that 'Democrats like to say that no one needs an AR-15', a military-grade assault rifle, 'for self-defence'. Davison's rural Western district has voted Republican since 2012 and the appeal of his message seems obvious, but with an unexpected twist.

Davison's video goes on to tell its audience that, 'when this rifle is the only thing standing between your family and a dozen angry Democrats in Klan hoods, you just might need that semi-automatic, and *all* thirty rounds'.[8] It is worth noting the 4th District is predominantly Hispanic, and Davison is Black. And while Davison's ad is undoubtedly over the top, there is no doubt that he's right. The Klan's support for the Second Amendment's protection of the right to bear arms has long had a deeply racial element.

Since its formative years in the Reconstruction South, the Klan argued firearms were for the protection of the white race. To white supremacists, arming the Black population was liable to lead to trouble. That didn't stop the Black community demanding colour-blind gun laws. Guns for self-defence became central to the civil rights struggle in the 1950s and 1960s.

The NAACP had supported the National Rifle Association (NRA) in its campaign to protect the right to bear arms, even founding Black chapters of the NRA linked to its own chapters. Martin Luther King applied for a concealed carry permit after his house was bombed in 1956. It was refused. In the late 1960s, one of the most prominent demands of the militant Black Panthers was the right to bear arms. They told new recruits, 'The gun is the only thing the pigs will understand. The gun is the only thing that will free us – gain us our liberation.'[9]

The scourge of gun violence in urban areas has made the Second Amendment a mixed-race issue. In 1976 in Atlanta, Georgia, the newly elected Black mayor attempted to get the federal government to ban the importing and sale of all handguns. In Gary, Indiana, another Black mayor declared he would deny all applications for concealed carry. By the twenty-first century, the NAACP sued a range of gun manufacturers on the grounds that they sold more guns to Black people living in deprived areas than other groups. It also petitioned the federal government to impose a blanket ban on handguns in Washington DC and Chicago. And the Black community leader and former presidential candidate Jesse Jackson bragged of his arrest for protesting the ease of *legal* gun sales.[10]

Moderate Black community leaders saw radicals' call for gun access for 'self-defence' as suicidal. They argued 10 million African Americans fighting 180 million white Americans could only have one result – an escalation of violence. Race war would certainly not end in their favour. They essentially agreed with the Klan on this issue. Both argued for gun control within the Black community, but the Klan was not about to relinquish that right for whites.

On abortion, immigration, expansion of the welfare system, gay rights, feminism and a host of other issues, the Klan's position had considerable backing but they were still very far from being 'mainstream' as they had been in the 1920s. The vast majority of Americans saw the Klan as violent and bigoted. They saw incidents like those in 2001 when skinheads and Klansmen beat up Black diners in front of families in Springfield, Missouri, hospitalising them – simply for eating alongside whites – as despicable.[11]

At other times – as it had been in the past – the Klan was denounced for its sheer stupidity. The Grand Dragon of Indiana's Church of the National Knights of the KKK, Richard Loy, arranged what he called a 'Christmas Unity Rally' at his smallholding in 2002. It started badly when he served pork to his Christian Identity guests, not realising they adhered to strict dietary requirements. He then compounded his idiocy by parading around as Klanta Klaus, grotesquely complete with a mouthful of missing and shattered stumps of teeth, mangled and bleeding gums and mashed-up lips – the result of a recent accident.

The accident itself was another indication of Loy's unrivalled stupidity. Earlier in the week, he'd decided to test a bullet-proof riot shield he'd somehow found. Unfortunately, the shield lived up to its name. The test bullet had bounced off the shield and ricocheted around his mouth. A true trier, as the light faded on his disastrous day, Loy decided to introduce a note of solemnity. Uttering sacred words, he lit a cross and a burning swastika, side by side. His guests looked on in dignified silence as the cross and swastika smoked. Then fizzled. Then fell over. Then went out. They couldn't be relit.[12]

Klansmen hit headlines for child molesting, domestic violence and drugs busts as often as they did for rallies, race hatred and violence. Their image was not one which would draw recruits or inspire imitators. Yet, in spite of their often spectacular incompetence, they were still capable of violence and they remained the most well known of all white power groups.

Soon, the basis of that power would be severely challenged.

# CHAPTER 85

The Klan and presidents have always had a rather unpredictable relationship with each other. Since 1865, the Klan has veered between overt support and overt condemnation. Yet few modern presidents have excited as much attention in connection with the Klan as the forty-fourth and forty-fifth presidents: Barack Obama and Donald Trump.

As the first African American president, Obama was bound to attract the attention of the Klan. The initial reactions to his election were predictably apocalyptic. Roy Larson of the Church of the National Knights of the KKK called for 'Yankee flags' to be flown upside down to signal distress, and got his Klansmen to parade with black armbands on Obama's inauguration day. David Duke tweeted that 'the country is not recognizable any more' and a posting on the Traditional Christian Knights of the Ku Klux Klan forum moaned that 'They might as well have put Bin Laden in the White House'.[1]

On the other hand, some Klansmen saw the election of Obama as beneficial to their cause. To Thom Robb, self-appointed National Director of the KKK:

> Every time the television shows an image of Obama, it will be a reminder that our people have lost power in this country. ... The betrayal will stare them in the face each time they watch the news and see little black children playing in the [White House] rose garden.[2]

As Obama campaigned, the allegations and falsehoods started. Right-wing media tried to undermine the president's legitimacy. He was depicted as an 'Arab', and many on the right chose to believe it. Fox News released figures claiming 20 per cent of Americans believed Obama was a practising

Muslim. A *Newsweek* poll claimed it was 24 per cent. But it was once he had been inaugurated that the accusations really started flying.

Even when the governor of Hawaii stated categorically that the president had been born in Honolulu, the rumours persisted that he'd been born in Kenya, making him ineligible to hold office. In spite of mounting proof to the contrary, a *Washington Post* poll claimed 20 per cent of white Americans believed Obama was not born in the USA. If that poll was limited to self-identified Republicans, the figure rose to 33 per cent.

'Birthers', as they became known, demanded to see Obama's long-form birth certificate, and they just got more strident as time went on. They referred to Obama by his middle name, Hussein, in order to make him sound less European and more Muslim. Republicans in states like Arizona and Tennessee demanded that all future presidential candidates must produce a long-form birth certificate, give sworn affidavits detailing the hospital, doctor, witnesses of the birth and details of where the candidate had resided for the last fourteen years.[3]

The issue rumbled on, reaching a new level when the then reality TV host Donald Trump waded in on prime-time TV. Appearing on Fox News' *O'Reilly Factor* chat show in March 2011, Trump made his concerns clear:

> I have a birth certificate. People have birth certificates. He [Obama] doesn't have a birth certificate. He may have one but there is something on that birth certificate – maybe religion, maybe it says he's a Muslim, I don't know. Maybe he doesn't want that. Or, he may not have one.[4]

Donald Trump was playing to a new and potentially powerful base of voters who seemed willing to ignore the obvious truth in favour of any message that suited their beliefs. It didn't seem to matter that Obama's staff produced and published documentation to prove his US birth. In fact, the more the president denied the rumours, the more it gave life to the birther rumour mill. Questioning these rumours was called an attack on the freedom of speech, unpatriotic. The birther attacks on Obama, originating largely from computer keyboards, foreshadowed a whole new level of hate in the digital age.

# CHAPTER 86

'Truthers', 'birthers' and other right-wing conspiracy theorists of today have come to believe they have been red-pilled. They see themselves as part of a rare group of enlightened souls who can see through the illusions put in place by the powers that be. But the spread of useful, paranoid conspiracy theories is nothing new to the Klan; the only difference is the speed of transmission. Today's conspiracists draw on that legacy more than they probably know.

In the autumn of 1923, North Manchester, Indiana, was a one of the leading Klan strongholds in the USA. Recruitment was easy in a place where locals were patriotic and wanted to protect their city. They especially wanted to keep it safe from the growing influence of the Roman Catholic Church.

Klan speeches, newspapers, pamphlets and Klavern meetings had convinced many Klansmen that the Pope was moving to the USA. He was setting up his HQ in Washington DC. While his million-dollar mansion was being completed, the Pope would need a temporary home, and patriotic residents of Indiana knew there was nowhere better than their own beautiful state. In December, word got out that the Pope was, in fact, arriving in North Manchester on an evening train. Some 1,500 true patriots lined the platform to make sure he didn't get off.

Riled up, the crowd boarded the northbound train and rampaged through the carriages looking for the Pope. There weren't many passengers, and no one seemed to fit their vision of the 'Tyrant of the Tiber'. Eventually they entered a compartment occupied by just one small, sweaty, bespectacled, man. He was sitting upright, clutching a leather bag, looking frightened and, to them, suspicious.

They forced the trembling 'Pope' off the train and grilled him. They didn't like his story that he was a corset salesman. But they told each other the Pope was bound to have a cover story, and besides, he looked shifty. His round tortoiseshell glasses looked fake. But when his bag turned out to be full of ladies' foundation wear, they reckoned that even the Pope – shameless as they knew he was – wouldn't risk carrying around such incriminating inventory. Warning him to be careful, they bundled the shaken man back onto the delayed train. They never found the *real* Pope that evening. No doubt he'd already been smuggled off the train.[1]

If the brief history of the twenty-first century teaches us anything, perhaps it should be that it isn't particularly hard to start a rumour. Largely unregulated social media, fake news, click-bait memes, chatbots, deep-fakes and trolling seem to have been created for that very purpose. This is what is meant by living in post-truth times. We seem to live in a world where conspiracy theories can attract hundreds of thousands of adherents – in weeks, or even days. Take the most famous of all of them, QAnon.

The mysterious 'Q Clearance Patriot' claimed to be a senior military intelligence officer who had decided to release information after realising the true extent of the machinations of the cabal that was running the so-called New World Order. This collection of Democrats, Hollywood celebrities, mass media, business leaders, liberal intellectuals, medical elites and Jews were so embedded that most Americans had no idea of their power, or their real intentions. But Q did, and he had high-security clearance. To alert other patriots he posted images of cryptic messages in which he purported to be telling his followers, so-called 'Anons', about how the Deep State was about to be exposed and purged by Donald Trump.

As with all effective conspiracy theories, QAnon had just enough elements which *could* have been true. For example, the government security clearance level 'Q' is actually genuine. A superficial reading of the Department of the Environment website would tell an interested reader that 'a final Top Secret clearance would support the granting of a Q access authorization'.[2] But reading further would show that such a clearance level would not grant access to the type of information the Q Clearance Patriot claimed to have.

It didn't matter. Q's true believers, his 'Digital Soldiers', had the same kind of unquestioning belief as the crowds rushing the train in North Manchester on that fateful night in 1923. The Pope was coming because Klan leadership had said so. Well, not in so many words, but their members knew what they were *implying*.[3] It is that vagueness, that need for interpretation, which is the most fertile breeding ground for conspiracy theories.

This very situation arose when, on 5 October 2017, Donald Trump spoke to the White House Press Corps about a vague and looming event: 'Maybe it's the calm before the storm.'

That was it.

There was no explanation of what 'it' was. No clarification of what the 'storm' might be. When pressed, the president simply winked and said, 'You'll find out.' The press corps was baffled.[4] QAnon wasn't.

At first, the messages posted on the unregulated Japanese image site, 4chan, seemed irrelevant to Trump's statements. A few weeks after the White House briefing, Q made 'Drop #1' – or his first posting. It read:

HRC [Hillary Rodham Clinton] extraction already in motion effective yesterday with several countries in case of cross border run. Passport approved to be flagged effective 10/30 @ 12:01am. Expect massive riots organized in defiance and others fleeing the US to occur. US M[arines]'s will conduct the operations while N[ational] G[uard] activated. Proof check: Locate a NG member and ask if activated for duty 10/30 across most major cities.

The posting referred to the bizarre Pizzagate scandal which had run for most of the presidential election cycle of 2016. It centred around accusations about the nefarious activities of Hillary Clinton and several other high-profile liberal figures. According to the online posts, this group was involved in a child-trafficking ring operating out of the Comet Ping Pong Pizza store in the Chevy Chase district of Washington DC. Q's Drop #1 told those connected that Hillary Clinton was soon to be arrested. But she was considered a flight risk, so security forces had been alerted.

To those already red-pilled to the Pizzagate conspiracy, this was proof that they had a new and powerful ally in their fight for justice – Q. Soon after Drop #1, other information began to flood the 4chan page '/pol/', giving the 'Soldiers' another new ally: none other than the President of the USA (POTUS). 4chan was now alive with drops from Q.

From Drop #2 onwards Q's 'Comms' addressed Trump's 'coming storm' remarks to the press corps. They came thick and fast, telling the Anons about how Trump anticipated a backlash to Hillary's arrest. In order to safeguard the state, the president had alerted the National Guard, the US Navy and the FBI. Q told his patriots that, when it was time for them to act, the president would post 'The Storm is upon us' on Twitter and the arrests would begin. Alongside the arrests there would be a temporary suspension of *habeas corpus*, the imposition of martial law and the spreading of deliberate disinformation to the mainstream media.

In Drop #60, Q really explained the mission of his soldiers. He told Anons that the full picture of the information he was sharing with them had only been seen by fewer 'than ten people ... and only three are non-military'.

At its height he'd be sharing with anything up to 100,000 readers and it ran for the next three years. Q posted his last drop in December 2020. It was Drop #4,953.

The drops would cover a wide range of issues ranging from political corruption and insider dealing to sexual abuse and the evils of feminism. Drops also appeared about the faking of JFK's assassination, COVID hoax and a huge variety of topics in between. QAnons began receiving prime-time TV coverage, while at the same time in private/online they were advocating extreme measures, such as calling for the hanging of Hillary Clinton. Their adoration of Donald Trump verged on the messianic, and certainly had elements of the cult about it. Yet like the Klan of the 1920s, QAnon is exceptionally difficult to define in general terms. It is not simply a political movement. Nor is it possible to see it as a religion or a secret society. It is all these things and more.[5]

QAnon owes more to the Klan than its fringe essence, antisemitic conspiracy theories and racism. Like the Klan in its heyday, QAnon had a great deal about it which was mainstream. Between 2018 and 2020, over 100 Republican candidates stood on a platform which openly supported QAnon.[6]

A *Newsweek* poll claimed that at the height of QAnon's influence some 25 per cent of white evangelists saw QAnon to be 'fundamentally correct'. Some 8 per cent of Americans felt the movement's beliefs were 'correct' and 10 per cent saw them as 'somewhat correct'.[7] A December 2020 NPR/Ipsos poll found that a third of Americans believed in a 'Deep State' which sought to overthrow democratically elected leaders and a surprising amount of Republicans believed there was a paedophile ring of 'Satan-worshipping elites' trying to control politics and the media.[8] And another YouGov poll claimed 30 per cent of Republicans had a 'favourable view' of QAnon.[9]

As QAnon used the Klan's core beliefs to take it to peaks the Klan could only dream of, the Klan's own membership seemed to be in free-fall. In 2016, as Donald Trump was about to enter the White House, the SPLC Hate Map showed the Klan as having only 130 Klaverns. By 2018 that number was down to fifty and, in 2021, the map showed only eighteen.[10] But that didn't mean it was irrelevant. It was, and still is, the grandfather of hate groups, with roots dating back to 1865.

To understand the importance of those roots in present-day terms it is worth looking at the actions of a neo-Nazi named Matthew Heimbach, the 'Little Führer'. Heimbach was the instigator of one of the most notorious events of the racist right in the last ten years, their rally in Charlottesville, Virginia, in 2017.

# CHAPTER 87

In 2017 Charlottesville's Lee Park was renamed Emancipation Park. The park had been bought a century before by a local philanthropist who'd made his money investing in the Chicago and New York stock markets. A proud Virginian, he'd erected a statue to Robert E. Lee, one of the state's greatest sons – at least that was the way it was seen by whites in 1917.

For those 100 years the Confederate military commander had sat imperiously on his famous horse, Traveller, right in the middle of the city. When the city council voted unanimously to change the name of the park in 2017, they also decided General Lee had to go. The removal was part of the current movement to reappraise Confederate history and address the legacy of Reconstruction, Jim Crow, segregation and ultimately white supremacy itself.

The divisiveness of these reappraisals is illustrated by the December 2015 New Orleans' Monuments Act. This ordinance to remove four Confederate statues from prominent locations around the city was passed by a thumping majority, sparking violence and protests. It was not until a second vote in May 2017 that the actual removal of the statues began. By this time similar removals had taken place in Austin, Texas, and Louisville, Kentucky. But in New Orleans the workers removing them wore bullet-proof vests and had police protection.

The decision to remove General Lee from his pedestal in Charlottesville was a part of this groundswell of public opinion. But, as in New Orleans, the removal was not unopposed. For many across the nation, the Confederacy was a foundation of their understanding of US history. In 2017, the SPLC identified over 1,500 Confederate monuments. They created a list of over 100 schools, and eighty counties and cities named after Confederate leaders and revealed that there were nine official Confederate state holidays in six separate states and ten US military bases named after Confederate commanders.[1]

There has been a tendency to see Dylann Roof's 2015 murderous rampage in a North Carolina church as a major catalyst of anti-Confederate protest.[2] He began his racist attack by announcing, 'I'm here to kill Black people', and ended leaving nine church members dead. Investigators found photos on Roof's phone of him standing with Confederate flags and posing alongside Confederate war graves, reinforcing the idea that the celebration of this history was a celebration of white supremacy. To the majority of Americans this was the tipping point; these monuments had to go.

Not surprisingly, it was the removal of the statue of the most iconic hero of the Confederacy, Robert E. Lee, that led to violence. The clash had been orchestrated by the leader of the Traditionalist Workers Party, 26-year-old Matthew Heimbach. Dedicated to 'stopping rampant multiculturalism', Heimbach also hoped to achieve the Holy Grail of white power, unifying the disparate elements of white nationalism and hopefully sparking a revival in their fortunes.[3]

The year 2017 started well for Heimbach. In January, he chaired a neo-Nazi and white supremacist forum in Pikesville, Kentucky. The gathering was a great success. With near-universal approval, the 150 attendees proclaimed Heimbach the 'Little Führer'. The far-right press saw him as the new face of white supremacy. On a high, Heimbach began to plan the now-infamous 'Unite the Right' rally, to be held in Charlottesville on 12 August 2017. Bringing together neo-Confederates, neo-Nazis, racist skinheads and Klansmen, its intention was to show that the 'movement is not just online, but growing physically' and to assert themselves 'as the voice of white America'.[4]

Central to this rally was the Alt-Right. In 2008, the term 'Alternative Right' was coined by a far-right commentator and leading white separatist named Richard B. Spencer. It was quickly shortened to the snappier Alt-Right. Spencer's sanitised coinage was a term for what was really the extreme right, dedicated to creating a white enthno-state. There was little new in this idea, it owed much to the theorising in William Gale's Posse Comitatus and William Pierce's *Turner Diaries*. But Spencer was different in his approach.

Spencer was from the David Duke mould. Like Duke, he was well groomed, articulate and seemingly affable. Like Duke, he flaunted his PhD and made much of his publications. He took to calling himself an 'academic racist', justifying his views with a 'quasi-intellectual approach to white supremacy'. Like Duke, Spencer drew on the thinking of Klansmen like Louis Beam, Thom Robb and Tom Metzger and their web-powered demands for a white homeland. But rather than using words like Duke's 'racialism' or more traditional white supremacist language, Spencer invoked a fight for 'white racial consciousness'. The goal was much the same.

Like Duke, Spencer abandoned the paramilitary fatigues and *never* used the Klan hood. Instead, he adopted the politician's camouflage, becoming the 'professional racist in khakis'.[5] Spencer told one interviewer in 2013, 'We have to look good' because 'being part of something that is crazed or ugly or vicious or just stupid, no one is going to want to be a part of it'. Unlike Duke, he did not opt for facelifts, perma-tan, dyed hair and body-sculptingly tight T-shirts. That was too downmarket. Spencer didn't want to appeal solely to 'redneck, tattooed, illiterate, no-teeth' people.[6] Without actually saying as much, he meant he didn't want to be associated with the Klan.

To Spencer, as to most other people on the racist right, the Klan was a liability. There might be Klaverns all over the nation, but most of these had fewer than a handful of members. They were a 'national' organisation only insofar as one sad little group of Klansmen travelled across the country to meet another sad little group. With their antiquated rituals, silly passwords and ridiculous costumes, the Klan was an embarrassment.

Spencer was speaking for many when he said the Klan's redneck image tended to attract only redneck members. He resented their continuously outspoken adherence to violence, a rhetoric which alienated all but the wildest of racists. Like Duke, Spencer frequently admitted there was a time and a place for 'talking the talk' – but it was not in public. To Spencer, what the movement needed was not the rednecked, but the red-pilled. And most of the Alt-Right shared his views.

Given this near-universal mistrust and dislike of the Klan, it is impressive that Heimbach managed to persuade both the Confederate Knights of KKK and the Loyal White Knights of the KKK to attend. He got them to accept that they would march, listen to speeches – and of course fight – alongside the Alt-Right, neo-Nazis, Proud Boys, Vanguard America, Identity Evropa – most of the main organisations of the racist right. The two groups' willingness to agree to Heimbach's terms was a tacit admission that the Klan had become, at best, peripheral to white supremacy. This would be glaringly obvious to anyone noting the Klan's collective turnout at the rally: a staggering ... twelve people.

The tone of the rally had been set the evening before when some 500 assorted white supremacists marched on the University of Virginia campus with tiki torches, chanting Nazi slogans like 'Blood and Soil' and the Trump slogan, 'Make America Great Again'. Others swore 'Jews will not replace us'.

They were intercepted by a thousand or so counter-protesters. Street brawls broke out all over the city, dying down as the sun set on the August night.

The bigotry, chanting and violence resumed the following morning. It was all too familiar. Only the chants had changed. It could have been New Orleans in 1874, Tulsa in 1921 or Selma in 1965. Now they shouted, 'White lives matter' alongside the more familiar 'Kill the Nigger'. The counter-protesters met them with equal aggression, chanting 'Punch a Nazi in the mouth' and 'Kill all Nazis'.[7]

By midday the situation had got so bad that the governor of Virginia declared a state of emergency and the police declared the rally unlawful. Two hours later a neo-Nazi drove his speeding car straight at a crowd of counter-protesters, killing Heather Heyer and injuring several others.

The rally will always be remembered for that hideous act of violence. The media tended to frame it as the Alt-Right baiting and attacking Antifa, an abbreviation of 'Anti-Fascist', itself a term coined by its enemies for the violent counter-movement against the Alt-Right.

But no one really mentioned the Klan. It seemed it was marginal to the white supremacy movement, only making the headlines when a Klansman was fined for discharging a handgun too close to a school. But though the Klan lacked any real power, it was vital in one respect: symbolism.

It was because of the Klan that Unite the Right had chosen Charlottesville. One neo-Nazi told reporters he was there to 'defend our history, our heritage and to protect our race'.[8] But the importance of Robert E. Lee had nothing to do with Nazis or the Alt-Right and everything to do with the history of the Klan. With his chivalrous, decorous calm under pressure, Lee became the personification of the 'Lost Cause' which was central to the Klan's very being. Legend has it that the 'Greatest Southerner' had been asked to lead the Klan in 1867. Lee politely declined, saying the Klan had his 'invisible support'.[9]

That Lost Cause presented an entirely false narrative about the Civil War and its importance to the USA.[10] It starts by depicting the South taking part in a 'War Between the States', a noble and just war which had erupted when brave men fought for the right of individual states to control all aspects of governance not *specifically* allocated to the federal government by the US Constitution. Those who believe in the Lost Cause will point out that in 1861 the US Constitution did not *expressly* say that a state could not leave the Union – and it still doesn't today.

In Lost Cause mythology, the issue of slavery as a cause of the war is peripheral, not least because adherents maintain that slavery was essentially a benign institution. The most fundamental – and deceitful – depiction of the Lost Cause, David Griffith's 1915 film *The Birth of a Nation*, shows happy, healthy, loyal slaves tending the cotton crop and demonstrating childlike devotion and loyalty to the slave-holder family. The film implies that, in freeing the slaves, Reconstruction carpetbaggers and their Republican overlords disrupted what was a kind of natural racial hierarchy. Of course, Griffith's epic film depicts that hierarchy from a white supremacist point of view with the Klan itself restoring the ideal of a 'natural order' to a grateful South.

By extension, belief in the Lost Cause justifies Jim Crow, segregation, disenfranchisement and racial violence. Underlying the Lost Cause is the heroism of the Confederacy, and the justification of Klan violence. To 'neo-Confederates', history should by no means celebrate the millions of Americans who fought and sometimes died opposing that cause.

Documents released to a British newspaper reveal that one of the leading neo-Confederate organisations has nearly 60,000 members. Ninety-one of the members of the Sons of Confederate Veterans (SCV) use a government email address and seventy-four use a military one. The SCV campaigned to keep the statue of Lee in its place – although the organisation is at pains to state it does not associate itself with white supremacy or white nationalism.[11]

Support for the legacy of the Confederacy is also evident in other spheres of US life. In the twenty-first century there are twice as many Civil War re-enactors choosing to be on the Confederate side as there are re-enactors 'serving' on the Union's. Just months after Roof's atrocity in South Carolina, a poll indicated that 43 per cent of Americans still opposed the removal of Confederate flags from government buildings and 41 per cent disagreed with the statement that 'slavery led the nation into the Civil War'.[12]

For all of the Alt-Right's attempts to disassociate itself from the Klan's redneck past and fossilised ways, many of those who took a stand at the Charlottesville rally would have understood the Klan's relevance. To paraphrase the journalist Vegas Tenold, what the organisers of Unite the Right were after was white nationalism 2.0. What they got was a mob which reverted to white nationalism 1.0.[13]

Klan numbers may well continue to decline, hopefully to a point of total irrelevance, but it is important to acknowledge that the Lost Cause is the *Klan's cause*. As in 1867, 1920 or 1954, the unifying cause in Charlottesville in 2017 was the Klan's cause.

# CHAPTER 88

The tragic events of Charlottesville had a noticeable impact on the Alt-Right, leading to a dissolution of what little unity the movement had achieved and, of course, a huge public backlash. As with the Klan in the 1930s and 1970s, while the Alt-Right was disgraced, it also became more newsworthy. In the splintering after Charlottesville, small but ultra-violent movements emerged.

The Boogaloo Bois are a loosely affiliated, heavily armed, far-right group dedicated to inciting a second Civil War. They have shot enemies dead, including police. They've infiltrated and acted as agents provocateurs at Black Lives Matter protests, as well as hatched plots to kidnap and assassinate leading political figures. The Proud Boys, a nationalist, misogynist, anti-Muslim hate group, fought a gun battle in the suburbs of Portland, Oregon. The Oath Keepers issued a threat of 'civil war' which was taken seriously enough to lead to the entire Oregon State Capitol at Salem being locked down.

On the other hand, the Unite the Right rally served to further unite the already coalescing opposition. Horror at the murder of Heather Heyer and the other violence at Charlottesville fed the seething groundswell of public outrage verging on revolution. Since the televised bludgeoning of Rodney King by the LAPD in 1991, a perpetual cycle of police violence provoked outrage, riots and promises of reform. Over the three decades since Rodney King's beating, police have faced off against protesters in LA, New York, St Louis, Ferguson (Missouri), Baltimore, Baton Rouge, St Paul and other cities.

But it was not until the 25 May 2020 murder of George Floyd in Minneapolis that the protests became national, if not global. By the end of May, protests had been held in 450 cities in every state in the Union. *The New York Times* estimated that up to 26 million Americans took part in the protests at some point over the summer of 2020, making them the largest in US history.[1] There were accusations of police using 'batons, tear gas, pepper spray and rubber bullets on protesters, bystanders and journalists, often without warning or seemingly unprovoked'. There were even eight accusations of police cars being driven into protesters.[2]

Police violence was seen as symptomatic of an inherent racism in US society. More subtle underpinnings of white supremacy were brought to the surface and questioned. Public displays of conservatism became flashpoints of anger, from standing for the national anthem at a sporting event, to cisgender intake forms, to the dinosaur-riding Jesus on display at a 'Biblical Science' museum. As society became more polarised, conservative culture was much more likely to be labelled backwards or racist, and conservatives much more likely to be called 'haters' or even white supremacists.

Such epithets didn't seem to bother the president. While some condemned Donald Trump as 'a race-baiting, xenophobic, religious bigot', he certainly didn't see himself in that light. With his characteristic lack of 'false' modesty, his response was to label himself 'the least racist person anybody is going to meet'.[3] He still managed to get the enthusiastic support of the Alt-Right. Richard Spencer gave an excited speech on hearing of Trump's election victory which he ended with 'Hail Trump! Hail our people! Hail victory!' while giving a Nazi salute.[4] The Klan also saw Trump's election as a cause for celebration.

David Duke tweeted, 'We did it! Congratulation[s] Donald J Trump President of the United States of America!'[5] Thom Robb's *Crusader* – 'The Political Voice of White Christian America' and the KKKK – saw the ousting of Obama and victory over Hillary Clinton in biblical terms. They'd represented 'a wicked and perverse generation'. Robb wholeheartedly supported Trump's campaign to 'Make America Great Again'.[6] The California Grand Dragon of the Loyal White Knights, Will Quigg, agreed. Quigg claimed membership of the LWKKKK had spiked since Trump's campaign started – a fact disputed by the SPLC.[7]

Quigg was not the only one who sensed Trump's victory was good for Klan growth. Across the nation, Klaverns planned rallies and stepped up leaflet drops to boost membership. It wasn't a great success. In Maine leaflets appeared reassuring the public that 'You can sleep tonight knowing the Klan is awake!' And while those who received these leaflets were worried, it turned out that only around twenty were actually dropped. It was hardly indicative of a Klan that was 'on the move'.[8]

The North Carolina LWKKKK in Pelham publicised their plans for a December 2016 celebration march. But although the Klavern was one of the largest in the country, with almost 200 members, the effect of their publicity was rather lost when they rolled out their triumphant but non-sensical slogan: 'TRUMP = TRUMP'S RACE UNITED MY PEOPLE'. The rally was never actually held.[9]

In 2020 over 1.5 million Americans signed an online petition to 'Change [the] status of the KKK to a terrorist organization'.[10] It was, in part, a response to President Trump's tweet signalling his intention to designate Antifa a terrorist group. The insinuation was that the president supported the Klan, a suspicion which had had currency ever since David Duke's triumphant tweet celebrating Trump's election in January 2017. Trump disingenuously denied any knowledge of Duke, shifting his attention back to Antifa. But the issue wouldn't go away that easily.

In a February 2016 interview on CNN, Trump was asked to denounce Duke, who was already supporting his candidacy. Trump swerved and ducked, saying, 'I will do research on them. And, certainly, I would disavow if I thought there was something wrong.' He would later blame his ambivalence on a faulty earpiece. Trump had already denounced Duke back in 2000, calling him 'a bigot, a racist, a problem'.[11] In 2016 he would tell Bret Baier on Fox News, 'I totally disavow the Ku Klux Klan. I totally disavow David Duke.'[12]

Once in office, Trump condemned the order despite the Klan's repeated statements of support. After Charlottesville Trump said, 'Racism is evil and those who cause violence in its name are criminals and thugs, including the KKK, neo-Nazis, white supremacists and other hate groups that are repugnant to all that we hold dear as Americans.' It is important and fitting that the best-remembered thing Trump said about Charlottesville was his comment that there were 'fine people on both sides'.[13]

The Trump White House came closer to supporting Klan-backed policies than any previous administration. Trump offered just the type of simple solutions the Klan and others on the racist right offered. His promise to ban the immigration of Muslims and his promise to 'build a wall' to exclude undocumented Mexicans drew heavily on the racial stereotypes so essential to the Klan. The 'exposure' of his opponents as corrupt and self-serving fed into New World Order conspiracy theories.

White supremacists also liked Trump's initial appointments. They were particularly fond of Trump's campaign adviser and chief strategist Steve Bannon. David Duke called his appointment 'excellent' and said he shared 'the ideological aspects of where we're going'. Bannon also bragged of his associations with the Alt-Right. As Richard Spencer told the *Daily Beast*, Bannon's mouthpiece, *Breitbart News*, had 'acted as a "gateway" to alt-right ideas and writers'.[14]

Given these ties to the Klan's allies, why did Trump disavow them? Quite simply, the Klan is electoral poison. The majority of Trump's constituency – in the rustbelt, the urban slums, the small rural towns – may well have agreed with the same policies as those who joined the Klan, but they would never *be* Klansmen or women.

Symbols of the Klan today – the hood, the burning cross and even the sound of its name pronounced out loud – are so synonymous with white supremacy that they are pretty much taboo. In 2016 three high-school seniors in Florida were suspended for wearing 'Klan-style' costumes at a homecoming parade. Two were of Hispanic background and one was an Arab.[15]

When it emerged in 2019 that the liberal, Democrat, governor of Virginia, Ralph Northam, had posed in a fancy-dress Klan costume for his 1984 East Virginia Medical School Yearbook photo, calls were made for his resignation.[16] He's never stood for political office since. And that taboo even extended beyond the USA. In 2020 in Birmingham, UK, ex-policeman James Watts posted racist pictures on WhatsApp. One showed his white dog in a Klan hood next to his black dog with a noose around its neck. In June 2022 he received a twenty-week prison sentence.[17]

# EPILOGUE

In the summer of 2022, as a Select Committee was completing the report on the 6 January 2021 attack on the Capitol, I looked up the website and I did what I always do: I tapped in the search-word 'Klan'.[1] It got *one* hit. On 9 June 2022, in his opening statement the Committee Chairman, Bennie Thompson, spoke of his upbringing in rural Mississippi:

> I'm from a part of the country where people justify the actions of slavery, Ku Klux Klan, and lynching. I'm reminded of that dark history as I hear voices today try and justify the actions of the insurrectionists of January 6, 2021.[2]

He was right. There are echoes of the Klan all over that shameful event. The pageantry, the wacky costumes and the holiday atmosphere bring to mind the carnival roots of the Reconstruction Klan. Most memorable of the 2021 debacle is the shirtless, tattooed 'QAnon Shaman', in his horned headdress with his stars-and-stripes-painted face. It echoes the Klan. It's an image which will forever be associated with that event.

Then of course we can draw parallels between the attempts to violently overthrow a legitimately elected President, and the Klan's insurgencies in Reconstruction. There are also the threats to hang Vice President Mike Pence on their homemade scaffold for his 'treasonous' denunciation of Donald Trump. Add the quest to find and shoot the House Speaker, Nancy

Pelosi, and the rioters look distinctly like a Klan lynch mob. Then, of course, it is possible to match the QAnon posts flying around social media, ranting about the 'stolen election', secret networks of paedophiles and voter fraud – all elements which resonated with Klan strategies down the ages.

But what is perhaps most telling in all this footage is the *absence* of Klan symbols. There are no white hoods or useless little shields emblazoned with the red, white and black 'Drop of Blood'. In fact, what is striking is the notable absence of the Klan at any of the events on 6 January 2021.

Yet the Klan is central to the events of 6 January in one vital way. Ironically it is the Klan's legacy that has led to the prosecution of many of the rioters. The federal government used the 1871 Klan Act to prosecute and bring to justice those involved in the rioting. This legislation has been, and will probably continue to be, a go-to means to halt 'insurrection, domestic violence, unlawful combinations, or conspiracies'. It was used in the 1870s, the 1960s and even by the NAACP in December 2021.[3] But arguably it is only the name of the Klan which seems to continue. By September 2023, not one of the 1,106 individuals charged with crimes related to the January 6th riot has – to my knowledge – been shown to have had known Klan affiliations.[4]

The news feeds I've received ever since I signed up in January 2018 for a Google Alert on 'the Ku Klux Klan' are almost entirely reminiscences by anti-Klan activists or musings on the Klan's irrelevance today. They concentrate on former Klan strongholds across the nation – Alabama, Mississippi, Oklahoma and Indiana – and celebrate the decline of the order in these areas. Some discuss the Klan's heyday in the 1920s. Others give personal accounts of the roles in fighting its violence in the 1960s. Journalists, academics and activists focus on the Klan's shrinking power. Others concentrate on Trump's racism and how his language, with its scapegoats and conspiracies, echoes that of the Klan in the 1920s.

From time to time, a journalist will report a rise in Klan leaflet drops in a certain area and see it as a sign the Klan is once more on the move. There are obituaries and biographies of leading Klan figures who've died or been sentenced for crimes they committed in the past. Sometimes it is to report prosecutions of Klansmen – often caught in drugs busts and frequently buying sex or committing domestic violence, alongside cross-burnings or other forms of intimidation. And then there is the constant round of Klan-associated statues being torn down and institutions and buildings being renamed because of past Klan associations.

When we see headlines of racist violence, like the massacres in May of 2022, where nineteen people were shot in a Uvalde, Texas, high school and ten at a supermarket in Buffalo, New York, there is no mention of the Klan. When race is suspected to be the motive, news reports no longer include the stock images of a Klan hood or a burning cross. In the early 2020s, the Proud Boys and Oath Keepers are news. The Klan is not.

The decline of the Klan does not mean white supremacy, white nationalism or white power has declined with it. During the Trump presidency, while Klan numbers declined, other hate groups expanded. They peaked in 2018 at 1,020, before dropping back down to about 730 in 2021. Yet, as the SPLC put it, 'the dropping numbers of organized hate and anti-government groups suggest that the extremist ideas that mobilize them now operate more openly'.[5] Donald Trump's outspoken time in office led to a shift in the boundaries of who and what it was 'acceptable' to hate.

Hate has gone mainstream.

Today it is possible for social media companies to analyse our taste, manipulate our decisions and pander to our politics. They can pick up our 'digital exhaust': the digital record of our website visits.[6] Like hounds on a trail, these scents can lead those who are interested to have a real understanding of what we love, what we support, what we'll pay for – and what we hate.

But there has been no 'Trump Bump' for the Klan. The situation today strongly echoes an observation in a 1968 Alabama newspaper editorial – 'Haters don't need to join a Klan when they have [the ultra-segregationist] George Wallace. If you want something hated, just name it – he'll hate it for you.'[7] Just substitute Steve Bannon, Richard Spencer or Donald Trump for George Wallace. Why parade around and openly air your views? Why subject yourself to vitriol, ridicule and quite probably violence when someone else can express what you feel? We live in a digital democracy. Retreat into cyberspace. Become a keyboard warrior. Retweet.

The result is that America feels more polarised now than ever. The Klan may be moribund, but other hate groups are surging. Yet the lessons of the Klan are important. Polarisation isn't built in a day, nor does it last forever, and it's not unique to any time in history. In the 1920s we saw a mix of politics which might be seen as very like today. Americans identified as native-born/immigrant; 'wet'/'dry'; rural/urban; Catholic/Protestant; Jewish/Gentile; modern/traditional. The categories may well be different, but the outlooks and conclusions seem all too familiar.

The Klan can teach us another significant lesson about the nature of polarisation. Polarisation seems to go hand in hand with a a sense of victimhood. Victim narratives give hate coherence. They are crucial for the white power movement. As we've seen, the Klan has victim narratives that keep reinventing themselves and reappearing: the Lost Cause; the flood of immigrants; positive discrimination; the White Holocaust. Hate groups thrive on victim narratives. But the premise of the white power victimhood is false. It relies on a false equivalence.

I repeat, white power's victimhood is false. It is not equivalent to say you have suffered or been excluded in the same way as people who were ripped from their continent, brought in chains, saw the destruction of their families on the auction block, tortured and worked to death and their ancestors treated as second-class citizens ever since. The condition of the freedmen in Reconstruction was not the same as that of the defeated Confederacy. White power is not the same as Black Power and Black Lives Matter is not an expression of identity politics: it is a civil rights movement. White power's victimhood is not 'equivalent' to those who experienced the industrialised murder of over 6 million of their families and faith. The White Holocaust is not *the* Holocaust.

It is the increasing realisation of these – and other – fundamental, ideological flaws which have played a major role in the collapse of the Klan. At the moment, the prevailing sense of the Klan is, rightly, one of ignorance, bigotry and cruelty. Only the most vile and extreme of society would want to be associated with the Klan. Only the most vile and extreme society could support it. But we live in times of increasing vitriol and polarisation. And we've been there before.

Today, the Klan feels like a threat that has passed. As the SPLC put it, 'the most noted Klan-related activity [in the 2020s] … will most likely be protests countering Klan events and community-based demonstrations against Klan flyer-ing incidents.'[8] But sadly we seem to be stuck in a moment where the lessons inherent in the seeming victory over the Klan are being ignored. It appears we feel that any mention of the Klan's history risks bringing it back. It seems the trauma is just too great.

However, on the anniversary of one of the Klan's most disgusting atrocities, the first Black female US Supreme Court Justice, Ketanji Brown Jackson, spoke out against this conspiracy of silence. Speaking at the 16th Street Baptist Church in Birmingham, Alabama, sixty years after four young girls were killed and dozens of others maimed, she reminded her audience that:

> The work of our time is maintaining that hard-won freedom, and to do that, we're going to need the truth – the whole truth – about our past. We must teach it to our children and preserve it for theirs. Knowledge of the past is what enables us to mark our forward progress. If we're going to continue to move forward as a nation, we can't allow concern about discomfort to displace knowledge, truth, or history.[9]

Let's hope we've learned the lessons which enabled us to understand the roots of the Klan's hatred. Let's hope they enable us to continue to neutralise, if not kill, the Klan. And let's hope we can continue to keep it that way.

# NOTES

## Preface

1 This (spurious) explanation has its roots in an anonymous 1868 account:
'[W]hen a Brother approaches the spot where a band is assembled, the sentinels,
always concealed, challenge him by bringing their rifles to a full cock. That
operation, as everyone knows, produces two sounds or clicks, one when the hammer
reaches the half cock, and the other when it comes to the full cock. These sounds or
clicks are represented by "Ku-Klux". The "Klan" is the sound of the hammer on the
nipple of the piece when the trigger is pulled, and the hammer snapped. Bringing
the piece to full cock is the challenge, and the answer is given by the challenged
party full-cocking his piece, and instantly pulling the trigger, snapping the hammer.'
Anonymous, *The Oaths, Signs, Ceremonies and Objects of the Ku-Klux-Klan: A Full
Expose by a Late Member* (Unknown Publisher, Cleveland, OH, 1868) pp.21–22.

2 It turns out this rumour had some pedigree and was well known in the African
American community, understandably tainting the brand's appeal to Black smokers
for some time and maybe in the process saving Black lives from smoking-related
deaths. For a discussion of the ideas behind this conspiracy see Rosemary J. Coombe,
*The Cultural Life of Intellectual Property: Authorship, Appropriation and the Law* (Duke
University Press, Durham, NC, 1998) pp.159–60.

3 David Holthouse, 'Motley Crews: With the Decline of the Hammerskins,
Independent Skinhead Groups Grow', *Intelligence Report* (October 2006)
www.splcenter.org/fighting-hate/intelligence-report/2006/motley-crews-decline-
hammerskins-independent-skinhead-groups-grow?page=0%2C1.

4 www.splcenter.org/fighting-hate/intelligence-report/2019/year-hate-rage-
against-change.

## Chapter 1

1 The best contemporary account of Sam Davis' trial and execution is in 'The
Execution of a Rebel Spy', *Cincinnati Daily Commercial* 8 December 1863. However,
neither this nor any other newspaper account of the time makes any mention of
Crowe. It seems the tale passed into Klan mythology later via the account of one
of the other friends present that night, John Lester, in John C. Lester and Daniel L.
Wilson, 'The Ku Klux Klan: Its Origin, Growth and Disbandment', *The Century
Illustrated Monthly Magazine*, 28:3 (July 1884). Details on the emergence of Davis as a

Confederate martyr are best found in Edward John Harcourt, '"The Boys Will Have to Fight the Battles without Me": The Making of Sam Davis, "Boy Hero of the Confederacy"', *Southern Cultures* 12:3 (Autumn, 2006) pp.29–54.

2   It is also probable that McCord was wounded at the Battle of Dallas or perhaps the Battle of Jonesboro, both halving the strength of the 9th Kentucky.

3   Information taken from the State Library and Archives, *Index to Tennessee Confederate Pension Applications* (Nashville, TN, 1964), Ancestry.com, 'Tennessee, U.S., Civil War Confederate Pension Applications Index' ,Provo, Utah, USA: Ancestry.com Operations Inc, 2005 and John C. Lester and Daniel L. Wilson, 'The Ku Klux Klan: Its Origin, Growth and Disbandment', *The Century Illustrated Monthly Magazine*, 28:3 (July 1884) p.19.

4   Craig L. Torbenson, 'College Fraternities and Sororities: A Historical Geography, 1776–1989' (Unpublished PhD Thesis, University of Oklahoma, Norman, OK, 1992) pp.28–32 and Nicholas L. Syrett, *The Company He Keeps: A History of White College Fraternities* (University of North Carolina Press, Chapel Hill, NC, 2011) pp.1–17.

5   Harriet W. McBride, 'The Golden Age of Fraternalism: 1870–1910', *Heredom*, 13 (2005) pp.1–31.

## Chapter 2

1   For some of the most extreme claims see Alma White, *Heroes of the Fiery Cross* (Good Citizen Press, Zarephat,h NJ, 1928).

2   The roots of this link come from Wyn Craig Wade's authoritative *Fiery Cross: The Ku Klux Klan in America* (Simon and Schuster, New York, 1984) p.454 n.33. However, he cites Mr and Mrs W.B. Romine's pamphlet *A Story of the Original Ku Klux Klan* (Pulaski Citizen, Pulaski, TN, 1924) p.7. Yet neither on that page nor on any other page of the text is there any mention of 'Cukulcan' or 'Kukulcan' as he is more properly known.

3   The Memphis Appeal in the *Savannah Daily News and Herald* 4 June 1868.

4   Nicholas Jackson Floyd, *Thorns in the Flesh: A Romance of the War and Ku-Klux Periods* (Hubbard Bros, Philadelphia, PA, 1884) pp.162–6.

5   Gladys-Marie Fry, *Night Riders in Black Folk History* (University of North Carolina Press, Chapel Hill, NC, 1975) pp.118–19.

6   Gladys-Marie Fry, *Night Riders in Black Folk History* (University of North Carolina Press, Chapel Hill, NC, 1975) pp.157–9.

7   Work Projects Administration: Federal Writers Project, Ex-Slave Narratives, MS.000149, Joseph Samuel Badgett, Arkansas State Archives, Little Rock, Arkansas p.81; genealogytrails.com/ark/slavenarrative_p2.html#badgett.

8   Work Projects Administration: Federal Writers Project, Ex-Slave Narratives, MS.000149, Joseph Samuel Badgett, Arkansas State Archives, Little Rock, Arkansas p.82.

9   J.T. Tims interviewed for the Federal Writers Project of the Works Progress Administration op.cit. Fry, p.121, also available from Library of Congress at www.loc.gov/resource/mesn.026/?sp=341.

10  R.J. Brunson, *Historic Pulaski, Birthplace of the Ku Klux Klan, Scene of Execution of Sam Davis* (The Methodist Publishing House, Nashville, TN, 1913) pp.14–16.

11  For a full account of this battle see David A. Blome, *Greek Warfare Beyond the Polis: Defense, Strategy, and the Making of Ancient Federal States* (Cornell University Press, New York, 2020) pp.9–28.

12 Allen Ward, 'A Note on the Origin of the Ku Klux Klan', *Tennessee Historical Quarterly*, 23:2 (June 1964) p.182.

13 Walter L. Fleming, *Civil War and Reconstruction in Alabama* (Columbia University Press, New York, 1905) p.661 n.1890.

## Chapter 3

1 William E. Dodd's *Cotton Kingdom* (1919) cited in James Taft Hatfield, 'Goethe and the Ku-Klux Klan Source', *Publications of the Modern Language Association*, 37:4 (December 1922) p.736.

2 John C. Lester and Daniel L. Wilson, *Ku Klux Klan: Its Origin, Growth and Disbandment* (Wheeler, Osborn and Duckworth Manufacturing Co., Nashville, TN, 1884) pp.24–26.

3 Elaine Frantz Parsons, 'Midnight Rangers: Costume and Performance in the Reconstruction-Era Ku Klux Klan', *The Journal of American History*, 92:3 (December 2005) pp.811–36.

4 James Crowe cited in the *Sandersville Herald* (Georgia) 3 April 1908 p.1.

## Chapter 4

1 Telegram from William T. Sherman to Ulysses S. Grant, 9 October 1864 in Jean V. Berlin and Brooks D. Simpson (eds), *Sherman's Civil War: Selected Correspondence of William T. Sherman, 1860–1865* (University of North Carolina Press, Chapel Hill, NC, 1999) p.731.

2 Cited in Allen C. Guelzo, *Fateful Lightning: A New History of the Civil War and Reconstruction* (Oxford University Press, New York, 2012), p.439.

3 A readable account of Sherman's March to the Sea is J.D. Dickey's *Rising in Flames: Sherman's March and the Fight for a New Nation* (Pegasus Books, New York, 2018).

4 Stephany McCurry, 'The Confederacy Was an Antidemocratic, Centralized State', *The Atlantic* 21 June 2020. www.theatlantic.com/ideas/archive/2020/06/confederacy-wasnt-what-you-think/613309/ and Edward Ball, *Life of a Klansman* (Farrar, Straus and Giroux, New York, 2020) p.182.

5 Figures taken from James L. Roark, *Masters Without Slaves: Southern Planters in the Civil War and Reconstruction* (Norton and Co., New York, 1977) pp.ix–xi.

6 James Stirling, *Letters from the Slave States* (J.W. Parker, London, 1857) pp.66 and 86.

## Chapter 5

1 The image was discovered by Bob Wamble of the Giles County Historical Society and shown to Elaine Franz Parsons who reproduces and analyses its significance in Elaine Frantz Parsons, *Ku-Klux: The Birth of the Klan During Reconstruction* (University of North Carolina Press, Chapel Hill, NC, 2015) pp.32–34.

2 Crowe quoted in 'The Origin of the Ku-Klux Klan: One of the Original Organizers Writes a Brief History of Organization' in the *Sandersville Herald* 3 April 1908 p.1.

3 'Magnolia County [Arkansas?] Record 1825' cited in J. Reuben Sheeler, 'Methods for Control of the Negro ... Mind, Soul and Body', *Negro History Bulletin*, 21:3 (December 1957) p.68.

4 Colin Edward Woodward, *Marching Masters: Slavery, Race and the Confederate Army During the Civil War* (University of Virginia Press, Charlottesville, VA, 2014) p.15.

5 For details of sabotage and other disruptions used by slaves and freedmen see James C. Scott, *Domination and the Arts of Resistance: Hidden Transcripts* (Yale University Press, New Haven, CT, 1990).

6   See, for example, Steven Hahn, '"Extravagant Expectations" of Freedom: Rumour, Political Struggle, and the Christmas Insurrection Scare of 1865 in the American South', *Past & Present* (1997) pp.151–52.
7   Sally E. Hadden, *Slave Patrols: Law and Violence in Virginia and the Carolinas* (Harvard University Press, Cambridge, MA, 2001) especially pp.203–20.

## Chapter 6

1   Because Lincoln was reluctant to impose a law of this kind on regions under his control, the Emancipation Proclamation could only be applied to areas not under federal (Washington's) control.
2   It is interesting that the Native Americans would not become 'citizens' of their country until 1924, and Chinese residents would have that right removed in 1882, not to regain it until 1943.
3   For details of the riot see US House of Representatives, *Memphis Riots and Massacres, US House of Representatives*, 39th Congress, 1st Session, Report No. 101 (Washington DC, 1866).
4   For a concise analysis see George C. Rable, *But There Was No Peace: The Role of Violence in the Politics of Reconstruction* (University of Georgia Press, Athens, GA, 1984) pp.187–9.
5   Quotations and details taken from Edward Ball, *Life of a Klansman* (Farrar, Straus and Giroux, New York, 2020) pp.200–11.
6   Details taken from Eric Foner, *Reconstruction: America's Unfinished Revolution 1863–1877* (Harper Collins, New York, 1988) pp.199–201.

## Chapter 7

1   *Lowell Daily Citizen and News* 25 August 1866.
2   President Johnson in *The New York Times* 30 May 1865.
3   Allen C. Guelzo, *Reconstruction: A Concise History* (Oxford University Press, New York, 2018) p.25.
4   Fourteenth Amendment, Section 3.
5   *Raleigh Sentinel* 9 June 1868.
6   Walter Lynwood Fleming, *The Sequel of Appomattox: A Chronicle of the Reunion of the States* (Yale University Press, New Haven, CT, 1919) p.244.

## Chapter 8

1   Herman Melville, *Battle-Pieces and Aspects of the War* (Harper Brothers, New York, 1866) p.264.
2   Federal Writers Project, *Slave Narratives: Volume XV Tennessee Narratives* (Washington DC, 1941) p.19.
3   Federal Writers Project, *Slave Narrative Project, Vol. XIV, South Carolina, Part 2* (Washington DC, 1941) pp.250–1 and Bradley D. Proctor, '"From the Cradle to the Grave": Jim Williams, Black Manhood, and Militia Activism in Reconstruction South Carolina', *American Nineteenth-Century History*, 19:1 (2018) pp.58–9.

## Chapter 9

1   Wyn Craig Wade, *The Fiery Cross: The Ku Klux Klan in America* (Touchstone Books, New York, 1987) pp.31–32 and Elaine Frantz Parsons, *Ku-Klux: The Birth of the Klan During Reconstruction* (University of North Carolina Press, Chapel Hill, NC, 2015) pp.49–50.

2  Thomas L. Connelly, *Five Tragic Hours: The Battle of Franklin* (University of Tennessee Press, Knoxville, TN, 1983).

3  Forrest Monument Association, *The Forrest Monument: Its History and Dedication; A Memorial in Art, Oratory and Literature* (Unknown Publisher, 1905) p.28 and Sumner Archibald Cunningham, *The Confederate Veteran*, 15 (January 1907) pp.21–3.

4  Enoch L. Mitchell, 'The Role of General George Washington Gordon in the Ku Klux Klan', *Western Tennessee Historical Society Papers*, 1 (1947) pp.73–80.

5  Stanley F. Horn, *The Invisible Empire: The Story of the Ku Klux Klan, 1866–1871* (Houghton Mifflin Co., Boston, MA, 1939) pp.32–3.

6  Taken from speeches made by James Garfield on 12 and 18 February 1867 cited in Burke A. Hinsdale (ed.), *The Works of James Abram Garfield*, 1 (James R. Osgood Co., Boston, MA, 1882) pp.254–5.

7  All quotes taken from The Original 1866 Ku Klux Klan Prescript cited in full in Patterson Smith Reprint Series in *Criminology 81: Law Enforcement and Social Problems* (Patterson Smith, Montclair, NJ, 1969) pp.383–408.

8  The term 'Invisible Empire', would become synonymous with the Klan throughout its history. Apparently the term comes from an incident early in the history of the Klan when Klansmen asked the legendary Confederate commander Robert E. Lee if he'd head up the order. Lee apparently said he didn't feel he could, but they would always have his 'invisible support'.

9  All quotes taken from The Original 1866 Ku Klux Klan Prescript cited in full in Patterson Smith Reprint Series in *Criminology 81: Law Enforcement and Social Problems* (Patterson Smith, Montclair, NJ, 1969) pp.383–408.

10 US Congress, *Report of the Joint Select Committee to Inquire into the Condition of Affairs in the Late Insurrectionary States: Georgia* (Govt Printing Office, Washington DC, 1872) p.453.

11 For a list of these, see Michael Newton, *White Robes and Burning Crosses* (McFarland, Jefferson, NC, 2014) p.9.

12 US Congress, *Report of the Joint Select Committee to Inquire into The Condition of Affairs in the Late Insurrectionary States: Georgia* (Govt Printing Office, Washington DC, 1872) p.453.

## Chapter 10

1  For details on Forrest's post-war life and the Edwards incident see Jack Hurst, *Nathan Bedford Forrest: A Biography* (Vintage, New York, 1993) pp.271–5 and Wyn Craig Wade, *The Fiery Cross: The Ku Klux Klan in America* (Touchstone Books, New York, 1987), pp.40–3.

2  Forrest cited in John A. Lynn, *Another Kind of War: The Nature and History of Terrorism* (Yale University Press, New Haven, CT, 2019) p.83. See also Klansman, John Watson Morton, *The Artillery of Nathan Bedford Forrest's Cavalry* (ME Church, Nashville, TN, 1909) pp.342–5.

## Chapter 11

1  Letter from Albion W. Tourgée to Senator Joseph C. Abbott, 24 May 1870, published in the *New York Tribune* 24 May 1870 and 26 February 1873.

2  Stephen E Massengill, 'The Detectives of William W. Holden, 1869–1870', *North Carolina Historical Review*, 62 (October 1985) pp.477–9, 486.

3  *The Anderson* [South Carolina] *Intelligencer* 26 October 1871.

4  *The Memphis Avalanche* 23 June 1866.

5   *Athens Post* 6 August 1868.
6   US Senate, *Report on the Alleged Outrages in the Southern States by the Select Committee of the Senate 10 March 1871* (US Printing Office, Washington DC, 1871) p.viii.
7   Cited in Michael W. Fitzgerald, *The Union League Movement in the Deep South: Politics and Agricultural Change During Reconstruction* (Louisiana State University Press, Baton Rouge, LA, 1989) p.217.
8   *Tuscaloosa Monitor* 18 August 1868.

## Chapter 12

1   Abraham Lincoln, 'A Proclamation, 4 July 1861' (Government Printing Office, Washington DC, 1861).
2   Stephen E. Massengill, 'The Detectives of William W. Holden, 1869–1870', *The North Carolina Historical Review*, 62:4 (October 1985) pp.448–87.
3   Cited in Otto H. Olsen, *Carpetbagger's Crusade: The Life of Albion Winegar Tourgée* (Johns Hopkins Press, Baltimore, 1965) p.130.
4   Reports of R.T. Bosher and G.R. Kimball cited in Stephen E. Massengill, 'The Detectives of William W. Holden, 1869–1870', *The North Carolina Historical Review*, 62:4 (October 1985) p.458.
5   The outrage was reported by detective John E. Williams in January 1869, Stephen E. Massengill, 'The Detectives of William W. Holden, 1869–1870', *The North Carolina Historical Review*, 62:4 (October 1985) p.461.
6   Stephen E. Massengill, 'The Detectives of William W. Holden, 1869–1870', *The North Carolina Historical Review*, 62:4 (October 1985) p.466.
7   Stephen E. Massengill, 'The Detectives of William W. Holden, 1869–1870', *The North Carolina Historical Review*, 62:4 (October 1985) p.462.
8   Jim D. Brisson, '"Civil Government Was Crumbling Around Me": The Kirk-Holden War of 1870', *The North Carolina Historical Review*, 8:2 (April 2011) pp.123–63.
9   Jim D. Brisson, '"Civil Government Was Crumbling Around Me": The Kirk-Holden War of 1870', *The North Carolina Historical Review*, 8:2 (April 2011) p.157.

## Chapter 13

1   Cited in E. Merton Coulter, *William G. Brownlow: Fighting Parson of the Southern Highlands* (University of Tennessee Press, Knoxville, TN, 1999) p.291.
2   Benjamin Horton Severance, 'Tennessee's Radical Army: The State Guard and Its Role in Reconstruction' (Unpublished PhD Thesis, University of Tennessee, Knoxville, 2002) pp.187–93.
3   Cited in the Nashville *Republican Banner* 3 August 1867.
4   For details of the parade and increased Klan activity see *Nashville Daily Press and Times* 6 March 1868.
5   Details of Fitzpatrick's lynching can be found in Donald Gordon Alcock, *A Study in Continuity: Maury County, Tennessee, 1850–1870* (University of California, Berkeley, CA, 1985) pp.238–9.
6   *Winchester Home Journal* 9 April 1868 and Nashville *Republican Banner* 21 March 1868.
7   *Winchester Home Journal* 9 April 1868 and Nashville *Republican Banner* 21 March 1868.

## Chapter 14

1   Allen W. Trelease, *White Terror: The Ku Klux Klan Conspiracy and Reconstruction* (Louisiana State University Press, Baton Rouge, LA, 1971) pp.xv–xlvii.

2   Thomas B. Alexander, 'Kukluxism in Tennessee, 1865–1869', *Tennessee Historical Quarterly*, 8:3 (September 1949) pp.203–5.

3   Benjamin Horton Severance, *Tennessee's Radical Army: The State Guard and Its Role in Reconstruction* (Unpublished PhD Thesis, University of Tennessee, Knoxville, 2002) p.178.

4   *Nashville Daily Press and Times* 5 March 1868.

5   Benjamin Horton Severance, *Tennessee's Radical Army: The State Guard and Its Role in Reconstruction* (Unpublished PhD Thesis, University of Tennessee, Knoxville, 2002) p.265.

6   Thomas B. Alexander, 'Kukluxism in Tennessee, 1865–1869' *Tennessee Historical Quarterly* 8:3 (September 1949) p.205.

7   Kathleen R. Zebley, 'Unconditional Unionist: Samuel Mayes Arnell and Reconstruction in Tennessee', *Tennessee Historical Quarterly*, 53 (1994) p.254.

8   Thomas B. Alexander, 'Kukluxism in Tennessee, 1865–1869' *Tennessee Historical Quarterly* 8:3 (September 1949) p.207.

9   *Nashville Daily Press and Times* 3 September 1868.

## Chapter 15

1   Paul David Wangsvick, 'The Contested Reputation of Nathan Bedford Forrest: A Case Study in Rhetoric and Regional Identity Formation' (Unpublished PhD Thesis, University of Memphis, TN, 2011) pp.20–25.

2   Benjamin Horton Severance, *Tennessee's Radical Army: The State Guard and Its Role in Reconstruction* (Unpublished PhD Thesis, University of Tennessee, Knoxville, 2002) pp.130 and 180.

3   For a discussion of this see Paul Ashdown and Edward Caudill, *The Myth of Nathan Bedford Forrest* (Rowman and Littlefield, New York, 2005) p.62.

## PART III

1   W.E.B. Dubois, *Black Reconstruction: An Essay Toward a History of the Part Which Black Folk Played in the Attempt to Reconstruct Democracy in America, 1860–1880* (Harcourt, Brace and Co., New York, 1935) p.674.

## Chapter 16

1   Albion W. Tourgée, *A Fool's Errand, by One of the Fools* (Fords, Howard & Hulbert, New York, 1879) p.246.

2   David W. Blight, *Race and Reunion: The Civil War in American Memory* (Harvard University Press, Cambridge, MA, 2001) pp.113–14.

3   *Raleigh Sentinel* 9 June 1868.

4   Allen W. Trelease, *White Terror: The Ku Klux Klan Conspiracy and Reconstruction* (Louisiana State University Press, Baton Rouge, 1971) pp.395–9.

5   *Columbia Daily Phoenix* 21 July 1871.

6   W.E.B. Dubois, *Black Reconstruction: An Essay Toward a History of the Part Which Black Folk Played in the Attempt to Reconstruct Democracy in America, 1860–1880* (Harcourt, Brace and Co., New York, 1935) pp.677 and 683.

7   Governor Scott to General Alfred Terry, 17 January 1871, in *Senate Executive Document No. 28*, serial 1440, 41st Congress, 3rd Session pp.1–2.

8   Taken from a letter sent by George H. Williams to Robert K. Scott 14 April 1869 cited in Lou Falkner Williams, *The Great South Carolina Ku Klux Klan Trials, 1871–1872* (University of Georgia Press, Athens, GA, 1996) p.17.

9   Cited in Louis F. Post, 'A "Carpetbagger" in South Carolina', *Journal of Negro History*, 10 (January 1925) pp.54 and 58.

10  James Michael Martinez, *Carpetbaggers, Cavalry, and the Ku Klux Klan: Exposing the Invisible Empire During Reconstruction* (Rowman & Littlefield, Lanham, MD, 2007) pp.1–5 and Jerry Lee West, *The Reconstruction Ku Klux Klan in York County, South Carolina, 1865–1877* (McFarland, Jefferson, NC, 2002) pp.126–30.

11  *Charleston Courier* 9 September 1871.

12  *Charleston Daily News* 9 September 1871.

## Chapter 17

1   Louis F. Post, 'A "Carpetbagger" in South Carolina', *Journal of Negro History*, 10 (January 1925) p.41.

2   *New York Daily Tribune* 13 November 1871.

3   Merrill's testimony to Joint Committee investigators cited in Allen W. Trelease, *White Terror: The Ku Klux Klan Conspiracy and Reconstruction* (Louisiana State University Press, Baton Rouge, 1971) p.370.

4   'Report of Major Merrill – Presentiments By the Grand Jury' US Senate, *Reports of the Committees* (US Government Printing Office, Washington DC, 1872) p.1602.

5   'Report of Major Merrill – Presentiments By the Grand Jury' US Senate, *Reports of the Committees* (US Government Printing Office, Washington DC, 1872) p.1600.

6   Cited in Lou Falkner Williams, *The Great South Carolina Ku Klux Klan Trials, 1871–1872* (University of Georgia Press, Athens, 1996) p.45.

7   Akerman cited in Charles Lane, *Freedom's Detective: The Secret Service, The Ku Klux Klan and the Man Who Masterminded America's First War on Terror* (Hanover Square Press, Toronto, 2019) p.150.

8   Akerman cited in *The New York Times* 30 October 1871.

## Chapter 18

1   'South Carolina – Court Proceedings' US Senate, *Reports of the Committees: Second Session of the Forty-Second Congress* (US Government Printing Office, Washington DC, 1872) p.1745.

2   Eric Foner, *Reconstruction: America's Unfinished Revolution 1863–1877* (Harper Collins, New York, 1988) pp.457–8.

3   George H. Williams to James M. Blount, 15 April 1873 cited in Charles Lane, *The Day Freedom Died: The Colfax Massacre, the Supreme Court and the Betrayal of Reconstruction* (Henry Holt and Co., New York, 2008) p.140.

4   Cited in Lou Falkner Williams, *The Great South Carolina Ku Klux Klan Trials, 1871–1872* (University of Georgia Press, Athens, 1996) p.147.

## Chapter 19

1   www.journalofthecivilwarera.org/2021/07/removing-the-white-supremacy-marker-at-colfax-louisiana-a-2021-success-story/#page.

2   Eric Foner, *Reconstruction: America's Unfinished Revolution, 1863–1877* (Perennial Library, New York, 1989) p.550.

3   Committee of 70, *History of the Riot at Colfax, Grant Parish, Louisiana, April 13th, 1873: With a Brief Sketch of the Trial of the Grant Parish Prisoners in the Circuit Court of the United States* (Clarke & Hofeline, New Orleans, LA, 1874) pp.10–13.

4 For details of the massacre see Leeanna Keith, *The Colfax Massacre: The Untold Story of Black Power, White Terror, & the Death of Reconstruction* (Oxford University Press, New York, 2007).

5 *New Orleans Bulletin* 30 June 1874.

6 For the legal arguments see supreme.justia.com/cases/federal/us/92/542/.

## Chapter 20

1 Letter to President Grant, 27 April 1874 cited in Otis A. Singletary, *Negro Militia and Reconstruction* (McGraw-Hill, New York, 1963) p.62.

2 T.J. Reed to James Redpath, 28 July 1876 cited in Nicholas Lemann, *Redemption: The Last Battle of the Civil War* (Farrar, Straus and Giroux Books, New York, 2006) p.171.

3 Quotations from US Senate, *Senate Documents*, 1st Session: 44th Congress vol. 1 (Govt Printing Office, Washington DC, 1876) p.247.

4 Vernon L. Wharton, *The Negro in Mississippi, 1865–1890* (University of North Carolina, Chapel Hill, NC, 1947) p.188.

5 Quotations taken from Dorothy Sterling (ed.), *The Trouble They Seen: The Story of Reconstruction in the Words of African Americans* (Da Capo Press, Cambridge, MA, 1994) pp.442–3, 447, 450.

6 US Grant to the Governor of South Carolina, 26 July 1876 cited in *Congressional Series of United States Public Documents*, 1729 (US Government Printing Office, Washington DC, 1877) pp.480 and 483.

## Chapter 21

1 Allan Peskin, 'Was There a Compromise of 1877?', *The Journal of American History*, 60:1 (June 1973) pp.63–75.

2 Clarence C. Clendenen, 'President Hayes' "Withdrawal" of the Troops – An Enduring Myth', *South Carolina Historical Magazine*, 70 (October 1969) pp.240–50.

3 Cited in Bradley David Proctor, 'Whip, Pistol, and Hood: Ku Klux Klan Violence in the Carolinas During Reconstruction' (Unpublished PhD Dissertation, University of North Carolina, Chapel Hill, NC, 2013) p.344.

## PART IV

1 'The South at the Bar', *Broad Ax* 4 September 1915. Under the editorship and ownership of the radical Julius F. Taylor *Broad Ax* was described as the 'the most controversial black newspaper in Chicago in the late nineteenth century', because it disagreed with many of the most popular conformist attitudes of the Black leadership of the time.

## Chapter 22

1 Quotation taken from C. Vann Woodward, *Origins of the New South, 1877–1913* (Louisiana State University Press, Baton Rouge, LA, 1951) p.271.

2 Hilary A. Herbert (ed.), *Why the Solid South?* (R.H. Woodward, Baltimore, MD, 1890) pp.250, 345 and 356.

3 Arguably the best-known and most consistent critic of the Dunning School was W.E.B. Dubois. A founding member of the National Association for the Advancement of Colored People (NAACP), he cogently and meticulously refuted nearly all aspects of the thesis in W.E.B. DuBois, *Black Reconstruction in America* (S.A. Russell, New York, 1935). There were also major contributions to an alternative view in the works of other, largely Black, scholars, including John R. Lynch,

'Some Historical Errors of James Ford Rhodes', *Journal of Negro History*, 2 (October 1917) pp.345–68; Howard K. Beale, *The Critical Year?* (Harcourt Brace, New York, 1930); Alrutheus A. Taylor, *The Negro in South Carolina During the Reconstruction* (The Association for the Study of Negro Life and History, Washington DC, 1924); and Francis B. Simkins and Robert H. Woody, *South Carolina During Reconstruction* (University of North Carolina Press, Chapel Hill, NC, 1932).

4  James Tice Moore, 'Redeemers Reconsidered: Change and Continuity in the Democratic South, 1870–1900', *Journal of Southern History*, 44:3 (August 1978) pp.357–78.

5  William A. Dunning, 'The Undoing of Reconstruction', *The Atlantic Monthly*, 88:528 (October 1901) pp.383–5.

6  John W. Burgess, *Reminiscences of an American Scholar: The Beginnings of Columbia University* (Columbia University Press, New York, 1934) p.3.

7  John W. Burgess, *Reconstruction and the Constitution, 1866–1876* (Scribners, New York, 1902) pp.1–7.

8  Eric Foner, 'Reconstruction Revisited', *Reviews in American History*, 10:4 (December 1982) p.83.

## Chapter 23

1  *The Jeffersonian* 5 August 1915 p.5.

2  Steve Olney, *And the Dead Shall Rise: The Murder of Mary Phagan and the Lynching of Leo Frank* (Random House, New York, 2004) pp.241–2 and 496 and *The Jeffersonian* 30 April 1914 p.9.

3  *The Jeffersonian* 2 September 1915 p.7.

4  *The Jeffersonian* 2 September 1915 p.1.

5  *The Jeffersonian* 2 September 1915 pp.1 and 7.

## Chapter 24

1  John Hope Franklinl, '"Birth of a Nation": Propaganda as History', *The Massachusetts Review*, 20:3 (Autumn, 1979) p.418.

2  Raymond Allen Cook, *Fire from the Flint: The Amazing Careers of Thomas Dixon* (John F. Blair, Winston-Salem, NC, 1968) pp.108–60.

3  *Virginia-Pilot* (Norfolk) 23 September 1905.

4  Griffiths cited in James Hart (ed.), *The Man Who Invented Hollywood: The Autobiography of D.W. Griffiths* (Touchstone, Louisville, KY, 1972) p.88.

5  For details of the film's production see Melvyn Stokes, *D.W. Griffith's The Birth of a Nation* (Oxford University Press, Oxford, 2007) pp.81–109.

6  Melvyn Stokes, *D.W. Griffith's The Birth of a Nation* (Oxford University Press, Oxford, 2007) p.125.

7  Mark E. Benbow, 'Birth of a Quotation: Woodrow Wilson and "Like Writing History with Lightning"', *Journal of the Gilded Age and the Progressive Era*, 9:4 (October 2010) p.509.

8  Woodrow Wilson, 'The Reconstruction of the Southern States', *The Atlantic* January 1901, pp.542–53.

9  *Variety* 19 March 1915.

10  Cited in James Vincent Lowry, 'Reconstructing the Reign of Terror: Popular Memories of the Ku Klux Klan' (Unpublished PhD, University of Mississippi, 2008) p.199.

11 Cited in National Association for the Advancement of Colored People, *Fighting a Vicious Film: Protest Against 'The Birth of a Nation'* (Boston Branch of the National Association for the Advancement of Colored People, 1915) p.26.

12 James Lowry Vincent, *Reconstructing the Reign of Terror: Popular Memories of the Ku Klux Klan, 1877–1921* (Unpublished PhD Thesis, The University of Mississippi, 2008) p.193.

13 Chester County, South Carolina *Semi-Weekly News* 26 May 1916.

14 *Spartanburg Herald* 22 October 1915.

15 *Orangeburg Times and Democrat* 6 April 1916.

## Chapter 25

1 William Joseph Simmons cited in 'An "Imperial Wizard" and His "Klan"', *The Literary Digest* 5 February 1921, p.41.

2 Quotations and details from Ralph McGill, *The South and the Southerner* (Little Brown, Boston, MA, 1959) pp.129–32.

3 William G. Shepherd, '"How I Put Over the Klan": Col William Joseph Simmons, Father of the Ku Klux Klan Tells His Story to William G. Shepherd', *Collier's* (14 July 1928) pp.5–7.

4 As the local theatre owner, Bill Sharpe, would later tell it: 'Doc told me many times he got the inspiration for the Klan revival from my free passes, a fact I lament no little.' Ralph McGill, *The South and the Southerner* (Little Brown, Boston, MA, 1959)p.132.

5 Littlejohn used the pseudonym Marion Mandeval for his *The Klan Inside Out* (Monarch Publishing Co., Claremore, OK, 1924).

## Chapter 26

1 For a discussion of the Spanish links see *El Pais* 25 April 2019.

2 Wyn Craig Wade, *The Fiery Cross: The Ku Klux Klan in America* (Touchstone Books, New York, 1987) p.147.

3 Pamphlet: W.J. Simmons, *Imperial Proclamation of the Imperial Wizard* (KKK, Atlanta, GA, 1917); Robert L. Duffus, 'How the Ku Klux Klan Sells Hate: How Salesmen Sold Packages of Hate at Ten Dollars Each', *The World's Work* (June 1923) pp.174–83; and Wyn Craig Wade, *The Fiery Cross: The Ku Klux Klan in America* (Touchstone Books, New York, 1987) p.147.

4 Michael Newton, *The Ku Klux Klan: History, Organization, Language, Influence and Activities of America's Most Notorious Secret Society* (McFarland, Jefferson, NC, 2007) pp.432–7.

5 Marion Mandeval, *The Klan Inside Out* (Monarch Publishing Co., Claremore, Oklahoma, 1924) p.11 and Ann Patton, *Unmasked: The Rise and Fall of the 1920s Ku Klux Klan* (APLcorps Books, Tulsa, OK, 2016) p.23.

6 Simmons cited in *The New York Times* 1 September 1918.

7 Cited in Henry P. Fry, *The Modern Ku Klux Klan* (Small, Maynard and Co., Boston, MA, 1922) p.36.

8 William J. Simmons, *America's Menace or the Enemy Within* (KKK, Atlanta, GA, 1926) p.64.

9 William J. Simmons in US House of Representatives, Committee on Rules, *The Ku Klux Klan Hearings* 67th Cong., 1st Sess. (1921) p.87.

10 Ward Greene, 'Notes for a History of the Klan', *American Mercury*, 5 (June 1925) p.241.

## Chapter 27

1   Charles O. Jackson, 'William J. Simmons: A Career In Ku Kluxism', *The Georgia Historical Quarterly*, 50:4 (December 1966) p.358.

2   For details, see *The Times Recorder* (Americus, Georgia) 24 September 1921 and *Athens Banner* (Georgia) 29 December 1921.

3   Henry P. Fry, *The Modern Ku Klux Klan* (Small, Maynard and Co., Boston, 1922) pp.36–8; Robert L. Duffus, 'How the Ku Klux Klan Sells Hate: How Salesmen Sold Packages of Hate at Ten Dollars Each', *The World's Work* (June 1923) pp.174–83; Wyn Craig Wade, *The Fiery Cross: The Ku Klux Klan in America* (Touchstone Books, New York, 1987) pp.152–5; Marion Mandeval, *The Klan Inside Out* (Monarch Publishing Co., Claremore, Oklahoma, 1924) pp.17–22; and 'For and Against the Klan', *Literary Digest*, 70 (24 September 1921) pp.36–40.

4   US House of Representatives, Committee on Rules, *The Ku Klux Klan Hearings* 67th Cong., 1st Sess. (1921) p.87 and Robert L. Duffus, 'How the Klan Was Built Up By Travelling Salesmen', *The World's Work*, 42 (May 1923) p.36.

5   US House of Representatives, Committee on Rules, *The Ku Klux Klan Hearings* 67th Cong., 1st Sess. (1921) pp.86–87.

## Chapter 28

1   US House of Representatives, Committee on Rules, *The Ku Klux Klan Hearings* 67th Cong., 1st Sess. (1921) p.14.

2   As stated before, Simmons kept no verifiable records of numbers, but his estimate ties in with most accounts.

3   Clarke cited in Dale W. Laackman, *Selling Hate: Marketing the Ku Klux Klan* (University of Georgia Press, Athens, GA, 2020) p.85.

4   The original contract signed on 7 June 1920 is reproduced in full in Henry P. Fry, *The Modern Ku Klux Klan* (Small, Maynard and Co., Boston, 1922) pp.38–40.

5   US House of Representatives, Committee on Rules, *The Ku Klux Klan Hearings* 67th Cong., 1st Sess. (1921) p.153.

6   Henry Peck Fry, *The Voice of the Third Generation: A Discussion of the Race Question for the Benefit of Those Who Believe that the United States is a White Man's Country and Should be Governed by White Men* (MacGowan-Cooke Printing Co., Chattanooga, TN, 1906) pp.7–8 and 16–17.

7   Quotes taken from Henry P. Fry, *The Modern Ku Klux Klan* (Small, Maynard and Co., Boston, 1922) pp.13–15.

## Chapter 29

1   Henry P. Fry to W.J. Simmons, cited in Henry P. Fry, *The Modern Ku Klux Klan* (Small, Maynard and Co., Boston, 1922) p.7.

2   Dale W. Laackman, *Selling Hate: Marketing the Ku Klux Klan* (University of Georgia Press, Athens, GA, 2020) p.110.

3   Cited in Dale W. Laackman, *Selling Hate: Marketing the Ku Klux Klan* (University of Georgia Press, Athens, GA, 2020) p.117.

4   *New York World* 6 September 1921.

5   *New York World* 6, 22 and 24 September 1921.

6   Dale W. Laackman, *Selling Hate: Marketing the Ku Klux Klan* (University of Georgia Press, Athens, GA, 2020) pp.122 and 134–5.

7 *Washington Times* 27 September 1921 and US Congress House Committee on Rules, *Hearings Before the Committee on Rules on the Ku Klux Klan* (Govt Printing, Washington DC, 1921) p.22. Henceforward *1921 KKK Hearings*.

8 *New York American* 15 September 1921.

9 *New York World* 17 and 18 September 1921 and *New York American* 17 and 18 September 1921.

10 *New York World* 19 September 1921 and *New York American* 19 September 1921.

## Chapter 30

1 *New York World* 6 and 7 September 1921.

2 *New York World* 27 September 1921.

3 William J. Simmons, telegram to congressmen cited in Wyn Craig Wade, *The Fiery Cross: The Ku Klux Klan in America* (Touchstone Books, New York, 1987) p.162.

4 *1921 KKK Hearings* pp.8–15.

5 *1921 KKK Hearings* pp.15–27.

6 *1921 KKK Hearings* pp.27–42.

7 *1921 KKK Hearings* pp.48–49.

8 *1921 KKK Hearings* pp.59–63.

9 *1921 KKK Hearings* pp.66–67.

## Chapter 31

1 *Hattiesburg American* 11 October 1921.

2 *1921 KKK Hearings* p.74.

3 *1921 KKK Hearings* p.73

4 *1921 KKK Hearings* p.94.

5 Wyn Craig Wade, *The Fiery Cross: The Ku Klux Klan in America* (Touchstone Books, New York, 1987) p.164.

6 *Kokomo Times* of Indiana and the *Nocona News* of Texas 14 October 1921 and *Washington Evening Star* 14 October 1921.

7 Wyn Craig Wade, *The Fiery Cross: The Ku Klux Klan in America* (Touchstone Books, New York, 1987) p.164.

## PART V

1 Arthur Corning White, 'An American Fascismo', *Forum*, 72:5 (November 1924) p. 637.

## Chapter 32

1 For the diversity of numbers see William Pierce Randel, *The Ku Klux Klan: A Century of Infamy* (Chilton Co., New York, 1969) p.191; Henry P. Fry, *The Modern Klan* (Small, Maynard and Co., Boston, 1922) p.37; and Linda Gordon, *Threat to Democracy: The Ku Klux Klan in the 1920s* (Amberley Publishing, Stroud, 2017) p.15.

2 Cited in William G. Shepherd, 'Ku Klux Koin', *Collier's*K 82 (21 July 1928) p.38.

3 Cited in Livia Gershon, 'The Ku Klux Klan Used to Be Big Business', *JStor Daily* 7 March 2016.

4 Stanley Frost, *The Challenge of the Klan* (Bobbs-Merrill and Co., New York, 1924) p.1.

5 John Moffat Mecklin, *The Ku Klux Klan: A Study of the American Mind* (Harcourt, Brace and Co., New York, 1924) p.31 and Wyn Craig Wade, *The Fiery Cross: The Ku Klux Klan in America* (Touchstone Books, New York, 1987) p.166.

6 Woodrow Wilson cited in Lisa L. Beckenbaugh, *Treaty of Versailles: A Primary Document Analysis* (ABC-Clio, Santa Barbara, CA, 2018) p.222.

7   *The Washington Post* 7 May 1919.

## Chapter 33

1   Cited in an interview with Simmons published in William G. Shepherd, 'How I Put over the Klan', *Collier's*, 82 (14 July 1928) p.7.

2   Merz, Charles, 'Sweet Land of Secrecy: The Strange Spectacle of American Fraternalism', *Harper's Magazine* February 1927, p.329.

3   Lila Lee Jones, 'The Ku Klux Klan in Eastern Kansas during the 1920s', *Emporia State Research Studies*, 23:3 (Winter, 1975) p.38.

4   Arthur Corning White, 'An American Fascismo', *Forum*, 72:5 (November 1924) p.638.

5   Kristofer Allerfeldt, 'Murderous Mumbo-Jumbo: The Significance of Fraternity to Three Criminal Organizations in Late Nineteenth-Century America', *Journal of American Studies*, 50:4 (November 2016) pp.1067–88.

6   *The New York Times* 2 September 1923.

7   Lynn Dumenil, *Freemasonry and American Culture: 1880–1930* (Princeton University Press, Princeton, NJ, 1984) p.101.

8   Kristofer Allerfeldt, 'Jayhawker Fraternities: Masons, Klansmen and Kansas in the 1920s', *Journal of American Studies*, 46:4 (November 2012) pp.1035–53.

9   Mark A. Tabbert, *American Freemasons: Three Centuries of Building Communities* (National Heritage Museum, Lexington, MA, 2005) p.162.

10  Figures taken from Alan Axelrod, *The International Encyclopedia of Secret Societies and Fraternal Orders* (Checkmark Books, New York, 1997) p.159.

11  Cited in Lynn Dumenil, *Freemasonry and American Culture: 1880–1930* (Princeton University Press, Princeton, NJ, 1984) p.122.

12  Kristofer Allerfeldt, 'Jayhawker Fraternities: Masons, Klansmen and Kansas in the 1920s', *Journal of American Studies*, 46:4 (November 2012) p.1047.

13  Figures taken from Craig Fox, *Everyday Klansfolk: White Protestant Life and the KKK in 1920s Michigan* (Michigan State University Press, East Lansing, MI, 2011) p.121.

14  Letter from Kansas Grandmaster J. McCullough to J.W. McDowell, Independence, Kansas, 19 June 1922, Correspondence Files, Records of the AF and AM Grand Lodge, Topeka.

15  Letter from Kansas Grand Master J. McCullough to J.S. Henderson, 28 March 1922, Correspondence Files, Records of the AF and AM Grand Lodge, Topeka.

## Chapter 34

1   Tyler Gregory Anbinder, *Nativism and Slavery: The Northern Know Nothings and the Politics of the 1850s* (Oxford University Press, New York, 1992).

2   Cited in Humphrey J. Desmond, *The APA Movement: A Sketch* (New Century Press, Washington DC, 1912) p.36.

3   Donald L. Kinzer, *An Episode in Anti-Catholicism: The American Protective Association* (University of Washington Press, Seattle, WA, 1964).

4   Knights of Columbus, *Report of Commission on Religious Prejudices* (Knights of Columbus Supreme Council, New Haven, CT, 1915).

5   Christopher S. Saladin, 'The End of the Small-Town Golden Age: A Rural Newspaper's Role in the Urban-Rural Clash of Anti-Catholicism', *Augustana Digital Commons* (Spring, 2015).

6   Martin Marty, *Righteous Empire: The Protestant Experience in America, Two Centuries of American Life* (Dial Press, New York, 1970) p.211.

7 For details of Helen Jackson, see Indiana Klan's newspaper, *The Fiery Cross* 8 December 1922 p.8.

8 Mark Paul Richard, '"This Is Not a Catholic Nation": The Ku Klux Klan Confronts Franco-Americans in Maine', *The New England Quarterly*, 82:2 (2009) pp.285–303.

9 Ernest R. Sandeen, *The Roots of Fundamentalism* (University of Chicago Press, Chicago, IL, 1970) pp.188–207.

10 Michael Williams, *The Shadow of the Pope* (McGraw-Hill and Co., New York, 1932) pp.317–18.

11 *Woodward News Bulletin* 2 December 1921.

12 *The New York Times* 1 December 1922. See also Robert Moats Miller, 'A Note on the Relationship Between the Protestant Churches and the Revived Ku Klux Klan', *The Journal of Southern History*, 22:3 (August 1956) pp.355–68.

## Chapter 35

1 H.W. Evans, 'Our Alien Crime-Plague and its Cure', *Kourier Magazine*, 2 (March 1926) p.2; 'Foreign Influences', *Fiery Cross* 25 July 1924; and Thomas R. Pegram, *One Hundred Percent Americanism: The Rebirth and Decline of the Ku Klux Klan in the 1920s* (Ivan R. Dee, Chicago, IL, 2011) pp.126–7.

2 Mark Thornton, *The Economics of Prohibition* (Mises Institute, Auburn, AL, 2007) pp.100–2.

3 Cited in US House of Representatives, Committee on Rules, *The Ku Klux Klan Hearings* 67th Cong., 1st Sess. (1921) p.6.

4 Richard Bain, *Convention Decisions and Voting Records* (The Brookings Institute, Washington DC, 1960) p.222.

## Chapter 36

1 Louis F. Post, *The Deportations Delirium of Nineteen Twenty* (Charles H. Kerr and Co., Chicago, IL, 1923) p.14.

2 *The New York Times* 13 and 21 December 1919 and 1 and 21 January and 1 February 1920. Also Emma Goldman, *My Disillusionment in Russia* (Doubleday, Page and Co., New York, 1923).

3 Mike Davis, *Buda's Wagon: A Brief History of the Car Bomb* (Verso Books, London, 2007) pp.9–12.

## Chapter 37

1 Leonard Schapiro, 'The Role of the Jews in the Russian Revolutionary Movement', *The Slavonic and East European Review*, 40:94 (December 1961) pp.148–67.

2 Andre Gerrits, *The Myth of Jewish Communism: A Historical Interpretation* (Peter Lang, New York, 2009) and Eliza Ablovatski, 'The 1919 Central European Revolutions and the Judeo-Bolshevik Myth', *European Review of History*, 17:3 (2010) pp.473–89.

3 Commentary in the *Imperial Night-Hawk* 23 April 1923.

4 Reuben H. Sawyer in the *Oregon Voter* 15 April 1922.

## Chapter 38

1 Chris M. Messer, Thomas E. Shriver and Alison E. Adams, 'The Destruction of Black Wall Street: Tulsa's 1921 Riot and the Eradication of Accumulated Wealth', *American Journal of Economics and Sociology*, 77:3–4 (May–September 2018) p.792.

2 Details taken from Scott Ellsworth, *Death in a Promised Land: The Tulsa Race Riot of 1921* (Louisiana State University Press, Baton Rouge, LA, 1982) and *Tulsa World* 3 June 1921.

3 Carter Blue Clarke, 'A History of the Ku Klux Klan in Oklahoma' (PhD Dissertation, University of Oklahoma, OK, 1976) pp.47–9.

4 Oklahoma Commission, *Tulsa Race Riot: A Report by the Oklahoma Commission to Study the Tulsa Race Riot of 1921* (CreateSpace Independent Publishing Platform, 2001) pp.37–103.

## Chapter 39

1 William Z. Ripley, *The Races of Europe: A Sociological Study* (D. Appleton and Co., New York, 1899).

2 Madison Grant, *The Passing of the Great Race or the Racial Basis of European History* (Charles Scribner's Sons, New York, 1916).

3 Hiram Wesley Evans, *The Menace of Modern Immigration* (The Knights of the Ku Klux Klan, Atlanta, GA, 1924) pp.7–12.

4 James Giesen, *Boll Weevil Blues: Cotton, Myth, and Power in the American South* (University of Chicago Press, Chicago, IL, 2011) pp.17–32.

5 James Grossman, 'Blowing the Trumpet: The "Chicago Defender" and Black Migration during World War I', *Illinois Historical Journal*, 2:78 (Summer, 1985) pp.82–96.

6 Roi Ottley, *The Lonely Warrior: The Life and Times of Robert S. Abbott, Founder of the Chicago Defender* (Henry Regnery Company, Chicago, IL, 1955) p.165.

7 Emmett J. Scott, *Negro Migration During the War* (Oxford University Press, New York, 1920) p.73

8 Cited in James R. Grossman, *Land of Hope: Chicago, Black Southerners, and the Great Migration* (University of Chicago, Chicago, IL, 1991) p.16.

9 United States Bureau of the Census, *Negroes in the United States, 1920–1930* (Government Printing Office, Washington DC, 1932) p.55.

## Chapter 40

1 *The New York Times* 1, 3, 5 and 8 August 1919 and Jonathan S. Coit, '"Our Changed Attitude": Armed Defense and the New Negro in the 1919 Chicago Race Riot', *Journal of the Gilded Age and Progressive Era*, 11 (April 2012), pp.225–56.

2 *Detroit Free Press* 12 July 1925.

3 Cited in Kevin Boyle, *Arc of Justice: A Saga of Race, Civil Rights, and Murder in the Jazz Age* (Henry Holt and Co., New York, 2004) p.19.

4 *Detroit News* 17 September 1925.

5 Official figures put the death toll at eight, of which two were white. Other estimates range as high as 200. The most complete account of the massacre is probably Edward Gonzalez-Tennant, *The Rosewood Massacre: An Archaeology and History of Intersectional Violence* (University of Florida Press, Gainesville, FL, 2018).

6 For details of the treatment of Turner see *Detroit Free Press* 8 July 1925. Links between the mob and the Klan can be found in the Cleveland *Gazette* 11 July 1925. See also Cited in Kevin Boyle, *Arc of Justice: A Saga of Race, Civil Rights, and Murder in the Jazz Age* (Henry Holt and Co., New York, 2004) pp.20–22.

7 John F. Wukovits, 'This Case is Close to My Heart', *American History* (December 1998) pp.26–32 and 66–8.

8  Cited in 'When the Ku Klux Klan Ruled Detroit', *The Journal of Blacks in Higher Education*, 47 (Spring, 2005) p.101.

9  Cited in *Detroit Times* 13 September 1925.

10 JoEllen McNergney Vinyard, *The Right in Michigan's Grass Roots: From the KKK to the Michigan Militia* (University of Michigan Press, Ann Arbor, MI, 2014) pp.87–90.

### Chapter 41

1  *The New York Times* 3 December 1921. See also the *Denver Post* 7 December 1925.

2  Paul Mere Winter, *What Price Tolerance?* (All-American Book, Lecture and Research Bureau, Newlett, New York, 1928) p.19.

3  The story went around the nation in no time. Papers which published variations included the *Wilmington Evening Journal* 2 April 1921; the *Baltimore Afro-American* 6 April 1921; and *The Meridian Times*, ID, 8 April 1921. No Texas papers published an account that month.

4  *The New York Times* 17 July 1922.

5  For full details of the coup from Simmons' perspective see William G. Shepherd, 'How I Put Over the Klan', *Collier's*, 83 (28 July 1928) pp.46–48. For a good historical approach see David M. Chalmers, 'Hooded Americanism: The First Century of the Ku Klux Klan' (Doubleday and Co., Garden City, NY, 1965) pp.26–9.

6  Wyn Craig Wade, *The Fiery Cross: The Ku Klux Klan in America* (Touchstone Books, New York, 1987) pp.186–9.

### PART VI

1  Cited in Edgar I. Fuller, *The Visible of the Invisible Empire* (Maelstrom Publishing Co., Denver, CO, 1925) p.78.

### Chapter 42

1  Kigy means 'Klansmen I Greet You'. Itsub means 'In The Sacred Unfailing Being'. These acronyms remind Klansmen of their bonds and allegiances. They served to identify Klansmen and exclude baffled 'Aliens'.

2  Details taken from Robert Coughlan, 'Konklave in Kokomo' in Isabel Leighton, *The Aspirin Age, 1919–1941: The Essential Events of American Life in the Chaotic Years Between the Two World Wars* (Simon and Schuster, New York, 1949) pp.105–10. Although only 10 years old at the time, Coughlan had been present at the massive rally.

3  *The Fiery Cross* 13 July 1923.

4  *The Fiery Cross* 6 July 1923.

5  Craig Fox, *Everyday Klansfolk: White Protestant Life and the Ku Klux Klan in 1920s Michigan* (Michigan State University Press, East Lansing, 2012) p.195.

6  Allen Safianow, 'Konklave in Kokomo Revisited', *The Historian*, 50:3 (May 1988) p.331.

7  Robert Coughlan, 'Konklave in Kokomo' in Isabel Leighton, *The Aspirin Age, 1919-1941: The Essential Events of American Life in the Chaotic Years Between the Two World Wars* (Simon and Schuster, New York, 1949) p.115.

### Chapter 43

1  The first full biography of Stephenson was Edgar Allen Booth, *The Mad Mullah of America* (Boyd Ellison, Columbus, OH, 1927) and many of the biographical details I used come from this, especially pp.7–10. See also Louis Francis Budenz, 'There's Mud on Indiana's White Robes', *The Nation* 27 July 1927 pp.81–82. Another interesting approach can be found in Harold Zink, 'A Case Study of a Political

Boss' *Psychiatry*, 1:4 (1938) pp.527–33. Since then the most thorough biography is M. William Lutholtz, *Grand Dragon: DC Stephenson and the Ku Klux Klan in Indiana* (Purdue University Press, West Lafayette, IN, 1991) and the most readable, dramatic and recent is Timothy Egan's *Fever in the Heartland: The Ku Klux Klan's Plot to Take Over America, and the Woman Who Stopped Them* (Viking, New York, 2023).

2  Karen Abbot, '"Murder Wasn't Very Pretty": The Rise and Fall of D.C. Stephenson', *The Smithsonian Magazine* 30 August 2012 p.50.

3  Edward A. Leary, *Indianapolis: The Story of a City* (Bobbs-Merrill Co., Indianapolis, IN, 1971) p.200. Leary added that Stephenson could also be 'as dangerous as a timber rattlesnake'.

4  Harold Zink, 'A Case Study of a Political Boss', *Psychiatry*, 1:4 (1938) p.530 and Karen Abbot, '"Murder Wasn't Very Pretty": The Rise and Fall of D.C. Stephenson', *The Smithsonian Magazine* 30 August 2012 p.50.

5  Leonard J. Moore, *Citizen Klansmen: The Ku Klux Klan in Indiana, 1921–1928* (University of North Carolina Press, Chapel Hill, NC, 1997) p.17.

## Chapter 44

1  Margaret Thatcher to the American Bar Association, 15 July 1985. Speech available in full at www.margaretthatcher.org/document/106096.

2  George C. Goble, 'The Obituary of a Machine: The Rise and Fall of Ottmar Mergenthaler's Linotype at US Newspapers' (Unpublished PhD Thesis, Indiana University, IN, 1984) pp.17–18 and Doug Wilson's 2012 documentary *Linotype: The Film – In Search of the Eighth Wonder of the World*.

3  Figures taken from Robert S. and Helen Lynd, *Middletown: A Study in Contemporary America* (Constable, London, 1929) pp.471–2.

4  Cited in Kenneth Jackson, *The Ku Klux Klan in the City, 1915–1930* (Ivan R. Dee, New York, 1968) p.39.

5  For details of Wood's editorship and attribution of quotes see Scott M. Cutlip, *The Unseen Power: Public Relations, A History* (Lawrence Erlbaum Associates, Hillsdale, NJ, 1994) pp.399–400.

6  *Chicago Defender* 21 October 1922 and *The New York Times* 21 December 1922.

7  The real figure was probably closer to 50,000. See Patricia Fogleson, 'The Fiery Cross', *The Encyclopedia of Indianapolis* beta.indyencyclopedia.org/the-fiery-cross-1921-1925/.

8  Cited in Linda Gordon, *The Second Coming of the KKK: The Ku Klux Klan of the 1920s and the American Political Tradition* (Liveright, New York, 2017) p.175.

9  *Searchlight* 28 March 1923.

10  *Imperial Night-Hawk* 28 March 1923 and 25 July 1923.

11  John M. Shotwell, 'Crystallizing Public Hatred: Ku Klux Klan Public Relations in the Early 1920s' (Unpublished MA Thesis, University of Wisconsin, Madison, WI, 1974) p.121.

12  Rory McVeigh, *The Rise of the Ku Klux Klan: Right-Wing Movements and National Politics* (University of Minnesota Press, Minneapolis, MN, 2009) p.13.

## Chapter 45

1  Figures taken from Michael Newton, *The Ku Klux Klan: History, Organization, Language, Influence and Activities of America's Most Notorious Secret Society* (McFarland, Jefferson NC, 2007) pp.197–224.

2  David M Chalmers, *Hooded Americanism: The History of the Ku Klux Klan* (Duke University Press, Durham, NC, 1981) pp.126–34 and Elise Melcher, 'The KKK Ruled Denver a Century Ago. Here's How the Hate Group's Legacy is Still Being Felt in 2021', *Denver Post* 6 June 2021.

3  Eckard V. Toy, 'Robe and Gown: The Ku Klux Klan in Eugene, Oregon during the 1920s', in Shawn Lay (ed.), *The Invisible Empire in the West: Toward a New Historical Appraisal of the Ku Klux Klan of the 1920s* (University of Illinois Press, Chicago, IL, 2004) pp.154–6; Linda Gordon, *The Second Coming of the KKK: The Ku Klux Klan of the 1920s and the American Political Tradition* (Liveright, New York, 2017) p.142; and Malcolm Clarke Jr, 'The Bigot Disclosed: 90 Years of Nativism', *Oregon Historical Quarterly*, 75 (June 1974) pp.109–90.

4  For details of Helen Jackson, see Indiana Klan's newspaper, *The Fiery Cross* 8 December 1922, p.8.

5  Kristofer Allerfeldt, *Race, Radicalism, Religion, and Restriction: Immigration in the Pacific Northwest, 1890–1924* (Praeger, Westport, CT, 2003) pp.186–189.

6  David M. Chalmers, *Hooded Americanism: The History of the Ku Klux Klan* (Duke University Press, Durham, NC, 1981) p.87.

7  Catherine Marie Saks, '"Real Americanism": Resistance to the Oregon Compulsory School Bill, 1920–1925' (Unpublished PhD Thesis, Portland State University, OR, 2010).

8  Kristofer Allerfeldt, *Race, Radicalism, Religion, and Restriction: Immigration in the Pacific Northwest, 1890–1924* (Praeger, Westport, 2003) p.103.

9  Carter Blue Clarke, *A History of the Ku Klux Klan in Oklahoma* (Unpublished PhD Thesis, University of Oklahoma, OK, 1976) p.181.

10 Howard A. Tucker, *History of Governor Walton's War on Ku Klux Klan, The Invisible Empire* (Southwest Publishing Co., Oklahoma City, OK, 1923).

11 *Imperial Night-Hawk* 29 August 1923 and 5 September 1923.

12 John M. Craig, '"There is Hell Going On Up There": The Carnegie Klan Riot of 1923', *Pennsylvania History* (Summer, 2005) pp.322–46.

13 David M. Chalmers, *Hooded Americanism: The History of the Ku Klux Klan* (Duke University Press, Durham, NC, 1981) p.41.

## Chapter 46

1  'C R C', 'Woman', *Southern Literary Journal*, 3 (November 1836) pp.181–2.

2  Mildred Lewis Rutherford, *A Measuring Rod to Test Text Books, and Reference Books in Schools, Colleges and Libraries* (United Confederate Veterans, Athens, GA, 1920).

3  Boulder *Daily Camera* 18 July 1925.

## Chapter 47

1  'Something for the Ladies', *The Fiery Cross* 9 March 1923.

2  For details, see Kenneth Barnes, *The Ku Klux Klan in 1920s Arkansas: How Protestant White Nationalism Came to Rule a State* (University of Arkansas Press, Fayetteville, AR, 2021) p.29.

3  Dwight D. Hoover, 'Daisy Douglas Barr: From Quaker to Queen "Kluckeress"', *Indiana Magazine of History* June 1991 pp.171–95.

4  'Bloodthirsty Women', *Muncie Post-Democrat* 2 January 1925.

5  Cited in Wendy P. Reilly Thorson, *Oregon Klanswomen of the 1920s: A Study in Tribalism, Gender and Women's Power* (Oregon State University Press, Corvalis, OR, 1997) p.38.

6  Taken from pamphlet, Robbie Gill-Comer, *American Women* (Imperial Headquarters of the Women's Ku Klux Klan, Little Rock, AR, 1924).

7  William F. Pinar, 'White Women in the Ku Klux Klan', *Counterpoints*, 163 (2001) p.582.

8  Cited in Kathleen M. Blee, *Women of the Klan: Racism and Gender in the 1920s* (University of California, Berkeley, CA, 1997) p.2.

9  Cited in William F. Pinar, 'White Women in the Ku Klux Klan', *Counterpoints*, 163 (2001) p.610.

10  Figures taken from William F. Pinar, 'White Women in the Ku Klux Klan', *Counterpoints*, 163 (2001) p.611.

11  Brochure from C.T. Gilliam and the Kool Koast Kamp, *To All the Klans and Klansmen of Texas Greetings: Kool Koast Kamp. The Healthiest Road to the Koolest Summer* (Rockport, MA, *c.*1924).

### Chapter 48

1  Quotations taken from 'Klansman OK Royal Riders' in the Pacific Northwest's own Klan weekly, *Watcher on the Tower* 18 August 1923 p.4.

2  Quotations taken from 'Klansman OK Royal Riders' *Watcher on the Tower* 18 August 1923, p.4; Michael Newton, *The Ku Klux Klan: History, Organization, Language, Influence and Activities of America's Most Notorious Secret Society* (McFarland, Jefferson NC, 2007) p.129; and Linda Gordon, *The Second Coming of the KKK: The Ku Klux Klan of the 1920s and the American Political Tradition* (Liveright, New York, 2017) pp.138 and 147.

3  Michigan Klan publication *Saginaw Night-Hawk* January 1928 cited in Craig Fox, *Everyday Klansfolk: White Protestant Life and the KKK in 1920s Michigan* (Michigan State University Press, Lansing, 2011) p.105.

4  Taken from Klan-published *The Kourier* magazine, October 1925 pp.11–13.

5  *The New York Times* 19 October 1924 and Michael Newton, *White Robes and Burning Crosses* (McFarland, Jefferson NC, 2014) p.52.

6  Julian Sher, *White Hoods: Canada's Ku Klux Klan* (New Star Books, Vancouver, 1983) and Allan Bartley, *The Ku Klux Klan in Canada: A Century of Promoting Racism and Hate in the Peaceable Kingdom* (Formac Publishing Ltd, Halifax, 2020).

7  Richard E. Frankel, 'Klansmen in the Fatherland: A Transnational Episode in the History of Weimar Germany's Right-Wing Political Culture', *Journal for the Study of Radicalism*, 7:1 (2013), pp.61–78.

### Chapter 49

1  *The Washington Post* 9 August 1925.

2  *Chicago Daily Tribune* 9 August 1925.

3  H.L. Mencken in the *New York Sun* in 'The Klan Walks in Washington', *Literary Digest* 22 August 1925 p.7.

4  *The Washington Post* 9 August 1925.

5  *The Washington Post* 9 August 1925.

6  'Klan Paraders Swarm to Capital as Marines Guard U.S. Buildings', *The New York Herald* 8 August 1925.

7  'The Klan Walks in Washington', *Literary Digest* 22 August 1925 pp.7–8.

8  *The New York Times* 9 August 1925.

### PART VII

1  Cited in Harold Zink, 'A Case Study of a Political Boss', *Psychiatry*, 1:4 (1938) p.529.

## Chapter 50

1 Leonard Lanson Cline, 'In Darkest Louisiana', *Nation*, 116 (14 March 1923) p.292.

2 *Report of Washington Bureau of Investigation agent A.E. Farland*, 2 November 1922 cited in Kenneth Earl Harrell, 'The Ku Klux Klan in Louisiana, 1920–1930' (Unpublished PhD, Louisiana State University, LA, 1966) p.195.

3 *The Morehouse Enterprise* 26 May 1922.

4 Reported in the *Baton Rouge State Times* 9 September 1922.

5 Leonard Lanson Cline, 'In Darkest Louisiana', *Nation*, 116 (14 March 1923) p.293.

6 Robert L. Duffus, 'How the Ku Klux Klan Sells Hate: How Salesmen Sold Packages of Hate at Ten Dollars Each', *The World's Work* (June 1923) p.177.

7 *New Orleans Times-Picayune* 25 December 1922. Klan newspapers went into damage limitation, running stories like 'Ol' Cap'n Skip' Tells Bastrop "Murder Facts"', *The Dawn* 25 August 1923 p.6., and '"Klan Victim" Seen Alive at Mer Rouge', *The Fellowship Forum* 3 November 1923 p.7.

8 *New Orleans Times-Picayune* 5 September and 28 December 1922.

9 E.W. Andrews, quoted in the *Baton Rouge State Times* 11 September 1922.

10 Quoted in *Shreveport Journal* 9 September 1922.

11 Cited in *New Orleans Times-Picayune* 17 March 1923.

12 Cited in Kenneth Earl Harrell, *The Ku Klux Klan in Louisiana, 1920–1930* (Unpublished PhD, Louisiana State University, 1966) pp.248 and 249.

13 Quoted in *The New York Times* 16 March 1923.

14 *New Orleans Times-Picayune* 8 January 1923.

## Chapter 51

1 Leonard Lanson Cline, 'In Darkest Louisiana', *Nation*, 116 (14 March 1923) p.293.

2 Michael Newton, *The Ku Klux Klan: History, Organization, Language, Influence and Activities of America's Most Notorious Secret Society* (McFarland, Jefferson NC, 2007) pp.221 and 371–2.

3 *Lakeland Evening Telegram*, Florida, 20 December 1920.

4 *Omaha Bee* 30 September 1921.

5 *Cincinnati Post* 22 July 1921.

6 William F. Mugleston, 'Julian Harris, the Georgia Press and the Ku Klux Klan', *The Georgia Historical Quarterly*, 59:3 (Autumn, 1975) pp.287–8.

7 'Brand Thugs are Sought by Klansmen', *The Fiery Cross* 25 July 1924 p.1.

8 For comments and a precis of the situation see *Arkansas Gazette* 29 April 1923.

9 Quoted in David M. Chalmers, *Hooded Americanism: The History of the Ku Klux Klan* (Duke University Press, Durham, NC, 1981) p.49.

10 Cited in R. Douglas Hurt, *The Big Empty: The Great Plains in the Twentieth Century* (University of Arizona Press, Tucson, AZ, 2011) p.48.

11 Howard A. Tucker, *The History of Governor Walton's War on Ku Klux Klan* (Southwest Publishing Group, Oklahoma City, OK, 1923) pp.3–6 and Charles C. Alexander, *The Ku Klux Klan in the Southwest* (University of Oklahoma Press, Norman, 1995) pp.49–50.

12 *Tulsa Tribune* 18 September 1923.

13 Howard A. Tucker, *The History of Governor Walton's War on Ku Klux Klan* (Southwest Publishing Group, Oklahoma City, OK, 1923) pp.25–26.

14 *The New York Times*, 17, 26, 28 and 31 August 1923; *Pittsburgh Sunday Post*, 26 August 1923; 'The Klan as the Victim of Mob Violence', *Literary Digest*, 78 (8 September) pp.12–13; and David J. Goldberg, 'Unmasking the Ku Klux Klan: The

Northern Movement against the KKK, 1920–1925', *Journal of American Ethnic History*, 15:4 (Summer, 1996) p.42.

15 *Papers Read at the Meeting of Grand Dragons, Knights of the Ku Klux Klan, at Their First Annual Meeting Held at Asheville, North Carolina, July 1923: Together with Other Articles of Interest to Klansmen* (Unknown publisher, 1923) p.13.

16 Cited in Howard A. Tucker, *The History of Governor Walton's War on Ku Klux Klan* (Southwest Publishing Group, Oklahoma City, OK, 1923) p.27.

## Chapter 52

1 Hiram Wesley Evans, *The Menace of Modern Immigration* (Knights of the Ku Klux Klan, Atlanta, 1923) p.4.

2 Martha Ragsdale, 'The National Origins Plan of Immigration Restriction' (Unpublished MA Thesis, Vanderbilt University, TN, 1928) and Kristofer Allerfeldt, '"And We Got Here First": Albert Johnson, National Origins and Self-Interest in the Immigration Debates of the 1920s', *Journal of Contemporary History*, 45:1 (January 2010) pp.7–26.

3 Laura J. Owen, 'Worker Turnover in the 1920s: What Labor-Supply Arguments Don't Tell Us', *The Journal of Economic History*, 55:4 (December 1995) pp.822–41.

4 Cited in Arthur Frank Wertheim, *Will Rogers at the Ziegfeld Follies* (University of Oklahoma Press, Norman, OK, 1992) pp.135–6.

5 Cited in Thomas R. Pegram, 'Hoodwinked: The Anti-Saloon League and the Ku Klux Klan in 1920s Prohibition Enforcement', *The Journal of the Gilded Age and Progressive Era*, 7:1 (January 2008) p.103.

6 For details see *LA Times* 24 and 29 April 1922 and David Chalmers, *Hooded Americanism: The History of the Ku Klux Klan* (Duke University Press, Durham, 1983) pp.118–21.

7 *The New York Times* 2 February 1925 and Masatomo Ayabe, 'Ku Kluxers in a Coal Mining Community: A Study of the Ku Klux Klan Movement in Williamson County Illinois, 1923–1926', *Journal of the Illinois State Historical Society*, 102:1 (Spring, 2009) pp.73–100.

8 Figures from Thomas R. Pegram, *One Hundred Percent Americanism: The Rebirth and Decline of the Ku Klux Klan in the 1920s* (Ivan R. Dee, Chicago, IL, 2011) p.199.

9 'Educators, Business and Political Leaders Unite in Vigilance Association', *The New York Times* 12 November 1923.

10 For a good analysis of the Supreme Court's ruling see *Jewish Daily Bulletin* 21 November 1923.

11 Cited in the Catholic, Indiana-based publication *Our Sunday Visitor* 18 February 1923.

## Chapter 53

1 A.J. Mann, Kligrapp (secretary) of the New Haven, Connecticut, Klan cited in *The New York Times* 5 January 1926.

2 'The "Invisible Empire" in the Spotlight', *Current Opinion*, 71 (November 1921) p.561 and Robert L. Duffus, 'Salesman of Hate: The Ku Klux Klan', *World's Work*, 46 (May 1923) p.33.

3 *The New York Times* 28 December 1923.

4 *The New York Times* 11 March 1924; *Houston Chronicle* 10, 16 and 21 March 1924; and Patricia Bernstein, *Ten Dollars to Hate: The Texas Man Who Fought the Klan* (Texas A&M University Press, College Station, TX, 2017) pp.169–71.

5 Lance Trusty, '"All Talk and No Kash": Valparaiso University and the Ku Klux Klan', *Indiana Magazine of History*, 82:1 (March 1986) pp.1–36.
6 Cited in Max Harrison, 'Gentlemen from Indiana', *Atlantic Monthly*, 141 (1928) p.680. Stephenson would later claim he told Evans this shooting of a group of Italians in Steubenville, Ohio, by masked Klansmen would turn people against the Klan. Evans retorted, 'Too bad it didn't kill every one of the wops.' See William Lutholtz, *Grand Dragon: DC Stephenson and The Ku Klux Klan in Indiana* (Purdue University Press, West Lafayette, IN, 1991) p.77.
7 For details see Edgar Allen Booth, *The Mad Mullah of America* (Boyd Ellison, Columbus, OH, 1927) pp.129–33.

## Chapter 54

1 Timothy Egan, *A Fever in the Heartland: The Ku Klux Klan's Plot to Take Over America, and the Woman Who Stopped Them* (Viking, New York, 2023) pp.94–6 and 264–66.
2 William Lutholtz, *Grand Dragon: DC Stephenson and the Ku Klux Klan in Indiana* (Purdue University Press, West Lafayette, IN, 1991) pp.178–206.
3 The indictment is cited in full in the *Indianapolis Times* 16 April 1925.
4 William Lutholtz, *Grand Dragon: DC Stephenson and the Ku Klux Klan in Indiana* (Purdue University Press, West Lafayette, IN, 1991)p.201.
5 *Tolerance* 6 June 1923.
6 *Indianapolis Times* 17 April 1925.
7 *Indianapolis Times* 16 November 1925.
8 For details, see D.C. Stephenson Collection, Box 3: Marion County Grand Jury Investigation, 1927–1928; Indiana Supreme Court, *Stephenson v. Indiana* housed at the Indiana Historical Society, Manuscripts and Archives, Indianapolis.
9 *The New York Times* 6, 7 and 15 November. For corrupt officials see *Indianapolis Times* 10 September 1927 and 8 February 1928. For rumour mill and other abuses of power see James H. Madison, *The Ku Klux Klan in the Heartland* (Indiana University Press, Bloomington, IN, 2020) pp.116–19; Wyn Craig Wade, *The Fiery Cross: The Ku Klux Klan in America* (Touchstone Books, New York, 1987) p.230; Louis Francis Budenz, 'There's Mud on Indiana's White Robes', *Nation*, 75 (July 1927) pp.81–2; and Robert R. Hull, 'The Klan Aftermath in Indiana', *America* 38, (October 1927) pp.8–9.

## Chapter 55

1 Figures taken from Edward J. Larson, *Summer for the Gods: The Scopes Trial and America's Continuing Debate over Science and Religion* (Rev. Ed. Basic Books, New York, 2008) p.48.
2 Memphis *Commercial Appeal* 28 January 1925.
3 John Moffat Mecklin, *The Ku Klux Klan: A Study of the American Mind* (Harcourt Brace & Co., New York, 1924) p.101.
4 Marquis James, 'Around Town at the Scopes Trial: A Small Hamlet in East Tennessee Enters the National Spotlight', *The New Yorker* 11 July 1925.
5 William Jennings Bryan, *The Prince of Peace* (Fleming H. Revell & Co., New York, 1914) p.16.
6 Walter Lippmann, *Drift and Mastery* (Michael Kennerley, New York, 1914) p.81.
7 *Chicago Evening Post* 6 and 19 August 1924.

8 Darrow in a letter to H.L. Mencken 5 August 1925 cited in Randall Tietjen (ed.), *In the Clutches of the Law: Clarence Darrow's Letters* (University of California Press, Berkeley, CA, 2013) p.395.

9 John Thomas Scopes, *The World's Most Famous Court Trial, State of Tennessee v. John Thomas Scopes* (National Book Co., Philadelphia, PA, 1925) p.294.

10 John Thomas Scopes, *The World's Most Famous Court Trial, State of Tennessee v. John Thomas Scopes* (National Book Co., Philadelphia, PA, 1925) pp.285–8 and 302.

11 Nebraska *Lincoln Star* 1 August 1925.

12 *The New York Times* 22 August 1925.

13 *The New York Times* 5 April and 24 May 1926.

## Chapter 56

1 *Baltimore Sun* cited in Felix Harcourt, *Ku Klux Kulture: America and the Klan in the 1920s* (University of Chicago Press, Chicago, IL, 2017) p.16.

2 *Tolerance* 6 June 1923.

3 *Tolerance* 8 and 15 July 1923 and Felix Harcourt, *Ku Klux Kulture: America and the Klan in the 1920s* (University of Chicago Press, Chicago, 2017) pp.190–1 notes 15 and 16.

4 *Emporia Gazette* 17 November 1923 and Kristofer Allerfeldt, 'Jayhawker Fraternities: Masons, Klansmen and Kansas in the 1920s', *Journal of American Studies*, 46:4 (November 2012) pp.1035–53.

5 *The New York Times* 9 November 1923.

6 Cited in Clement Charlton Moseley, 'The Political Influence of the Ku Klux Klan in Georgia, 1915–1925', *Georgia Historical Quarterly*, 57:2 (Summer, 1973) pp.238 and 245–6. See also Arnold Shankman, 'Julian Harris and the Ku Klux Klan', *The Mississippi Quarterly*, 28:2 (Spring, 1975) pp.147–69 and William F. Mugleston, 'Julian Harris, the Georgia Press and the Ku Klux Klan', *Georgia Historical Quarterly*, 59:3 (Autumn, 1975) pp.284–95.

7 *Columbus Enquirer-Sun* 24 September 1921.

8 Arnold Shankman, 'Julian Harris and the Ku Klux Klan', *The Mississippi Quarterly*, 28:2 (Spring, 1975) pp.152–5.

9 Cited in *Columbus Enquirer-Sun* 22 June 1921.

10 After the Klan launched a fundraising campaign for its 'Americanisation' programme in Atlanta in 1941, *The American Scholar* asked Harris to comment. He excused himself, using the cited reasons; see Arnold Shankman, 'Julian Harris and the Ku Klux Klan', *The Mississippi Quarterly*, 28:2 (Spring, 1975) p.169.

11 Citation for the 1926 Pulitzer Prize for Public Service www.pulitzer.org/prize-winners-by-year/1926.

12 *Indiana Catholic and Record* 28 July and 3 November 1922.

13 Ron F. Smith, 'The Klan's Retribution Against an Indiana Editor: A Reconsideration', *Indiana Magazine of History*, 106 (December 2010) pp.381–400.

14 *The Fiery Cross* 5 September and 14 November 1924.

15 James H. Madison, 'The Klan's Enemies Step up, Slowly', *Indiana Magazine of History*, 116:2 (June 2000) pp.113–17.

16 Wyn Craig Wade, *The Fiery Cross: The Ku Klux Klan in America* (Simon and Schuster, New York, 1984) p.492, n.247.

17 Klan numbers are a nightmare to calculate. For a well-informed and intelligent discussion of Indiana membership, see Linda Gordon, *Threat to Democracy: The Rise of the Ku Klux Klan in the 1920s, A Warning from History* (Amberley Books, Stroud, 2017) pp.18–19 and 69.

## Chapter 57

1   *The New York Times* 1 June 1927.
2   For full details, see the *Brooklyn Daily Eagle* 31 May 1927 and *Long Island Daily Press* 2 June 1927.
3   Michael Newton, *The Ku Klux Klan: History, Organization, Language, Influence and Activities of America's Most Notorious Secret Society* (McFarland, Jefferson, NC, 2007) p.17.
4   *The New York Times* 1 June 1927.
5   *The New York Times* 22 September 2015.
6   *Long Island Daily Press* 2 June 1927 and 22 January 1936.
7   *The Richmond Hill Record* 3 June 1927.
8   Paul A Carter, 'The Campaign of 1928 Re-Examined: A Study in Political Folklore', *The Wisconsin Magazine of History*, 46:4 (Summer, 1963) pp.263–72.

## PART VIII

1   Michael Hale, '15 Leading Jews Marked for Death', *New Masses* 25 August 1936, p.8.

## Chapter 58

1   *The New York Times* 14 April 1928.
2   *The New York Times* 31 May 1927.
3   *The New York Times* 25 July 1927.
4   *The New York Times* 4 September 1927.
5   *Mobile News-Item* 18 October 1927.
6   *Richmond Planet* 10 September 1927.
7   Michael Newton, *The Ku Klux Klan: History, Organization, Language, Influence and Activities of America's Most Notorious Secret Society* (McFarland, Jefferson, NC, 2007) p.380 and *Mobile News-Item* 4 August 1927.
8   *The New York Times* 11 October 1927.
9   *The New York Times* 11 October 1927 and *Decatur Daily* 15 October 1927.
10  *The New York Times* 20 October 1927.
11  Judge R.F. Elmore, cited in Glenn Feldman, *Politics, Society and the Klan in Alabama, 1915–1949* (University of Alabama Press, Tuscaloosa, AL, 1999) p.142.
12  archive.tuskegee.edu/.

## Chapter 59

1   *The Daily Worker* 26 May 1928.
2   James Ford to the Sixth Comintern, Moscow July cited in Oscar Berland, 'The Emergence of the Communist Perspective on the "Negro Question" in America: 1919–1931: Part Two', *Science & Society*, 64:2 (Summer, 2000) p.196.
3   Biographic and other details taken from 'Negro Worker Nominated for Vice President', *Negro Worker*, 2:4 (June 1932) pp.25–26 and Walter T. Howard (ed.), *We Shall Be Free! Black Communist Protest in Seven Voices* (Temple University Press, Philadelphia, PA, 2013) pp.57–8.
4   For examples of this thinking, see William C. White, 'Has the Depression Missed Russia?', *The North American Review*, 234:3 (September 1932) pp.256–62.
5   Cited in Wyn Craig Wade, *The Fiery Cross: The Ku Klux Klan in America* (Touchstone Books, New York, 1987) p.258.
6   Robin D.G. Kelley, *Hammer and Hoe: Alabama Communists During the Great Depression* (University of North Carolina Press, Chapel Hill, NC, 1990) pp.59–61.

7   Cited in Robin D.G. Kelley, *Hammer and Hoe: Alabama Communists During the Great Depression* (University of North Carolina Press, Chapel Hill, NC, 1990) p.60.

8   Editorial, 'Another Retreat', *The New Masses* 25 August 1936, p.3.

9   Cited in *Birmingham Post* 13 October 1934 and also Robert P. Ingalis, 'Antiradical Violence in Birmingham During the 1930s', *The Journal of Southern History*, 47:4 (November 1981) pp.521–44.

10  See the Klan monthly *The Kourier* November 1932; the *Baltimore Afro-American* 12 March 1932; Leroy Davis and John Hope Franklin, *A Clashing of the Soul: John Hope and the Dilemma of African American Leadership and Black Higher Education in the Early Twentieth Century* (University of Georgia Press, Athens, GA, 1998); and Wyn Craig Wade, *The Fiery Cross: The Ku Klux Klan in America* (Touchstone Books, New York, 1987) p.258.

11  Ward H. Rogers, Southern Tenant Farmers Union activist, cited in the Workers Party weekly *New Militant* 18 May 1935.

12  *Party Organizer*, 6:1 (1933) p.16 cited in Timothy V. Johnson, '"We Are Illegal Here": The Communist Party, Self-Determination and the Alabama Share Croppers Union', *Science and Society*, 75:4 (October 2011) p.470.

13  *Birmingham News* 16 July 1931; *The New York Times* 18 July 1931; and Timothy V. Johnson, '"We Are Illegal Here": The Communist Party, Self-Determination and the Alabama Share Croppers Union', *Science and Society*, 75:4 (October 2011) pp.454–79.

14  Ward H. Rogers in *New Militant*, 18 May 1935.

15  *Chicago Tribune* 5 April 1936.

16  *Boston Globe* 21 April 1936. See also *The New York Times* 23 April 1936.

17  *Chicago Tribune* 5 April 1936.

18  *The New York Times* 13 October 1937.

## Chapter 60

1   Arnold Rice, *The Ku Klux Klan in American Politics* (Public Affairs Press, Washington DC, 1962) p.102 and Michael Newton, *White Robes and Burning Crosses* (McFarland, Jefferson, NC, 2014) p.77.

2   Evans in *Literary Digest* July 1934 cited in Wyn Craig Wade, *The Fiery Cross: The Ku Klux Klan in America* (Touchstone Books, New York, 1987) p.259.

3   Evans in *The Kourier* cited in the *Brooklyn Times Union* 28 March 1934.

4   'Attacks Advisors of the President', *The New York Times* 17 September 1934, which lists a hit list of fifteen prominent Jewish advisors to FDR who antisemite William True argued should be dismissed from office.

5   An Editorial written by Klan allies, the Knights of the White Camellia, in 'Who Controls Our Government', *The White Knight: Jew Deal Issue* 15 August 1936, p.8.

6   Birmingham, Alabama, *Age-Herald* 22 January 1932.

7   William F. Pinar, 'The Communist Party/NAACP Rivalry in the Trials of the Scottsboro Nine', *Counterpoints*, 163 (2001) pp.753–811.

8   Klan letter to George Maurer, cited in the *Chicago Defender* 9 May 1931.

9   *Chicago Defender* 29 August 1931.

10  Dan T. Carter, *Scottsboro: A Tragedy of the American South* (Louisiana State University Press, Baton Rouge, LA, 2007) pp.54–5.

11  Frank L. Owsley, 'Scottsboro: Third Crusade; Sequel to Abolitionism and Reconstruction', *American Review*, 1 (1933) pp.267–8.

## Chapter 61

1 Charles Vibbert, 'La Generation Présente aux Etats-Unis', *Revue des Deux Mondes*, 58 (1930) p.332.
2 Richard E. Frankel, 'Klansmen in the Fatherland: A Transnational Episode in the History of Weimar Germany's Right-Wing Political Culture', *Journal for the Study of Radicalism*, 7:1 (2013) pp.61–78.
3 *The Kourier* February 1925.
4 *The Kourier* March 1934.
5 Cited in Johnpeter Horst Grill and Robert L. Jenkins, 'The Nazis and the American South in the 1930s: A Mirror Image?', *The Journal of Southern History*, 58:4 (November 1992) p.672.
6 Americanism Committee of the American Legion, *Report 1: Subversive Activities in America First Committee in California* (Los Angeles, CA, 1941) pp.6–7, 11–12 and 15–16.
7 *The Washington Post* 6 October 1938.
8 Quotes and details taken from John Roy Carlson, *Undercover: My Four Years in the Nazi Underworld of America* (E.P. Button and Co., New York, 1943) pp.152–3 and *The New York Times* 19 August 1940.
9 *The New York Times* 20 August 1940 and *Christian Science Monitor* 24 August 1940.
10 George Lewis, '"An Amorphous Code": The Ku Klux Klan and Un-Americanism, 1915–1965', *Journal of American Studies*, 47:4 (November 2013) pp.979–81 and Wyn Craig Wade, *The Fiery Cross: The Ku Klux Klan in America* (Simon and Schuster, New York, 1984) pp.273–4.

## Chapter 62

1 For details of this see Samuel D. Brunson, 'Addressing Hate: Georgia, the IRS, and the Ku Klux Klan' (31 July 2020). Available at SSRN: ssrn.com/abstract=3664799 or dx.doi.org/10.2139/ssrn.3664799.
2 Kristofer Allerfeldt, 'Jayhawker Fraternities: Masons, Klansmen and Kansas in the 1920s', *Journal of American Studies*, 46 (2012) pp.1049–50.
3 University of California, Santa Barbara, *American Presidency Project* at www.presidency.ucsb.edu/documents/state-the-union-message-congress.
4 Kristofer Allerfeldt, *Organized Crime in the United States, 1865–1941* (McFarland, Jefferson, NC, 2018) pp.140–3.
5 Colescott recalled this unpleasant moment to the undercover investigator Stetson Kennedy who retold it in *I Rode with the Ku Klux Klan* (Hamilton & Co., London, 1958) p.87.
6 For the annual breakdown of the figures see the Washington DC *Evening Star* 15 June 1946.
7 Cited in Ben Haas, *The Ku Klux Klan* (Greenleaf Classics, San Diego, 1963) p.93.
8 Stetson Kennedy, *I Rode with the Ku Klux Klan* (Hamilton & Co., London, 1958) p.87.
9 Colescott to *The New York Times* 5 June 1944.

## Chapter 63

1 *The New York Times* 27 and 29 October 1944 and Michael Newton, *White Robes and Burning Crosses* (McFarland, Jefferson NC, 2014) p.88.
2 Quotes taken from William Leuchtenburg, 'The Conversion of Harry Truman', *American Heritage* (November 1991) p.55 and *Arizona Daily Star* 17 July 1983.
3 Cited in Karen Tani, *States of Dependency: Welfare, Rights, and American Governance, 1935–1972* (Cambridge University Press, Cambridge, 2016) p.104.

4  Barton J. Berstein, 'The Ambitious Legacy: The Truman Administration and Civil Rights' in Barton J. Berstein (ed.), *Politics and Policies of the Truman Administration* (Quadrangle Books, Chicago, IL, 1970) pp.712–13.
5  *LA Times* 21 October 1945 and Michael Newton, *White Robes and Burning Crosses* (McFarland, Jefferson NC, 2014) p.90.
6  Michael Newton, *The Ku Klux Klan: History, Organization, Language, Influence and Activities of America's Most Notorious Secret Society* (McFarland, Jefferson NC, 2007) p.241 and *The Washington Post* 19 June 2005. Byrd would go on to be one of West Virginia's most influential politicians in a career spanning fifty years on Capitol Hill. He would hold posts including Senate majority Leader, chair of the Senate Democratic Caucus, president pro tem of the US Senate and Senate majority whip.
7  *The New York Times* 22 June 1946.
8  'The Governor of Georgia Remembers He Was Once a Flogger Himself', *Life* 8 December 1941) p.40.,
9  William Anderson, *The Wild Man from Sugar Creek: The Political Career of Eugene Talmadge* (Louisiana State University, Baton Rouge, LA, 1975) and Michael Newton, *The Ku Klux Klan: History, Organization, Language, Influence and Activities of America's Most Notorious Secret Society* (McFarland, Jefferson, NC, 2007) pp.253–4.
10  Cited in David M. Chalmers, *Hooded Americanism: The History of the Ku Klux Klan* (Duke University Press, Durham, NC, 1981) pp.330–1.
11  Melody Lehn, 'Liminal Protest: Eleanor Roosevelt's "Sit-Between" at the 1938 Southern Conference for Human Welfare' in Sean Patrick O'Rourke (ed.), *Like Wildfire: The Rhetoric of the Civil Rights Sit-Ins* (University of South Carolina Press, SC, 2000) pp.17–34.
12  Michael Newton, *Ku Klux Terror: Birmingham Alabama from 1866 to the Present* (Schiffer, Atglen, PA, 2013) pp.51 and 55.

## Chapter 64

1  *The New York Times* 9 August 2022.
2  'American Experience; The Murder of Emmett Till; Interview with John Herbers, Journalist', 2003, GBH Archives openvault.wgbh.org/catalog/V_DDA9FECDBFD44A8D9FA7775B8511900E.
3  Timothy B. Tyson, *The Blood of Emmett* (Simon and Schuster, New York, 2017) pp.160–77.
4  William Bradford Huie, 'The Shocking Story of Approved Killing in Mississippi', *Look Magazine* 24 January 1956.

## Chapter 65

1  Cited in Thomas P. Brady, *Black Monday* (Association of Citizens' Councils, Brookhaven, MI, 1955) p.18 and *The Atlanta Constitution* 28 May 1954.
2  *Norfolk Journal and Guide* 29 May 1954; *Christian Science Monitor* 25 May 1954; *The New York Times* 27 May 1954; and Michael Newton, *The Ku Klux Klan: History, Organization, Language, Influence and Activities of America's Most Notorious Secret Society* (McFarland, Jefferson, NC, 2007) p.388.
3  'Mysterious Bomb Blasts Black Electrical Engineer Andrew Wade IV's Home in Louisville, Kentucky', *Jet Magazine* 15 July 1954 and Michael Newton, *The Ku Klux Klan: History, Organization, Language, Influence and Activities of America's Most Notorious Secret Society* (McFarland, Jefferson NC, 2007) p.388.

4   'Is Mississippi Hushing Up a Lynching? Rev. George Lee Murdered in Belzoni', *Jet Magazine* 26 May 1955.

5   Michael Newton, *The Ku Klux Klan: History, Organization, Language, Influence and Activities of America's Most Notorious Secret Society* (McFarland, Jefferson NC, 2007) pp.388–9.

6   Figures cited in Wyn Craig Wade, *The Fiery Cross: The Ku Klux Klan in America* (Simon and Schuster, New York, 1984) p.300.

7   C. Vann Woodward, 'From the First Reconstruction to the Second', *Harper's*, 230 (April 1965) p.129.

## Chapter 66

1   Cited in Dan Wakefield, *Revolt in the South* (Grove Press, New York, 1960) p.3.

2   Dan Wakefield, *Revolt in the South* (Grove Press, New York, 1960) p.3.

3   Wyn Craig Wade, *The Fiery Cross: The Ku Klux Klan in America* (Simon and Schuster, New York, 1984) pp.299–300.

4   Figures taken from James W. Vander Zanden, 'The Klan Revival', *American Journal of Sociology*, 65:5 (March 1960) p.456.

5   Larry J. Fisk and John Schellenberg, *Patterns of Conflict, Paths to Peace* (Broadview Press, Peterborough, Ontario, 1999) p.115.

6   Michael Newton, *The Ku Klux Klan: History, Organization, Language, Influence and Activities of America's Most Notorious Secret Society* (McFarland, Jefferson, NC, 2007) p.389.

7   *News Journal*, Radford, VA 11 April 1956.

8   *Commentary*, 29 (January 1960) pp.45–51; *New York Herald Tribune* 16 and 24 April 1960; Wayne Greenhaw, *Fighting the Devil in Dixie: How Civil Rights Activists Took on the Ku Klux Klan in Alabama* (Lawrence Hill Books, Chicago, IL, 2011) pp.97–9; and Wyn Craig Wade, *The Fiery Cross: The Ku Klux Klan in America* (Simon and Schuster, New York, 1984) p.303.

9   Patsy Sims (rev. ed.), *The Klan* (Kentucky University Press, Lexington, KY, 1996) p.151 and Michael Newton, *The Ku Klux Klan: History, Organization, Language, Influence and Activities of America's Most Notorious Secret Society* (McFarland, Jefferson, NC, 2007) pp.86–7.

10  Wyn Craig Wade, *The Fiery Cross: The Ku Klux Klan in America* (Simon and Schuster, New York, 1984) pp.303–4.

## Chapter 67

1   Governor Big Jim Folsom in a radio address, Christmas 1949 cited in Wayne Greenhaw, *Fighting the Devil in Dixie: How Civil Rights Activists Took on the Ku Klux Klan in Alabama* (Lawrence Hill Books, Chicago, IL, 2011) p.71.

2   www.shoppbs.pbs.org/wgbh/amex/wallace/peopleevents/pande02.html.

3   Imperial Wizard of the United Klans of America, Robert 'Bob' Shelton cited in Wayne Greenhaw, *Fighting the Devil in Dixie: How Civil Rights Activists Took on the Ku Klux Klan in Alabama* (Lawrence Hill Books, Chicago, IL, 2011) p.154.

4   Figures taken from Lawrence Leamer, *The Lynching: The Epic Courtroom Battle That Brought Down the Klan* (William Morrow, New York, 2017) p.122.

5   Civil rights activist Charles Morgan Jr cited in Howell Raines, *My Soul is Rested: The Story of the Civil Rights Movement in the Deep South* (Penguin Books, New York, 1983) p.180.

## Chapter 68

1  Andrew Cohen, 'The Speech That Shocked Birmingham the Day After the Church Bombing' *The Atlantic* (13 September 2013).
2  See the autobiography of Robert Chambliss' sister-in-law Elizabeth H. Cobbs, *Long Time Coming* (Crane Hill Publishers, Birmingham, AL, 1994) p.81.
3  Elizabeth H. Cobbs, *Long Time Coming* (Crane Hill Publishers, Birmingham, AL, 1994) p.41.
4  Letter from Robert Chambliss to Flora Chambliss (28 May 1979) in File No. 1969.1.2 of the Chambliss, Robert E., Papers, Birmingham Public Library, Department of Archives and Manuscripts.
5  *Summary of Investigation, Bombing of 16th Street Baptist Church, Birmingham, Alabama, September 15, 1963* p.9 in Birmingham, Alabama Police Department Surveillance Files, 1947–1980, Collection Number 1,125, Archives Department 1125.3.3A.
6  *Birmingham News*, 17 November 1977 and *The New York Times* 24 July 1983.

## Chapter 69

1  Figures and quotes taken from Civil Rights Movement Archive, *The Struggle for Voting Rights in Mississippi – The Early Years* www.crmvet.org/info/voter_ms.pdf.
2  Congress of Racial Equality CORE; Student Non-Violent Coordinating Committee: SNCC; Southern Christian Leadership Conference: SCLC and National Association for the Advancement of Colored People: NAACP.
3  *The New York Times* 21 June 1964.
4  Cited in Don Whitehead, *Attack on Terror: The FBI Against the Ku Klux Klan in Mississippi* (Ishi Press International, New York, 2012) pp.202–3.
5  Wyn Craig Wade, *The Fiery Cross: The Ku Klux Klan in America* (Simon and Schuster, New York, 1984) pp.337–8.
6  John R. Rachal, '"The Long, Hot Summer": The Mississippi Response to Freedom Summer, 1964', *The Journal of Negro History*, 84:4 (Autumn, 1999) pp.315–39.
7  Florence Mars, *Witness in Philadelphia* (LSU Press, Baton Rouge, LA, 1977) p.108.
8  Cited in Wyn Craig Wade, *The Fiery Cross: The Ku Klux Klan in America* (Simon and Schuster, New York, 1984) p.344.
9  Don Whitehead, *Attack on Terror: The FBI Against the Ku Klux Klan in Mississippi* (Ishi Press International, New York, 2012) pp.202–3.
10  Don Whitehead, *Attack on Terror: The FBI Against the Ku Klux Klan in Mississippi* (Ishi Press International, New York, 2012) p.260.
11  Douglas O Linder, 'Bending Toward Justice: John Doar and the Mississippi Burning Trial' *Mississippi Law Review* 72:2 (Winter, 2002) pp.776 and 777.

## Chapter 70

1  Garry Thomas Rowe, *Undercover Years with the Ku Klux Klan* (Bantam Books, New York, 1976) pp.3–5; US Department of Justice, *Task Force Report on Garry Thomas Rowe Jnr* (Govt Printing, Washington DC, 1979) pp.33–39 and Gary May, *The Informant: The FBI, the Ku Klux Klan, and the Murder of Viola Liuzzo* (Yale, Newhaven, 2008) pp.1–13.
2  Renata Adler, 'The Selma March: On the Trail to Montgomery' *The New Yorker* (10 April 1965).
3  Garry Thomas Rowe, *Undercover Years with the Ku Klux Klan* (Bantam Books, New York, 1976) pp.174–175.
4  *Washington Evening Star* 26 March 1965.

5  Charles Longstreet Weltner, *Southerner* (J.B. Lippincott Co., New York, 1966) p.180.
6  For details of the Hearings, see US Congress, House. Committee on Un-American Activities. *Report: The Present-Day Ku Klux Klan Movement* 90th Congress, 1st Session (1967).
7  *The New York Times* 5 December 1965.

## Chapter 71

1  Renee Romano, 'No Diplomatic Immunity: African Diplomats, the State Department, and Civil Rights, 1961–1964' *Journal of American History*, 87:2 (September 2000) pp.546–551.
2  Wyn Craig Wade, *The Fiery Cross: The Ku Klux Klan in America* (Touchstone Books, New York, 1987) p.361.
3  *Fort Lauderdale News* 25 April 1969 and John Drabble, 'To Ensure Domestic Tranquility: The FBI, COINTELPRO-WHITE HATE and Political Discourse, 1964–1971' *Journal of American Studies* 38 (2004) pp.310–312.
4  John Drabble, 'To Ensure Domestic Tranquility: The FBI, COINTELPRO-WHITE HATE and Political Discourse, 1964–1971' *Journal of American Studies* 38 (2004) p.311.
5  John Drabble, 'To Ensure Domestic Tranquility: The FBI, COINTELPRO-WHITE HATE and Political Discourse, 1964–1971' *Journal of American Studies* 38 (2004) p.313 and *The New York Times* 17 March 1970.
6  Details and quote from John Drabble, 'To Ensure Domestic Tranquility: The FBI, COINTELPRO-WHITE HATE and Political Discourse, 1964–1971' *Journal of American Studies* 38 (2004) p.326.

## Chapter 72

1  Roi Ottley, 'I Met the Grand Dragon' *The Nation* 169 (2 July 1949) pp.10–11.
2  Cited in Wayne Greenhaw, *Fighting the Devil in Dixie: How Civil Rights Activists Took on the Ku Klux Klan in Alabama* (Lawrence Hill Books, Chicago, 2011) p.172.
3  *The New York Times*, 12 March 1965.
4  Michael Newton, *Ku Klux Terror: Birmingham, Alabama, from 1866-Present* (Schiffer Books, Atglen, PA, 2013) p.152 and Hoggle's obituary in *The New York Times* 5 September 2016.

## Chapter 73

1  For the intellectual underpinnings of this movement, see Stokely Carmichael and Charles V. Hamilton, *Black Power: The Politics of Liberation in America* (Vintage, New York, 1967).
2  Jelani Cobb (ed.), *The Essential Kerner Commission Report* (Liveright Publishing Co., New York, 2021) pp.7–37.
3  Figures taken from Michael Newton, *The Ku Klux Klan: History, Organization, Language, Influence and Activities of America's Most Notorious Secret Society* (McFarland, Jefferson, NC, 2007) pp.24–26.

## PART X

1  Louis Beam in essay, *New World Order* (1983).

## Chapter 74

1 Rick Bowers, *Superman Versus the Klan: The True Story of How the Iconic Superhero Battled the Men of Hate* (National Geographic, Washington DC, 2012) pp.133–141. *Klan of the Fiery Cross* available at www.youtube.com/watch?v=1ol8Gmi57DI.
2 'Its Superfight' *Newsweek* 29 April 1946 p.162.
3 *The Washington Post* 20 April 1947.
4 Stetson Kennedy, *The Klan Unmasked* (University of Alabama Press, Tuscaloosa, 1990) p.20.
5 Stetson Kennedy, *Southern Exposure* (Doubleday, New York, 1946) p.364.
6 Stetson Kennedy, *I Rode with the Ku Klux Klan* (Arco Publishers, New York, 1954) p.94.

## Chapter 75

1 Kenneth S. Stern, 'David Duke: A Nazi in Politics' *Issues in National Affairs* 1:4 (1991) p.3.
2 Figures taken from Anti-Defamation League cited in Patsy Sims, *The Klan* (Stein and Day, New York, 1978) p.163.
3 Duke cited in Michael Newton, *The Ku Klux Klan: History, Organization, Language, Influence and Activities of America's Most Notorious Secret Society* (McFarland, Jefferson, NC, 2007) p.65.
4 Patsy Sims, *The Klan* (Stein and Day, New York, 1978) p.4.
5 David Duke cited in *Newsweek*, 90 (14 November 1977) p.45.
6 Taken from Bill Stanton, *Klanwatch: Bringing the Klan to Justice* (Grove Weidenfeld, New York, 1991) p.86.
7 Robert Shelton in *The Fiery Cross*, 13 (1978) cited in Wyn Craig Wade, *Fiery Cross: The Ku Klux Klan in America* (Simon and Schuster, New York, 1984) p.370.
8 David Duke to Patsy Sims, July 1976 cited in Patsy Sims, *The Klan* (Stein and Day, New York, 1978) p.163.
9 Howard Schuman et al. (rev. ed.), *Racial Attitudes in America* (Harvard University Press, Cambridge, MA, 1997) p.184.
10 Patsy Sims, *The Klan* (Stein and Day, New York, 1978) p.184 and Michael Newton, *The Ku Klux Klan: History, Organization, Language, Influence and Activities of America's Most Notorious Secret Society* (McFarland, Jefferson, NC, 2007) p.62.
11 *The Daily Telegraph* 23 October 2009.
12 For details of the incident see Julia Reed, 'His Brilliant Career' *New York Review of Books* 9 April 1992, p.20.
13 For quotations and details see Southern Poverty Law Center www.splcenter. org/fighting-hate/extremist-files/individual/david-duke and www.youtube.com/ watch?v=Qwnqv44rMXM.

## Chapter 76

1 *The New York Times* 21 March 1979.
2 According to Miles the Reconstruction Klan had been the first era; the 1920s, the second; then came the Civil Rights; then Duke; and finally his Klan. See Leonard Zuskind, *Blood and Politics* (Farrar, Straus and Giroux, New York, 2009) p.86.
3 Louis Beam, *Understanding the Struggle, or Why We have to Kill the Bastards* (Aryan Nations, Church of Jesus Christ Christian, Hayden Lake, ID, no date) p.5.
4 Cited in Michael Newton, *The Ku Klux Klan: History, Organization, Language, Influence and Activities of America's Most Notorious Secret Society* (McFarland, Jefferson, NC, 2007) p.91.

5   Louis R. Beam (ed.), *Essays of a Klansman* (AKIA [A Klansman I Am] Publications, Hayden Lake, ID, 1983) pp.vi–vii.

6   Quotes and details taken from Kathleen Belew, *Bring the War Home* (Harvard University Press, Cambridge, MA, 2018) p.46.

7   Louis R. Beam (ed.), *Essays of a Klansman* (AKIA [A Klansman I Am] Publications, Hayden Lake, ID, 1983) p.22.

8   *Chicago Tribune* and *The New York Times* 24 November 1980.

9   'Border Watch Continues: Anatomy of an Apprehension' on the front page of the KKKK's in-house newspaper *The Crusader*, 28 (1977).

10  www.brennancenter.org/our-work/research-reports/posse-comitatus-act-explained.

11  *The New York Times* 17 November 2002.

12  D.J. Mulloy, *Years of Rage: White Supremacy in the United States from the Klan to the Alt-Right* (Rowman and Littlefield, Lanham, Boulder, CO, 2021) p.109.

13  Louis Beam, 'Leaderless Resistance', *Inter-Klan Newsletter & Survival Alert* (undated, *c.* May 1983). The document doesn't have page numbers but can be read in full at firstmonday.org/ojs/index.php/fm/article/view/1040/961.

## Chapter 77

1   Kathleen Belew, *Bring the War Home* (Harvard University Press, Cambridge, MA, 2018) pp.6–7.

2   Klansman Coleman Pridmore, cited in *The Washington Post* 19 November 1980.

3   John Drabble, 'From White Supremacy to White Power: The FBI, COINTELPRO-WHITE HATE, and the Nazification of the Ku Klux Klan in the 1970s', *American Studies*, 43:3 (January 2007) pp.49–51.

4   Gorrell Pierce cited in Daniel Byman, *Spreading Hate: The Global Rise of White Supremacist Terrorism* (Oxford University Press, Oxford, 2022) p.57.

5   United Klans of America, 'Why Revolution?', *The Fiery Cross*, 7:10 (1972) p.6.

6   www.splcenter.org/fighting-hate/hate-incidents?f%5B0%5D=field_hate_incident_type%3A12&page=37; www.adl.org/resources/news/white-supremacists-sentenced-missouri-racial-assault.

## Chapter 78

1   www.adl.org/resources/backgrounders/turner-diaries and www.britannica.com/topic/The-Turner-Diaries.

2   Kevin Flynn and Gary Gerhardt, *The Silent Brotherhood: Inside America's Racist Underground* (Free Press, New York, 1989).

3   Figures taken from Michael Newton, *The Ku Klux Klan: History, Organization, Language, Influence and Activities of America's Most Notorious Secret Society* (McFarland, Jefferson, NC, 2007) p.27.

4   L.J. Lawrence, 'Ballad of an American Terrorist: A Neo-Nazis Dream of Order', *Harper's Magazine*, 273 (July 1986) p.60.

5   Bill Stanton, *Klanwatch: Bringing the Ku Klux Klan to Justice* (Grove Weidenfeld, New York, 1991) pp.184–6.

6   Michael Newton, *The FBI and the KKK: A Critical History* (McFarland and Co., Jefferson, NC, 2005) pp.186–8.

7   Michael Newton, *The Ku Klux Klan: History, Organization, Language, Influence and Activities of America's Most Notorious Secret Society* (McFarland, Jefferson, NC, 2007) p.190.

## Chapter 79

1   Morris Dees and Steve Fiffer, *A Season For Justice: The Life and Times of Civil Rights Lawyer Morris Dees* (Charles Scribner's Sons, New York, 1991) p.98.

## Chapter 80

1   Lawrence Leamer, *The Lynching: The Epic Courtroom Battle That Brought Down the Klan* (William Morrow, New York, 2017) p.304.
2   William Vincent Hunt, 'A Sheet and a Cross: A Symbolic Analysis of the Ku Klux Klan' (Unpublished PhD Thesis, Tulane University, LA, 1975).
3   Kelly J. Baker, *The Gospel According to the Klan: The KKK's Appeal to Protestant America, 1915–1930* (University of Kansas Press, Lawrence, KS, 2011).
4   Tom Metzger cited in James Ridgeway, 'Unholy Terrorists', *Village Voice* 25 January 1985.
5   Cited in Eckard V. Toy, Jr, 'The Ku Klux Klan in Oregon: Its Program and Character' (Unpublished MA Thesis, University of Oregon, OR, 1959) p.137.
6   Wesley Swift cited in the Anti-Defamation League, 'The Identity Churches: A Theology of Hate', *ADL Facts*, 6 available at archive.org/details/TheidentityChurchesATheologyOfHate/page/n1/mode/2up?view=theater.

## Chapter 81

1   Barry J. Balleck, *Allegiance to Liberty: The Changing Face of Patriots, Militias and Political Violence in America* (Praeger, Westport, CT, 2015) p.18.
2   Barry J. Balleck, *Allegiance to Liberty: The Changing Face of Patriots, Militias and Political Violence in America* (Praeger, Westport, CT, 2015) p.172.
3   Barry J. Balleck, *Allegiance to Liberty: The Changing Face of Patriots, Militias and Political Violence in America* (Praeger, Westport, CT, 2015) pp.172–3.
4   Cited in *Baltimore Sun* 15 April 2009.
5   Mark Potok cited in Bill Morlin, 'Ruby Ridge Carved a Niche in History', *Hatewatch* 21 August 2012 cited at www.splcenter.org/hatewatch/2012/08/21/ruby-ridge-carved-niche-history?gclid=Cj0KCQjw8O-VBhCpARIsACMvVLNPNhT9X5hlxc308RodIJVt8Y3Hs_1NhQMEcqciOjPl7T4kkJfnO1waAlIAEALw_wcB.
6   For details of the hearings, see law2.umkc.edu/faculty/projects/ftrials/weaver/weaversenate.html.
7   *The New York Times* and *LA Times* 16 August 1995.
8   Lou Michel and Dan Herbeck, *American Terrorist: Timothy McVeigh and the Oklahoma Bombing* (Harper, New York, 2001) p.128.
9   Cited in *San Diego Union-Tribune* 14 April 1996 and *Boston Globe* 19 April 2005.

## PART XI

1   Itay Hod, 'An Ex-KKK Grand Wizard Tells Us How Donald Trump Dog-Whistles to Closet Racists', *The Wrap* 25 August 2016.

## Chapter 82

1   Aaron Winter, 'Online Hate: From the Far-Right to the "Alt-Right", and from the Margins to the Mainstream' in Karen Lumsden and Emily Harmer (eds), *Online Othering: Exploring Violence and Discrimination on the Web* (Palgrave, London, 2019) pp.39–63.

2 Louis Beam, 'Computers and the American Patriot', *The Inter-Klan Newsletter and Survival Alert* (March 1984) pp.1 and 3.

3 Kathleen Belew, *Bring the War Home* (Harvard University Press, Cambridge, MA, 2018) p.121.

4 Quotation taken from *Miami New Times* 19 February 1998. For details of Operation Red Dog, see 'Bayou of Pigs: A Coup that Fizzled', *Time* 11 May 1981.

5 Jesse Daniels, 'Race, Civil Rights, and Hate Speech in the Digital Era', *CUNY Academic Works* (2008) pp.133–4 and www.splcenter.org/fighting-hate/extremist-files/group/stormfront.

6 Jesse Daniels, *Cyber Racism: White Supremacy Online and the New Attack on Civil Rights* (Rowman and Littlefield, Lanham, MD, 2009) pp.42–48.

7 www.kkk.com.

8 Todd Schroer, *White Racialists, Computers and Internet*, a paper presented at the Annual Meeting of the American Sociological Association in 1997 available at digitalcommons.unl.edu/dissertations/AAI9912694/.

## Chapter 83

1 R.L. Hilliard and M.C. Keith, *Waves of Rancor: Tuning in the Radical Right* (M.E. Sharpe, New York, 1999) p.112.

2 Cited in J. McDevitt, J. Levin & S. Bennett, 'Hate Crime Offenders: An Expanded Typology', *Journal of Social Issues*, 58:2 (2002) p.307.

3 Cited in *The New York Times* 20 June 2015.

4 www.splcenter.org/fighting-hate/extremist-files/group/euro.

5 Kathleen Belew, *Bring the War Home* (Harvard University Press, Cambridge, MA, 2018) p.6.

6 Booth Gunter and Caleb Kieffer, 'Islamophobia After 9/11: How a Fearmongering Fringe Movement Exploited the Terror Attacks to Gain Political Power', *SPLC* 21 September 2021.

## Chapter 84

1 webarchive.loc.gov/legacy/20011016155005/http://www.kukluxklan.org/index.htm.

2 Southern Illinois KKK leader, Basil 'Red' Sitzes cited in *Belleville News–Democrat* 30 September 2001.

3 Cited in *The New York Times* 1 March 2003.

4 *Pittsburgh Post-Gazette* 14 February 2003.

5 *The New York Times* 4 March 1994.

6 casetext.com/statute/code-of-alabama/title-26-infants-and-incompetents/chapter-23h-the-alabama-human-life-protection-act/section-26-23h-2-legislative-findings.

7 Senator Dennis Baxley cited in *South Florida Sun-Sentinel* 29 May 2019.

8 twitter.com/Jerone4Congress/status/1544700948164972546.

9 Cited in Curtis J. Austin, *Up Against the Wall: Violence in the Making and Unmasking of the Black Panther Party* (University of Arkansas Press, Fayetteville, AR, 2006) p.94.

10 Nicholas Johnson, *Negroes and the Gun: The Black Tradition of Arms* (Prometheus Books, Amherst, New York, 2014) pp.283–5.

11 www.trendsinhate.com/dateinhate.html.

12 www.muckrock.com/foi/united-states-of-america-10/church-of-the-national-knights-of-the-ku-klux-klan-31223/.

## Chapter 85

1  www.splcenter.org/fighting-hate/intelligence-report/2015/
   their-words-hating-barack-obama.
2  tarobb.blogspot.com/2008/11/obama-electred-president.html.
3  Terence G. Fitzgerald, *Black Males and Racism* (Routledge, New York, 2015) pp.47–49.
4  *The Washington Post* 28 April 2011.

## Chapter 86

1  Thomas M Conroy, 'The Ku Klux Klan and the American Clergy', *Ecclesiastical Review*, 70:1 (January 1924) pp.55 and Wyn Craig Wade, *The Fiery Cross: The Ku Klux Klan in America* (Touchstone Books, New York, 1987) p.227.
2  www.energy.gov/ehss/security-policy-guidance-reports/
   departmental-personnel-security-faqs.
3  aleteia.org/2019/10/25/the-ku-klux-klan-vs-catholics-a-sad-chapter-in-american-
   history/.
4  www.youtube.com/watch?v=VrF7alkwdHw.
5  For details on QAnon, see Mike Rothschild, *The Storm Is Upon Us: How QAnon Became a Movement, Cult, and Conspiracy Theory of Everything* (Monoray, London, 2021).
6  www.axios.com/2020/08/19/
   trump-praises-qanon-supporters-i-understand-they-like-me-very-much
7  www.newsweek.com/topic/conspiracy-theory?page=4.
8  www.ipsos.com/en-us/news-polls/npr-misinformation-123020.
9  today.yougov.com/politics/articles/
   41873-which-groups-americans-believe-conspiracies
10 www.splcenter.org/fighting-hate/intelligence-report/2019/year-hate-rage-
   against-change and www.splcenter.org/fighting-hate/extremist-files/ideology/
   ku-klux-klan; and www.splcenter.org/sites/default/files/splc-2021-year-in-hate-
   extremism-report.pdf.

## Chapter 87

1  Shodai Sennin J.A. Overton Guerra, *Message to America: Why We Need to Finally Win the War Against White Supremacy* (Mamba-Ryu Publications, 2017) p.6.
2  www.aljazeera.com/news/2018/6/17/
   dylann-roof-rampage-3-years-on-confederate-debate-still-evolving.
3  Vegas Tenold, *Everything You Love Will Burn: Inside the Rebirth of White Nationalism in America* (Bold Type Books, New York, 2018).
4  Heimbach in *The New York Times* 13 August 2017.
5  *The Washington Post* 22 November 2021.
6  www.salon.com/2013/09/29/the_hatemonger_next_door/.
7  D.J. Mulloy, *Years of Rage: White Supremacy in the United States from the Klan to the Alt-Right* (Roman and Littlefield, New York, 2021) pp.203–5.
8  *The Washington Post* 13 August 2017.
9  imperialglobalexeter.com/2014/07/07/
   invisible-empire-an-imperial-history-of-the-kkk/.
10 For a detailed refutation of the Lost Cause, see Adam H. Domby, *The False Cause: Fraud, Fabrication and White Supremacy in Confederate Memory* (University of Virginia Press, Charlottesville, VA, 2000).
11 *The Guardian* 28 June 2021.

12 maristpoll.marist.edu/wp-content/misc/usapolls/us150722/CivilWar/ McClatchy-Marist%20Poll_National%20Release%20and%20Tables_ The%20Confederate%20Flag_August%202015.pdf.

13 Vegas Tenold, *Everything You Love Will Burn: Inside the Rebirth of White Nationalism in America* (Bold Type Books, New York, 2018) p.290.

## Chapter 88

1 *The New York Times* 14 June and 3 July 2020 and *Wall Street Journal* 19 June 2020.

2 *The New York Times* 1 June 2020.

3 www.bbc.co.uk/news/av/uk-42830165.

4 edition.cnn.com/videos/politics/2015/12/08/lindsey-graham-donald-trump-xenophobic-bigot-interview-newday.cnn and edition.cnn.com/2016/11/21/politics/ alt-right-gathering-donald-trump/index.html.

5 *New York Daily News* 20 January 2017.

6 *The Washington Post* 2 November 2016.

7 www.splcenter.org/fighting-hate/intelligence-report/2016/year-hate-and-extremism.

8 *New York Daily News* 31 January 2017.

9 See *LA Times* 11 November 2016

10 www.change.org/p/department-of-counterterrorism-change-kkk-status-into-terrorist-organization.

11 www.politifact.com/factchecks/2019/aug/27/joe-biden/ biden-wrong-when-he-says-trump-hasnt-condemned-dav/.

12 *The Washington Post* 3 March 2016.

13 *The Washington Post* 14 August 2017.

14 ADL, Steve Bannon: 'Five Things to Know', www.adl.org/resources/backgrounder/ steve-bannon-five-things-know.

15 *Tampa Bay Times* 30 September 2016.

16 *The Washington Post* 1 February 2019.

17 *The Guardian* 14 June 2022.

## Epilogue

1 www.govinfo.gov/committee/house-january6th?path=/browsecommittee/chamber/ house/committee/january6th/collection/CRPT

2 www.npr.org/2022/08/16/1117762232/the-unspoken-role-of-race-in-the-jan-6-riot.

3 See *Washington Post* 18 February 2021.

4 See Department of Justice website www.justice.gov/opa/pr/proud-boys-leaders-sentenced-prison-roles-jan-6-capitol-breach.

5 www.splcenter.org/20220309/year-hate-extremism-report-2021#hate-group-numbers.

6 See Shoshona Zuboff, *The Age of Surveillance Capitalism* (Profile Books, London, 2019).

7 *Birmingham Post-Herald* cited in Robert Sherrill, 'A Look Inside the Invisible Empire', *New South*, 23 (Spring, 1968) p.8.

8 Southern Poverty Law Center, *The Year in Hate and Extremism: 2021* (SPLC, Montgomery, AL, 2022) p.46.

9 'Justice Ketanji Brown Jackson Says "Whole Truth" About Black History Must be Taught', *ABC News*, 15 September 2023 abcnews.go.com/Politics/ justice-ketanji-brown-jackson-truth-black-history-taught/story?id=103220003.

# BIBLIOGRAPHY

## Books and Pamphlets

Donald Gordon Alcock, *A Study in Continuity: Maury County, Tennessee, 1850–1870* (University of California, Berkeley, CA, 1985)

Charles C. Alexander, *The Ku Klux Klan in the Southwest* (University of Oklahoma Press, Norman, OK, 1995)

Kristofer Allerfeldt, *Race, Radicalism, Religion, and Restriction: Immigration in the Pacific Northwest, 1890–1924* (Praeger, Westport, CT, 2003)

Kristofer Allerfeldt, *Organized Crime in the United States, 1865–1941* (McFarland, Jefferson, NC, 2018)

Tyler Gregory Anbinder, *Nativism and Slavery: The Northern Know Nothings and the Politics of the 1850s* (Oxford University Press, New York, 1992)

William Anderson, *The Wild Man from Sugar Creek: The Political Career of Eugene Talmadge* (Louisiana State University, Baton Rouge, LA, 1975)

Anonymous, *The Oaths, Signs, Ceremonies and Objects of the Ku-Klux-Klan: A Full Expose. by a Late Member* (Unknown Publisher, Cleveland, OH, 1868)

Paul Ashdown and Edward Caudill, *The Myth of Nathan Bedford Forrest* (Rowman and Littlefield, New York, 2005)

Richard Bain, *Convention Decisions and Voting Records* (The Brookings Institute, Washington DC, 1960)

Kelly J. Baker, *The Gospel According to the Klan: The KKK's Appeal to Protestant America, 1915–1930* (University of Kansas Press, Lawrence, KS, 2011)

Edward Ball, *Life of a Klansman* (Farrar, Straus and Giroux, New York, 2020)

Barry J. Balleck, *Allegiance to Liberty: The Changing Face of Patriots, Militias and Political Violence in America* (Praeger, Westport, CT, 2015)

Kenneth Barnes, *The Ku Klux Klan in 1920s Arkansas: How Protestant White Nationalism Came to Rule a State* (University of Arkansas Press, Fayetteville, AR, 2021)

Allan Bartley, *The Ku Klux Klan in Canada: A Century of Promoting Racism and Hate in the Peaceable Kingdom* (Formac Publishing Ltd, Halifax, 2020)

Louis Beam, *Understanding the Struggle, or Why We have to Kill the Bastards* (Ayran Nations, Church of Jesus Christ Christian, Hayden Lake, ID, no date)

Louis R. Beam (ed.), *Essays of a Klansman* (AKIA Publications, Hayden Lake, ID, 1983)

Kathleen Belew, *Bring the War Home* (Harvard University Press, Cambridge, MA, 2018)

Jean V. Berlin and Brooks D. Simpson (eds), *Sherman's Civil War: Selected Correspondence of William T. Sherman, 1860–1865* (University of North Carolina Press, Chapel Hill, NC, 1999)

Patricia Bernstein, *Ten Dollars to Hate: The Texas Man Who Fought the Klan* (Texas A&M University Press, College Station, TX, 2017)

Kathleen M. Blee, *Women of the Klan: Racism and Gender in the 1920s* (University of California, Berkeley, CA, 1997)

David W. Blight, *Race and Reunion: The Civil War in American Memory* (Harvard University Press, Cambridge, MA, 2001)

Edgar Allen Booth, *The Mad Mullah of America* (Boyd Ellison, Columbus, OH, 1927)

Rick Bowers, *Superman Versus the Klan: The True Story of How the Iconic Superhero Battled the Men of Hate* (National Geographic, Washington DC, 2012)

Kevin Boyle, *Arc of Justice: A Saga of Race, Civil Rights, and Murder in the Jazz Age* (Henry Holt and Co., New York, 2004)

Thomas P. Brady, *Black Monday* (Association of Citizens' Councils, Brookhaven, MS, 1955)

R.J. Brunson, *Historic Pulaski, Birthplace of the Ku Klux Klan, Scene of Execution of Sam Davis* (The Methodist Publishing House, Nashville, TN, 1913)

William Jennings Bryan, *The Prince of Peace* (Fleming H. Revell & Co., New York, 1914)

John W. Burgess, *Reconstruction and the Constitution, 1866–1876* (Scribners, New York, 1902)

John W. Burgess, *Reminiscences of an American Scholar: The Beginnings of Columbia University* (Columbia University Press, New York, 1934)

John Roy Carlson, *Undercover: My Four Years in the Nazi Underworld of America* (E.P. Button and Co., New York, 1943)

David M. Chalmers, *Hooded Americanism: The First Century of the Ku Klux Klan* (Doubleday and Co., Garden City, NY, 1965)

Jelani Cobb (ed.), *The Essential Kerner Commission Report* (Liveright Publishing Co., New York, 2021)

Elizabeth H. Cobbs, *Long Time Coming* (Crane Hill Publishers, Birmingham, AL, 1994)

Committee of 70, *History of the Riot at Colfax, Grant Parish, Louisiana, April 13th, 1873: With a Brief Sketch of the Trial of the Grant Parish Prisoners in the Circuit Court of the United States* (Clarke & Hofeline, New Orleans, LA, 1874)

Thomas L. Connelly, *Five Tragic Hours: The Battle of Franklin* (University of Tennessee Press, Knoxville, TN, 1983)

Allen Cook, *Fire from the Flint: The Amazing Careers of Thomas Dixon* (John F. Blair, Winston-Salem, NC, 1968)

E. Merton Coulter, *William G. Brownlow: Fighting Parson of the Southern Highlands* University of Tennessee Press, Knoxville, TN, 1999)

Scott M. Cutlip, *The Unseen Power: Public Relations, A History* (Lawrence Erlbaum Associates, Hillsdale, NJ, 1994)

Jesse Daniels, *Cyber Racism: White Supremacy Online and the New Attack on Civil Rights* (Rowman and Littlefield, Lanham, MD, 2009)

Leroy Davis and John Hope Franklin, *A Clashing of the Soul: John Hope and the Dilemma of African American Leadership and Black Higher Education in the Early Twentieth Century* (University of Georgia Press, Athens, GA, 1998)

Morris Dees and Steve Fiffer, *A Season For Justice: The Life and Times of Civil Rights Lawyer Morris Dees* (Charles Scribner's Sons, New York, 1991)

Humphrey J. Desmond, *The APA Movement: A Sketch* (New Century Press, Washington DC, 1912)

J.D. Dickey, *Rising in Flames: Sherman's March and the Fight for a New Nation* (Pegasus Books, New York, 2018)

Adam H. Domby, *The False Cause: Fraud, Fabrication and White Supremacy in Confederate Memory* (University of Virginia Press, Charlottesville, VA, 2000)

W.E.B. Dubois, *Black Reconstruction: An Essay Toward a History of the Part Which Black Folk Played in the Attempt to Reconstruct Democracy in America, 1860–1880* (Harcourt, Brace and Co., New York, 1935)

Scott Ellsworth, *Death in a Promised Land: The Tulsa Race Riot of 1921* (Louisiana State University Press, Baton Rouge, LA, 1982)

Hiram Wesley Evans, *The Menace of Modern Immigration* (The Knights of the Ku Klux Klan, Atlanta, GA, 1924)

Federal Writers Project, *Slave Narratives* (Washington DC, 1941)

Michael W. Fitzgerald, *The Union League Movement in the Deep South: Politics and Agricultural Change During Reconstruction* (Louisiana State University Press, Baton Rouge, LA, 1989)

Terence G. Fitzgerald, *Black Males and Racism* (Routledge, New York, 2015)

Walter Lynwood Fleming, *Civil War and Reconstruction in Alabama* (Columbia University Press, New York, 1905)

Walter Lynwood Fleming, *The Sequel of Appomattox: A Chronicle of the Reunion of the States* (Yale University Press, New Haven, CT, 1919)

Nicholas Jackson Floyd, *Thorns in the Flesh: A Romance of the War and Ku-Klux Periods* (Hubbard Bros, Philadelphia, PA, 1884)

Kevin Flynn and Gary Gerhardt, *The Silent Brotherhood: Inside America's Racist Underground* (Free Press, New York, 1989)

Eric Foner, *Reconstruction: America's Unfinished Revolution 1863–1877* (Harper Collins, New York, 1988)

Forrest Monument Association, *The Forrest Monument: Its History and Dedication; A Memorial in Art, Oratory and Literature* (Unknown Publisher, 1905)

Gladys-Marie Fry, *Night Riders in Black Folk History* (University of North Carolina Press, Chapel Hill, NC, 1975)

Henry Peck Fry, *The Voice of the Third Generation: A Discussion of the Race Question for the Benefit of Those Who Believe that the United States is a White Man's Country and Should be Governed by White Men* (MacGowan-Cooke Printing Co., Chattanooga, TN, 1906)

Henry P. Fry, *The Modern Ku Klux Klan* (Small, Maynard and Co., Boston, MA, 1922)

Andre Gerrits, *The Myth of Jewish Communism: A Historical Interpretation* (Peter Lang, New York, 2009)

Edward Gonzalez-Tennant, *The Rosewood Massacre: An Archaeology and History of Intersectional Violence* (University of Florida Press, Gainesville, FL, 2018)

Linda Gordon, *The Second Coming of the KKK: The Ku Klux Klan of the 1920s and the American Political Tradition* (Liveright, New York, 2017)

Linda Gordon, *Threat to Democracy: The Ku Klux Klan in the 1920s* (Amberley Publishing, Stroud, 2017)

Madison Grant, *The Passing of the Great Race or the Racial Basis of European History* (Charles Scribner's Sons, New York, 1916)

James R. Grossman, *Land of Hope: Chicago, Black Southerners, and the Great Migration* (University of Chicago, Chicago, IL, 1991)

Allen C. Guezlo, *Fateful Lightning: A New History of the Civil War and Reconstruction* (Oxford University Press, New York, 2012)

Allen C. Guelzo, *Reconstruction: A Concise History* (Oxford University Press, New York, 2018)

Ben Haas, *The Ku Klux Klan* (Greenleaf Classics, San Diego, CA, 1963)

Sally E. Hadden, *Slave Patrols: Law and Violence in Virginia and the Carolinas* (Harvard University Press, Cambridge, MA, 2001)

Felix Harcourt, *Ku Klux Kulture: America and the Klan in the 1920s* (University of Chicago Press, Chicago, IL, 2017)

James Hart (ed.), *The Man Who Invented Hollywood: The Autobiography of D.W. Griffith* (Touchstone, Louisville, KY, 1972)

R.L. Hilliard and M.C. Keith, *Waves of Rancor: Tuning in the Radical Right* (M.E. Sharpe, New York, 1999)

Stanley F. Horn, *The Invisible Empire: The Story of the Ku Klux Klan, 1866–1871* (Houghton Mifflin Co., Boston, MA, 1939)

Walter T. Howard (ed.), *We Shall Be Free! Black Communist Protest in Seven Voices* (Temple University Press, Philadelphia, PA, 2013)

Jack Hurst, *Nathan Bedford Forrest: A Biography* (Vintage, New York, 1993)

Kenneth Jackson, *The Ku Klux Klan in the City, 1915–1930* (Ivan R. Dee, New York, 1968)

Leeanna Keith, *The Colfax Massacre: The Untold Story of Black Power, White Terror, & the Death of Reconstruction* (Oxford University Press, New York, 2007)

D.G. Kelley, *Hammer and Hoe: Alabama Communists During the Great Depression* (University of North Carolina Press, Chapel Hill, NC, 1990)

Stetson Kennedy, *I Rode with the Ku Klux Klan* (Hamilton & Co., London, 1958)

Donald L. Kinzer, *An Episode in Anti-Catholicism: The American Protective Association* (University of Washington Press, Seattle, WA,1964)

Knights of Columbus, *Report of Commission on Religious Prejudices* (Knights of Columbus Supreme Council, New Haven, CT, 1915)

Dale W. Laackman, *Selling Hate: Marketing the Ku Klux Klan* (University of Georgia Press, Athens, GA., 2020)

Charles Lane, *The Day Freedom Died: The Colfax Massacre, the Supreme Court and the Betrayal of Reconstruction* (Henry Holt and Co., New York, 2008)

Charles Lane, *Freedom's Detective: The Secret Service, The Ku Klux Klan and the Man Who Masterminded America's First War on Terror* (Hanover Square Press, Toronto, 2019)

Shawn Lay (ed.), *The Invisible Empire in the West: Toward a New Historical Appraisal of the Ku Klux Klan of the 1920s* (University of Illinois Press, Chicago, IL, 2004)

Lawrence Leamer, *The Lynching: The Epic Courtroom Battle That Brought Down the Klan* (William Morrow, New York, 2017)

Nicholas Lemann, *Redemption: The Last Battle of the Civil War* (Farrar, Straus and Giroux Books, New York, 2006)

John C. Lester and Daniel L. Wilson, *Ku Klux Klan: Its Origin, Growth and Disbandment* (Wheeler, Osborn and Duckworth Manufacturing Co., Nashville, TN, 1884)

Walter Lippmann, *Drift and Mastery* (Michael Kennerley, New York, 1914)

Karen Lumsden and Emily Harmer (eds), *Online Othering: Exploring Violence and Discrimination on the Web* (Palgrave, London, 2019)

M. William Lutholtz, *Grand Dragon: DC Stephenson and the Ku Klux Klan in Indiana* (Purdue University Press, West Lafayette, IN, 1991)

Robert S. and Helen Lynd, *Middletown: A Study in Contemporary America* (Constable, London, 1929)

John A. Lynn, *Another Kind of War: The Nature and History of Terrorism* (Yale University Press, New Haven, CT, 2019)

Ralph McGill, *The South and the Southerner* (Little Brown, Boston, MA, 1959)

Rory McVeigh, *The Rise of the Ku Klux Klan: Right Wing Movements and National Politics* (University of Minnesota Press, Minneapolis, MN, 2009)

James H. Madison, *The Ku Klux Klan in the Heartland* (Indiana University Press, Bloomington, IN, 2020)

Marion Mandeval, *The Klan Inside Out* (Monarch Publishing Co, Claremore, Oklahoma, OK, 1924)

Florence Mars, *Witness in Philadelphia* (LSU Press, Baton Rouge, LA, 1977)

Michael Martinez, *Carpetbaggers, Cavalry, and the Ku Klux Klan: Exposing the Invisible Empire During Reconstruction* (Rowman & Littlefield, Lanham, MD, 2007)

Martin Marty, *Righteous Empire: The Protestant Experience in America, Two Centuries of American Life* (Dial Press, New York, 1970)

Gary May, *The Informant: The FBI, the Ku Klux Klan, and the Murder of Viola Liuzzo* (Yale, New Haven, CT, 2008)

John Moffat Mecklin, *The Ku Klux Klan: A Study of the American Mind* (Harcourt, Brace and Co., New York, 1924)

Herman Melville, *Battle-Pieces and Aspects of the War* (Harper Brothers, New York, 1866)

Lou Michel and Dan Herbeck, *American Terrorist: Timothy McVeigh and the Oklahoma Bombing* (Harper, New York, 2001)

Leonard J. Moore, *Citizen Klansmen: The Ku Klux Klan in Indiana, 1921–1928* (University of North Carolina Press, Chapel Hill, NC, 1997)

D.J. Mulloy, *Years of Rage: White Supremacy in the United States from the Klan to the Alt-Right* (Rowman and Littlefield, Lanham, Boulder, CO, 2021)

National Association for the Advancement of Colored People, *Fighting a Vicious Film: Protest Against 'The Birth of a Nation'* (Boston Branch of the National Association for the Advancement of Colored People, 1915)

Michael Newton, *The FBI and the KKK: A Critical History* (McFarland and Co., Jefferson, NC, 2005)

Michael Newton, *The Ku Klux Klan: History, Organization, Language, Influence and Activities of America's Most Notorious Secret Society* (McFarland, Jefferson, NC, 2007)

Michael Newton, *Ku Klux Terror: Birmingham Alabama from 1866 to the Present* (Schiffer, Atglen, PA, 2013)

Michael Newton, *White Robes and Burning Crosses* (McFarland, Jefferson, NC, 2014)

Sean Patrick O'Rourke (ed.), *Like Wildfire: The Rhetoric of the Civil Rights Sit-Ins* (University of South Carolina Press, SC, 2000)

Oklahoma Commission, *Tulsa Race Riot: A Report by the Oklahoma Commission to Study the Tulsa Race Riot of 1921* (CreateSpace Independent Publishing Platform, 2001)

Steve Olney, *And the Dead Shall Rise: The Murder of Mary Phagan and the Lynching of Leo Frank* (Random House, New York, 2004)

Otto H. Olsen, *Carpetbagger's Crusade: The Life of Albion Winegar Tourgée* (Johns Hopkins Press, Baltimore, MD, 1965)

Roi Ottley, *The Lonely Warrior: The Life and Times of Robert S. Abbott, Founder of the Chicago Defender* (Henry Regnery Company, Chicago, IL, 1955)

Elaine Frantz Parsons, *Ku-Klux: The Birth of the Klan During Reconstruction* (University of North Carolina Press, Chapel Hill, NC, 2015)

Ann Patton, *Unmasked: The Rise and Fall of the 1920s Ku Klux Klan* (APLcorps Books, Tulsa, OK, 2016)

Thomas R. Pegram, *One Hundred Percent Americanism: The Rebirth and Decline of the Ku Klux Klan in the 1920s* (Ivan R. Dee, Chicago, IL, 2011)

Louis F. Post, *The Deportations Delirium of Nineteen Twenty* (Charles H. Kerr and Co., Chicago, IL, 1923)

George C. Rable, *But There Was No Peace: The Role of Violence in the Politics of Reconstruction* (University of Georgia Press, Athens, GA, 1984)

Howell Raines, *My Soul is Rested: The Story of the Civil Rights Movement in the Deep South* (Penguin Books, New York, 1983)

William Pierce Randel, *The Ku Klux Klan: A Century of Infamy* (Chilton Co., New York, 1969)

Arnold Rice, *The Ku Klux Klan in American Politics* (Public Affairs Press, Washington DC, 1962)

William Z. Ripley, *The Races of Europe: A Sociological Study* (D. Appleton and Co., New York, 1899)

James L. Roark, *Masters Without Slaves: Southern Planters in the Civil War and Reconstruction* (Norton and Co., New York, 1977)

Mr and Mrs W.B. Romine, *A Story of the Original Ku Klux Klan* (Pulaski Citizen, Pulaski, VA, 1924)

Mike Rothschild, *The Storm Is Upon Us: How QAnon Became a Movement, Cult, and Conspiracy Theory of Everything* (Monoray, London, 2021)

Garry Thomas Rowe, *Undercover Years with the Ku Klux Klan* (Bantam Books, New York, 1976)

Mildred Lewis Rutherford, *A Measuring Rod to Test Text Books, and Reference Books in Schools, Colleges and Libraries* (United Confederate Veterans, Athens, GA, 1920)

Ernest R. Sandeen, *The Roots of Fundamentalism* (University of Chicago Press, Chicago, IL, 1970)

Howard Schuman et al (rev. ed.), *Racial Attitudes in America* (Harvard University Press, Cambridge, MA, 1997)

Emmett J. Scott, *Negro Migration During the War* (Oxford University Press, New York, 1920)

James C. Scott, *Domination and the Arts of Resistance: Hidden Transcripts* (Yale University Press, New Haven, CT, 1990)

Julian Sher, *White Hoods: Canada's Ku Klux Klan* (New Star Books, Vancouver, 1983)

W.J. Simmons, *Imperial Proclamation of the Imperial Wizard* (KKK, Atlanta, GA, 1917)

Patsy Sims, *The Klan* (Stein and Day, New York, 1978)

Patsy Sims (rev. ed.), *The Klan* (Kentucky University Press, Lexington, KY, 1996)

Bill Stanton, *Klanwatch: Bringing the Klan to Justice* (Grove Weidenfeld, New York, 1991)

James Stirling, *Letters From the Slave States* (J.W. Parker, London, 1857)

Melvyn Stokes, *D.W. Griffith's The Birth of a Nation* (Oxford University Press, Oxford, 2007)

Nicholas L. Syrett, *The Company He Keeps: A History of White College Fraternities* (University of North Carolina Press, Chapel Hill, NC, 2011)

Vegas Tenold, *Everything You Love Will Burn: Inside the Rebirth of White Nationalism in America* (Bold Type Books, New York, 2018)

Mark Thornton, *The Economics of Prohibition* (Mises Institute, Auburn, AL, 2007)

Wendy P. Reilly Thorson, *Oregon Klanswomen of the 1920s: A Study in Tribalism, Gender and Women's Power* (Oregon State University Press, Corvalis, OR, 1997)

Randall Tietjen (ed.), *In the Clutches of the Law: Clarence Darrow's Letters* (University of California Press, Berkeley, CA, 2013)

Albion W. Tourgée, *A Fool's Errand, by One of the Fools* (Fords, Howard & Hulbert, New York, 1879)

Allen W. Trelease, *White Terror: The Ku Klux Klan Conspiracy and Reconstruction* (Louisiana State University Press, Baton Rouge, LA, 1971)

Howard A. Tucker, *History of Governor Walton's War on Ku Klux Klan, The Invisible Empire* (Southwest Publishing Co., Oklahoma City, OK, 1923)

Timothy B. Tyson, *The Blood of Emmett* (Simon and Schuster, New York, 2017)

US Congress, *Report of the Joint Select Committee to Inquire into The Condition of Affairs in the Late Insurrectionary States* (Govt Printing Office, Washington DC, 1872)

US Congress: House Committee on Un-American Activities, *Report: The Present-Day Ku Klux Klan Movement* 90th Congress, 1st Session (1967)

US Department of Justice, *Task Force Report on Gary Thomas Rowe Jnr* (Govt Printing, Washington DC, 1979)

US House of Representatives, *Memphis Riots and Massacres, US House of Representatives*, 39th Congress, 1st Session, Report No. 101 (Washington DC, 1866)

US House of Representatives, Committee on Rules, *The Ku Klux Klan Hearings* 67th Congress, 1st Session. (1921)

JoEllen McNergney Vinyard, *The Right in Michigan's Grass Roots: From the KKK to the Michigan Militia* (University of Michigan Press, Ann Arbor, MI, 2014)

Wyn Craig Wade, *Fiery Cross: The Ku Klux Klan in America* (Simon and Schuster, New York, 1984)

Dan Wakefield, *Revolt in the South* (Grove Press, New York, 1960)

Jerry Lee West, *The Reconstruction Ku Klux Klan in York County, South Carolina, 1865–1877* (McFarland, Jefferson, NC, 2002)

Vernon L. Wharton, *The Negro in Mississippi, 1865–1890* (University of North Carolina, Chapel Hill, NC, 1947)

Alma White, *Heroes of the Fiery Cross* (Good Citizen Press, Zarephath, NJ, 1928)

Don Whitehead, *Attack on Terror: The FBI Against the Ku Klux Klan in Mississippi* (Ishi Press International, New York, 2012)

Lou Falkner Williams, *The Great South Carolina Ku Klux Klan Trials, 1871–1872* (University of Georgia Press, Athens, GA, 1996)

Michael Williams, *The Shadow of the Pope* (McGraw-Hill and Co., New York, 1932)

Colin Edward Woodward, *Marching Masters: Slavery, Race and the Confederate Army During the Civil War* (University of Virginia Press, Charlottesville, VA, 2014)

C. Vann Woodward, *Origins of the New South, 1877–1913* (Louisiana State University Press, Baton Rouge, LA,1951)

Shoshona Zuboff, *The Age of Surveillance Capitalism* (Profile Books, London, 2019)

Leonard Zuskind, *Blood and Politics* (Farrar, Straus and Giroux, New York, 2009)

## Articles

Karen Abbot, '"Murder Wasn't Very Pretty": The Rise and Fall of D.C. Stephenson', *The Smithsonian Magazine* 30 August 2012

Thomas B. Alexander, 'Kukluxism in Tennessee, 1865–1869' *Tennessee Historical Quarterly*, 8:3 (September 1949)

Kristofer Allerfeldt, '"And We Got Here First": Albert Johnson, National Origins and Self-Interest in the Immigration Debates of the 1920s', *Journal of Contemporary History*, 45:1 (January 2010)

Kristofer Allerfeldt, 'Jayhawker Fraternities: Masons, Klansmen and Kansas in the 1920s', *Journal of American Studies*, 46:4 (November 2012)

Kristofer Allerfeldt, 'Murderous Mumbo-Jumbo: The Significance of Fraternity to Three Criminal Organizations in Late Nineteenth-Century America', *Journal of American Studies*, 50:4 (November 2016)

Louis Beam, 'Computers and the American Patriot', *The Inter-Klan Newsletter and Survival Alert* (March 1984)

Mark E. Benbow, 'Birth of a Quotation: Woodrow Wilson and "Like Writing History with Lightning"', *Journal of the Gilded Age and the Progressive Era*, 9:4 (October 2010)

Jim D. Brisson, '"Civil Government Was Crumbling Around Me": The Kirk-Holden War of 1870', *The North Carolina Historical Review*, 8:2 (April 2011)

Louis Francis Budenz, 'There's Mud on Indiana's White Robes', *The Nation* 27 July 1927

Malcolm Clarke Jr, 'The Bigot Disclosed: 90 Years of Nativism', *Oregon Historical Quarterly*, 75 (June 1974)

Clarence C. Clendenen, 'President Hayes' "Withdrawal" of the Troops – An Enduring Myth', *South Carolina Historical Magazine*, 70 (October 1969)

Leonard Lanson Cline, 'In Darkest Louisiana', *Nation*, 116 (14 March 1923)

Andrew Cohen, 'The Speech That Shocked Birmingham the Day After the Church Bombing', *The Atlantic* 13 September 2013

Jonathan S. Coit, '"Our Changed Attitude": Armed Defense and the New Negro in the 1919 Chicago Race Riot', *Journal of the Gilded Age and Progressive Era*, 11 (April 2012)

Thomas M. Conroy, 'The Ku Klux Klan and the American Clergy', *Ecclesiastical Review*, 70:1 (January 1924)

John M. Craig, '"There is Hell Going On Up There": The Carnegie Klan Riot of 1923', *Pennsylvania History* (Summer, 2005)

Jesse Daniels, 'Race, Civil Rights, and Hate Speech in the Digital Era', *CUNY Academic Works* (2008)

John Drabble, 'To Ensure Domestic Tranquillity: The FBI, COINTELPRO-WHITE HATE and Political Discourse, 1964–1971', *Journal of American Studies*, 38 (2004)

John Drabble, 'From White Supremacy to White Power: The FBI, COINTELPRO-WHITE HATE, and the Nazification of the Ku Klux Klan in the 1970s', *American Studies*, 43:3 (January 2007)

Robert L. Duffus, 'How the Klan Was Built Up By Travelling Salesmen', *The World's Work*, 42 (May 1923)

Robert L. Duffus, 'How the Ku Klux Klan Sells Hate: How Salesmen Sold Packages of Hate at Ten Dollars Each', *The World's Work* (June 1923)

William A. Dunning, 'The Undoing of Reconstruction', *The Atlantic Monthly*, 88:528 (October 1901)

H.W. Evans, 'Our Alien Crime-Plague and its Cure', *Kourier Magazine*, 2 (March 1926)

Craig Fox, *Everyday Klansfolk: White Protestant Life and the KKK in 1920s Michigan* (Michigan State University Press, East Lansing, MI, 2011)

Richard E. Frankel, 'Klansmen in the Fatherland: A Transnational Episode in the History of Weimar Germany's Right-Wing Political Culture', *Journal for the Study of Radicalism*, 7:1 (2013)

John Hope Franklin, '"Birth of a Nation": Propaganda as History', *The Massachusetts Review*, 20:3 (Autumn, 1979)

David J. Goldberg, 'Unmasking the Ku Klux Klan: The Northern Movement against the KKK, 1920–1925', *Journal of American Ethnic History*, 15:4 (Summer, 1996)

Ward Greene, 'Notes for a History of the Klan', *American Mercury*, 5 (June 1925)

Wayne Greenhaw, *Fighting the Devil in Dixie: How Civil Rights Activists Took on the Ku Klux Klan in Alabama* (Lawrence Hill Books, Chicago, IL, 2011)

Johnpeter Horst Grill and Robert L. Jenkins, 'The Nazis and the American South in the 1930s: A Mirror Image?', *The Journal of Southern History*, 58:4 (November 1992)

James Grossman, 'Blowing the Trumpet: The "Chicago Defender" and Black Migration during World War I', *Illinois Historical Journal*, 2:78 (Summer, 1985)

Booth Gunter and Caleb Kieffer, 'Islamophobia After 9/11: How a Fearmongering Fringe Movement Exploited the Terror Attacks to Gain Political Power', *SPLC* 21 September 2021

Michael Hale, '15 Leading Jews Marked for Death', *New Masses* 25 August 1936

Edward John Harcourt, '"The Boys Will Have to Fight the Battles without Me": The Making of Sam Davis, "Boy Hero of the Confederacy"', *Southern Cultures*, 12:3 (Autumn 2006)

James Taft Hatfield, 'Goethe and the Ku-Klux Klan Source', *Publications of the Modern Language Association*, 37:4 (December 1922)

Itay Hod, 'An Ex-KKK Grand Wizard Tells Us How Donald Trump Dog-Whistles to Closet Racists', *The Wrap*, 25 August 2016

William Bradford Huie, 'The Shocking Story of Approved Killing in Mississippi', *Look Magazine* 24 January 1956

Robert P. Ingalis, 'Antiradical Violence in Birmingham During the 1930s', *The Journal of Southern History*, 47:4 (November 1981)

Charles O. Jackson, 'William J. Simmons: A Career In Ku Kluxism', *The Georgia Historical Quarterly*, 50:4 (December 1966)

Timothy V. Johnson, '"We Are Illegal Here": The Communist Party, Self-Determination and the Alabama Share Croppers Union', *Science and Society*, 75:4 (October 2011)

Lila Lee Jones, 'The Ku Klux Klan in Eastern Kansas during the 1920s', *Emporia State Research Studies*, 23:3 (Winter, 1975)

L.J. Lawrence, 'Ballad of an American Terrorist: A Neo-Nazi's Dream of Order', *Harper's Magazine*, 273 (July 1986)

William Leuchtenburg, 'The Conversion of Harry Truman', *American Heritage* (November 1991)

George Lewis, '"An Amorphous Code": The Ku Klux Klan and Un-Americanism, 1915–1965', *Journal of American Studies*, 47:4 (November 2013)

Douglas O. Linder, 'Bending Toward Justice: John Doar and the Mississippi Burning Trial, *Mississippi Law Review*, 72:2 (Winter, 2002)

Harriet W. McBride, 'The Golden Age of Fraternalism: 1870–1910', *Heredom* ,13 (2005)

Stephany McCurry, 'The Confederacy Was an Antidemocratic, Centralized State', *The Atlantic* 21 June 2020

J. McDevitt, J. Levin & S. Bennett, 'Hate Crime Offenders: An Expanded Typology', *Journal of Social Issues*, 58:2 (2002)

James H. Madison, 'The Klan's Enemies Step up, Slowly', *Indiana Magazine of History*, 116:2 (June 2000)

Stephen E. Massengill, 'The Detectives of William W. Holden, 1869–1870', *North Carolina Historical Review*, 62 (October 1985)

Charles Merz, 'Sweet Land of Secrecy: The Strange Spectacle of American Fraternalism', *Harper's Magazine* February 1927

Chris M. Messer, Thomas E. Shriver and Alison E. Adams, 'The Destruction of Black Wall Street: Tulsa's 1921 Riot and the Eradication of Accumulated Wealth', *American Journal of Economics and Sociology*, 77:3–4 (May–September 2018)

Robert Moats Miller, 'A Note on the Relationship Between the Protestant Churches and the Revived Ku Klux Klan', *The Journal of Southern History*, 22:3 (August 1956)

Enoch L. Mitchell, 'The Role of General George Washington Gordon in the Ku Klux Klan', *Western Tennessee Historical Society Papers*, 1 (1947)

James Tice Moore, 'Redeemers Reconsidered: Change and Continuity in the Democratic South, 1870–1900', *Journal of Southern History*, 44:3 (August 1978)

Bill Morlin, 'Ruby Ridge Carved a Niche in History', *Hatewatch*, 21 August 2012

Roi Ottley, 'I Met the Grand Dragon', *The Nation*, 169, 2 July 1949

Elaine Frantz Parsons, 'Midnight Rangers: Costume and Performance in the Reconstruction-Era Ku Klux Klan', *The Journal of American History*, 92:3 (December 2005)

Thomas R. Pegram, 'Hoodwinked: The Anti-Saloon League and the Ku Klux Klan in 1920s Prohibition Enforcement', *The Journal of the Gilded Age and Progressive Era*, 7:1 (January 2008)

Allan Peskin, 'Was There a Compromise of 1877?', *The Journal of American History*, 60:1 (June 1973)

William F. Pinar, 'White Women in the Ku Klux Klan', *Counterpoints*, 163 (2001)

Louis F. Post, 'A "Carpetbagger" in South Carolina', *Journal of Negro History*, 10 (January 1925)

Bradley D. Proctor, '"From the Cradle to the Grave": Jim Williams, Black Manhood, and Militia Activism in Reconstruction South Carolina', *American Nineteenth Century History*, 19:1 (2018)

John R. Rachal, '"The Long, Hot Summer": The Mississippi Response to Freedom Summer, 1964', *The Journal of Negro History*, 84:4 (Autumn, 1999)

Julia Reed, 'His Brilliant Career', *New York Review of Books* 9 April 1992

Mark Paul Richard, '"This Is Not a Catholic Nation": The Ku Klux Klan Confronts Franco-Americans in Maine', *The New England Quarterly*, 82:2 (2009)

James Ridgeway, 'Unholy Terrorists', *Village Voice* 25 January 1985

Allen Safianow, 'Konklave in Kokomo Revisited', *The Historian*, 50:3 (May 1988)

Christopher S. Saladin, 'The End of the Small-Town Golden Age: A Rural Newspaper's Role in the Urban-Rural Clash of Anti-Catholicism', *Augustana Digital Commons* (Spring, 2015)

Leonard Schapiro, 'The Rôle of the Jews in the Russian Revolutionary Movement', *The Slavonic and East European Review*, 40:94 (December 1961)

Arnold Shankman, 'Julian Harris and the Ku Klux Klan', *The Mississippi Quarterly*, 28:2 (Spring, 1975)

J. Reuben Sheeler, 'Methods for Control of the Negro … Mind, Soul and Body', *Negro History Bulletin*, 21:3 (December 1957)

William G. Shepherd, '"How I Put Over the Klan": Col William Joseph Simmons, Father of the Ku Klux Klan Tells His Story to William G. Shepherd', *Collier's* 14 July 1928

Robert Sherrill, 'A Look Inside the Invisible Empire', *New South*, 23 (Spring, 1968)

Ron F. Smith, 'The Klan's Retribution Against an Indiana Editor: A Reconsideration', *Indiana Magazine of History*, 106 (December 2010)

Kenneth S. Stern, 'David Duke: A Nazi in Politics', *Issues in National Affairs*, 1:4 (1991)

Lance Trusty, '"All Talk and No Kash": Valparaiso University and the Ku Klux Klan', *Indiana Magazine of History*, 82:1 (March 1986)

Allen Ward, 'A Note on the Origin of the Ku Klux Klan', *Tennessee Historical Quarterly*, 23:2 (June 1964)

Woodrow Wilson, 'The Reconstruction of the Southern States', *The Atlantic* (January 1901)

C. Vann Woodward, 'From the First Reconstruction to the Second', *Harper's*, 230 (April 1965)

John F. Wukovits, 'This Case is Close to My Heart', *American History* (December 1998)

James W. Vander Zanden, 'The Klan Revival', *American Journal of Sociology*, 65:5 (March 1960)

Kathleen R. Zebley, 'Unconditional Unionist: Samuel Mayes Arnell and Reconstruction in Tennessee', *Tennessee Historical Quarterly*, 53 (1994)

Harold Zink, 'A Case Study of a Political Boss', *Psychiatry*, 1:4 (1938)

## Unpublished Works

Carter Blue Clarke, 'A History of the Ku Klux Klan in Oklahoma' (PhD Dissertation, University of Oklahoma, OK, 1976)

Kenneth Earl Harrell, 'The Ku Klux Klan in Louisiana, 1920–1930' (Unpublished PhD, Louisiana State University, LA, 1966)

William Vincent Hunt, 'A Sheet and a Cross: A Symbolic Analysis of the Ku Klux Klan' (Unpublished PhD thesis, Tulane University, LA, 1975)

James Vincent Lowry, 'Reconstructing the Reign of Terror: Popular Memories of the Ku Klux Klan' (Unpublished PhD, University of Mississippi, MS, 2008)

Bradley David Proctor, 'Whip, Pistol, and Hood: Ku Klux Klan Violence in the Carolinas During Reconstruction' (Unpublished PhD Dissertation, University of North Carolina, Chapel Hill, NC, 2013)

Martha Ragsdale, 'The National Origins Plan of Immigration Restriction' (Unpublished MA Thesis, Vanderbilt University, TN, 1928)

Catherine Marie Saks, '"Real Americanism": Resistance to the Oregon Compulsory School Bill, 1920–1925' (Unpublished PhD Thesis, Portland State University, OR, 2010)

Benjamin Horton Severance, 'Tennessee's Radical Army: The State Guard and Its Role in Reconstruction' (Unpublished PhD Thesis, University of Tennessee, Knoxville, TN, 2002)

Eckard V. Toy, Jr, 'The Ku Klux Klan in Oregon: Its Program and Character' (Unpublished MA Thesis, University of Oregon, OR, 1959)

Paul David Wangsvick, 'The Contested Reputation of Nathan Bedford Forrest: A Case Study in Rhetoric and Regional Identity Formation' (Unpublished PhD Thesis, University of Memphis, TN, 2011)

# INDEX

You may also enjoy …

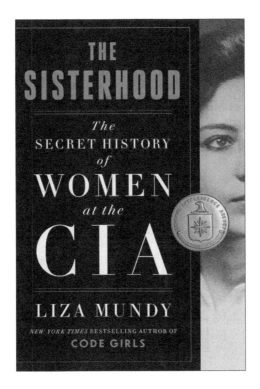

978 0 7509 9929 8

A revelatory history of three generations at the CIA – the women who
fought to become operatives, transformed spycraft, and tracked down
Osama bin Laden.

'Ignore this book – and these astonishing
women – at your peril.' – Kate Moore,
bestselling author of *The Radium Girls*

**You may also enjoy ...**

978 0 7509 9880 2

Every day, the President of the United States receives a bespoke, top-secret briefing document from the Central Intelligence Agency. Truman started them, Kennedy came to rely on them and Trump hardly read them.

*Current Intelligence* charts almost a century of history and politics, revealing for the first time the day-to-day intelligence that lands on the Oval Office desk.